NEGOTIATING JERUSALEM

SUNY series in Israeli Studies
Russell Stone, editor

Negotiating Jerusalem

Jerome M. Segal
Shlomit Levy
Nader Izzat Sa'id
Elihu Katz

STATE UNIVERSITY OF NEW YORK PRESS

Published by
State University of New York Press, Albany

For information, address State University of New York Press,
State University Plaza, Albany, N.Y., 12246

Production by Cathleen Collins
Marketing by Patrick Durocher

Library of Congress Cataloging in Publication Data

Negotiating Jerusalem / Jerome M. Segal . . . [et al.].
        p.   cm. — (SUNY series in Israeli studies)
      Includes bibliographical references and index.
      ISBN 0-7914-4537-2 (alk. paper) — ISBN 0-7914-4538-0 (pbk.: alk. paper)
      1. Jerusalem—International status.   2. Arab-Israeli conflict—1993—Peace.
    I. Segal, Jerome M., 1943–   II. Series.
    DS109.94.N45   2000
    341.2'9'09569442—dc21   99-041586

10 9 8 7 6 5 4 3 2 1

Contents

v

Preface

It is widely believed that the Jerusalem issue is unique, the one issue on which the two peoples are so far apart that any political leadership which even sought to compromise would be swept aside. Within Israel, Jerusalem is viewed as the third rail of Israeli politics. To date, no major political party has proposed sharing sovereignty with the Palestinians. Yet, among Palestinians, some 94% say that even if it were the only way that a Palestinian state could come into being, they would not accept Israel's claim that it alone is sovereign over all of Jerusalem. Were the PLO to abandon Jerusalem, Palestinians would abandon the PLO.

Negotiating Jerusalem explores the potential (and limits) for resolving the Jerusalem issue. Unlike much writing on the Jerusalem question, it does not concern itself with the positions of the Israeli government or the PLO. Nor does it seek to identify theoretically possible solutions to the Jerusalem question. Instead, it focuses on the beliefs, values, and attitudes of ordinary people, specifically Israeli Jews living in Israel and in settlements in the West Bank and Gaza, and Palestinians living in Jerusalem, the West Bank, and Gaza. Only after examining the orientations of the two peoples does the book turn to the question of policy: Is it possible to arrive at a negotiated solution to the Jerusalem question, and if so, what might such a solution look like?

The final policy section of the book, "Is Jerusalem Negotiable?", was written by Jerome Segal (speaking only for himself). It builds on the study of Israeli Jews undertaken by Shlomit Levy, Elihu Katz, and Jerome Segal and the study of Palestinians undertake by Nader Sa'id and Jerome Segal, each of which involved an extensive research effort that went far beyond any previous studies of public attitudes toward Jerusalem. On the Israeli side, some 1,530 door-to-door interviews were conducted. Each interview consisted of almost 100 questions, all focused on the Jerusalem issue. On the Palestinian side, a parallel effort was undertaken, interviewing some 870 Palestinians.

These two studies emerged from distinct and separate research efforts, one representing an Israeli-American collaboration and one representing a Palestinian-

American collaboration. While distinct investigations, they form a coherent body of inquiry. The Israeli Jewish study was conducted first, in 1995–96 and in developing the Palestinian study, to enable comparison, a very similar questionnaire, often with identical questions, was used in 1996. Jerome Segal was a member of both research teams.

The overall product is unique. Standing individually, each of the research projects provides a major leap forward in what was known about the attitudes of both Palestinians and Israeli Jews toward Jerusalem. Taken together, and with the final section "Is Jerusalem Negotiable?", the volume offers a comprehensive assessment of the extent to which public opinion constitutes a barrier to the potential negotiability of the Jerusalem question.

Some of what we found confirms the widespread belief that it will be extraordinarily difficult to successfully negotiate the permanent status of Jerusalem. For instance, we found that the overwhelming majority of Israeli Jews are opposed to negotiations on Jerusalem and a majority say that no concessions should be made at all. On the Palestinian side, as already noted, we found that 94% of Palestinians would not be willing to accept Israel's claim that it alone is sovereign over all of Jerusalem, even if this were the only way a Palestinian state could come into being. And parallel to Israeli Jewish attitudes, the overwhelming majority of Palestinians said there should be no concessions at all with respect to Jerusalem.

The key to understanding this strong anticoncession response is to note that such questions were asked about Jerusalem as a whole. One of the central features of our studies is that we "disaggregated" the Jerusalem question, asking many questions about specific parts of the city. Once that was done, a quite different picture emerged.

- A plurality of Israeli Jews (45%) would seriously consider Palestinian sovereignty over Arab settlements and villages previously in the West Bank which are now within the borders of Jerusalem (e.g., Shuafat, Um Tuba, Zur Baher, Beit Hanina).
- Most Palestinians would seriously consider a proposal in which West Jerusalem would be under Israeli sovereignty and East Jerusalem would be under Palestinian sovereignty, with a special arrangement for Israeli control of the Jewish neighborhoods in East Jerusalem. The Old City would be dealt with separately.

More generally we found, that once you disaggregate the city, contrary to popular belief, there is no overall consensus among either Israelis or Palestinians on Jerusalem. Thus, the Jerusalem issue begins to look much more like the other issues in the conflict (i.e., both Israelis and Palestinians are split on what to do).

In an effort to better understand the nature of the strong Israeli and Palestinian attachments to the city, we asked people how important to them "as Jerusalem" various parts of the city were. Here the responses were quite striking:

- The vast majority of both Israeli Jews and Palestinians prioritize, distinguishing certain parts of the city as far more important "as Jerusalem" than other parts.
- Among Israeli Jews, the priorities of diverse subgroups of the population, quite remarkably, are virtually identical. Every subgroup puts very high value on where Israeli Jews live and on Jewish religious sites. Every subgroup views the residential areas of Palestinians as of much lower importance "as Jerusalem."
- Among Palestinians we find a parallel pattern of prioritization— high value on where fellow nationals live and on one's own religious sites, much lower value on where Israeli Jews live and on their religious sites.

This prioritization and the fact that only a small part of the city overlaps as very important ("as Jerusalem") to both peoples provides a potential basis for a negotiated solution. The catch, however, is that this "small part" geographically speaking (the Old City and the Mount of Olives) is huge symbolically speaking.

It is important for the reader to be aware that the study of Israeli Jews was carried out in Hebrew and the study of Palestinians in Arabic, and that in Hebrew and Arabic the names for Jerusalem differ. Thus, the word "Jerusalem" was never used in the interviews. Israelis were asked about "Yerushalayim" and Palestinians about "Al-Quds." While both names allude to the sacred center, the fact that there are two names makes it easier to think about the nonoverlapping parts of the mental maps in the minds of each population. Moreover, we found that, for both peoples, the current municipal boundaries are neither sacrosanct nor definitive. There is reason to believe that it may be possible to make Yerushalayim and Al-Quds either smaller or larger.

In "Is Jerusalem Negotiable?"—the final section of the book—Jerome Segal lays out his own ideas for a negotiated settlement. Segal offers a "two-cities" approach in which Yerushalayim and Al-Quds would both be redefined, overlapping on "only" 1% to 2% of the area within the current Israeli municipal boundaries. He also considers various approaches that might defuse the sovereignty issue with respect to the Old City.

The extent to which Jerusalem is negotiable will, no doubt, change over time. In our studies we sought to identify the factors that disposed individuals toward compromise. For Israeli Jews, the data suggest that willingness to compromise is strongly dependent on whether a person believes that a peace treaty will lead to real peace. At the time of these studies—it should be noted—only a minority so believed.

For both Palestinians and Israelis, believing that the other side has "some legitimate rights in regard to Jerusalem" appears to make a very big difference in people's willingness to compromise. For the minority of Israeli Jews, who so believe, this effect was equal in power to the effect of believing that a peace treaty will lead to real peace. These findings are of particular relevance for those seeking to expand the realm of negotiability.

Many of these findings—the importance of disaggregating, the prioritization of areas of the city, the openness to boundary changes, the significance of believing that real peace is possible and of believing that the other side has legitimate rights in regard to Jerusalem—are matters that are unlikely to change rapidly over time. While the degree of public support for specific compromise proposals will likely shift with changing political circumstance, these features constitute relatively enduring parameters within which such changes will occur.

Altogether there are four authors involved, and each has written their own contributions to the volume. The two Israelis, Shlomit Levy and Elihu Katz, are sociologists, as is our Palestinian colleague, Nader Sa'id. By contrast, Jerome Segal comes from a policy background and has been an activist engaged with issues of Israeli-Palestinian peacemaking for the past sixteen years. As the reader may surmise, these diverse backgrounds are reflected in our respective contributions.

Because of these diverse backgrounds and perspectives, the book can be read in a variety of ways. Those who read it cover to cover, will find separate sociological and policy analyses of both the Israeli and Palestinian data. For those less interested in policy matters and more interested in the structure of Israeli and Palestinian attitudes, it is possible to focus on the analyses by the three sociologists. And for those primarily interested in matters of policy, the three sections by Jerome Segal, one on Israeli-Jews, one on Palestinians, and one bringing the data together, offer the reader a coherent policy analysis in a single voice, which does not presume to represent the other three authors.

The authors are indebted to many individuals for assistance and funding. For the study of Israeli Jews, we wish to thank the Bydale Foundation, The Ford Foundation, The Tides Foundation, and The United States Institute of Peace for their generous assistance. Along the way several individuals provided us with wise counsel; we wish to give special thanks in this regard to Fran Burwell, Alouphe Hareven, Sharon Lang, Tamar Liebes, Ian Lustick, Moshe Maoz, Naomi Nim, and Thomas Schelling.

For the study of Palestinians and for "Is Jerusalem Negotiable?", the authors greatly appreciate the support received from the MacArthur Foundation, and specifically extend their thanks to Fran Burwell, Kevin Curow, Robert O. Freedman, Mark Lopez, Ian Lustick, Ayoub Mustafa, Naomi Nim, Lara Sao Pedro, Ziad Said, and Thomas Schelling for various forms of assistance. Thanks also to the Foundation for Middle East Peace for its general support of the University of Maryland's Jerusalem Project.

— Jerome M. Segal

PART I

The Status of Jerusalem in the Eyes of Israeli-Jews and Palestinians

A Policy Perspective

JEROME M. SEGAL

The Olso Accord signed in September 1993, identified Jerusalem as one of several issues to be taken up by Israelis and Palestinians in the permanent status negotiations. It is widely believed that of all the permanent status issues, Jerusalem will prove the most difficult.

The negotiations on Jerusalem began in November 1999, six years after Oslo. During that interval Palestinian statehood became a near fait accompli—but on Jerusalem there was virtually no movement whatsoever. Israelis political leaders showed no willingness to accept Palestinian sovereignty over any part of Jerusalem, and the PLO continued to affirm that Jerusalem will be the capital of the Palestinian state.

The common wisdom on Jerusalem is that it differs from the other issues of the conflict. On Jerusalem (it is believed) the two peoples are so far apart, that even if the political leaders wanted to make major concessions, they would be unable to do so.

But is the common wisdom correct? The two studies, one of Israeli-Jews, the other of Palestinians, were undertaken in order to ascertain whether in fact the outlooks of the two peoples do impose limits to the negotiability of Jerusalem, and if so, what kinds of limits. Are they insuperable? What aspects of the Jerusalem question are negotiable? What factors might tend to expand negotiability? What kind of approaches might allow gaps to be bridged?

1

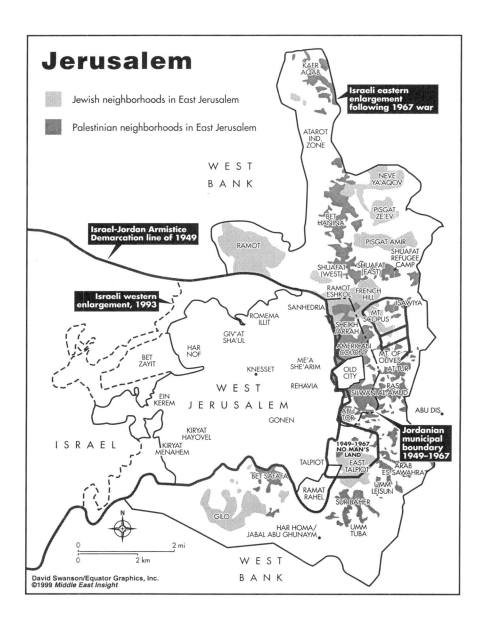

Jerusalem

Jewish neighborhoods in East Jerusalem

Palestinian neighborhoods in East Jerusalem

KAFR AQAB

Israeli eastern enlargement following 1967 war

ATAROT IND. ZONE

WEST BANK

NEVE YA'AQOV

Israel-Jordan Armistice Demarcation line of 1949

BET HANINA

PISGAT ZE'EV

RAMOT

PISGAT AMIR

SHUAFAT REFUGEE CAMP

SHUAFAT (WEST)

SHUAFAT (EAST)

Israeli western enlargement, 1993

RAMOT ESHKOL

FRENCH HILL

ISAWIYA

SANHEDRIA

ROMEMA ILLIT

MT. SCOPUS

GIV'AT SHA'UL

SHEIKH JARRAH

HAR NOF

AMERICAN COLONY

MT. OF OLIVES

BET ZAYIT

ME'A SHE'ARIM

OLD CITY

AT-TUR

KNESSET

REHAVIA

RAS AL-AMUD

SILWAN

EIN KEREM

WEST JERUSALEM

ABU DIS

GONEN

ABU TOR

Jordanian municipal boundary 1949–1967

ISRAEL

KIRYAT HAYOVEL

KIRYAT MENAHEM

1949–1967 NO MAN'S LAND

TALPIOT

EAST TALPIOT

ARAB ES-SAWAHRA

BET SAFAFA

UMM LEISUN

RAMAT RAHEL

SUR BAHER

GILO

HAR HOMA/ JABAL ABU GHUNAYM

UMM TUBA

N

0   2 mi

0   2 km

WEST BANK

These are the kind of policy questions that motivated the empirical research. The studies we undertook were far more extensive than any previous research on either Israeli or Palestinian attitudes towards Jerusalem. They have produced a wealth of information and have deepened understanding of the complexity of the issue. And they have been shared with political leaders on both sides.

In what follows, from the perspective of negotiability, I examine the research data, taking each population separately. A detailed discussion of the methodology of the studies of Israeli-Jews and Palestinians can be found respectively in the analyses by Shlomit Levy and Nader Sa'id. The questionnaires and cross-tabulations can be found in the Appendixes at the end of the book. In Part IV, in a separate essay, "Is Jerusalem Negotiable?" I bring the data from the two studies together, seeking to identify both the limits and the potential for successful negotiation. I close by offering a model for a permanent status agreement on Jerusalem, one that is grounded in the reality of the two peoples.

A. Israeli Jews

Introduction: The News on Negotiability*

A defining feature of this study is that it approaches Jerusalem in both an aggregate and a disaggregate manner, that is, it asks some questions about Jerusalem as a whole, and then asks many questions about specific parts of the city.

The study clearly demonstrates that disaggregation makes a major difference. For instance, when asked, "How important is Jerusalem to you personally?", 98% of Israeli Jewish respondents answered that it is "important" or "very important"; yet when asked how important to you "as part of Jerusalem" are the non-Jewish quarters of the Old City, the percentage answering "very important" or "important" fell to 59%. This percentage was below 50% for areas populated by Palestinians outside the Old City.

When asked their view on negotiations on Jerusalem, 78% stated that they were opposed to negotiations; yet when queried with respect to specific proposals dealing with particular areas of the city, the response was considerably more open.

It is a central conclusion of the study that when the city is approached in a disaggregated fashion, a substantial proportion of Israeli Jews are willing to consider "transferring to Palestinian sovereignty"** those non-Jewish areas of the city that have only limited importance in their subjective map of what constitutes Jerusalem.

The results of the study, however, are complex and tend in opposite directions on the prospects for negotiations on Jerusalem.

---

* Throughout the discussion, the assumption is made that a Palestinian state will come into being. The issue is whether that state will have sovereignty over some part of Jerusalem, and secondarily whether Jerusalem (in part) will be the capital of that state. Interestingly, while 67% of the respondents oppose establishment of a Palestinian state, 78% believe that it will be established.

** The phrase "transfer to Palestinian sovereignty" was used in the questions put to the Israeli public; its use does not imply any position on the part of the author with respect to outstanding issues in international law pertaining to sovereignty over Jerusalem.

Findings Militating Against Negotiability

1. Seventy-eight percent of Israeli Jews are against negotiations on Jerusalem.
2. Ninety-eight percent of Israeli Jews say that Jerusalem is "important" or "very important" to them personally.
3. Sixty percent of Israeli Jews say that no concessions over Jerusalem should be made, "even if we have to give up on peace with the Arabs."
4. Eighty percent of Israeli Jews object (including 50% who "definitely object") to the designation of an Arab region in East Jerusalem as the capital of the Palestinian state.
5. With respect to East Jerusalem as a whole, as well as with respect to sections taken separately, a clear majority of Israeli Jews oppose transferring sovereignty to the Palestinians.
6. If an Israeli government that "lacks a Zionist majority in the Knesset" (as was true of the previous Labor government) arrives at a compromise that the respondent thinks is wrong, 40% say they view nonviolent actions that disrupt the functioning of society as a justified form of protest.
7. Twenty-seven percent say they would participate in action against a compromise on Jerusalem with which they disagree, and an additional 27% say that they probably would.

In sum, the study offers considerable comfort to those opposed to or fearful of a negotiated compromise on Jerusalem. Their point of view is a clear majority position among Israeli Jews; it is a very strongly felt position, and any Israeli government that fails to pay heed to this point of view can expect major and forceful public protest and general disruption of society.

If we make the assumptions that when it comes to final, permanent, and comprehensive negotiation of the Jerusalem question, that no Palestinian leadership would agree to sole Israeli sovereignty over the Old City and that none would accept less than part of East Jerusalem as the sovereign capital of Palestine, it seems clear that a final and comprehensive agreement is unattainable, given current attitudes among the Israeli Jewish public.

At the same time, one cannot conclude from this that Jerusalem is non-negotiable. Even if a final, permanent, and comprehensive agreement is not possible, something less may be consistent with current Israeli Jewish opinion. For instance, it may be possible to negotiate the permanent status of parts of the city, leaving other parts for the future. And with respect to areas where permanent agreement cannot be reached, it may be possible to negotiate agreements that hold for a specified interim period, or even indefinitely, with both sides agreeing to disagree on ultimate status.

Indeed, other findings support the conclusion that aspects of the Jerusalem question are negotiable.

Findings That Support Negotiability:

1. While Israeli Jews overwhelmingly view Jerusalem as "important" or "very important," when asked about specific places and parts of the city ("to what extent is or isn't it important to you as part of Jerusalem?"), Israeli Jews, across the ideological spectrum, judge certain areas as much less important than other areas.

2. The non-Jewish quarters of the Old City were judged "not so important" or "not important at all" as "part of Jerusalem" by 40%.

3. The neighborhoods in downtown East Jerusalem were deemed "not so important as part of Jerusalem" or "not important at all" by 52% of Israeli Jews, with more saying it was "not important at all" than said it was "very important." As for the outlying Arab areas of the city, 53% said "not important" as opposed to 41% who said these are important to them "as part of Jerusalem."

4. Thirty-nine percent of Israeli Jews disagree with the "no concessions on Jerusalem" position, even when Jerusalem is treated as a single unit. When Jerusalem is disaggregated and people are asked about specific areas of the city, willingness to make compromises rises.

5. Forty-two percent would cede the Arab neighborhoods of East Jerusalem to the Palestinians if the Old City, the Mount of Olives, all the Jewish neighborhoods of East Jerusalem, and Mount Scopus remain in Jerusalem.

6. Forty-five percent would seriously consider transferring outlying areas of Jerusalem such as Shuafat, Um Tuba, Zur Baher, and Beit Hanina to Palestinian sovereignty, while only 36% flatly reject such an idea.

7. A clear majority of Israeli Jews do not view the boundaries of Jerusalem as sacrosanct. In order to ensure a Jewish majority in the city, 59% would support boundary changes so that outlying areas of the city populated by Palestinians are redefined as outside the city; only 7% "definitely object" to such an idea.

8. Thirty-nine percent believe that Palestinians have legitimate rights with regard to Jerusalem.

Thus, it may be reasonably inferred from the study that while current Israeli Jewish public opinion precludes a comprehensive agreement that establishes the permanent status of all parts of the city, it does allow room for the negotiation of agreements on the permanent status of parts of the city.

The Complex Pattern of Consensus and Discord on Jerusalem

The term "consensus" is lacking in precision, and it can be used in many ways. In this chapter, it will be differentiated from other strong majority positions. As will become clear, there are many areas of the Jerusalem question about which Israeli Jews share a consensus—issues with respect to which, say, 85 out of 100 Israeli Jews agree. This, however, must be distinguished from positions to which 60% or 70% or 80% of Israelis adhere. The importance of these distinctions becomes apparent when one realizes that a position held by, say, 30% of Israeli Jews, may be held by 50% of those within a major political faction or may command majority support from the Israeli public in a government-supported referendum, when the votes of Israeli Arabs and the significance of government support are factored in. This outcome, however, is distinctly unlikely on the "true consensus" issues.

In presenting the areas of agreement and disagreement among Israeli Jews, responses to the survey questionnaire have been merged so as to identify a stance shared by at least 50% of the population. By inverting the formulation, minority positions ranging from negligible to strong can also be identified.

Responses have been grouped as follows:

1. High consensus: 85% or more of the population hold these positions or characteristics. (Only a negligible minority position exists.)
2. Overwhelming majority: 70% to 85% of the population hold these positions or have these characteristics. (A weak minority position exists.)
3. Substantial Majority: 60% to 70% of the population hold these positions. (A substantial minority position exists.)
4. Mere majority: 50% to 60% of the population hold these positions. (The opposing position is almost equally strong.)

The areas of consensus and discord are as follows:*

Areas of high consensus
(only a negligible minority position exists)

Q:	Position	Percentage
17.	The Western Wall is important to me as part of Jerusalem**	99%
8.	Jerusalem is important to me personally	98%
9.	Feel a sense of belonging to Jerusalem	98%
11.	Jerusalem is important to me from Jewish national/historic viewpoint	97%
15.	Jerusalem is important to me as symbol of State of Israel	97%

* To see the actual wording of the questions, consult Appendix A.
** "Important" in these listings includes "very important" as well.

24. Old Jewish areas (e.g., Rehavia) important to me as part of Jerusalem	97%
25. The Old City is important to me as part of Jerusalem	97%
83. Lawful demonstrations are a legitimate response to "wrong" decision on Jerusalem made by a government lacking a Zionist majority in the Knesset	96%
18. Mount of Olives is important to me as part of Jerusalem	94%
19. Jewish quarter of Old City is important to me as part of Jerusalem	94%
23. New Jewish neighborhoods (e.g., Ramot) important to me as Jerusalem	94%
26. New Jewish neighborhoods as much a part of Jerusalem as old ones	94%
87. Violence against Jews not legitimate response to "wrong" decision on Jerusalem made by a government lacking a Zionist majority in the Knesset	94%
16. Temple Mount is important to me as part of Jerusalem	93%
10. Jerusalem is important to me from Jewish/religious point of view	89%
6. Follows the Jerusalem question within the peace process	88%

Areas of overwhelming majority
(a weak minority position exists)

Q:	Position	Percentage
75.	Important to me that Jews be able to pray on Temple Mount	84%
85.	Unlawful force not legitimate response to "wrong" decision on Jerusalem made by a government lacking a Zionist majority in the Knesset	83%
86.	Violence against Palestinians not okay response to "wrong" decision on Jerusalem by a government lacking a Zionist majority in the Knesset	83%
71.	Would not take seriously proposal to internationalize Old City*	82%
72.	Not take seriously: East Jerusalem under Palestinian sovereignty with special status for Jewish neighborhoods under Israeli control	81%
62.	Palestinian claim to East Jerusalem as capital not justified	80%
80.	Object to Palestinian capital in Arab area of East Jerusalem	80%
42.	Do not see Jerusalem compromise as key to peace with Arab states	80%
43.	Do not believe that for true peace with Palestinians it is necessary to make a compromise on Jerusalem	80%
44.	Do not believe thst to co-exist with Arabs in Jerusalem compromise must be made	79%
38.	Did not know that East Jerusalem today much bigger than under Jordanians	79 %
70.	Not take seriously Palestinian sovereignty of Temple Mount in exchange for Palestinian recognition of Israeli sovereignty of Western Wall	79%
78.	Opposed to negotiation over Jerusalem in the peace process	79%
7.	Opposed to negotiation over Jerusalem in the peace process	78%
79.	Expect that there will be a Palestinian state	78%
13.	Jerusalem is important to me as center for all religions	75%
39.	Assuming the existence of Palestinian state, significant problem: that Arab residents of East Jerusalem may become Palestinian citizens	75%

---

* "Not seriously consider" in these listing merges those who flatly rejected the proposal with those who said they would consider it "not so seriously."

Areas of substantial majority
(a substantial minority position exists)

Q:	Position	Percentage
47.	Oppose a wall in Jerusalem separating Israelis from Palestinians	70%
29.	Never visited Arab village areas inside Jerusalem (e.g., Zur Baher, Um Tuba, Beit Hanina)	70%
69.	Not seriously consider: Temple Mount under Wakf control as now	70%
27.	Visit Jerusalem a lot	69%
41.	Do not see peace agreement with Palestinians leading to true peace	67%
77.	Object to establishment of Palestinian state	67%
73.	Not seriously consider autonomy for Arab areas in East Jerusalem	66%
82.	Jerusalem issue is more important than other issues in negotiations	66%
74.	Not seriously consider: joint Israeli-Palestinian administration of the Old City with Israel not yielding its claim to sovereignty	66%
35.	Support restricting housing for Arabs in Jerusalem to prevent majority	65%
76.	Reject "sovereignty belongs to God" formula for Temple Mount	65%
48.	See separation between Jews and Arabs in Jerusalem as a fact	64%
40.	Do not believe there can be true peace with Arab world	64%
15.	Do not believe Jerusalem is important to the Palestinians	63%
33.	Knew % of Palestinians in Jerusalem had not increased greatly	63%
61.	Palestinians do not have legitimate rights with regard to Jerusalem	61%
34.	Disturbed that 28% of population of Jerusalem is Palestinian	61%
31.	Oppose concessions on Jerusalem even if must give up on peace with Arabs	60%
84.	Nonviolent disruptions not legitimate response to "wrong" decision on Jerusalem made by a government lacking a Zionist majority in the Knesset	60%

Areas of mere majority
(an almost equally strong opposing opinion exists)

Q:	Position	Percentage
20.	Non-Jewish quarters of Old City "important to me as part of Jerusalem"	59%
36.	To ensure Jewish majority: support redefining city limits so that Arab settlements and villages that are now within the borders of Jerusalem (such as Shuafat, Um Tuba, Zur Baher) will be outside the city	59%
50.	Oppose ceding Arab neighborhoods in East Jerusalem even if Old City, Mount of Olives, Mount Scopus and Jewish neighborhoods remain Israeli	57%
66.	Not seriously consider: the Arab settlements and villages previously in the West Bank that are now within Jerusalem will come under Palestinian sovereignty in exchange for Jewish regions in the West Bank such as Maale Adomin and Givat Ze'ev becoming part of Jerusalem	56%
56.	Do not see better chance of co-existence with Palestinians in Jerusalem than West Bank	56%
65.	Not seriously consider: Palestinian sovereignty over the Arab settlements and villages previously in the West Bank which are now within the borders of Jerusalem (e.g., Shuafat, Um Tuba, Zur Baher, Beit Hanina)	55%

89. Probably participate in some action against wrong Jerusalem decision	54%
64. Would find regular commerce with Arabs convincing sign of real peace	53%
22. Arab settlements and villages previously in the West Bank which are now included within Jerusalem (e.g., Um Tuba, Zur Baher) "not important to me as part of Jerusalem"	53%
21. Arab neighborhoods in downtown East Jerusalem (Wadi Jos, Sheikh Jarah) "not important to me as part of Jerusalem"	52%
46. Security requires wall between Israel and territories	52%
49. Jewish/Arab separation in daily life in Jerusalem is desirable	52%
37. Did not know substantial areas added to East Jerusalem for policy reasons	51%
32. Did not know Palestinians constitute about 30% of Jerusalem population	51%

There is high consensus (85% or stronger) concerning the importance to Israeli Jews of the city's Jewish neighborhoods, whether old or new, whether in the Old City or elsewhere. There is also consensus with respect to the importance of the Old City, the Mount of Olives, the Western Wall, and the Temple Mount.

Certain reasons for the importance of Jerusalem (national/historic, symbol of the State of Israel) are also consensual. And so is the legitimacy accorded to lawful demonstrations and the refusal to grant legitimacy to violence against other Jews, "even in the event that a government with a non-Zionist majority in the Knesset approves an unpopular agreement on Jerusalem."

At the same time, on other questions dealing with which sections of the city are subjectively important "as part of Jerusalem" considerable disagreement was found. The greatest disagreement arose with respect to the Arab sections of the city, whether in the Old City, in downtown East Jerusalem, or in outlying village areas. And, as might be expected (given disagreement with respect to the importance of these areas as "part of Jerusalem") there was substantial disagreement on proposals to transfer such areas to Palestinian sovereignty, or more generally, to redefine the city boundaries so as to exclude certain Arab areas.

While there is both consensus and discord among Israeli Jews when it comes to how "important as part of Jerusalem" certain areas of the city may be, *two structural features characterized every subgroup of the population that we examined, regardless of whether the population was broken down by ideological tendency, degree of religiosity, place of residence, or place of birth. First, each subgroup sharply distinguished the relative importance of different areas of the city. Second, broadly speaking, the various subgroups all share the same prioritization of the different areas of Jerusalem.*

This can be seen in Table 1.1.

Viewed from this perspective of group membership, it appears that there is almost complete consensus among Israeli Jewish groupings as to the relative importance of different areas of the city.

One of the few points at which there is some variance in prioritization occurs when the population is considered in terms of residence. Interestingly, Jerusalemites attribute considerably less relative (and absolute) importance to the

Table 1.1

Percentage answering "very important" when asked to what extent the area in question "is important to you as part of Jerusalem"

	Western Wall	Old City	Old Jewish neighborhoods	Jewish quarter in Old City	Mount of Olives	Temple Mount	New Jewish neighborhoods	Non-Jewish quarters in Old City	Arab downtown	Arab village areas
National	91	85	81	79	77	76	76	33	24	22
Settlers	92	86	84	79	80	81	79	42	32	32
Labor	85	79	78	71	67	64	71	23	14	10
Meretz	72	62	63	59	49	49	48	17	9	8
Likud	95	90	83	85	83	82	79	38	28	26
Right of Likud	95	92	90	88	85	82	83	54	38	35
Religious Parties	100	91	84	88	94	94	83	39	38	34
Tel Avivans	86	89	73	78	73	82	75	40	29	22
Jerusalemites	89	70	84	78	72	59	77	32	23	24
Israel-born	91	85	81	79	77	75	75	34	25	22
Soviet-born	88	85	73	78	69	64	67	27	20	16
North African-born	96	86	83	80	84	82	80	29	25	23
Totally non-observant	82	79	76	70	65	65	69	32	21	18

Temple Mount and the Old City than do Israelis as a whole. Analogously, Tel Aviv residents attribute higher relative and absolute importance to these areas than do Israelis as a whole. This suggests that the attachment to these parts of Jerusalem is a symbolic matter that is at its strongest when proximity and familiarity are at their weakest. In this regard it is interesting to note that a greater percentage of the totally nonobservant viewed the Temple Mount and the Old City as "very important" than did Jerusalem residents.

From this group perspective there is almost complete consensus that the areas of Arab residence are of significantly less importance than other areas of the city. With the exception of settlers and those whose ideological tendency is closer to parties to the right of Likud, not more than 40% of any subgroup categorized the non-Jewish quarters of the Old City as "very important" to them "as part of Jerusalem." Those who view Arab sections of the city outside the walls as "very important as part of Jerusalem" fall to very low numbers. For instance, within those who identified themselves as "closer to the Labor Party," 86% did not characterize the Arab neighborhoods in downtown areas of East Jerusalem as "very important." Among those "closer to Likud," 72% did not characterize this area as "very important." Even among those "closer to the parties to the right of Likud," only 38% characterized the Arab downtown as "very important to them as part of Jerusalem."

Consensus and Discord on Policy Options

As part of the study, respondents were asked to imagine that they were a member of the negotiating team and then to indicate how seriously they would consider each of ten specific proposals. The possible responses were "very seriously," "seriously," "not so seriously," "not at all," and a fifth response which was not read indicating refusal to consider compromises. Included were proposals to transfer to Palestinian sovereignty one or another of five areas of the city.

In Table 1.2 the percentages willing to consider a proposal seriously are contrasted to those that reject it flat out (responses 1 and 2 compared to 4 and 5). The proposals are organized into three groups, according to their relative negotiability.

These results closely parallel the answers given to the questions about the importance to the respondent of specific areas of the city. Thus, the areas of the city of least importance to Israeli Jews—the outlying areas of Arab residence that were only added to East Jerusalem after 1967—are the areas that received the most serious consideration for transfer to Palestinian sovereignty. Here, those seriously considering Palestinian sovereignty were greater than those flatly rejecting it (Q. 65, Q. 66).

The second least important areas for Israeli Jews, the central urbanized Arab areas of East Jerusalem outside the Old City (56% said "not so important," "not important at all," or "did not hear of this place"), received the second highest level of serious consideration for transfer to Palestinian sovereignty (34%), with

Table 1.2
Relative negotiability of ten proposals

	Percentage	
	Seriously consider	*Outright rejection*
Group I: Serious consideration > outright rejection		
65. Palestinian sovereignty over Arab settlements and villages previously in the West Bank which are now within the borders of Jerusalem (e.g., Shuafat, Um Tuba, Zur Baher, Beit Hanina)	45	36
66. Palestinian sovereignty for Arab village areas in Jerusalem, (e.g., Um Tuba) in exchange for Jewish areas of West Bank such as Maale Adomim becoming part of Jerusalem.	44	40
Group II: Serious consideration > 30%, outright rejection < 50%		
73. Autonomy for Arab areas in East Jerusalem	35	44
67. Arab areas in East Jerusalem outside Old City to Pal. sovereignty	34	44
74. Joint administration of Old City without yielding claim to sovereignty	34	41
69. Temple Mount under Wakf control as now	31	48
Group III: Serious consideration < 25%, outright rejection > 50%		
68. Palestinian sovereignty over Arab neighborhoods in Old City	23	55
70. Palestinian sovereignty over Temple Mount, Israeli over Western Wall	20	58
72. East Jerusalem under Palestinian sovereignty, with Jewish neighborhoods of East Jerusalem given special status under Israeli control	19	62
71. Old City internationalized under UN	18	64

less than half of the respondents flatly rejecting such transfer (Q. 67). Similarly, three proposals that did not transfer sovereignty to the Palestinians fall into this group of proposals receiving serious consideration from over 30% and flat rejection from less than 50% of Israelis (Q. 73, 74, 69).

For these first two groups of proposals there was substantial disagreement among Israeli Jews. When, however, it came to considering transferring sovereignty over the Arab quarters of the Old City to the Palestinians, the rejection was considerably stronger. Here only 23% were willing to give the proposal serious consideration (Q. 68). The willingness to consider Palestinian sovereignty over East Jerusalem as a whole or the Temple Mount was even lower (Q. 70, 72).

These national averages mask the full discord on the policy proposals that is found when responses are examined in terms of political identification. This is considered in Table 1.3.

Table 1.3

Percentage willing to consider specific proposals "seriously" or "very seriously" ("SC") and (second line) percentage responding with outright rejection ("OR")

	Meretz	Labor	Likud	Right of Likud	Religious parties
			Closer to		
Group I:					
65. Palestinian sovereignty over Arab settlements and villages previously in the West Bank which are now within the borders of Jerusalem (e.g., Shuafat Um Tuba, Zur Baher, Bet Hanina)					
Serious consideration	75	64	35	26	19
Outright rejection	13	20	45	56	56
66. Pal. sovereignty for Arab village areas in Jerusalem, (e.g., UmTuba) in exchange for Jewish areas of West Bank IMaale Adomim) becoming part of Jerusalem.					
Serious consideration	71	61	35	23	24
Outright rejection	17	22	48	58	62
Group II:					
73. Autonomy for Arab areas in East Jerusalem					
Serious consideration	61	45	30	22	17
Outright rejection	21	29	51	57	63
67. Arab areas in East Jerusalem outside Old City to Palestinian sovereignty					
Serious consideration	73	50	24	17	15
Outright rejection	14	26	53	66	66
74. Joint administration of Old City without yielding claim to sovereignty					
Serious consideration	52	47	26	22	17
Outright rejection	24	28	49	57	53
69. Temple Mount under Wakf as now					
Serious consideration	61	46	23	14	14
Outright rejection	20	32	55	68	73
Group III:					
68. Palestinian sovereignty over Arab neighborhoods in Old City					
Serious consideration	54	34	14	8	8
Outright rejection	25	40	65	80	74

Table 1.3 (continued)

			Closer to		
	Meretz	Labor	Likud	Right of Likud	Religious parties
70. Palestinian sovereignty over Temple Mount Israeli over Western Wall					
Serious consideration	59	31	12	7	5
Outright rejection	32	44	67	80	77
72. East Jerusalem under Palestinian sovereignty with Jewish neighborhood of East Jerusalem given a special status under Israeli control					
Serious consideration	37	27	12	11	10
Outright rejection	36	49	70	80	79
71. Old City internationalized under UN					
Serious consideration	35	25	13	10	8
Outright rejection	36	55	70	79	80

The table makes clear the existence of thoroughgoing differences among Israelis with respect to the policy proposals considered. The public that identifies with the parties at the two ends of the political spectrum—Meretz and parties to the right of Likud—occupy radically disparate positions on most of these proposals. Thus, 73% of those who identified as "closer to Meretz" would give serious consideration to giving the Palestinians sovereignty over Arab areas of East Jerusalem outside the Old City, with 14% flatly rejecting the idea. In contrast, only 17% of those "closer to parties to the right of Likud" would seriously consider the proposal, while 66% flatly reject consideration.

Even between those who identify with one of the two major parties, Labor and Likud, the degree of disagreement is striking. For instance, 34% of those closer to Labor would seriously consider a proposal to give Palestinians sovereignty over Arab neighborhoods in the Old City, while 40% would reject it outright. Among those closer to Likud, this is seriously considered by only 14% and rejected flat out by 65%. In short, Israeli Jews strikingly disagree on what to do about Jerusalem, and these disagreements are sharply visible in terms of party identification.

All the proposals in the second group (those where the population as a whole gives serious consideration greater than 30% and flat rejection less than 50%) show dominant support for serious consideration by those identifying with Labor, and they are majority positions for those identifying with Meretz.

These dramatic differences between political groupings with respect to policy cannot be fully explained by differences in the degree of attachment to areas of the city. For instance, 22% of those "closer to Likud" indicated that outlying Arab areas in East Jerusalem were "very important" and 35% were willing to take seriously a proposal to transfer these areas to Palestinian sovereignty. For those closer to Labor, 10% indicated these areas as "very important" and 64% were willing to seriously consider a transfer of sovereignty.

From a rationalist point of view, one that conceives of opinion as built upon a structure of "reasons," the extent of willingness to transfer any part of Jerusalem to Palestinian sovereignty should depend on a multiplicity of factors in addition to degree of attachment to that part of the city. For instance, a rationalist perspective would predict that such willingness also depends on people's beliefs about whether true peace is possible, whether a compromise on Jerusalem is necessary for peace, and whether Palestinians are perceived as having any rightful claims to Jerusalem.

Views on these issues are displayed in Table 1.4.

Previously, strong differences were noted in the responses when different groupings are asked how important to them "as part of Jerusalem" different parts of the city are. Yet those differences are not nearly as marked as those we see in Table 1.4, which displays, more strikingly than anywhere else, the way in which Israelis across the political spectrum have essentially different worldviews.

In Table 1.4 the first two questions deal with matters central to sound argumentation either for or against making compromises on the Jerusalem question, when such compromises are considered as a means to achieving true peace. One can assume that regardless of location on the political spectrum, all Israelis have a strong self-interest in "true, long-term peace." Where they would be expected to

Table 1.4
Percentage answering "yes" or "definitely yes" to questions relevant to the reasonableness (or unreasonableness) of compromising

	Closer to					
	Meretz	*Labor*	*Likud*	*Right of Likud*	*Religious parties*	*Total population*
41. Do you believe that a peace agreement with the Palestinians will bring a true, long-term peace?	77	63	14	7	10	33
43. To what extent do you believe that in order to make possible a true peace with the Palestinians we must make a compromise over Jerusalem?	56	37	10	7	9	20
61. In your opinion do the Palestinians have any sort of legitimate rights with regard to Jerusalem?	82	55	27	22	22	39

differ is over how to achieve peace, over what concessions are or are not necessary for peace, and over how much loss a person feels when taking such steps.

Given that there is wide support in Israel for continuing the peace process, one might have thought that most (although not all) Israelis believe a peace agreement with the Palestinians will bring true peace. However, only 33% of the population hold this view. Viewed in terms of party identification, Table 1.4 shows a striking degree of disagreement, with 63% of those closer to Labor believing that a peace agreement will bring true peace, while only 14% of those closer to Likud have this view.

Indeed, attitudes toward every one of the policy proposals divide quite sharply by positions on this key question of the relation of a peace agreement to true, long-term peace. This can be seen in Table 1.5, which considers the percentage of Israelis who would seriously consider or flatly reject each proposal.

The numbers in Table 1.5 should be read as answers to the question, "Of those who believe (or do not believe) that a peace agreement will lead to true peace, what percentage would seriously consider (or reject outright) the proposal?"

Table 1.5 shows how powerfully the issue of the efficacy of a peace agreement divides Israeli Jews. Of those who believe it will bring true peace, a majority are willing to seriously consider negotiating Palestinian sovereignty over Arab neighborhoods in Jerusalem outside the Old City, and even with respect to the Old City, those willing to seriously consider negotiating Palestinian sovereignty over Arab neighborhoods are greater than those who flatly reject the idea.

Looking at those who believe a peace agreement will lead to true peace, there is considerable openness to the proposals. It is only with the last three ideas—Palestinian sovereignty over the Temple Mount, Palestinian sovereignty over Jewish neighborhoods, and internationalization of the Old City—that we find those flatly rejecting the idea outnumbering those who would seriously consider it. These issues can be viewed as red lines that most Israeli Jews will not cross, even for the sake of genuine peace.

On the other hand, for those who do not believe a peace agreement will lead to true peace, the percentage flatly rejecting each proposal is greater than the percentage who would seriously consider it.

While it is perilous to attribute a causal relationship on the basis of correlations, it remains the case that not believing that a peace agreement will yield long-term peace is a very good reason for not making painful compromises.

Returning to Table 1.4, which deals with questions relevant to the reasonableness of compromise, the final question in the table considers the issue of the "legitimate rights" of Palestinians and the extent to which their claims are "justified." These issues enter into arguments based not on self-interest but on a person's sense of what is right. Here, too, we find strong differences across the political spectrum, with 82% of those who identify with Meretz and 55% of those who identify with Labor believing that Palestinians have legitimate rights with

Table 1.5
Percentage willing to consider specific proposals "seriously" or "very seriously" (top line) and percentage outrightly rejecting consideration (bottom line), in relation to beliefs about whether a peace agreement with the Palestinians will lead to true, long-term peace

		Will a peace agreement lead to peace?	
		Believe it will	*Do not believe it will*
Group I:			
65. Palestinian sovereignty over Arab village areas in East Jerusalem (e.g., Shuafat, Um Tuba, Zur Baher, Beit Hanina)	Serious Consideration	67	35
	Outright Rejection	16	46
66. Palestinian sovereignty for Arab village areas in Jerusalem, (e.g., Um Tuba) in exchange for Jewish areas of West Bank such as Maale Adomim becoming part of Jerusalem.	Serious Consideration	63	34
	Outright Rejection	20	49
Group II:			
73. Autonomy for Arab areas in East Jerusalem	Serious Consideration	50	28
	Outright Rejection	28	51
67. Arab areas in East Jerusalem outside Old City to Palestinian sovereignty	Serious Consideration	53	24
	Outright Rejection	24	54
74. Joint administration of Old City without yielding on claim to sovereignty	Serious Consideration	50	26
	Outright Rejection	26	49
69. Temple Mount under Wakf as now	Serious Consideration	48	23
	Outright Rejection	30	56
Group III:			
68. Palestinian sovereignty over Arab neighborhoods in Old City	Serious Consideration	41	13
	Outright Rejection	35	65
70. Palestinian sovereignty over Temple Mount, Israeli over Western Wall	Serious Consideration	37	13
	Outright Rejection	42	67
72. East Jerusalem under Palestinian sovereignty with Jewish neighborhoods of East Jerusalem given a special status under Israeli control	Serious Consideration	33	12
	Outright Rejection	43	71
71. Old City internationalized under UN	Serious Consideration	30	12
	Outright Rejection	47	72
	Percentage of total population	33	67

regard to Jerusalem, as opposed to approximately 25% who hold this view among those on the right. It is interesting to note that the disagreement over factual issues (e.g., whether a peace agreement will lead to true peace) is considerably stronger than the disagreement over the moral issue (whether the Palestinians have legitimate rights with regard to Jerusalem). On this issue, even though there remains a major right/left divide, those on the right and left take a step toward each other. For instance, 27% of those identified with Likud and 55% of those identified with Labor believe that Palestinians have some legitimate rights with respect to Jerusalem; with respect to the efficacy of a peace agreement, the Likud/Labor split was 14/63.

Here, as with those who believe that a peace agreement will lead to true peace, there is a marked willingness to compromise on Jerusalem among those who believe that Palestinians have legitimate rights vis-à-vis Jerusalem.

Question 50 in the survey was designed to probe Israeli Jewish willingness to give up parts of East Jerusalem provided that Israel retain those areas of the city it was cut off from when Jerusalem was divided. While it is distinctly unlikely that the Palestinians would find this proposal acceptable, it does allow us to examine the extent to which Israelis are willing to yield Arab neighborhoods provided that they retain their most cherished areas:

> Q. 50: To what extent would you agree to cede the Arab neighborhoods of East Jerusalem to the Palestinians if the Old City, the Mount of Olives, all of the Jewish neighborhoods of East Jerusalem, and Mount Scopus remain in Jerusalem as they are today?

Forty-two percent of Israeli Jews "agreed" or "definitely" agreed with this proposal. Table 1.6 shows how agreement to this proposal divides according to beliefs in the efficacy of a peace treaty, and beliefs with respect to Palestinian rights.

Looking at either those who believe in the efficacy of a treaty or those who believe that Palestinians have rights with respect to Jerusalem, the table shows *strong majorities in favor of the proposal.* Among those that hold opposite perspectives on these two key issues, there is a parallel strong opposition.

In sum, as noted earlier, when asked about the city as a whole, there is very strong opposition to negotiations on Jerusalem (78%). Yet when looked at in terms of their underlying beliefs, Israelis fall into multiple camps on key aspects of the Jerusalem question. Within each camp there is great internal consistency of empirical beliefs, value judgments, and attitudes toward various proposals.

As we move across the political spectrum from left to right, we find that each step to the right indicates greater attachment to the Arab-populated parts of the city, lesser belief that a peace treaty means peace, lesser belief that peace requires compromise on Jerusalem, and lesser belief that Palestinians have valid moral claims to Jerusalem, and, quite logically given these beliefs, each step to the right brings less willingness to compromise.

Table 1.6

Percentage willing to cede Arab neighborhoods if Israel retains the Old City, Mount of Olives, Mount Scopus, and Jewish neighborhoods

	Agree to cede Arab neighborhoods outside Old City	*Disagree to ceding Arab neighborhoods outside Old City*	
Believe a peace treaty will lead to true peace	66	34	(100%)
Believe Palestinians have legitimate rights with regard to Jerusalem	63	37	(100%)
Don't believe peace treaty will lead to true peace	30	70	(100%)
Don't believe Palestinians have legitimate rights with regard to Jerusalem	29	71	(100%)

How Negotiable Is Jerusalem?: An Interpretation

The study makes clear that an Israeli government that refuses to negotiate seriously on Jerusalem is not going to encounter major public opposition on that score. If the Jerusalem issue is to be successfully negotiated, even in part, it will require a government that believes in the possibility of true peace and in the importance of negotiating on Jerusalem to obtain that peace.

The population of Israeli Jews who identify with the Likud and parties to the right of Likud do not share these beliefs. Only 14% of those who identify with Likud believe that a peace agreement with the Palestinians will lead to true, long-term peace, and only 10% believe that a compromise on Jerusalem must be made for true peace with the Palestinians to ensue.

The question that remains open is this: To what extent does Israeli public opinion constitute a limit on potential Jerusalem accords beyond which even a government that sought to, could not go? There are two primary ways in which the government might be constrained by public opinion. The first is through the voting process if, as promised by Prime Minister Barak there is a referendum on any final status agreement. The second way a government would be constrained is if it feared unacceptable levels of societal discord in reaction to specific potential agreements.

As stated above, it is reasonable to assume that agreements unpopular with large segments of the Jewish community would result in major protests. This does not constitute anything new. Further, no Israeli government would allow itself to be blackmailed by a limited group of violent extremists. However, if a situation arose in which large segments of the population either engaged in extreme actions or viewed them sympathetically, then Israel would be faced with the prospect of a "meltdown" of civic order. It is doubtful that any government, even for the sake of a peace agreement, would be willing to take Israel down this path.

The study shows that in the event of a "wrong" compromise by a Knesset lacking a Zionist majority, among Likud-identified persons, 49% believe that nonviolent but disruptive actions would be justified, 24% believe that violent actions directed against Palestinians would be justified, and 8% believe that violent actions directed against other Jews would be justified. Interestingly, those identifying with parties to the right of Likud showed slightly less support for violent actions.

These are impressive numbers that would not be taken lightly by any government. Just how forceful public opposition would be of course depends enormously on the kind of agreement that was reached, whether it was viewed as merely wrong or crossed critical red lines.

The possibility that the government would submit a Jerusalem agreement to a referendum offers a way of sorting out the political viability of different proposals. If one makes the assumption that 10% of the voters in a national referendum are Israeli Arabs, and if it is assumed that the full 10% votes in favor of the proposal, then the proposal would have to win the support of roughly 45% of the Jewish vote in order to be accepted by 50% of the voters.

Only the proposal to give the Palestinians sovereignty over the outlying areas of Jerusalem received this level of Jewish support (45%). On the other hand, it is widely believed that with an actual proposal supported by the government, Israeli voters would show stronger support than in a hypothetical survey question. There is no way of knowing how great this additional support would be, but suppose we arbitrarily said that government support would add 10% of total Jewish voters to those who already supported the measure. On such assumptions, proposals such as giving up Arab areas in East Jerusalem outside the Old City (outlying and central), and joint administration of the Old City without Israel giving up its claim to sovereignty, are within the realm of possibility. Remaining out of reach even with these assumptions are proposals such as Palestinian sovereignty over Arab neighborhoods within the Old City and Palestinian sovereignty over the Temple Mount in exchange for Israeli sovereignty over the Western Wall.

The point here is not to speculate seriously about which proposals could win a referendum, but to get a sense of where to draw the line among proposals that are "do-ables," those that are "possibles" under favorable circumstances, and those that remain "nonstarters." These three characterizations correspond broadly to the three groupings of proposals in Tables 1.2, 1.3, and 1.5.

It is not possible to draw inferences as to the exact limits of negotiability imposed by Israeli Jewish opinion. A plausible case can be made that a determined government could transfer to Palestinian sovereignty the outlying areas of the city populated by Palestinians, and might further be able to transfer to Palestinian sovereignty the other Arab neighborhoods and downtown sections of East Jerusalem as well.

For any Israeli government to seek public approval along these lines would certainly be taking things to the edge of what is possible, both with respect to the results of a referendum and with respect to the carrying capacity of Israeli civility. *Yet, it is important to recognize that some openness exists even on the right and far right. For instance, Table 1.3 shows that serious consideration would be given to Palestinian sovereignty in the outlying areas of Jerusalem by 19% of those identifying with religious parties, by 26% of those identifying with parties to the right of Likud, and by 35% of those identifying with Likud.* This willingness on the part of some of those identified with parties on the right to seriously consider transferring to Palestinian sovereignty certain parts of East Jerusalem is particularly surprising given that 90% of those "closer to Likud" and 94% of those "closer to the parties to the right of Likud" indicated that they were "against" or "definitely against" negotiations on Jerusalem.

More generally, the data show that *opposition in principle to negotiations on Jerusalem does not imply rejection of specific disaggregated proposals, even those that would transfer specific areas to Palestinian sovereignty.* This conclusion is further supported by the fact that while 79% said they were against negotiations on Jerusalem, 42% indicated agreement with the proposal in Question 50:

> To what extent would you agree to cede the Arab neighborhoods of East Jerusalem to the Palestinians if the Old City, the Mount of Olives, all of the Jewish neighborhoods of East Jerusalem, and Mount Scopus remain in Jerusalem, as they are today?

Answers to two other questions also support this general conclusion that Israeli Jewish opinion does not rule out transferring certain areas of East Jerusalem to Palestinian sovereignty. Without postulating what would happen to excluded territories, the study probed attitudes toward redefinition of the boundaries of Jerusalem in order to ensure a Jewish majority:

> Q. 36: In order to ensure a Jewish majority, do you support or object to redefining the city limits so that Arab settlements and villages which are now within the borders of Jerusalem (such as Shuafat, Um Tuba, Zur Baher) will be outside the city?

1. Definitely support	17
2. Support	42
3. Object	34
4. Definitely object	7

*This majority in favor of redefinition of the boundaries (59% to 41%) clearly demon-
strates that the current boundaries do not have a sacrosanct place in Israeli conscious-
ness. Indeed, only 7% of the population "definitely objected" to redefinition.*

If a Palestinian state comes into being, this may tend to increase interest in
making the city more Jewish through redefinition of the boundaries. It can be
expected that a Palestinian government will extend Palestinian citizenship to all
Palestinians living in East Jerusalem. This was clearly foreshadowed by the fact
that these Palestinians (who are not Israeli citizens) were allowed to vote in the
Palestinian elections established by the Oslo Accord. Thus, if there is a Palestinian
state, Israelis may find that 190,000 Palestinian citizens are living in Jerusalem.

Question 39 probed Israeli Jewish responses to exactly this situation:

> Let's assume that a Palestinian state is established and Jerusalem remains
> united under Israeli sovereignty. In such circumstances, there is a rea-
> sonable chance that the Arab residents of East Jerusalem will become
> citizens of a Palestinian state. To what extent do you consider this a
> problem?

1. A very big problem	41
2. Some problem	34
3. A small problem	10
4. No problem at all	13
5. On the contrary, it is very desirable	3

Given this substantial Israeli discomfort with having 190,000 citizens of the
State of Palestine living within the Israeli capital, it is quite possible that Israelis
would favor redefining Jerusalem so that some of these residential areas were
outside Jerusalem, and indeed, outside Israel.

Thus, various aspects of the study point to the possibility of negotiating
Palestinian sovereignty over some parts of East Jerusalem. This, however, must be
sharply distinguished from Jewish Israeli opposition on two central Palestinian
objectives: that East Jerusalem become the Palestinian capital, and that the Palestinians obtain sovereignty over parts of the Old City, including the Temple
Mount. These require separate consideration and are taken up below.

Opposition to Jerusalem as the Palestinian Capital

Thus far the discussion has centered around Israeli Jewish attitudes toward proposals for Palestinian sovereignty over at least some part of East Jerusalem. Having
sovereignty, however, does not necessarily imply that East Jerusalem (or some part
of it) would be the Palestinian capital. On this latter issue, Israeli Jews are even
more opposed than with respect to sovereignty per se.

Table 1.7
Questions on Jerusalem as Palestinian capital

	Definitely justified	Justified	Not justified	Definitely not justified
62. To what extent, in your opinion, is the Palestinian claim for East Jerusalem as a capital justified?	2	18	43	37

80–81. Let's assume that with time a Palestinian state will be established. If that is the case, to what extent do you support or object to each of the following?

	Definitely support	Support	Object	Definitely object
80. That an Arab region in East Jerusalem will be designated as the capital of the Palestinian state.	4	16	30	50
81. That the Palestinian capital will be in a new city consisting of two parts: an area of East Jerusalem plus an area of the West Bank adjoining Jerusalem (such as Abu Dis) and will be named "Al-Quds."	4	19	29	48

The questions that addressed the issue of a Palestinian capital are displayed in Table 1.7.

It is noteworthy just how strongly respondents objected to these proposals. In response to the straightforward designation of part of East Jerusalem as a capital for the Palestinians, not only did 80% object, but 50% indicated that they "strongly object." This weak (20%) support for part of East Jerusalem as the Palestinian capital might be compared to the responses to Questions 50 and 67, which probed Israeli Jewish attitudes toward Palestinian sovereignty over Arab neighborhoods of East Jerusalem (outside the Old City) without addressing the issue of the Palestinian capital. Responses to these two questions showed that from 34% to 42% of Israeli Jews were open to Palestinian sovereignty, depending on how the option was framed.

It is also striking how little difference there was between the answers to Questions 80 and 81. The distinction between the proposals in 80 and 81 can be seen in two ways. On the one hand, the proposal in Question 81 can be seen as a "two-cities" approach, in which each side sees itself as retaining Jerusalem. Israel redefines its borders so as to exclude certain areas of Arab residence. These excluded areas are combined with a region outside present-day Jerusalem (Abu Dis) and together they form a new and different capital city, with a different name, "Al-Quds" (the Arabic name used to refer to Jerusalem).

On the other hand, the proposal in Question 81 can be seen as really the same as that in 80, with the different name for Jerusalem and the addition of Abu Dis as of little significance. The responses suggest that most Israelis saw little difference between the proposals, possibly because they were in sequence in the questionnaire.

Shortly after Israel's 1996 elections, the press reported on secret informal permanent status discussions that had occurred between the previous Labor government and the PLO. In those discussions, it appears that it was agreed that a Palestinian capital would be established in Abu Dis. The "Abu Dis" question in the survey should be sharply distinguished from that reported agreement.

That proposal did not transfer any part of present-day Jerusalem to Palestinian sovereignty; instead, it allowed the Palestinians to simply establish their capital in the Abu Dis suburb. Furthermore, that reported agreement was essentially a way of circumventing difficult final status questions about Palestinian sovereignty over East Jerusalem, as it allowed both sides to maintain their respective claims. Thus, it can be viewed as an interim proposal.

Given the responses to Question 81, the decision of Israeli negotiators not to go further appears to be borne out. *The Israeli public is not prepared to accept a proposal for a Palestinian capital that combines Abu Dis with part of East Jerusalem*, although conceivably they would accept a proposal making Abu Dis alone the Palestinian capital. Presumably, the Israeli government would then say the Palestinians had backed off their claim to East Jerusalem and the Palestinians would note that they have not accepted Abu-Dis-as-the-capital as permanent status. The study did not ask about a simple Abu-Dis-as-the-capital proposal, and it is possible that even this would lack sufficient public support.

Negotiability of the Old City and the Temple Mount

What remains to be discussed is the very heart of the matter, the Old City and the Temple Mount. Here, as elsewhere, the extent to which Israeli Jewish opinion constitutes a barrier to negotiability depends on the nature of the Palestinian bottom line position. With respect to the Temple Mount and the Old City, I make the following assumptions: (a) No Palestinian government could or would recognize Israeli sovereignty over the Old City as a whole, and (b) No Palestinian government could or would recognize Israeli sovereignty over the Temple Mount.

Three alternatives to negotiation deadlock are possible consistent with these Palestinian red lines:

1. A permanent status agreement on the Old City/Temple Mount is reached.

2. An interim agreement is reached.
3. Negotiations are postponed indefinitely, with the Old City/Temple Mount dispute sitting as one of perhaps many unresolved international issues separating the State of Israel from the State of Palestine.

The Old City was the subject of several specific questions. The study strongly suggests that it is not possible to reach a permanent agreement on the Old City. Consider Table 1.8:

Table 1.8
"Importance to you as part of Jerusalem" of the Old City and its elements

	Importance to you as part of Jerusalem			
	Very important	*Important*	*Not so important*	*Not at all important*
The Temple Mount	75	18	5	2
The Western Wall	91	8	1	1
The Jewish Quarter in Old City	79	15	4	2
The Old City	85	12	2	1
Non-Jewish Quarters of Old City	33	26	25	15

The table shows a consensus among Israeli Jews that the Old City (as a whole) is "important" or "very important" "as part of Jerusalem" and that the Jewish quarter, the Western Wall, and the Temple Mount are similarly so. Only with respect to the non-Jewish quarters is there a break with this pattern, and even here 59% view the area as a subjectively important part of the city.

These attitudes are reflected in the responses to policy proposals:

	I would consider the proposal				*Object to*
	Very seriously	*Seriously*	*Not so seriously*	*Not at all*	*compromise, won't consider*
68. Give the Palestinians sovereignty over the Arab neighborhoods of the Old City	7	16	22	36	19
69. The control of the Temple Mount will be under the Wakf as is now	9	22	22	29	19
70. The Palestinians will get sovereignty of the Temple Mount in exchange for Palestinian recognition of Israel's sovereignty of the Western Wall	5	15	21	36	22

71. Turn the Old City into an international city under the United Nations	5	13	18	40	24
72. Establish a joint Palestinian-Jewish administration for the Old City without Israel having to yield its claim to sovereignty	9	25	25	41	*

For each of these options, those flatly rejecting the proposal outnumbered those willing to give it serious consideration. This was even true of seemingly moderate proposals such as formalization of the current policy of Wakf administration of the Temple Mount (70) and establishment of a joint administration without yielding Israel's claim to sovereignty (72).

No more than 23% of the respondents were willing to consider seriously any proposal that would rescind Israeli sovereignty over any element of the Old City. And the proposal that received 23% (to give the Palestinians sovereignty over the Arab neighborhoods in the Old City) was flatly rejected by 55% of the respondents.

It seems clear that the negotiation of Palestinian sovereignty over part of the Old City is not possible, given the state of Israeli Jewish opinion. Thus, a permanent status agreement on the Old City cannot be fully negotiated at this point.

The proposal for joint administration, if accepted by both parties, could be part of a decision to postpone indefinitely the issue of sovereignty. While those flatly rejecting this idea outnumbered those willing to consider it seriously, the 41% to 34% ratio places this approach within the realm of the possible. It is likely, however, that any joint administration acceptable to the Israeli public would have to involve concessions from the Palestinians with respect to the present arrangements for the administration of the Temple Mount. This is suggested not just by the fact that formalization of the current policy of Wakf control was flatly rejected by 48% of the respondents, but also by responses to Question 75:

To what extent is it important to you that Jews can pray on the Temple Mount?

1. Very important   59%
2. Important   27%
3. Not so important   10%
4. Not at all important   4%

---

* This response category was mistakenly combined with "Not at all."

Under current Israeli policy, Jews are not allowed to pray on the Temple Mount, and it seems clear that there would be major opposition to the formalization of this arrangement in an agreement with the Palestinians. As noted earlier, it is striking that even among the totally nonobservant, 73% rank it as "important" or "very important" that Jews be allowed to pray on the Temple Mount.

The study considered one proposal to sidestep the issue of sovereignty over the Temple Mount. This proposal emerged from a formulation suggested by King Hussein that was deemed intriguing by Foreign Minister Peres during the Rabin government:

> There is a proposal that each side should stop arguing about sovereignty over the Temple Mount and agree that sovereignty belongs to God. Is this approach acceptable to you?

1. Definitely yes	9%
2. Yes	26%
3. No	32%
4. Definitely no	33%

This 65% to 35% rejection is interesting when compared to the mere 20% willing to seriously consider Palestinian sovereignty over the Temple Mount in exchange for recognition of Israeli sovereignty over the Western Wall.

Despite the strong level of rejection, the "sovereignty belongs to God" formulation may in fact hold promise. It is striking that rejection of this approach was highest among the totally nonobservant, and acceptance was highest among the strictly observant:

| | | To a great extent | Observe somewhat | Totally nonobservant |
	Strictly observant			
76. There is a proposal that each side should stop arguing about sovereignty over the Temple Mount and agree that sovereignty belongs to God. Is this approach acceptable to you?				
1. Definitely yes	20	8	8	8
2. Yes	22	28	27	23
3. No	30	37	33	28
4. Definitely no	28	28	32	41
Total	100%	100%	100%	100%
Number	140	268	712	356

In this regard it is also worth noting that as religious observance decreased so did the personal importance attributed to the Temple Mount. The more important the Temple Mount was to respondents the more likely they were to find some merit in the "sovereignty belongs to God" approach.

Whether the "sovereignty belongs to God" formulation will prove to be a fruitful approach to taking the sharp edge off conflicting Israeli and Palestinian claims to sovereignty over the Temple Mount remains to be seen. What is not speculative, however, is the fact that the permanent status of the Temple Mount will be an extraordinarily difficult obstacle to a comprehensive and permanent solution to the Jerusalem question.

Summary

These conclusions may be reached on negotiability in relation to Israeli Jewish public opinion:

1. There is no majority support for any proposal which would give Palestinians sovereignty over any part of Jerusalem.

2. Opposition to Jerusalem as the capital of Palestine is even greater than it is to partial sovereignty, and appears beyond the realm of possibility given current Israeli Jewish opinion.

3. The degree of opposition to Palestinian sovereignty differs very widely depending on the area of Jerusalem in question.

4. It is possible that public opinion could support an agreement that gave Palestinians sovereignty over the outlying regions within Jerusalem, and possibly even the urbanized areas of East Jerusalem outside the Old City.

5. The opposition to Palestinian sovereignty over areas within the Old City is sufficiently great as to make resolution of the sovereignty question thoroughly unlikely. However, joint administration is possible while leaving the issue of sovereignty unresolved. This solution becomes more likely if Jewish prayer on the Temple Mount is accommodated.

6. Thus, the final status of parts of Jerusalem may be negotiable, with the Old City and the Temple Mount subject to administrative agreements reached through the negotiating process.

One Major Caveat

This consideration of reactions to various policy proposals indicates that Israelis might accept dealing with sovereignty in a piecemeal fashion, and dealing with different elements at different points.

There is one main caveat to be noted to this conclusion, and it emerged when we considered how convincing the respondents found various arguments for or against making compromises on Jerusalem.

Of the various reasons against making any compromises on Jerusalem there was one in particular that resonated broadly—even more broadly than the belief that a peace agreement would not lead to true peace. Israeli Jews were asked how convincing they found the following assertion:

> There should not be a compromise over Jerusalem because concessions in Jerusalem will only enhance the Palestinians' demand for more concessions.

In response, 58% found this to be very convincing, and an additional 25% found it convincing. Thus, 83% of the respondents made clear their concern that the demand for concessions would be never-ending. This, no doubt, is part of the reason why there is much greater opposition to negotiating on Jerusalem in general than there is to various specific proposals (78% oppose negotiations, while support for certain proposals runs over 40%).

And this is indeed the dilemma. Even assuming that for the Palestinians there are potential negotiated outcomes that they would treat as comprehensive, final, and permanent, these ask from Israelis more than they are willing to give. And while the Palestinians may be willing to take less on a partial or interim basis, the Israeli public believes that it is better to make no concessions at all than to start down this road.

If Jerusalem is to be negotiable a way will have to be found to solve this dilemma. The problem is compounded by the marked skepticism of those on the right that a peace agreement will lead to true and lasting peace. The study suggests that to the extent that Israeli public opinion precludes the negotiability of Jerusalem, there is a twofold explanation. With respect to some areas of the city, the explanation is to be found simply in a deep Israeli Jewish attachment that tends towards non-negotiability. For other areas the explanation is not primarily a matter of powerful attachment, but rather the simple logic of not negotiating away valued areas when you believe that concessions will only result in further demands or when you believe that even a peace treaty will not lead to peace.

These two concerns—that concessions lead to further demands and that a peace treaty will not bring true peace—are intertwined. If demands are always escalating, then true peace is indeed an impossibility. And if true peace, for whatever reason, is not possible, this may express itself in a continued escalation of demands.

Clearly then, beliefs with respect to the possibility of true peace are central to the degree of negotiability of Jerusalem. How fixed are these beliefs and what factors do they respond to? These are critical questions not just for Jerusalem, but for the peace process as a whole.

The study probed responses to two hypothetical developments: that Saudi Arabia would open an embassy in Jerusalem, and that regular commercial relations

with the Arab states would emerge. Table 1.9 shows the extent to which those
with differing beliefs as to current prospects for true peace indicated they would
find such events convincing evidence that true peace was really possible.

The columns of numbers in the table should be read as answering the
question: Of those who believe strongly (or other column heading) that true
peace will result from a peace agreement, how convincing of "long-term peace"
would they find "opening of a Saudi embassy in Jerusalem" or "regular commercial
relations with Arab states"?

Table 1.9
Would it convince you that real, long-term peace is possible?

	To what extent do you believe there can be true peace between Israel and the Arab world in the foreseeable future?				
	Believe strongly	*Believe*	*Don't believe so much*	*Don't believe at all*	*Total*
63. To what extent would it convince you that long-term peace with the Arab world is possible if Saudi Arabia opens an embassy in Jerusalem?					
Very convincing	30%	16%	7%	4%	10%
Convincing	34%	38%	22%	16%	26%
Not so convincing	25%	21%	42%	31%	32%
Not at all convincing	11%	25%	29%	49%	32%
Total	100%	100%	100%	100%	100%
N	97	441	542	426	1506
64. To what extent would it convince you that long-term peace with the Arab world is possible if there were regular commercial relations with Arab States?					
Very convincing	45%	26%	10%	8%	16%
Convincing	39%	50%	38%	23%	38%
Not so convincing	11%	17%	34%	30%	26%
Not at all convincing	5%	7%	18%	38%	20%
Total	100%	100%	100%	100%	100%
N	96	441	545	426	1508

The table shows that those who already hold strong beliefs ("believe strongly" or "don't believe at all") with respect to the possibility of peace are either strongly supported in their beliefs or relatively unaffected in their beliefs by the hypothetical developments. Thus, of those that "believe strongly" that peace is possible, 64% would find the opening of a Saudi embassy in Jerusalem "convincing" or "very convincing," and 84% would find regular commercial relations "convincing" or "very convincing." Similarly, of those that "don't believe at all" in the possibility of peace, 80% would find the opening of a Saudi embassy "not so convincing" or "not at all convincing," and 68% would find regular commercial relations "not so convincing" or "not at all convincing."

Perhaps of more interest than those with very strong beliefs with respect to the possibility of true peace are those two groups in the middle—those that "believe" and those that "don't believe so much" that peace is possible. These groups make up roughly two-thirds of the population. Of those who presently "don't believe so much" that there can be true peace in the foreseeable future, 29% would find it "convincing" or "very convincing" if Saudi Arabia opened an embassy in Jerusalem, and 48% would find it "convincing" or "very convincing" if there were regular commercial relations with Arab states. And of those that say they "believe" (as opposed to "believe strongly") in the possibility of peace, 54% would be strengthened in that belief by the opening of a Saudi embassy in Jerusalem, and 76% strengthened in that belief by regular commercial relations.

The larger picture suggested by the data is that, while for all groups the possibility of peace is central to the willingness to compromise over Jerusalem, for the bulk of Israeli Jews—those who do not hold strong beliefs as to whether peace is possible—there is a readiness to examine potential evidence. Presumably events can drive these beliefs either way. Thus a process of unfolding peace will tend to be self-perpetuating, and similarly a collapsing peace process will destroy the belief that peace is possible, leading to further collapse. In the end, while the negotiability of Jerusalem may be a necessary condition for lasting peace, successful negotiation may depend heavily on the prior emergence of the hallmarks of peace.

B. Palestinians

As with the study of Israeli Jews, the study of Palestinian attitudes does not yield a single, simple message. The Jerusalem question is complex, and the study results are equally complex. Study findings can be grouped in terms of those that point toward the negotiability of the Jerusalem question and those that suggest that it will not be possible to successfully negotiate the issues involved.*

For the reader it is important to attempt to grasp the results in their entirety. Focusing on any specific question may prove to be misleading. In particular, because of the powerful symbolism attached to the term "Jerusalem," it is important to set responses to aggregate questions about Jerusalem as a whole in the context of responses to disaggregated questions about specific parts of the city, or to specific proposals for dealing with aspects of the Jerusalem issue. For example, when you ask Palestinians whether there should be any concessions over Jerusalem, 82% say that there should not be, even if it means giving up achieving a Palestinian state. Yet when specific compromises are put forward, there is considerable support for many of them.

Findings Militating Toward Negotiability
1. Eighty percent of Palestinians are either "for" or "definitely for" negotiations on Jerusalem within the peace process.
2. Forty-two percent of Palestinians say they do not consider the large areas first included by the Israelis within the municipal boundaries after 1967 as part of Jerusalem.

---

* It should be remembered that questions were posed in Arabic. Thus, Palestinians were asked about Al-Quds, the term used to refer to Jerusalem, but which to Palestinians may not always have either the same denotations or connotations as does "Jerusalem" in English or "Yerushalayim" in Hebrew. Similarly, in the study of Israeli Jewish attitudes, people were asked about "Yerushalayim." In what follows, "Jerusalem" is used to refer to the area within the current Israeli municipal boundaries.

3. Forty-six percent of Palestinians consider the Western Wall as "not so important" or "not at all important" to them "as part of Jerusalem."

4. Fifty-nine percent of Palestinians consider the Jewish quarter of the Old City as "not so important" or "not at all important" to them "as part of Jerusalem."

5. Fifty-three percent of Palestinians consider the new Jewish neighborhoods established after 1967 which are included by Israelis in Jerusalem (e.g., Gilo, Ramot, Pisgat Zeev) as "not so important" or "not at all important" to them "as part of Jerusalem."

6. Fifty-three percent of Palestinians would accept as a permanent solution of the Jerusalem question that Israel has sovereignty over West Jerusalem and the State of Palestine has sovereignty over East Jerusalem.

7. Thirty-eight percent of Palestinians, in order to attain a Palestinian majority in the city, would support redefining the city limits so that Jewish areas built after 1967 on areas that had been outside the city are again outside the city. Among Palestinian Jerusalemites, this rises to 46%.

8. Seventy percent of Palestinians support genuine and lasting peace with Israel in exchange for recognition of a Palestinian state with its capital in East Jerusalem and resolution of the refugee issue, "even though this will inevitably fall short of full justice for the Palestinians."

9. Sixty-five percent of Palestinian "agree" or "strongly agree" that "certain compromises could be made on Jerusalem in order to bring peace."

10. Sixty-four percent favor some compromises on Jerusalem "if doing so gains more favorable outcomes on other issues in the negotiations, such as statehood, refugees, and borders."

11. Forty percent "agree" or "strongly agree" that "a compromise on Jerusalem is the right thing to do because Israelis also have deep historical and religious attachments to Jerusalem."

12. Sixty-four percent of Palestinians find acceptable the proposal that "each side should stop arguing about sovereignty over holy sites in Jerusalem and agree that ultimate sovereignty belongs to God."

13. Forty percent of Palestinians would "seriously" or "very seriously" consider a proposal for the Old City in which Israel would get sovereignty over the Jewish neighborhoods and Palestine would get sovereignty over the Palestinian neighborhoods.

14. Fifty percent of Palestinians would "seriously" or "very seriously" consider a proposal in which the Palestinians would get sovereignty

over the Haram al-Sharif in exchange for Palestinian recognition of Israeli sovereignty over the Western Wall.

15. Forty-one percent of Palestinians would "seriously" or "very seriously" consider a proposal in which Palestinians would have sovereignty over the al-Aqsa mosque and the Dome of the Rock. But, with respect to the plateau itself, sovereignty would be shared with the Israelis, although day-to-day administration of the plateau would be in Palestinian hands.

Other findings underscore just how difficult it will be to negotiate the Jerusalem question.

Findings Militating Against Negotiability

1. Eighty-seven percent of Palestinians would advise Palestinian negotiators to be "less" or "much less" compromising in negotiations with the Israelis over Jerusalem. (*Note:* Formal negotiations on Jerusalem had not yet started at the time this question was asked.)
2. Nineth-four percent of Palestinians would not support recognizing Israel's claim that it alone is sovereign over Jerusalem, even if that was the only way a Palestinian State could come into being.
3. Ninety-two percent of Palestinians say that Jerusalem is "very important" to them personally.
4. Eighty-six percent of Palestinians do not believe that it is true that Jerusalem is important to Israelis "as a national center."
5. Sixty-four percent of Palestinians do not believe that it is true that Jerusalem is important to Israelis "as a religious center."
6. Ninety-four percent of Palestinians consider the Haram al-Sharif (the Temple Mount) as "very important" to them "as part of Jerusalem."
7. Sixty-six percent of Palestinians consider the Mount of Olives as "very important" to them "as part of Jerusalem" with an additional 29% considering it "important" as part of Jerusalem.
8. Eighty-six percent of Palestinians consider the Old City as "very important" to them "as part of Jerusalem" with an additional 12% considering it "important" as part of Jerusalem.
9. Eighty-two percent of Palestinians "agree" or "strongly agree" that there should be "no concessions at all over Jerusalem," even if it means giving up achieving a Palestinian State.
10. Seventy percent of Palestinians "agree" with the claim that "because Judaism is a religion, Jews should not be thought of as constituting a people and therefore are lacking in national rights."
11. Eighty-five percent find "convincing" or "very convincing" that there should not be any compromise on Jerusalem because "Jerusalem in its entirety is the heart of Palestine."

12. Seventy-three percent find "convincing" or "very convincing" that there should not be any compromise on Jerusalem because "Israel has no right to Jerusalem at all."

13. Eighty percent of Palestinians say "no" or "definitely no" when asked if Jews have "any sort of legitimate rights with regard to Jerusalem."

14. Ninety percent of Palestinians say that beyond attaining Palestinian sovereign rights in East Jerusalem it is "very important" that, in addition, East Jerusalem be a Palestinian capital.

15. Sixty-two percent of Palestinians say they would participate in some action against an agreement on Jerusalem of which they don't approve.

16. Seventy-two percent agree that "in the case of an unacceptable agreement on Jerusalem, Palestinians have the right to use all means necessary to block its implementation."

17. Seventy-six percent would "not take seriously" or would "totally reject" a proposal to allow Jews to pray on the Haram al-Sharif.

18. Fifty-seven percent would "not seriously consider" or would "totally reject" a proposal in which West Jerusalem and the Jewish neighborhoods in East Jerusalem would be under Israeli sovereignty and the rest of East Jerusalem under Palestinian sovereignty with the Old City dealt with separately.

19. Seventy-one percent would "not seriously consider" or would "totally reject" a proposal in which Israel would exercise sovereignty over East Jerusalem, but Palestinians would be given a special self-rule status.

The Importance of Jerusalem to Palestinians

The parallel study of Israeli Jews ("The Status of Jerusalem in the Eyes of Israeli Jews" by Elihu Katz, Shlomit Levy, and Jerome Segal) revealed that only 19% of Israeli Jews believe that Jerusalem is "very important to the Palestinians as a national center," with an additional 44% believing that for Palestinians it is "important as a national center."

When Palestinians are asked about the importance of Jerusalem to themselves, they present a strikingly different picture. Ninety-two percent say that Jerusalem is "very important" to them personally, and an additional 7% say that it is "important." When asked about the perspectives from which they find Jerusalem important, 90% find it "very important" from an "Islamic religious" point of view. But rather than this constituting the core of Palestinian engagement with Jerusalem, the same percentage, 90%, judge it "very important" as "a symbol of the future Palestinian state."

Indeed, when asked, "Assume that a satisfactory agreement giving the Palestinians sovereign rights in East Jerusalem can be reached, how important to you is it that, in addition, East Jerusalem be a Palestinian capital?", again, 90% say that it is "very important."

These attitudes are reflected in responses given to other questions as well. When asked, "If the only way a Palestinian state could come into existence was by recognizing Israel's claim that it alone is sovereign over all of Jerusalem, would you support that?", 75% said "definitely no," and an additional 19% said "no." When asked, "In comparison with other topics that are being negotiated with the Israelis, such as water rights, return of Palestinian refugees, and the status of settlements, is the topic of Jerusalem more or less important than these other topics?", the response was:

1.	Much more important	47%
2.	More important	11%
3.	As important	41%
4.	Less important	1%
5.	Much less important	0%

And when asked, "If a Palestinian government accepts a compromise on Jerusalem that you don't approve of, how will you react?", the response was:

1.	Will definitely oppose	31%
2.	Will oppose	35%
3.	Will accept with reservations	28%
4.	Will accept	6%

Further, some 62% said that they would participate in some action against an agreement on Jerusalem of which they did not approve.

Thus the picture that emerges is that Jerusalem is of great importance to almost all Palestinians; the nature of this importance is not confined to the religious dimension, but also encompasses issues of sovereignty and of Jerusalem as the capital and symbol of a Palestinian state.

The Subjective Importance of Different Parts of the City to Palestinians

A defining feature of this study is that Jerusalem was approached in a disaggregated manner. While some questions were asked about Jerusalem as a whole, we specifically sought to understand Palestinian attitudes toward different parts of the city, and found that disaggregation matters. Thus when asked, "How important is Jerusalem to you personally?", 92% said that it was "very important" and an additional 7% said that it was "important." But when we asked about the "importance as part of Jerusalem" of varying sections of the city, the response was much more complex.

Table 1.10 shows that there is a sharp degree of prioritization when it comes to what is "important as Jerusalem." Of the greatest importance is the Old City, and in particular the al-Aqsa mosque, the Haram al-Sharif (the Temple Mount), and the Islamic quarter within the Old City. When attention is turned to areas of Jewish residence, the percentage of Palestinians that view these areas as "very important as Jerusalem" drops to below 30%. This is even true with respect to the Jewish quarter within the Old City.

From Table 1.10 it can be seen that prioritization is a feature of the Palestinian experience of Jerusalem independent of region, religion, religiosity, or political affiliation. People in all groupings make major distinctions in the degree of importance of the different areas of the city. Moreover, with the exception of Palestinian Christians, different areas basically receive the same priority ranking.

This can be seen, perhaps even more dramatically, in Table 1.11, which shows the percentage of Palestinians who answered "not so important" or "not important at all" when asked the same question.

Table 1.11 shows that for every grouping considered, the percentage of Palestinians that view Jewish residential areas, whether in West Jerusalem, East Jerusalem, or the Old City, as "not so important" or "not important at all as part of Jerusalem" is typically half or more. Although to a somewhat lesser extent, this even applies to the Western Wall, an area judged by Israeli Jews to be of the highest importance. In interpreting these numbers, it is important to remember that people were answering with respect to how important a specific area is "as part of Jerusalem." To say that it is "not important at all as part of Jerusalem" is not the same as saying that it is not important. Rather, it is to say that it does not partake in the special importance of Jerusalem and, as such, is likely to be more amenable to compromise.

Palestinian Responses to Specific Proposals

When asked broad *aggregate* questions about "concessions on Jerusalem" (as opposed to questions on specific compromises), Palestinians are strongly opposed. For instance:

Q. 44: There are people who say that we should make no concessions at all over Jerusalem even if we have to give up achieving a Palestinian state. To what extent do you agree or disagree with this statement?

1. definitely agree	64%
2. agree	18%
3. disagree	12%
4. disagree	6%

Table 1.10

Percentage answering "very important" when asked to what extent the area
in question "is important to you as part of Jerusalem"

	AA	HS	Old City	Isl Qtr	MT. O	Arab downtown	Chr Qtr	WW	New Jewish Neigh	Old Jewish Neigh	JQtr OC
National	95	94	86	85	66	59	47	34	29	26	24
West Bank	93	92	87	83	62	54	55	38	26	22	27
Gaza	98	98	85	89	72	66	33	26	35	32	17
Jerusalem	91	89	96	83	65	70	62	36	30	26	33
Very religious	98	99	92	94	76	73	50	41	31	39	21
Not at all religious	79	78	88	70	60	57	69	38	31	23	33
Muslims	96	96	87	87	64	59	46	35	31	26	24
Christians	67	65	80	64	75	43	80	36	7	15	29
Islamists	98	98	87	91	65	59	44	38	32	29	23
Leftists	81	81	82	75	58	51	67	33	26	23	28
Fatah	97	97	86	86	70	62	47	35	29	26	24
Independents	92	91	86	82	61	56	44	35	28	25	25

Key: al-Aqsa (AA); Haram al-Sharif (HS); Islamic quarter of Old City (Isl Qtr); Mount of Olives (MT O); Palestinian neighborhoods in downtown East Jerusalem such as Wadi Jos, Sheikh Jarah (Arab downtown); Christian quarter of the Old City (Chr Qtr); Western Wall (WW); Jewish neighborhoods of East Jerusalem built since 1967 (New Jewish Neigh); Jewish neighborhoods of West Jerusalem (Old Jewish Neigh); Jewish quarter of the Old City (J Qtr. OC).

Table 1.11

Percentage answering "not so important" or "not at all important" when asked to what extent the area in question "is important to you as part of Jerusalem"

	AA	HS	Old City	Isl Qtr	MT. O	Arab downtown	Chr Qtr	WW	New Jewish Neigh	Old Jewish Neigh	JQtr OC
National	0	1	2	2	5	8	23	46	53	56	59
West Bank	1	1	2	3	5	9	14	39	55	58	56
Gaza	0	0	1	1	5	6	39	59	49	52	51
Jerusalem	2	2	0	1	2	3	10	41	45	45	51
Very religious	1	1	2	0	4	2	26	41	54	50	64
Not at all religious	4	4	1	6	8	9	5	41	54	50	64
Muslims	0	0	1	1	5	8	23	45	51	55	58
Christians	7	9	3	9	7	11	4	55	77	77	56
Islamists	0	0	2	0	5	8	26	39	52	53	62
Leftists	5	5	3	8	5	12	11	46	62	56	53
Fatah	0	1	4	2	3	7	25	48	54	58	56
Independents	1	1	4	2	7	11	24	44	48	55	56
Support genuine peace	1	1	1	1	5	8	21	45	54	60	58
Not support genuine peace	1	1	4	3	4	9	28	51	52	48	63

Key: al-Aqsa (AA); Haram al-Sharif (HS); Islamic quarter of Old City (Isl Qtr); Mount of Olives (MT O); Palestinian neighborhoods in downtown East Jerusalem such as Wadi Jos, Sheikh Jarah (Arab downtown); Christian quarter of the Old City (Chr Qtr); Western Wall (WW); Jewish neighborhoods of East Jerusalem built since 1967 (New Jewish Neigh); Jewish neighborhoods of West Jerusalem (Old Jewish Neigh); Jewish quarter of the Old City (J Qtr. OC).

And when asked, "If you were able to advise Palestinian negotiators with respect to Jerusalem, with respect to their willingness to reach a compromise with the Israelis, how would you advise them?", the response was:

1. Be much less compromising   62%
2. Be less compromising   25%
3. Be more compromising   14%

If this were all there were to Palestinian views on potential compromise, one could have little hope indeed about the possibility of arriving at a negotiated solution. But, as was found with the Israeli public, the Palestinian public responds in one fashion when asked about Jerusalem as a whole and in a more nuanced and flexible manner when asked about specific parts of the city and specific proposals.

As part of the study, Palestinians were asked to assume that they were part of the negotiating team considering Jerusalem. They were asked how seriously they would consider each of ten proposals. This is shown in Table 1.12.

The proposals in Table 1.12 are organized into three groups. Those in the first group received very strong support. In each case, at least 50% would "seriously consider" or "very seriously" consider the proposal, and no more than roughly one-third of the Palestinian population indicated that they would either "not take the proposal seriously" or "totally reject it."

Of particular interest within this first group is the strong support for two proposals involving a measure of compromise. The proposal contained in Question 61 would deal with the Old City separately; Israel would have sovereignty over West Jerusalem, and control, but not sovereignty over the Jewish neighborhoods in East Jerusalem outside the Old City. Fifty-two percent of Palestinians would give serious consideration to this proposal and 36% dismiss it. The proposal contained in Question 64 also received very strong support (50% seriously consider, 35% dismiss). Here the Palestinians would get sovereignty over the Haram al-Sharif in exchange for Palestinian recognition of Israeli sovereignty over the Western Wall.

The proposals in the second group lack majority support, but they are certainly within the realm of what might ultimately prove to be acceptable to Palestinians. At least 40% of Palestinians would "seriously" or "very seriously" consider these proposals, and less than 50% dismiss them as not worthy of consideration.

The proposal in Question 68 draws a particularly important distinction between the mosques on the Haram al-Sharif and the plateau itself. According to this proposal Palestinians would have sovereignty over the mosques, but would share sovereignty over the plateau with the Israelis. Day-to-day administration of the plateau would (as is presently the case) be in Palestinian hands. Forty-one percent indicated a willingness to seriously or very seriously consider the proposal.

Table 1.12
Relative negotiability of ten proposals

	Percentage	
	Seriously consider	*Reject/not seriously consider*
Group I: Serious consideration > reject/not seriously consider		
69. The control of the Haram al-Sharif would be under the Wakf as it is now.	60	28
67. Abu Dis would be added to Jerusalem and the Palestinian Parliament would be located in that region of the expanded city.	53	36
61. West Jerusalem would be under Israeli sovereignty and East Jerusalem would be under Palestinian sovereignty, with a special arrangement for Israeli control of the Jewish neighborhoods in East Jerusalem. The Old City would be dealt with separately.	52	32
64. The Palestinians would get sovereignty over the Haram al-Sharif in exchange for Palestinian recognition of Israeli sovereignty over the Western Wall.	50	35
Group II: Serious consideration > 30%, reject/not seriously consider < 50%		
68. Palestinians would have sovereignty over the al-Aqsa mosque and the Dome of the Rock, but with respect to the plateau itself, sovereignty would be shared with the Israelis, although day-to-day administration of the plateau would be in Palestinian hands alone.	41	47
60. Israel and Palestine together would exercise joint sovereignty over an undivided city.	40	45
62. In the Old City, Israel would get sovereignty over the Jewish neighborhoods, and Palestine would get sovereignty over the Palestinian neighborhoods.	40	47
Group III: Serious consideration < 30%, reject/not seriously consider > 50%		
66. West Jerusalem and the Jewish neighborhoods in East Jerusalem would be under Israeli sovereignty and the rest of East Jerusalem under Palestinian sovereignty, with the Old City dealt with separately.	28	57
65. Israel would exercise sovereignty over East Jerusalem, but Palestinian neighborhoods would be given a special self-rule status.	20	71
63. Jews would be allowed to pray on the Haram al-Sharif, which would be under operational authority of the Wakf.	17	76

Similar percentages would also give serious consideration to the two other proposals in this group: joint sovereignty over an undivided city and Israeli sovereignty over the Jewish neighborhoods in the Old City and Palestinian sovereignty over the Palestinian neighborhoods.

In the third group there are three proposals that received rather thorough rejection. The first, contained in Question 66, would provide for Israeli sovereignty over the Jewish neighborhoods in East Jerusalem. Strikingly, only 28% of Palestinians are prepared to "seriously consider" this, while 57% dismiss it. Receiving even less support were the two remaining proposals: that Palestinians would have a "self-rule" status under Israeli sovereignty in East Jerusalem and that Jews would be allowed to pray on the Haram al-Sharif.

In Table 1.13 the responses to these proposals are broken down by political affiliation. The table shows that the greatest support comes from those identifying with Fatah, and second, from those identifying as independents. Those identifying as leftists or Islamists are significantly less willing to seriously consider any of these proposals.

Table 1.13 illustrates several points worth noting:

- There is a significant, yet not vast, degree of difference to be found in the acceptability of these proposals across the political spectrum.
- With minor exceptions, all the political groupings show the same rank ordering of the proposals.
- Those who identify with Fatah find these proposals more acceptable than those identifying with any of the other political orientations.
- Those who identify themselves as independents show the second highest willingness to seriously consider the proposals.
- The Islamists and the leftists show the least willingness to seriously consider the proposals. Between them, they differ proposal by proposal.
- Among those who identify with Fatah, more would "seriously consider" the three proposals in Group II than would dismiss ("not seriously consider" and "reject totally") the proposal. This includes their response to Question 68, which would give Israel sovereignty over the Jewish neighborhoods in the Old City.
- Thirty-nine percent of the Islamists would seriously consider shared sovereignty over the Haram al-Sharif plateau, provided that there was Palestinian sovereignty over the mosques and day-to-day Palestinian administration of the plateau.
- Even among Islamists, Proposal 64, according to which Israel would have sovereignty over the Western Wall (in exchange for Palestinian sovereignty over the Haram al-Sharif), would be seriously considered by 41% and is rejected by less than 50%.

Table 1.13

Percentage willing to consider specific proposals "seriously" or "very seriously" ("SC") and (second line) percentage that would "reject totally" or "not seriously consider" (R), by political orientation

		Closer to			
		Fatah	Independent	Islamist	Leftist
Group I: Seriously consider > reject/not seriously consider					
69. The control of the Haram al-Sharif would be under the Wakf as it is now.	SC	63	60	59	37
	R	23	39	28	56
67. Abu Dis would be added to Jerusalem and the Palestinian Parliament would be located in that region of the expanded city.	SC	61	50	49	44
	R	25	39	44	45
61. West Jerusalem under Israeli sovereignty and East Jerusalem under Palestinian sovereignty, with special arrangement for Israeli control of the Jewish neighborhoods in East Jerusalem. Old City dealt with separately.	SC	59	53	41	48
	R	27	29	41	33
64. The Palestinians would get sovereignty over the Haram al-Sharif in exchange for Palestinian recognition of Israeli sovereignty over the Western Wall.	SC	57	51	41	41
	R	27	36	46	40
Group II: Serious consideration > 30%, reject/not seriously consider < 50%					
68. Palestinians would have sovereignty over the al-Aqsa mosque and the Dome of the Rock, but with respect to the plateau itself, sovereignty would be shared with the Israelis, although day-to-day administration of the plateau would be in Palestinian hands alone.	SC	45	39	39	23
	R	43	47	51	70
60. Israel and Palestine together exercise joint sovereignty over an undivided city.	SC	45	42	30	30
	R	36	43	60	51
62. In the Old City, Israel sovereignty over the Jewish neighborhoods, and Palestine sovereignty over the Palestinian neighborhoods.	SC	44	41	31	37
	R	41	47	57	49

Group III: Serious consideration < 30%, reject/not seriously consider > 50%

66. West Jerusalem and the Jewish neighborhoods in East Jerusalem under Israeli sovereignty, and the rest of East Jerusalem under Palestinian sovereignty; Old City dealt with separately.	SC	33	28	20	23
	R	55	54	66	61
65. Israel would exercise sovereignty over East Jerusalem, but Palestinian neighborhoods would be given a special self-rule status.	SC	21	20	14	22
	R	69	72	77	68
63. Jews would be allowed to pray on the Haram al-Sharif, which would be under operational authority of the Wakf.	SC	21	15	17	19
	R	72	77	77	70
Percentage of total population		36	33	21	11

- Even among those identifying with Fatah, Proposal 66, in which the Jewish neighborhoods in East Jerusalem would be under Israeli sovereignty, is rejected by more than 50%.
- The two least attractive proposals, 65 (self-rule but not sovereignty over Palestinian neighborhoods) and 63 (Jewish prayer on the Haram al-Sharif) receive no significant level of support from any political grouping. Indeed, on these proposals, Fatah supporters are indistinguishable from the leftists.

Palestinian Support for Genuine Peace with Israel

In the parallel study of Israeli Jews it was found that those who believe that peace with the Palestinians would result in genuine peace were considerably more willing to compromise. However, it was also found that two-thirds of Israeli Jews do not believe that a peace agreement with the Palestinians will lead to real peace. Thus, among Israeli Jews there is widespread doubt and skepticism as to whether Palestinians and the Arab nations truly seek lasting peace with Israel. These perceptions play a powerful role in determining the extent to which Jerusalem is negotiable.

It is important to bear in mind the distinction between support for the peace process and support for genuine and lasting peace. From an Israeli point of view, the fear is that Palestinian support for the peace process is largely tactical, not an expression of an underlying willingness to make genuine peace with Israel.

In the study of Palestinian opinion we asked about their attitudes toward lasting peace with Israel. Their responses are reflected in Table 1.14.

Table 1.14 shows that support for genuine and lasting peace with Israel (provided that there is a Palestinian state with East Jerusalem as its capital and resolution of the refugee issue) is quite high, and even among Islamists, it reaches almost 50%.

In reading Table 1.14 it is worth noting that:

- Seventy percent of Palestinians support genuine peace. This support is almost as high in Gaza as it is in the West Bank, and it is about the same level for Jerusalemites.
- Support for genuine and lasting peace varies considerably among political factions, ranging from a high of 82% for those identified with Fatah, to a low of 48% for the Islamists.
- On this issue there is a wide gap between the 67% support among leftists and the 48% support among Islamists, even though they were at similar levels with respect to specific proposals considered for Jerusalem.

Table 1.14
Q. 44: Do you support genuine and lasting peace with Israel in exchange for recognition of a Palestinian state with its capital in East Jerusalem, and resolution of the refugee issue, even though this will inevitably fall short of full justice for the Palestinians?

	Definitely yes or yes	Definitely yes	Yes	No	Definitely no
National	70	26	44	17	13
Islamist	48	17	31	26	26
Left	67	20	47	24	9
Fatah	82	33	49	12	6
Independents	72	23	49	16	12
Very Religious	60	25	35	18	22
Religious	67	25	42	17	16
Not Religious	74	25	49	19	7
Not at All Religious	73	24	49	19	8
West Bank	71	21	50	16	13
Gaza	68	35	33	19	13
Jerusalem	68	25	43	15	17
Muslim	69	26	43	18	14
Christian	85	18	67	13	2

- Support for genuine and lasting peace varies inversely with religiosity, however; even among the very religious it is 60%.
- Among Christians it is 85% and among Muslims it is 69%.

Those who say that they would not support genuine and lasting peace with Israel, even if there were a Palestinian state with Jerusalem as its capital and even if there were resolution of the refugee issue, make up some 30% of the Palestinians. Whether this represents a group that would under no conditions give up the struggle, we do not know. However, the operative question is whether Israel can make peace with the 70% of the Palestinians who at present, at least in principle, are willing to do so.

Resolving the Jerusalem question will be central to being able to do this. It is thus particularly interesting to see how this 70% who support genuine peace is both similar to and different from the 30% who reject it.

Who are the 70% who support genuine and lasting peace? This is addressed in Table 1.15.

Table 1.15
Characteristics of Palestinians who support genuine and lasting peace with Israel and those who do not

Q. 44: Do you support genuine and lasting peace with Israel in exchange for recognition of a Palestinian state with its capital in East Jerusalem, and resolution of the refugee issue, even though this will inevitably fall short of full justice for the Palestinians?

		Percentage Distribution	
	Yes/no split	*of those saying "Yes"*	*of those saying "No"*
Gender			
1. Male	71/29	55	50
2. Female	67/33	45	50
Religion			
1. Islam	68/32	92	96
2. Christianity	85/33	8	3
Religiosity			
1. Very religious	62/38	12	16
2. Religious	67/32	46	50
3. To some extent	75/25	33	25
4. Not at all religious	72/28	10	9
Education			
1. Illiterate	80/20	8	4
2. 4 yrs. schooling	68/31	5	5
3. 5–8	70/30	14	13
4. 9–10	68/31	11	11
5. 11 yrs.	70/30	8	8
6. 12 yrs.	69/31	27	27
College	69/31	14	14
Bachelor's	62/39	11	16
Place of birth			
1. Inside 1948 boundaries	75/15	7	6
2. Inside West Bank or Gaza	69/31	88	91
3. Outside region	60/40	2	3
Political orientation			
1. Islamist	51/50	15	35
2. Leftist	65/35	9	12
3. Fatah	82/18	43	22
4. Independent	71/29	33	31

From Table 1.15 it can be seen that of the 70% of Palestinians who support genuine and lasting peace with Israel (given the conditions specified), most (92%) are Muslim, a majority (55%) are male, a majority (58%) are religious or very religious, and most (76%) identify politically in terms of either Fatah or as independents.

At the same time, it is interesting to note that support for genuine peace is strong across all divisions of gender, religion, religiosity, level of education, and place of birth or political orientation, with the exception of Islamists. *And even here there is an even split between those who support genuine peace and those who do not.*

How do the beliefs and attitudes of those who support peace with Israeli compare to those who do not? This is addressed in Table 1.16.

Table 1.16 reveals that those who support genuine and lasting peace with Israel are quite similar to those who do not, regarding (1) what they would tell Palestinian negotiators, (2) their unwillingness to forgo Palestinian sovereignty in Jerusalem, and (3) the importance to them of Jerusalem as the Palestinian capital.

Similarly, when it comes to awareness of the importance of Jerusalem to Israelis, perceptions of Judaism, and the rights of Jews with respect to Jerusalem, there are only marginal differences between those who support genuine peace and those who do not.

- Those who support peace show a marginally greater acknowledgment (37% as opposed to 32%) of the importance, from a religious point of view, of Jerusalem to Israelis.
- The two groups are identical in their broad agreement (70%) with the claim that "because Judaism is a religion, Jews should not be thought of as a people and therefore are lacking in national rights."
- The two groups are quite similar in denying that Jews have "any sort of legitimate rights with regard to Jerusalem" (78% of peace supporters deny this claim, and 83% of those that do not support peace deny it).

Thus, what distinguishes those who support peace from those who do not is not a lesser attachment to Jerusalem, nor a greater understanding of the meaning of Jerusalem to Israelis, nor a greater acceptance of claims about either the national rights of Jews as a people or the specific rights of Jews with regard to Jerusalem.

Further, those who deny that Jews have "any sort of legitimate right to Jerusalem" are almost as strongly supportive of genuine peace with Israel (68%) as are those who believe Jews do have some rights with regard to Jerusalem (75% of whom support genuine peace.) Thus it appears that the widespread support for "genuine and lasting peace" (given the satisfaction of the identified conditions) while reflecting a desire for peace, does not rest on a broad perception of the partial validity of the perspective of the other side.

On a range of other issues, however, significant differences emerge between those that support genuine peace and those that do not:

- Overall, only 35% of Palestinians believe that there can be true peace between Israel and the Arab world in the foreseeable future.

Table 1.16
Differences and similarities between Palestinians who support genuine and lasting peace with Israel and those who do not

		"Do you support genuine peace . . . ?" Percentage distribution	
		Yes	No
5.	If you were able to advise Palestinian negotiators with respect to Jerusalem with respect to their willingness or unwillingness to reach a compromise with the Israelis, how would you advise them?		
	1. Be much less compromising	58	70
	2. Be less compromising	27	18
	3. Be more compromising	15	12
7.	If the only way a Palestinian state could come into being was by recognizing Israel's claim that it alone is sovereign over all of Jerusalem, would you support that?		
	1. Definitely no	70	83
	2. No	23	10
	3. Yes	6	3
	4. Definitely yes	1	3
59.	Assume that a satisfactory agreement giving the Palestinians sovereign rights in East Jerusalem can be reached. How important to you is it, that in addition, East Jerusalem be a Palestinian capital?		
	1. Very important	92	83
	2. Important	7	10
	3. Not important	1	3
	4. Not important at all	0	3
46.	Do you agree with the claim that because Judaism is a religion, Jews should not be thought of as constituting a people, and therefore are lacking in national rights?		
	1. Agree	70	70
	2. Disagree	31	31
58.	In your opinion do Jews have any sort of legitimate rights with regard to Jerusalem?		
	1. Yes (75/25)	22	17
	2. No (68/32)	78	83
45.	Do you believe that a genuine Israeli willingness to compromise on Jerusalem would lead to true and lasting peace between Israel and the Arab world?		
	1. Definitely agree	9	5
	2. Agree	44	19
	3. Disagree	37	43
	4. Definitely disagree	10	33

However, of those that do support genuine peace on the identified conditions, 43% believe that peace is possible whereas only 18% of those that do not support genuine peace believe it is possible.

- Of those that believe peace is possible, 84% support it (given the conditions); of those who don't think it is possible, 62% support it.
- Of those that support peace, 53% believe that a genuine Israeli willingness to compromise on Jerusalem would lead to true peace whereas of those that do not support genuine peace, only 24% hold this view.
- Interestingly, there is more strong support (56% to 43%) among those who do not support genuine peace for a proposal to stop arguing over sovereignty of the holy sites and instead say that "ultimate sovereignty belongs to God."

In Table 1.17, the two groups are compared in terms of their willingness to seriously consider specific proposals.

Table 1.17 allows for an examination of the responses of the 70% of the Palestinians who support genuine and lasting peace with Israel (on the condition of a Palestinian state with East Jerusalem as its capital and resolution of the refugee problem) and of the 21% of Palestinians who believe that Jews have "some sort of legitimate rights in regard to Jerusalem." Several points may be noted:

- While the 70% of Palestinians that support genuine peace are considerably more favorably disposed to most of the proposals, with one exception, those that support genuine peace rank the various proposals in the same order as those that do not.
- The one exception is the proposal for Palestinian sovereignty over East Jerusalem with a special status allowing for Israeli control over Jewish neighborhoods in East Jerusalem and dealing with the Old City separately. This received the greatest support by those in favor of genuine peace; 62% would seriously consider it.
- With respect to the Old City, those that support genuine peace are equally divided between those that would seriously consider Israeli sovereignty over Jewish neighborhoods and Palestinian sovereignty over Palestinian neighborhoods.
- When it comes to Israeli sovereignty over the Jewish neighborhoods in East Jerusalem outside the Old City, willingness to seriously consider the proposal drops off to 32% of those that support genuine peace.
- Even among those who support genuine peace there is little willingness to seriously consider Palestinian self-rule within the context of Israeli sovereignty over East Jerusalem, and even less support for allowing Jewish prayer on the Haram al-Sharif.

Table 1.17

In relation to beliefs about peace and rights of Jews, percentage willing to consider specific proposals "seriously" or "very seriously" ("SC") and (second line) percentage that would "reject totally" or "not seriously consider" (R)

		Support Genuine Peace		Jews have some legitimate rights in regard to Jerusalem	
		Yes	*No*	*Yes*	*No*
Group I: Serious consideration > reject/not seriously consider					
69. The control of Haram al-Sharif would be under the Wakf as it is now.	SC	cross tab data not available			
	R				
67. Abu Dis would be added to Jerusalem and the Palestinian Parliament would be located in that region of the expanded city.	SC	57	47	52	55
	R	32	42	35	36
61. West Jerusalem under Israeli sovereignty and East Jerusalem under Palestinian sovereignty, with special arrangement for Israeli control of the Jewish neighborhoods in East Jerusalem. Old City dealt with separately.	SC	62	32	68	48
	R	24	48	20	35
64. The Palestinians would get sovereignty over the Haram al-Sharif in exchange for Palestinian recognition of Israeli sovereignty over the Western Wall.	SC	54	43	64	47
	R	31	45	20	39
Group II: Serious consideration >30%, reject/not seriously consider < 50%					
68. Palestinians would have sovereignty over the al-Aqsa mosque and the Dome of the Rock, but with respect to the plateau itself, sovereignty would be shared with the Israelis, although day-to-day administration of the plateau would be in Palestinian hands alone.	SC	cross tab data not available			
	R				
60. Israel and Palestine together exercise joint sovereignty over an undivided city.	SC	44	30	57	35
	R	38	60	30	50
62. In the Old City, Israeli sovereignty over the Jewish neighborhoods, and Palestine sovereignty over the Palestinian neighborhoods.	SC	44	31	46	38
	R	43	57	36	50

Group III: Serious consideration < 30%, reject/not seriously consider > 50%

66. West Jerusalem and the Jewish neighborhoods in East Jerusalem under Israeli sovereignty, and the rest of East Jerusalem under Palestinian sovereignty; Old City dealt with separately.	SC	32	18	29	27
	R	56	70	52	59
65. Israel would exercise sovereignty over East Jerusalem, but Palestinian neighborhoods would be given a special self-rule status.	SC	20	16	23	19
	R	69	77	67	72
63. Jews would be allowed to pray on the Haram al-Sharif, which would be under operational authority of the Wakf.	SC	18	17	21	17
	R	75	77	67	78
Percentage of total population		70	30	20	80

The division of the population into those that recognize some Jewish rights vis-à-vis Jerusalem and those that do not follows the pattern seen in dividing the population into those that support genuine peace and those that do not. Thus, those that recognize Jewish rights and those that do not, have essentially the same ranking of proposals. Those that recognize Jewish rights are systematically more disposed to seriously consider the proposals than those that do not recognize Jewish rights, with the exception of the three proposals in Group III. Here, even those that recognize Jewish rights show very little willingness to seriously consider the proposals, and have hardly more willingness to do so than those that do not recognize Jewish rights.

Of those who recognize some Jewish rights vis-à-vis Jerusalem, 75% also support genuine peace with Israel. Of those that support genuine peace with Israel, 78% do not recognize Jewish rights in regard to Jerusalem. The supporters of peace constitute a substantial majority of the Palestinians (70%). Palestinians who recognize Jewish rights constitute only a small minority (20%) of Palestinians. Yet when we compare these two groups (those that support genuine peace and those that recognize some Jewish rights vis-à-vis Jerusalem), we find that their responses to the various proposals are quite similar. Those that recognize Jewish rights are somewhat more favorably disposed to the proposals in Groups I and II than are those who support peace. Yet, for both of these populations, these varied proposals receive a plurality that would give them serious consideration. Strikingly, almost two-thirds of those that recognize Jewish rights would recognize Israeli sovereignty over the Western Wall in exchange for recognition of Palestinian sovereignty over the Haram al-Sharif. And 57% of those that recognize Jewish rights would support joint sovereignty over an undivided city.

But when it comes to the proposals in Group III, including Proposal 66, which gives Israel sovereignty over the Jewish neighborhoods in East Jerusalem, those that support Jewish rights are no more willing to seriously consider these proposals than those that support genuine peace. Both groups reject them forcefully.

The Palestinian data is brought together with the Israeli Jewish data to assess the implications for negotiability in Part IV, "Is Jerusalem Negotiable?"

PART II

The Status of Jerusalem in the Eyes of Israeli-Jews

A Survey Research Perspective

SHLOMIT LEVY AND ELIHU KATZ

An Analysis of Israeli Jewish Opinion
on the Status of Jerusalem

SHLOMIT LEVY

Introduction

In 1995, the Center for International and Security Studies of the University of Maryland developed a project entitled "Jerusalem: Exploring the Limits of Negotiability." The purpose of the project was to explore the attitudes, beliefs, and values of the Israeli and Palestinian publics toward the possibility of reaching a permanent status agreement on Jerusalem. The project was also concerned with developing policy recommendations bearing on Jerusalem, for both governmental and nongovernmental actors seeking to promote resolution of the Israeli-Palestinian conflict.

Within this larger project, "The Status of Jerusalem in the Eyes of Israeli Jews" was the first subproject. Under the leadership of Jerome M. Segal, the Maryland team sought the collaboration of the Guttman Institute of Applied Social Research. Located in Jerusalem, the Guttman Institute is one of Israel's leading survey research institutions. A research team was constituted, consisting of Elihu Katz and Shlomit Levy from the Guttman Institute, and Jerome Segal from the University of Maryland.

The study that we undertook together establishes a new baseline for understanding how Israeli Jews conceive the multiple dimensions of the Jerusalem issue. Prior to undertaking the interviews, with the assistance of Tamar Liebes, we conducted six focus groups sessions with Israeli Jews from across the political spectrum. We then developed a lengthy questionnaire consisting of eighty-five substantive questions, plus a series of background questions that was used in over 1,500 face-to-face interviews. Unlike other inquiries, which have approached Jerusalem as an undifferentiated entity, or as a symbol, the present study is an effort to understand

Israeli attitudes more concretely-towards different parts of the city as well as towards the city as a whole. The survey, in effect, invites respondents to step into the shoes of the negotiators (or to refuse to do so), and to consider what is, and what is not, negotiable.

The study is unique in another respect: the assassination of Prime Minister Rabin was perpetrated while fieldwork was being conducted. Interviewing of a national sample of Israeli Jews had begun on September 17, 1995, was suspended for about three weeks for the high holidays, and resumed on October 17, only to be interrupted, traumatically, by Rabin's assassination on November 4. Although the fieldwork was formally continued, the country was in such a state of shock and mourning that very little work was accomplished before December 5, 1995, the end of the official mourning period, and was completed only several weeks later.

The sample represents all Jewish adults over 20 years of age, in all types of communities except kibbutzim. The sampling procedure involved three stages. In the first stage, cities, towns and villages were sampled, following the guidelines of Israel's Central Bureau of Statistics. Within the sampled towns, households were sampled from election rosters, and within households, the individual to be interviewed was chosen according to the Kish method (L. Kish, 1967, *Survey Sampling,* New York: John Wiley and Sons, pp. 396–401). Respondents were interviewed in their homes by trained interviewers working under the supervision of field supervisors. The original design called for interviews with 1,200 respondents.

Prior to the assassination, 850 interviews had been completed. Since it seemed likely that the assassination would affect attitudes toward the peace process and the linked question of Jerusalem, it was decided to augment the remaining 350 interviews with a further national sample of 300, drawing on the same settlements and the same criteria for selecting households and interviewees, in order to make "before" and "after" comparison possible. Thus, the augmented sample comprises 1,530 respondents, of whom 850 were interviewed before the assassination and 680 afterward. The "before" and "after" interviews should not be regarded as separate samples, however, but as two subgroups, like any other group division in the data analysis. For most purposes, the combined sample of 1,530 are treated as a single national sample. Where appropriate, comparisons are made between "before" and "after" subgroups, in an effort to spell out the effects of the Rabin assassination from very close up.

In addition to the national sample, data were gathered on a special sample of 121 settlers in the territories, employing the same questionnaire. Almost all of them were interviewed following the Rabin assassination.

The settlers constitute a distinct population. They are concentrated in the younger age groups; only 4% of them are over 55 years old, compared to 21% in the national sample. They are better off socioeconomically, compared to the population as a whole, especially with regard to education and gross income: only 6% of the settlers have less than 12 years of schooling, compared to 25% in the regular population; and 31% of the settlers have a gross monthly income of over 8,000 NIS, compared to 14% in the national sample.

The proportion of observant respondents within the settlers' sample is considerably higher than in the national sample. Over half (57%) identify themselves as religiously observant (27% as "strictly observant"), and only 14% are "totally nonobservant." Appendix A presents the questionnaire together with the percentage distribution of the responses, for the settler sample and the national sample.

In addition to these two samples, we have supplemented the SHAS political group (religiously observant Sepharadis) beyond the fourteen who identified themselves in the national sample in answer to the question, "If elections were held today, for which party would you vote?" Thus, the total number of SHAS supporters has been enlarged to seventy. It should be noted that this is only a "convenient sample," rather than a representative one, and is analyzed separately in order to understand the unique attitudes of this party, an ethnic-religious faction that has been gaining power in recent years.

The majority of SHAS supporters in this group are of eastern origin, mainly North African, and all are religiously observant (77% strictly observe the religious tradition, and 23% "observe to a great extent"). Ideologically, almost all (93%) feel closer to the religious parties. A great majority of them (80%) have no more than a high school education, and the remaining fifth have more than thirteen years of schooling, with only 4% having a full academic education. The great majority is in the lower-income brackets (the gross family income of 90% of SHAS supporters is less than 5,000 shekels per month). Thus, from a religious viewpoint, SHAS supporters are more similar to the settler sample than to the national sample, with an even higher proportion of observance. Their socioeconomic status, on the other hand, is lower than that of the settler sample.

What follows is a detailed analysis of the survey data by Shlomit Levy, consisting of six brief sections. Section 1 presents an overview of findings from the national sample, including a comparative analysis of findings "before" and "after" the assassination. Section 2 compares attitudes of Jewish Jerusalemites toward the status of their city with the attitudes of Jewish residents of other Israeli cities. Sections 3 and 4 consider the influence of personal, social, and political affiliations on attitudes toward the status of Jerusalem. Section 5 elaborates on the issues relating to negotiations on Jerusalem within the peace process, and section 6 considers how the attitudes expressed by the settlers and by the enlarged SHAS sample differ from those of the national sample.

The reader interested in the language and methodology of the survey will wish to consult the appendices. Appendix A-1 presents the questions asked and marginal distributions of the replies. Appendix A-2 cross-tabulates these replies by ideological tendency as defined by political affiliation and voting intentions. Appendix A-3 cross-tabulates religious observance.

Elihu Katz concludes this part by highlighting and commenting on the analysis.

1. The Status of Jerusalem in the Eyes of Israeli Jews: An Overview Before and After the Rabin Assassination

This chapter presents an overview of the study as a whole, beginning with the nature of involvement of Israeli Jews with the city of Jerusalem, and the nature of their involvement in the peace process. These two commitments, it will be seen, do not always sit well with each other. Wherever appropriate, the findings of the survey are analyzed to highlight the effect of the Rabin assassination on the distribution of attitudes.

Involvement with the Peace Process

About 80% of Israeli Jews consider themselves involved in the peace negotiations: one-third are involved "to a great extent." When the topic of Jerusalem is broached, involvement increases to 90%, of whom *half* choose the affirmative answer "to a great extent" (Appendix A, Q. 5, 6).

The Meaning of Jerusalem

For the vast majority of Israeli Jews (77%), Jerusalem is "very important" personally, even more so after Rabin's assassination (75% and 80% respectively). Only for a tiny minority (2%) Jerusalem is "not so important." Most Israeli Jews also feel a sense of belonging to the city: 69% chose the extreme answer "definitely yes" (Q. 8, 9), both before and after Rabin's assassination.

The respondents were asked to indicate the importance of Jerusalem to them personally, from five points of view (Q. 10–14). Table 2.1 presents the ranking of these five points of view according to their importance, as well as a before and after comparison.

Almost all points of view are "very important" to the majority of Israeli Jews, both before and after the assassination. The highest importance is attributed to "Jerusalem as a symbol of the State of Israel" (83%), followed immediately by the "national-historical" viewpoint (80%) and "as a center for the Jewish people and Judaism" (77%). Somewhat less importance is attributed to the Jewish religious point of view (68%). Each of these aspects systematically gained in importance after the assassination. Thus, for Israeli Jews, Jerusalem is considered the symbolic center of the Jews and Judaism, even more from a national-historic point of view and as symbolic of the State than from the religious point of view. Least of all is Jerusalem symbolized as "a center for world religions."

However, this least important aspect (48%) underwent a dramatic change following Rabin's assassination—its importance increased from a minority of 38%

Table 2.1
Ranking of importance of Jerusalem from five points of view
before and after Rabin's assassination
(percentage answering "very important")

	To what extent is Jerusalem important to you?		
Points of view	Before Rabin's assassination	After Rabin's assassination	Total sample
As a symbol of the State of Israel	83	84	83
Jewish national-historical point of view	78	82	80
As a center for the Jewish people and Judaism	75	80	77
Jewish religious point of view	65	71	68
As a world center for all religions	38	61	48

who considered it "very important" to a majority of 61% who considered it "very important." Despite this change, its location is still at the bottom of the ranking. Moreover, it should be noted that this point of view, in contrast to the others, is unrelated to attitudes concerning the status of Jerusalem. The assassination, apparently, illuminated the universality of Jerusalem alongside its Jewish centrality. Along the same lines, the percentage of those saying that Jerusalem is "not at all important" to the Palestinians as a national center decreased from 22% before the assassination to only 11% afterward, while many more consider it "important" for the Palestinians after the assassination. However, even after the assassination only a small minority think that Jerusalem is "very important" as a national center for the Palestinians (21% and 17% respectively). As we shall soon see, for the Palestinians, too, Jerusalem symbolizes "the future Palestinian state," first and foremost (90%). Even if 77% of Palestinians also consider the city important "as a center for world religions," this aspect of Jerusalem was at the bottom of the scale for Palestinians too.

The meaning of Jerusalem was further examined by asking respondents to assess those areas of the city "that you consider important as part of the city" (Q. 16–25). The assassination did not change the relative importance attributed to these sites, as Table 2.2 makes evident. Almost all Israeli Jews (91%) consider the Western Wall to be "very important" as part of Jerusalem, followed immediately by the Old City (85%). A great majority (76% to 81%) consider all Jewish neighborhoods (the old and the new), the Mount of Olives, and the Temple Mount to be "very important" as part of Jerusalem. Only a negligible minority (1% to 5%) consider each of these to be "not so important" or "not at all important" as part of Jerusalem. On the other hand, one-third consider the non-Jewish quarters in the

Table 2.2
Ranking of importance of sites in Jerusalem as part of the city
before and after Rabin's assassination
(percentage answering "very important")

| | Importance of sites as part of Jerusalem Percentage answering "very important" | | |
The site	Before Rabin's assassination	After Rabin's assassination	Total sample
The Western Wall	91	91	91
The Old City	84	86	85
Old Jewish neighborhoods	82	79	81
The Jewish quarter in the Old City	80	78	79
Mount of Olives	77	77	77
The Temple Mount	77	74	76
New Jewish neighborhoods (established after 1967)	76	76	76
Non-Jewish quarters in the Old City	36	31	33
Arab neighborhoods in downtown East Jerusalem	26	22	24
Arab settlements and villages previously in the West Bank	23	20	22

Old City to be "very important" as part of Jerusalem, and only about one-fifth consider the Arab neighborhoods outside the Old City to be "very important" as part of Jerusalem. As for the non-Jewish neighborhoods outside the Old City, the pattern is roughly 45% ("very important" and "important") versus 55% ("not so important" and "not important"), while for the non-Jewish quarters inside the Old City the pattern is the opposite: 60% versus 40%. The rank order in Table 2.2 is shared by almost all groups in the population, demographically and politically, even when the extent of attributed importance varies, as will be elaborated below.

A similar list of parts of the city was presented to Palestinian respondents (see above, p. 41). For them, the Jewish quarters in West Jerusalem and sites in the Old City that are holy to Jews and Christians (but not to Moslems) are not accorded high importance as parts of the city. Thus, the two "maps" of the city—the one of the Jews, the other of Palestinians—do not completely overlap, except for the Old City generally speaking, and the Temple Mount, specifically. It follows that the heart of the problem lies in the similar *national* meaning attributed to

Jerusalem as symbol of statehood (Israel, and the future Palestine) whose most concrete expression is the walled Old City in general and some of its holy places.

Visits to Jerusalem

Almost all Israeli Jews (99%) residing outside Jerusalem have visited Jerusalem, the majority (65%) "quite a lot of times," or more (Q. 27). Noteworthy is the outstanding increase of "one-time" visitors after Rabin's assassination, probably due to the masses of people who came to Jerusalem to pay their respects at Rabin's coffin and grave throughout the thirty days of mourning; for many of them this may have been their first visit to Jerusalem. The number of visits to the Old City of Jerusalem was not changed by Rabin's assassination. Almost all Israeli Jews (98%) residing outside Jerusalem have visited the Old City at one time or another, most of them (84%) *after* the intifada, with 40% of the visits being recent, namely, "a few months ago" and "in the past month" (Q. 28).

Seventy-three percent have never visited Arab villages that are now included within the borders of Jerusalem, and a similar proportion have never visited the Arab neighborhoods of Wadi Jos or Sheikh Jarah of East Jerusalem. Most of those who have visited these neighborhoods have done so quite rarely, "once" or "a few times" (Q. 30). Only a minority, about 5%, have visited these places many times. This pattern remains unchanged after the assassination.

The Demography and Size of Jerusalem

Did the demography of Jerusalem undergo any change since 1967, with regard to its two main population groups, Jews and non-Jews? According to the 1995 statistical yearbook of Jerusalem, the proportion of Jews vis-à-vis non-Jews remained principally the same throughout the years, as can be seen from the following table (Table 2.3), extracted from the yearbook.

Table 2.3 points to the fact that the proportion of non-Jews (Arabs) in Jerusalem remained virtually the same, with minor oscillations of 2.5% or less. Thus, the Arab population increased by 2.5% from 1967 to 1993, now amounting to 28%. Indeed, the majority of Israeli Jews (56%) gave a correct estimate regarding the proportion of the Arab population of Jerusalem (Q. 32).

Surprisingly, the number of respondents who chose the correct answer increased from 48% before the assassination to 65% after the assassination (respondents answering "don't know" were omitted from the calculations). The remainder of the sample and of each group mostly underestimated the proportion of Arabs, assessing the percentage to be 15% to 20%. Hence, almost all Israeli Jews (92%) know that the Jews constitute a majority in Jerusalem, and most indicated the correct proportion. However, only a small minority (7%) are aware of the fact that the proportion of Arabs in Jerusalem has remained essentially the same since

Table 2.3*
Population of Jerusalem by population group
in selected years since 1967 (in percentages)

End of year	Jews	Non-Jews**
1967	74.2	25.8
1972	73.4	26.6
1983	71.4	28.6
1985	71.6	28.4
1990	72.1	27.9
1991	72.2	27.8
1992	72.1	27.9
1993	71.7	28.3

* From Table III/1 of the *1993 Statistical Yearbook of Jerusalem*, edited by M. Choshen and N. Shahar, Jerusalem: The Municipality of Jerusalem and The Jerusalem Institute for Israel Studies, 1995, p. 25.
** "Non-Jews" is the term used in the yearbook; this group, however, is principally Arab.

1967. The majority believe that the proportion of Arabs increased "somewhat" or even "greatly" (Q. 33). After the assassination, the percentage of respondents who think that the proportion of Arabs "increased greatly" dropped from 35% to 17%, giving way to the answer "increased somewhat." Here again, the estimate after the assassination seems to be more realistic.

Sixty-one percent of the respondents are "disturbed" by the fact that 28% of the inhabitants of Jerusalem are Arabs (Q. 34). When asked about possible means to avoid an Arab majority, two thirds—before as well as after the assassination—are in favor of restricting housing construction for Arabs (Q. 35). A similar majority (64%) were in favor *before* Rabin's assassination of redefining the city limits so that Arab settlements and villages that are now within the borders of the city will be excluded from the city limits. *After* the assassination a division of opinion with regard to this issue is apparent, when support for redefining the city limits drops to 53%. Support for this option in the entire sample is 59% (Q. 36).

As to the size of Jerusalem (Q. 37), many more respondents stated after the assassination, compared to previously, that Jerusalem nowadays consists of the two parts of the city that were united in 1967 plus additional regions that were added for reasons of security and other political considerations (65% and 48% respectively). However, the percentage saying that *East Jerusalem* is "much bigger" nowadays compared to 1967 dropped from 33% before to 18% after the assassination. Respondents answering "don't know" (about 19%) were not included in the calculations. Only a minority (16%) think that the size of East Jerusalem is about the same as in 1967 (Q. 38).

The Role of Jerusalem in Achieving Peace

Two-thirds of Israeli Jews consider the topic of Jerusalem to be more important ("much more" or "more") than other topics to be negotiated with the Palestinians (Q. 82). At the end of 1995, after the Oslo Accord, the majority of Israeli Jews did not believe that true peace between Israel and the Arab world is possible in the foreseeable future, nor that a peace agreement with the Palestinians will bring about a true and lasting peace. However, many more came to believe in the prospect for peace after Rabin's assassination. While before, the proportion of peace believers versus nonbelievers was 29% versus 71%, the proportion after the assassination changed to 42% versus 58% respectively. Especially notable is the drop in the extreme negative answer "Don't believe at all," from 36% to 18% for "peace with the Arab world." There is a corresponding drop from 39% to 22% in the proportion that strongly disbelieves in the possibility of "a true and lasting peace with the Palestinians."

Despite the increased belief in the prospects for peace following Rabin's assassination, only a minority of 20% continue to agree that a compromise on Jerusalem is the key to true peace between Israel and the Arab states, and that only such a compromise will make possible a true peace with the Palestinians. Also, a similar minority (21%) believe that for the sake of co-existence between Arabs and Jews in Jerusalem there must be a compromise over Jerusalem—this, in spite of the increased optimism following Rabin's assassination (from 39% to 51%) regarding the chances of arriving at a peaceful co-existence with the Palestinians in Jerusalem than with the Palestinians of the West Bank.

A vast majority of Israeli Jews (80%) object ("definitely against" and "against") to negotiations on Jerusalem within the peace process. The question was posed twice: at the very beginning of the interview, and toward the end (Q. 7, 78). The percent distribution of responses to this question at the beginning and at the end of the interview, before and after the assassination, is as follows:

	Before Rabin's assassination		After Rabin's assassination	
	Beginning of interview	End of interview	Beginning of interview	End of interview
Are you for or against negotiations on Jerusalem within the peace process?				
1. Definitely for	6	3	5	3
2. For	14	17	19	19
3. Against	43	32	41	41
4. Definitely against	37	48	35	37
Total (%)	100	100	100	100

The location of the question did not reveal much change in the overall proportion of opponents and supporters of negotiations over Jerusalem. Specifically, there was no difference, following Rabin's assassination, in the distribution of replies to the question when asked at the beginning of the interview; but when asked at the end, a change occurred in the intensity of the opposition: while before the assassination 48% chose the most extreme negative answer ("definitely against") and 32% chose the more moderate negative answer ("against"), after the assassination 41% chose the moderate answer and only 37% chose the extreme negative answer; that is, the same distribution that was obtained for this question at the beginning of the interview.

In other words, raising the awareness of respondents to the issue of Jerusalem in the process of interviewing contributed to a clarification of the topic and to second thoughts, which in turn led to different results before and after the assassination. Before the assassination, at the end of the interview negative responses became more extreme, while after the assassination negative responses did not increase, repeating the same level as that obtained at the beginning of the interview. This suggests that Rabin's assassination prevented the possible rise in the extreme negative response from the beginning to the end of the interview, but had no effect on the overall proportion of supporters (20%) and opponents (80%) of the negotiations on Jerusalem within the peace process. (A discussion of the joint distribution of the two questions is given in section 5.) Moreover, both before and after Rabin's assassination, 60% agree ("definitely agree" and "agree") with the statement "that we should make no concessions over Jerusalem even if we have to give up on peace with the Arabs" (Q. 31).

Opinions are divided concerning the desirability of a separation between Jews and Arabs in Jerusalem (Q. 49). At the same time, the proportion of respondents who believe that such a separation is desirable dropped from 56% before the assassination to 45% afterward. The vast majority (70%) object to putting up a wall to separate between Jews and Arabs in Jerusalem (Q. 47).

In summary, most Israeli Jews prefer not to negotiate over Jerusalem within the peace process, and do not believe that a compromise over Jerusalem is an absolute condition for achieving peace, yet they have become more optimistic regarding the prospects for peace.

Reasons for and Against Compromise on Jerusalem

Respondents were presented with six possible reasons why it is worthwhile to compromise on Jerusalem and four additional arguments against such a compromise. They were asked to indicate to what extent each of the arguments was convincing. The results are presented in Table 2.4.

Inspection of Table 2.4 reveals that the arguments for a compromise on Jerusalem convince only a minority of Israeli Jews while the majority are convinced

Table 2.4
Arguments for and against a compromise on Jerusalem
before and after Rabin's assassination
(percentage answering "very convincing" and "convincing")

The argument	Percentage answering "very convincing" and "convincing"		
	Before Rabin's assassination	After Rabin's assassination	Total sample
Arguments for compromise			
A compromise on Jerusalem will enhance personal safety of Israelis in Jerusalem	31	29	31
A compromise on Jerusalem will lead to international recognition of Jerusalem as the capital of Israel	27	30	29
A compromise on Jerusalem will honor the religious national rights of Palestinians in Jerusalem	23	24	23
Without a compromise on Jerusalem Muslim extremists will strengthen	22	24	23
Without a compromise on Jerusalem any Palestinian leadership that makes peace with Israel will be discredited among Palestinians	22	22	22
A compromise on Jerusalem will improve peace with Egypt	17	20	19
Arguments against compromise			
There should not be a compromise on Jerusalem because concessions in Jerusalem will enhance Palestinian demands	85	81	83
There should not be a compromise on Jerusalem because Jews will not have free access to the Old City	79	75	77
There should not be a compromise on Jerusalem because a city should not be divided because of a minority	68	71	70
There should not be a compromise on Jerusalem because Jerusalem is much more important for Judaism than for Islam	64	70	67

by the arguments against a compromise. Rabin's assassination scarcely had an effect on attitudes in this regard. It follows, then, that the public holds robust political attitudes with regard to fundamental issues related to Jerusalem and those are crystallized by long-term relevant considerations. If any changes did occur in this regard immediately after Rabin's assassination, they disappeared in the months following. The extent to which each argument is convincing or not varies from one argument to another.

The most convincing arguments for a compromise (about 30% are convinced) are personal safety in the city and the possibility of international recognition of Jerusalem as the capital of Israel. The least convincing is the argument that a compromise on Jerusalem will improve peace with Egypt. The remaining three arguments, referring to peace with the Moslem world and with the Palestinians, convince less than one-quarter of the respondents (22% to 24%).

The vast majority are convinced that there should not be a compromise on Jerusalem—because concessions will exacerbate Palestinian demands (83%), and because Jews will not have free access to the Old City (77%). A smaller majority—over two-thirds—are convinced that there should not be a compromise on Jerusalem since a city should not be divided because of a minority, and because Jerusalem is much more important for Judaism than for Islam.

The Status of Jerusalem

What should be the status of Jerusalem within the final agreement with the Palestinians? Who should have control or sovereignty over which parts of the city?

These questions were posed to the respondents. Ten options regarding the future of Jerusalem were presented, and the respondents were requested to state to what extent they would consider each of them if they were part of the negotiating team. The options with the percentage answering "consider very seriously" and "consider seriously" are given in Table 2.5.

The data in Table 2.5 reveal that no option of the ten presented gained the support of a majority of Israeli Jews. The highest consideration (about 45%) is given to the two options that propose Palestinian sovereignty over those regions that were previously part of the West Bank, namely, "Transfer to Palestinian sovereignty the Arab settlements and villages previously in the West Bank which are now within the borders of Jerusalem," and "The Arab settlements and villages previously in the West Bank will come under Palestinian sovereignty in exchange for the Jewish regions in the West Bank such as Ma'aleh Adumim, etc." Consideration of the second proposed option has dropped somewhat after Rabin's assassination. Actually, these two options are similar, except that the second one binds transfer to Palestinian authority with an exchange with Jewish areas in the West Bank.

Table 2.5
Options for the status of Jerusalem
(percentage answering "would consider very seriously" and "seriously" before and after Rabin's assassination)

To what extent would you consider each of the following proposals?	Consider "very seriously" and "seriously"		Total sample
	Before Rabin's assassination	After Rabin's assassination	
Transfer to Palestinian sovereignty Arab settlements now within Jerusalem	45	46	45
Arab settlements now in Jerusalem go to Palestinian sovereignty in exchange for Jewish regions in the West Bank	45	40	44
Retain Israeli sovereignty over East Jerusalem, while Arab neighborhoods in East Jerusalem have special status under Palestinian control	35	35	35
Transfer Arab neighborhoods of East Jerusalem, except those inside the walls of the Old City, to Palestinian sovereignty	34	33	34
Establish a joint Palestinian-Jewish administration of the Old City without Israel having to yield sovereignty	33	35	34
Control of Temple Mount will be under the Wakf as is now	28	35	31
Give the Palestinians sovereignty over the Arab neighborhoods of the Old City	20	26	23
Palestinians will get sovereignty of Temple Mount in exchange for Palestinian recognition of Israel's sovereignty of the Western (Wailing) Wall	18	23	20
Give East Jerusalem to Palestinian sovereignty while Jewish neighborhoods in East Jerusalem have special status under Israeli control	16	22	19
Turn the Old City into an international city under the United Nations	14	23	18

Thus, in spite of the fact that a large majority (80%) objects in principle to negotiations over Jerusalem, it is also the case that a sizable proportion (45%) would be prepared to consider specific proposals for Palestinian sovereignty over Arab settlements and villages in East Jerusalem. This readiness contradicts the prevailing image that there exists a broad consensus among Israeli Jews against transferring sovereignty over any area included in the present borders of Jerusalem. Moreover, only 36% objected categorically to considering such proposals. This readiness to relate to the possibility of Palestinian control of various Arab areas in the eastern part of the city stems, apparently, from the fact that the Israeli public distinguishes clearly between these areas of the city to which it attributes high importance as "part of Jerusalem" and those areas to which it does not attribute such importance.

About one-third of the respondents (34% to 35%) would consider seriously the following three proposals: "Transfer to Palestinian sovereignty the Arab neighborhoods of East Jerusalem except those inside the walls of the Old City"; "Establish a joint Jewish-Palestinian administration of the Old City, without Israel having to yield sovereignty"; and "Retain Israeli sovereignty over East Jerusalem, while Arab neighborhoods in East Jerusalem have special status under Palestinian control." Note that the opposite proposal, namely, "Give East Jerusalem to Palestinian sovereignty while Jewish neighbrhoods in East Jerusalem have special status under Israeli control" is considered seriously by only 19% of the respondents (14% before and 22% after the assassination). Least serious consideration (18%) is accorded to the proposal "To turn the Old City into an international city under the United Nations" (14% before and 23% after the assassination). This result is similar to the one obtained twenty-five years ago,* when 21% "agreed" to that option; at that time, too, this option was located toward the end of the options-ranking (although the options differed then from those in the present study). It should also be noted that the options accorded least consideration gained a few more supporters after Rabin's assassination, yet still not exceeding 25%. Most of these are concerned with proposals referring to the Old City and the holy places. On the whole, the picture concerning the options before and after Rabin's assassination is that of stability.

In addition to the proposals for the future of Jerusalem, respondents were asked whether they would agree to "cede the Arab neighborhoods of East Jerusalem to the Palestinians if the Old City, the Mount of Olives, all of the Jewish neighborhoods of East Jerusalem, and Mount Scopus remain in Jerusalem, as they are today" (Q. 50). A majority of 57% disagree with this possibility. Rabin's assassination did not change that attitude.

Attitudes Toward a Palestinian State and its Capital

Two-thirds of Israeli Jews object to the establishment of a Palestinian State. Nevertheless, the vast majority (78%) believe that a Palestinian State will eventually be

---

* Guttman, L., and Levy, S. (1973). "Religious Freedom and the Status of Jerusalem." Jerusalem: Israel Institute of Applied Science Research and Communications Institute of the Hebrew University.

established (Q. 77, 79). This belief strengthened somewhat after Rabin's assassination (76% to 82%).

Thirty-nine percent of Israeli Jews agree that "the Palestinians have *some sort* of legitimate rights with regard to Jerusalem," but only a tiny minority (5%) are definite in this opinion (Q. 61). On the other hand, only 20% think that the Palestinians' claim to East Jerusalem as a capital is justified, and only 2% chose the answer "very justified" (Q. 62). After Rabin's assassination, a few more respondents (17% versus 23%) believe that this claim is justified.

Two possibilities regarding the capital of a Palestinian State, if established, were presented, and respondents were requested to indicate the extent of their support for each (Table 2.6).

Table 2.6
Proposals for the capital of a Palestinian state
(percentage answering "definitely support" and "support"
before and after Rabin's assassination)

	Percentage answering "definitely support" and "support"		
	Before Rabin's assassination	After Rabin's assassination	Total sample
The capital of the Palestinian State will be an Arab region in East Jerusalem	21	17	20
The Palestinian capital will be a new city consisting of two parts: an area of East Jerusalem plus an area of the West Bank adjoining Jerusalem (such as Abu Dis) and will be named "Al-Quds"	26	19	23

As evident from Table 2.6, only a minority support each of the two proposals that involve part of East Jerusalem as a capital of the Palestinian State. This meager support suffered a further drop after Rabin's assassination. In other words, Israeli Jews strongly oppose any proposal that the capital of the Palestinian State, if established, be part of Jerusalem or any area adjoining Jerusalem. This objection even increased by a few percentages after Rabin's assassination.

Protest Acts Against a Compromise on Jerusalem

Even prior to Rabin's assassination, which, obviously, could not have been anticipated, the interviews included questions on violent as well as nonviolent protest acts. Two sets of questions were posed to the respondents regarding various protest acts they would consider justified if the government were to decide on a compromise—which is not acceptable to them—on Jerusalem on the basis of a Knesset decision. The question was posed under two conditions: decision of (a) a non-

Zionist Knesset majority,* and (b) a Zionist Knesset majority. Five possible acts of protest were posed to the respondents, and they were asked to indicate to what extent each of them was justified under such circumstances (Table 2.7).

Table 2.7
Justifying acts of protest
before and after Rabin's assassination
(percentage answering "very justified" and "justified")

	Percentage answering "very justified" and "justified"		
The act of protest	*Before Rabin's assassination*	*After Rabin's assassination*	*Total sample*
Lawful demonstrations	96	96	96
Nonviolent actions that disrupt the functioning of society	51	26	40
Use of force if necessary to prevent implementation	23	8	17
Violent actions directed toward Palestinians	18	15	16
Violent actions against other Jews, if necessary	8	2	6

The acts in Table 2.7, with regard to a decision of a non-Zionist Knesset majority, are ordered by degree of severity, from the relative harmless lawful demonstrations to violent actions against Jews. As evident from the table, the more violent the act the less it is justified. Almost all Israeli Jews (96%) justify lawful demonstrations, both before and after Rabin's assassination. As for most of the remaining acts, justification drops dramatically after the assassination. While before the assassination half of the respondents justified acts that disrupt the functioning of society even though nonviolent, only 26% justify this form of protest after the assassination. A dramatic decline occurred with regard to use of force (from 23% to 8%) and also with respect to violent actions against Jews (from 8% to 2%). However, when Palestinians are the object of the violent actions, the percentages remain almost unchanged (18% and 15% respectively).

With regard to a decision for a compromise on Jerusalem, which is unacceptable to the respondents but based on a *Zionist Knesset majority*, a similar trend of lesser justification of violent protest acts is apparent. The data show that both before as well as after Rabin's assassination only 6% to 7% do not justify any kind of protest act. The majority justifies lawful demonstrations, and this majority even

---

* Refers to a decision whose majority depends on the votes of Arab and ultra-religious MKs.

rose, from 63% to 80%, after the assassination. Justification of unlawful and violent acts declined considerably after the assassination. This trend of decline in justification of unlawful and of violent acts goes hand in hand with the trend shown above in the case of a *non-Zionist Knesset majority*.

Also, after Rabin's assassination, compared to previously, fewer respondents said that they personally would participate ("definitely yes" and "yes") in an action against a compromise on Jerusalem (21% and 31% respectively).

Summary

For Israeli Jews, Jerusalem symbolizes, first and foremost, the birthplace of the Jewish people and Judaism (not necessarily in its religious sense), placing emphasis on its national-historic components, and, above all, as a symbol of the State of Israel. Jerusalem symbolizes (future) statehood for the Palestinians, too. Thus, the problem is the parallel national symbolism of the two nations, which is concretized in the Old City within the walls and some of its holy places, especially the Temple Mount. No such overlap exists with respect to the rest of the city, where different mental maps characterize the two populations, according to the importance they attribute to the various quarters "as part of" the city.

Only one-third of the Jewish public believes that a peace agreement with the Palestinians will bring true and long-lasting peace. Most Israeli Jews prefer not to negotiate over Jerusalem within the peace process, and do not believe that compromise over Jerusalem is a necessary condition for achieving peace. Nevertheless, and apart from the influence of the assassination, a sizable proportion of Israeli Jews (45%) is prepared to give serious consideration to the idea of Palestinian control over settlements and villages in and around East Jerusalem. This stands in contrast to the prevalent image that there exists a broad consensus against transfer of any part of the present boundaries of Jerusalem to Palestinian sovereignty. Only 36% objected categorically to giving consideration to such proposals. The readiness for such consideration stems, apparently, from the fact that the Israeli public makes a sharp distinction between those parts of the city that are important components in their view, and those parts that are of lesser centrality. Moreover, the study suggests that most Israeli Jews do not consider the present boundaries of the city sacrosanct. Fifty-nine percent of the respondents say that in order to ensure a Jewish majority in the city, they would be willing "to redefine the city boundaries" to exclude certain Arab settlements and villages that are presently within the city limits. On the other hand, a similar percentage (60%) supports the statement that "no concessions should be made in Jerusalem, even if we have to abandon peace with the Arabs." These positions are not experienced as contradictory, however, in the sense that there is no negative correlation between them.

The research also finds strong opposition to a Palestinian State in Israeli public opinion, even if most Israeli Jews (78%) believe that it will be established.

There is also strong opposition to the establishment of a Palestinian capital in any part of East Jerusalem and there is only the most minimal support for compromise in the Old City, especially with respect to the Temple Mount (18% to 20%).

An overview of these findings leads to the conclusion that pragmatic considerations, not only principled ones, play a significant role in the extent to which Israeli Jews are prepared to consider compromise with respect to the boundaries of Jerusalem. This follows from the different degrees of centrality that are assigned, subjectively, to their perceptions of different parts of the city. Analysis of the data reveals that these pragmatic considerations neither contradict, nor even weaken, the principled ones. The fact remains that 80% of the respondents object in principle to negotiation over Jerusalem on both occasions that the question was put— at the beginning, and at the end, of the interview.

Rabin's assassination illuminated the universality of Jerusalem in the eyes of Israeli Jews, especially by attributing more importance to the city as "a world center for all religions." However, this viewpoint remains the least important for Israeli Jews, and is not related to almost any of the attitudes concerning the future status of Jerusalem.

Following the assassination, Israeli Jews have become more optimistic regarding the prospects for peace, but the assassination scarcely had an effect on political attitudes with regard to fundamental issues related to Jerusalem. These are probably crystallized by long-term, relevant considerations, as evident from the analysis of the reasons for and against a compromise on Jerusalem, and from the options proposed for the future status of the city. The assassination did weaken Israeli Jews' rejection of the idea that there are "any sort of legitimate rights of the Palestinians with regard to Jerusalem." Moreover, the vast majority of Israeli Jews strongly oppose any proposal that the capital of the Palestinian State, if established, be part of Jerusalem or any area adjoining Jerusalem. This objection even increased by a few percentage points after Rabin's assassination. Nevertheless, alongside this strong opposition to compromise on Jerusalem, the signs of openness to the other side that followed Rabin's assassination are apparently persistent enough to permit the continuity of the peace process as was evident at the Wye Plantation, for example.

Rabin's assassination greatly influenced Israeli Jews' attitudes with respect to protest actions directed toward preventing implementation of an unacceptable agreement regarding Jerusalem. Following the assassination there occurred a steep decline in justification of unlawful, even though nonviolent, protest actions. Especially noteworthy is the drastic decline in justification of use of force and in justification of actions to be directed against Jews in order to prevent an unacceptable agreement over Jerusalem. Such decline was not recorded for justification of violent actions against Palestinians.

2. The Status of Jerusalem
in the Eyes of Jerusalemites and Those Residing Elsewhere

In the previous section, various aspects of the future of Jerusalem were studied for the entire sample, comparing respondents' attitudes before and after Rabin's assassination. An additional central issue is the attitudes of Jerusalemites with regard to the Jerusalem problem compared to the attitudes of respondents residing elsewhere. The national sample was scattered throughout thirty-five settlements, including the large cities. Since only the samples of the three large cities consist of a sufficient number of respondents for a comparative analysis, the respondents were classified into four groups: Residents of (1) Jerusalem (N = 149), (2) Tel Aviv (N = 156), (3) Haifa (N = 99) (the results pertaining to the three cities should be taken with caution in view of the small numbers), and (4) the remaining respondents. These four groups enable us not only to compare the attitudes of Jerusalemites with those of respondents residing elsewhere, but also with those residing in other large cities.

In order to examine in concise fashion the differences between Jerusalemites and the others, we have calculated monotonicity coefficients (further explanation in section 3) between place of residence (Jerusalemites versus all others combined) and the research questions; these are given in Table 2.11. We shall refer to them here, too, when necessary, for the sake of clarification.

Involvement with the Peace Process

Over 80% of the residents of each of the three cities—Jerusalem, Tel Aviv, and Haifa—are involved, at least "to some extent," in the peace negotiations. However, many more Jerusalemites are involved "to a great extent" compared to residents of Tel Aviv (44% and 28% respectively). Haifa residents are more similar to Jerusalemites in their involvement in the peace process, with 39% choosing the extreme answer "to a great extent." The high involvement of Jerusalemites, compared to residents of Tel Aviv and Haifa, is even more striking when "Jerusalem" is specifically mentioned. While 71% of Jerusalemites answered "to a great extent" to the question "To what extent do you follow the topic of the future of Jerusalem within the peace process?", only 40% of residents of Tel Aviv and Haifa chose this reply. However, while the involvement of both Jerusalemites and Tel Avivans increased when the topic of Jerusalem was raised (90% chose the two extreme positive answers), residents of Haifa remained unchanged.

The Meaning of "Jerusalem"

Jerusalem is "very important" to Israelis personally, wherever they live. The data show that Jerusalem is "very important" personally to residents of Tel Aviv and

Table 2.8
Ranking of importance of Jerusalem
from five points of view by residents of the large cities
(percentage answering "very important")

Points of view	Importance of Jerusalem		
	Jerusalem	Tel Aviv	Haifa
As a symbol of the State of Israel	79	82	81
Jewish national-historical point of view	73	76	76
As a center for the Jewish people and Judaism	73	75	62
Jewish-religious point of view	60	68	52
As a world center for all religions	39	68	26

Haifa no less than to Jerusalemites. But, as expected, more Jerusalemites feel a stronger sense of belonging to the city. Compared to residents of Haifa and Tel Aviv, 82%, 68%, and 62% respectively chose the answer "definitely yes" to the question "Do you feel a sense of belonging to Jerusalem?" Only a tiny proportion (2% to 4%) in each of the large cities—Jerusalem, Tel Aviv, and Haifa—do not feel a sense of belonging to Jerusalem. In other words, Jerusalem is important to *all* Israeli Jews, whether residing in Jerusalem or not, and the great majority also feel a sense of belonging to the city.

Moreover, Jerusalem is "very important" to most Israelis, no matter where they live, with respect to four out of the five points of view that were investigated—the exception being "a world center for all religions." In the latter case, Jerusalem is "very important" to most Tel Avivans (68%), to 40% of Jerusalemite residents, but only to 26% of Haifa residents as shown in Table 2.8.

Apparently, Haifa residents and, to a lesser extent, also Jerusalemites were not part of the dramatic change that took place after Rabin's assassination in the assessment of the importance of Jerusalem as a "world center for all religions" (see section 1). The increase in the importance of Jerusalem as a world center for all religions prevailed only among the Tel Aviv residents and those living outside the large cities. It is worth recalling that this aspect remained least important also after Rabin's assassination, and it appears at the bottom of the ranking of "importance" for each individual city.

Examining the importance attributed to various sites in Jerusalem as part of the city, we find that there are scarcely any differences between the Jerusalemites and the others, except for two sites, "The Old City" (in general), and "The Temple Mount." Table 2.9 shows that fewer Jerusalemites consider these two sites "very important," compared to residents of Tel Aviv, Haifa, and other parts of Israel. This difference is also apparent in the sizes of the coefficients of monotonicity between place of residence and assessment of importance of the various sites as

Table 2.9
Ranking of importance of sites in Jerusalem as part of the city
by residents of the three large cities
(percentage answering "very important")

The site	Importance of sites as part of Jerusalem Percentage answering "very important"		
	Jerusalem	Tel Aviv	Haifa
The Western Wall	89	86	89
The Old City	70	89	85
Old Jewish neighborhoods	84	73	86
The Jewish quarter in the Old City	78	78	82
Mount of Olives	72	73	72
The Temple Mount	59	82	76
New Jewish neighborhoods (established after 1967)	77	75	80
Non-Jewish quarters in the Old City	32	40	35
Arab neighborhoods in downtown East Jerusalem	23	29	22
Arab settlements and villages previously in the West Bank	24	24	21

part of the city (see Table 2.11). While most of these coefficients are very low, mostly around zero, the monotonicity coefficients for "the Temple Mount" and for "the Old City" are –0.44 and –0.46 respectively. That means that fewer Jerusalemites believe that these sites are "very important" as part of Jerusalem, as compared to Israelis living elsewhere in the country. We can conclude, therefore, that for Jerusalemites the city is more a place of residence—albeit a problematic one—than a "symbol"; for the others it is more of a "symbol," a fact that is expressed in the great importance attributed by the others to the Temple Mount and the Old City. Support for this conclusion may be seen in responses to the question "To what extent is it important to you that Jews be able to pray on the Temple Mount?" Fewer Jerusalemites and Haifa residents (49%) considered it "very important," compared to Tel Avivans and Israelis living elsewhere (58% to 61%).

It should be noted that in each of the large cities, the ranking of Jerusalem sites by their importance as part of the city is very similar to that obtained for the overall sample (Table 2.9 is ranked according to the overall national sample, as is Table 2.2), with but small and nonsystematic differences. The exception, of course, is the lower ranking of the centrality of "the Old City" among Jerusalem Jews. Also, no meaningful differences were found among cities concerning the importance of Jerusalem "as a national center for Palestinians," although compared to elsewhere, Jerusalemites are slightly more ready to acknowledge this. But the difference is very slight (see also Table 2.11).

Similarly, no noteworthy differences are apparent between Jerusalemites and residents of the other large cities in the assessment of the size of Jerusalem. But Jerusalemites, compared to respondents residing elsewhere, tend to say that the proportion of Arab residents of the city is smaller. Fifty-eight percent of Jerusalemites think that the proportion of Arabs in the city does not exceed 20%, while only somewhat over one-third in the rest of the country think so. The Jerusalemites are disturbed no more than the others by the fact that the proportion of Arabs in Jerusalem is 28%.

Attitudes Toward the Negotiations on Jerusalem and Assessment of the Prospects for Peace

The question then arises: To what extent are the attitudes of Jerusalem residents similar to or different from the attitudes of the others with respect to the various aspects of the status of Jerusalem? Above all, what is their attitude toward the actual conduct of negotiations on Jerusalem within the peace process?

Seventy-nine percent of Jerusalemites object to conducting negotiations on Jerusalem within the peace process; in this they are similar to the Tel Avivans and other Israelis, but with one difference: somewhat more Jerusalemites, compared to Tel Avivans, chose the most extreme negative response "definitely against" (39% and 32% respectively). Haifa residents are somewhat more inclined to approve the negotiations. It should be recalled that the proportion of the latter in the sample is particularly small, hence caution should be taken in reaching conclusions regarding Haifa residents. In general, then, Jerusalemites do not differ from other Israelis on this issue. The absence of correlation between this question and place of residence (Jerusalem versus elsewhere) is also apparent in the –0.01 monotonicity coefficient in Table 2.11. Also, there are hardly any differences between Jerusalemites and the others in assessment of the prospects for peace with the Arab countries and with the Palestinians, and in the assessment of the prominence of Jerusalem in achieving a lasting peace (see Table 2.11 monotonicity coefficients). Nevertheless, Tel Avivans are systematically less negative than Jerusalemites and other Israeli residents in their assessment of prospects for peace (21% versus 27% to 31%) and of the prominence of Jerusalem in achieving a lasting peace.

Reasons for and Against a Compromise on Jerusalem

Hardly any differences were found between Jerusalemites and the others in assessing the various pros and cons that were presented to them with regard to a compromise on Jerusalem (see Table 2.11 monotonicity coefficients). Most of the coefficients are around zero, and never exceed 0.19. A weak but systematic trend was found with respect to three of the four reasons that were presented *against* a compromise on Jerusalem. According to this trend, Jerusalemites, compared to the others, are somewhat less convinced of the validity of these reasons, except for the reason "there should not be a compromise over Jerusalem because concessions in Jerusalem will only enhance the Palestinians' demands for more concessions," with respect to which Jerusalemites do not differ from other Israeli citizens. Inspection of the distribution of responses by place of residence reveals that the slight differences mentioned above are due to the fact that somewhat more Jerusalemites chose the answer "a not at all convincing reason" (15% to 21% of Jerusalemites versus 4% to 9% of others); and also that, for some of the questions, somewhat fewer Jerusalemites chose the answer "a very convincing reason" (36% to 52% of Jerusalemites versus 42% to 60% of those who reside elsewhere).

In general, little difference was found between Jerusalemites and residents of the rest of the country in the assessment of the reasons for reaching a compromise on Jerusalem. However, residents of Tel Aviv are systematically more inclined to approve each of these reasons than are residents of Jerusalem or the rest of the country. To clarify, we present below the proportion of approvals of each of the reasons for a compromise by residents of Jerusalem and of Tel Aviv (Table 2.10).

Table 2.10
Arguments for a compromise on Jerusalem
among Jerusalemites and Tel Avivians
(percentage answering "very convincing" and "convincing")

The argument	Percent answering "very convincing" and "convincing"	
	Jerusalem	Tel Aviv
A compromise on Jerusalem will enhance personal safety of Israelis in Jerusalem	23	36
A compromise on Jerusalem will lead to international recognition of Jerusalem as the capital of Israel	28	42
A compromise on Jerusalem will honor the religious and national rights of Palestinians in Jerusalem	25	39
Without a compromise on Jerusalem Moslem extremists will strengthen	20	39
Without a compromise on Jerusalem any Palestinian leadership that makes peace with Israel will be discredited among Palestinians	27	30
A compromise on Jerusalem will improve peace with Egypt	14	30

The ranking of the pros in Table 2.10 is according to their "persuasive" power as obtained for the general sample (Table 2.4). The Tel Avivans express stronger support for each of the reasons for a compromise on Jerusalem. Even in Tel Aviv, however, only a minority (30% to 40%) approve each of the reasons.

Overall, we can see that Tel Avivians are somewhat more optimistic than the others in assessing the prospects for peace, and are more inclined to support each of the pro-reasons presented to them. It is also of interest that residents of both Tel Aviv and Jerusalem—unlike other Israelis—attribute greater importance to "international recognition" than to "personal safety" as justifications for compromise.

The Status of Jerusalem Within a Peace Agreement

The monotonicity coefficients (Table 2.11) show that in general Jerusalemites do not differ greatly from the other Israeli residents in their attitudes toward the various options relating to the status of Jerusalem within a final peace arrangement. All the coefficients are around zero, and never exceed μ = 0.18. However, as in the case of the reasons for a compromise on Jerusalem, so, too, in the options for the future status of Jerusalem, Tel Avivians are more inclined to seriously consider the various options. Conversely, among the cities, Tel Aviv had the lowest proportion of respondents who chose the extreme negative answer for each of the options ("Object to compromise, won't consider"—a response that was not even openly presented to respondents). Among Jerusalemites we find the highest proportion who chose that response (7% to 13% among Tel Avivians, versus 25% to 40% among Jerusalemites). The rest of the Israeli residents fall between these two extremes.

Attitudes Toward a Palestinian State and Its Capital

Two-thirds of Israeli residents object to the establishment of a Palestinian State, with the exception of Jerusalem and Haifa, where a somewhat smaller majority (58% and 54% respectively) expressed an objection. Jerusalem residents do not differ from the others in their assessment of the importance of the issue of Jerusalem, as compared to other issues relating to negotiations with the Palestinians. Neither do Jerusalem residents differ from the others in their attitudes regarding the rights of the Palestinians in Jerusalem: 45% of Jerusalemites believe that "Palestinians have any sort of legitimate rights with regard to Jerusalem." As for the Palestinians' claim to East Jerusalem as a capital, more Tel Avivans, compared to all other Israeli residents, justify this claim: 34% of Tel Avivans believe this claim is justified, compared to 20% who think so in the rest of the country. However, when the two options for situating a Palestinian capital were presented, no differences were found by place of residence: the majority (about 80%) throughout the country object to both options.

Protest Activities Against a Compromise on Jerusalem

Respondents were asked about five possible protest actions they might take against a compromise on Jerusalem if it were made by an Israeli government that lacks a Zionist majority in the Knesset. In general, there are hardly any differences by place of residence in attitudes toward these actions, with the exception of two: (1) "nonviolent actions that disrupt the functioning of society"—to which many more Tel Avivans objected compared to the others (63% versus 35% to 38%), and, conversely, (2) "violent actions directed against Palestinians"—which is less justified by Jerusalemites, compared to the others (μ = –0.38—see Table 2.11 monotonicity coefficients): 22% of Tel Avivians justify such actions, versus only 6% of Jerusalemites. This difference may stem from the fact that Jerusalem is a mixed city, as is Haifa, whose residents responded in similar fashion, with only 7% who justify violent actions against Palestinians.

More of the Jerusalem residents, compared to the others, would "definitely" personally participate in a protest action against a compromise on Jerusalem that is not acceptable to them: 23% of Jerusalemites versus 5% to 12% of other Israelis.

3. Background Variables

Do different strata of the population vary with respect to their assessments of the future status of Jerusalem? Differences by residence have been discussed in detail in the second section of this chapter. Throughout the discussion reference is made to the relevant correlation coefficients given in Table 2.11 below, and will therefore not be discussed further here.

Differences among other strata can be studied in the same fashion by calculating monotonicity coefficients* for each of the assessments by background characteristics whose categories are ordered. For the present research, we concentrate on six background variables that have ordered categories, so that monotonicity coefficients can be calculated for their relations with the attitudes. These background variables are:

1. *Gender*—ordered arbitrarily from "male" to "female";
2. *Education*—ordered from "low" to "high";

---

* The correlation coefficient used is μ_2 for weak monotonicity. This coefficient expresses the extent to which replies to one question increase in a particular direction as the replies to the other questions, without assuming that the increase is exactly according to a straight line. All such coefficients vary between –1 and +1. μ = 1 implies a full monotone relationship with positive or rising trend; μ = 0 expresses complete lack of a monotone relationship; and μ = –1 implies a full monotone relationship which is of a negative or descending trend. (For details, see L. Guttman, 1986, "Coefficients of Politonicity and Monotonicity," in *Encyclopedia of Statistical Sciences*, VII, pp. 80–87, New York: John Wiley & Sons, Inc.).

Table 2.11

Monotonicity coefficients between various issues pertaining to the status of Jerusalem and ordered background characteristics

	Gender	Education	Age	Religious observance	Time in Israel	Voting intention	Residence
	Male to female	Low to high	Young to old	Observant to nonobservant	Veteran to newcomer	Labor Likud	Jerusalem to other
Involvement with the peace process (high to low)							
Follow negotiations with Palestinians	0.29	-0.27	-0.19	-0.02	0.11	0.26	0.17
Follow "Jerusalem" topic within peace process	0.18	-0.29	-0.14	0.14	0.09	0.16	0.37
Attitude toward negotiations on Jerusalem (pos. to neg.)	-0.12	-0.04	-0.06	-0.48	-0.03	0.64	-0.01
The meaning of Jerusalem ("very important" to "not at all")							
Jerusalem is important personally	0.02	0.10	-0.19	0.49	0.12	-0.30	0.21
From Jewish-religious point of view	0.06	0.29	-0.01	0.71	0.12	-0.59	-0.34
Jewish national-historical point of view	0.08	0.05	-0.17	0.35	-0.08	-0.32	-0.22
As center of Jewish people and Judaism	0.03	0.20	-0.13	0.51	-0.01	-0.43	-0.12
As world center of all religions	-0.11	0.09	-0.05	-0.13	0.00	0.19	-0.22
As symbol of the State of Israel	-0.05	0.16	-0.03	0.24	0.01	-0.51	-0.23
Feel sense of belonging to Jerusalem ("definitely yes" to "definitely no")	0.11	0.05	-0.16	0.49	0.10	-0.30	0.37
Jerusalem important to Palestinians as national center ("very important" to "not at all")	-0.08	-0.28	0.15	-0.32	0.10	0.49	0.19

Important as part of Jerusalem
("very important" to "not at all")

The Temple Mount	0.04	0.18	0.06	0.34	-0.01	-0.53	-0.44
The Wailing Wall	0.08	0.20	0.08	0.59	0.00	-0.51	-0.23
Mount of Olives	0.01	0.14	-0.07	0.42	0.02	-0.39	-0.29
The Jewish quarter in the Old City	0.00	0.07	-0.10	0.43	0.05	-0.41	-0.02
Non-Jewish quarters in the Old City	0.09	-0.09	0.01	0.09	0.01	-0.31	0.07
Arab neighborhoods in downtown East Jerusalem	0.06	0.01	0.03	0.13	0.07	-0.38	0.05
Arab villages previously in the West Bank	0.08	0.06	0.04	0.18	0.07	-0.40	0.07
New Jewish neighborhoods (established after 1967)	0.06	0.13	-0.07	0.26	0.00	-0.29	0.04
Old Jewish neighborhoods	0.10	-0.01	-0.07	0.20	0.00	-0.15	0.18
The Old City	0.07	0.17	0.04	0.34	-0.02	-0.51	-0.46
New Jewish neighborhoods are part of Jerusalem as the older ("definitely yes" to "definitely no")	0.13	-0.02	0.02	0.27	0.09	-0.22	0.15
Demography and size of Jerusalem							
Proportion of Arabs in Jerusalem ("very small" to "most")	0.10	-0.15	-0.04	0.21	0.00	0.06	0.47
Proportion of Arabs increased or decreased since Six-Day War ("increased" to "decreased")	-0.08	0.28	-0.15	0.10	-0.03	-0.16	-0.29
Disturbed that 28% are Arabs ("very much" to "not at all")	-0.01	0.16	0.13	0.28	0.06	-0.61	-0.21

Table 2.11 (continued)

	Gender Male to female	Education Low to high	Age Young to old	Religious observance Observant to nonobservant	Time in Israel Veteran to newcomer	Voting intention Labor Likud	Residence Jerusalem to other
Demography and size of Jerusalem (continued)							
Restricting housing construction for Arabs ("support" to "object")	-0.07	0.21	0.01	0.40	-0.04	-0.42	-0.25
Redefining city limits— Arab villages outside ("support" to "object")	-0.09	0.06	-0.14	0.16	-0.06	0.15	-0.01
Borders of Jerusalem (two parts as in 1967 to two parts + additional regions)	-0.10	0.18	0.05	0.12	-0.18	-0.21	-0.18
Size of Jerusalem ("about the same" to "much bigger")	-0.05	-0.12	0.01	-0.03	0.06	0.17	0.12
Prospects for peace and the role of Jerusalem in achieving peace							
We should make no concessions over Jerusalem even if we have to give up peace ("definitely agree" to "definitely disagree")	0.08	0.08	0.06	0.33	-0.03	-0.35	-0.18
Can be true peace with Arab world in foreseeable future ("believe" to "don't believe")	0.04	-0.18	-0.10	-0.38	0.03	0.81	0.12
Peace agreement with Palestinians will bring true, lasting peace ("believe" to "don't believe")	-0.04	-0.18	-0.12	-0.46	-0.02	0.87	-0.03
Compromise on Jerusalem is key to true peace with Arab States ("agree" to "disagree")	-0.08	-0.07	-0.11	-0.38	-0.01	0.68	-0.05
For true peace with Palestinians must compromise over Jerusalem ("believe" to "don't believe")	-0.05	-0.14	0.00	-0.43	0.01	0.70	0.07

For co-existence in Jerusalem, must make compromise over Jerusalem ("believe" to "don't believe")	-0.05	-0.13	-0.02	-0.43	0.02	0.66	0.00
Reasons FOR compromise on Jerusalem ("very convincing" to "not at all convincing")							
Without compromise Moslem extremists will strengthen	-0.09	0.05	-0.07	-0.23	0.01	0.44	0.01
Without compromise Palestinian leadership that makes peace will be discredited among Palestinians	-0.02	-0.10	0.01	-0.27	0.07	0.59	0.19
Compromise will improve peace with Egypt	-0.14	0.06	-0.06	-0.24	0.02	0.48	-0.03
Compromise will honor religious and national rights of Palestinians in Jerusalem	-0.06	-0.12	0.01	-0.32	0.10	0.58	0.09
Compromise will enhance personal safety of Israelis in Jerusalem	-0.12	-0.02	-0.02	-0.25	-0.05	0.53	-0.01
Compromise will lead to international recognition of Jerusalem as capital of Israel	-0.05	0.00	-0.09	-0.18	-0.03	0.49	0.13
Reasons AGAINST compromise on Jerusalem ("very convincing" to "not at all")							
No compromise—Jerusalem is much more important for Judaism than for Islam	-0.10	0.40	-0.19	0.45	-0.17	-0.54	-0.18
No compromise—a city should not be divided because of a minority	-0.04	0.28	-0.12	0.36	-0.09	-0.53	-0.05
No compromise—concessions on Jerusalem will enhance Palestinians' demands	0.00	0.22	-0.07	0.45	-0.23	-0.64	-0.18
No compromise—Jews will not have free access to Old City	-0.08	0.28	-0.04	0.38	-0.10	-0.64	-0.19

Table 2.11 (continued)

	Gender Male to female	Education Low to high	Age Young to old	Religious observance Observant to nonobservant	Time in Israel Veteran to newcomer	Voting intention Labor Likud	Residence Jerusalem to other
Options for the status of Jerusalem ("consider very seriously" to "won't consider")							
Transfer to Palestinian sovereignty Arab settlements now within Jerusalem	−0.16	−0.06	−0.03	−0.34	0.02	0.61	0.08
Arab settlements now in Jerusalem go to Palestinian sovereignty in exchange for Jewish regions in West Bank	−0.17	−0.15	−0.04	−0.33	0.02	0.57	−0.02
Transfer Arab neighborhoods of East Jerusalem except those inside the walls of Old City to Palestinian sovereignty	−0.22	−0.04	−0.03	−0.34	0.04	0.63	−0.08
Give Palestinians sovereignty over Arab neighborhoods of the Old City	−0.19	0.02	−0.05	−0.31	0.06	0.55	−0.13
Control of Temple Mount will be under Wakf as is now	−0.03	−0.11	0.01	−0.40	0.03	0.57	−0.13
Palestinians will get sovereignty of Temple Mount in exchange for Palestinian recognition of Israeli sovereignty over Wailing Wall	−0.13	0.01	−0.01	−0.37	0.07	0.55	−0.13
Turn Old City into international city under the United Nations	−0.16	−0.03	0.04	−0.37	0.03	0.43	−0.18
Give East Jerusalem to Palestinian sovereignty while Jewish neighborhoods in East Jerusalem have special status under Israeli control	−0.10	0.03	−0.01	−0.30	0.09	0.47	−0.16

	1	2	3	4	5	6	7
Retain Israeli sovereignty over East Jerusalem while Arab neighborhoods in East Jerusalem have special status under Palestinian control	-0.10	-0.10	0.02	-0.34	0.05	0.53	-0.09
Joint Palestinian-Jewish administration for Old City without Israel having to yield claim to sovereignty	-0.08	-0.10	0.03	-0.23	0.06	0.50	0.00
Conditions for real, long-term peace with Arab world ("very convincing" to "not at all")							
Saudi Arabia open an embassy in Jerusalem	0.04	-0.17	-0.06	-0.21	-0.04	0.47	0.14
Regular commercial relations with Arab States	-0.02	-0.19	-0.05	-0.28	0.04	0.60	0.09
Attitudes toward a Palestinian State and its capital (from positive to negative)							
Palestinians have any legitimate rights with regard to Jerusalem	-0.11	-0.16	-0.06	-0.37	0.03	0.64	0.19
Palestinians' claim for East Jerusalem as capital is justified	-0.17	-0.13	0.05	-0.35	0.10	0.61	0.10
Do you support or object to the establishment of a Palestinian State?	-0.12	-0.23	0.03	-0.51	0.04	0.79	0.17
An Arab region in East Jerusalem will be designated as capital of Palestinian State	-0.04	-0.16	0.15	-0.25	0.16	0.42	0.17
Palestinian capital will be a new city consisting of an area of East Jerusalem plus an area of the West Bank adjoining Jerusalem	-0.03	-0.21	0.13	-0.25	0.14	0.43	0.12
Sovereignty over Temple Mount belongs to God	-0.09	0.23	-0.10	0.17	-0.09	0.00	0.12

Table 2.11 (continued)

	Gender	Education	Age	Religious observance	Time in Israel	Voting intention	Residence
	Male to female	Low to high	Young to old	Observant to nonobservant	Veteran to newcomer	Labor Likud	Jerusalem to other
Protest acts against compromise on Jerusalem ("very justified" to "not at all justified")							
Lawful demonstrations	0.14	0.09	-0.03	0.15	0.08	-0.22	-0.18
Nonviolent actions that disrupt the functioning of society	0.12	0.06	0.16	0.39	0.04	-0.47	-0.13
Use of force to prevent implementation	0.19	0.16	0.19	0.37	0.13	-0.58	0.07
Violent actions directed against Palestinians	0.10	0.32	0.07	0.21	0.06	-0.60	-0.38
Violent actions against Jews, if necessary	0.12	0.29	0.11	0.23	0.06	-0.58	-0.12
Would participate in action against compromise on Jerusalem ("yes, definitely" to "definitely no")	0.18	-0.14	0.34	0.18	0.15	-0.45	0.16

   3. *Age*—ordered from "young" to "old";
   4. *Religious observance*—ordered from "very observant" to "nonobservant";
   5. *Time in Israel*—ordered from "veteran" to "newcomer";
   6. *Political tendency*—ordered arbitrarily from "Labor" to "Likud" (these
       two categories are from the question on the intention to vote).

Table 2.11 presents monotonicity coefficients that correlate the ordered background variables with attitudes toward the Jerusalem issue, grouped by the topics studied. The order of the response categories for each assessment is given in parentheses, alongside the topic heading for each of the assessments separately. Hence, a positive coefficient means that on the average the closer the respondent is to the starting-point of the ordered background continuum, the closer he is to the starting-point of the assessment continuum. A coefficient with a negative sign (–) implies that the closer the respondent is to the starting-point of the ordered background continuum, the farther he is from the starting-point of the assessment continuum. A coefficient of zero means that there is no difference by the background characteristics with respect to the specific assessment. For example, with respect to the dichotomous variable "gender," a positive sign means that men are closer to the starting-point of the assessment continuum than are women, as, for instance, in the "involvement" section, where men are somewhat more involved than women in the negotiations. A negative sign means that women are closer to the starting-point of the assessment continuum than are men, as, for instance, in the section on options for the status of Jerusalem, where somewhat more women than men would consider some of the options. A coefficient of zero means that there is no difference between women and men in their views on the specific topic.

The use of correlation coefficients such as those in Table 2.11 permits better comprehension of the lawfulness of the correlations than studying the joint frequencies on which the coefficients are based.

The coefficients in Table 2.11 show that the demographic variables—gender, education, age, time in the county—are hardly related to assessments regarding the status of Jerusalem. All the coefficients are very low, never exceeding 0.29, and a majority fall around zero. Thus, the personal-social attributes of the respondents do not contribute much to prediction of their assessments on a topic that is perceived as entirely political. Political inclination, on the other hand, in the sense of intention to vote for Labor or Likud, was closely correlated with most of the topics that were studied. Another background variable that was found to be related to the topics under study is religiosity, which, as is well known, also correlates with the political inclinations of Israelis.

Religious Observance

Among social-personal characteristics, religious observance is the only one that strongly correlates with the various aspects relating to Jerusalem. Given that religious-national Jewishness is also identified with political viewpoints, such a correlation is, of course, to be expected.

Involvement with the Peace Process

There are no differences, by religious observance, in the extent of involvement in the peace negotiations in general, and in the status of Jerusalem in particular. However, a sizable correlation (μ = –0.48) was found between extent of observance and support for negotiations over Jerusalem in the framework of the peace process (Table 2.11). With decreased observance there is greater support for such negotiations ("definitely for" and "for"), from 5% among the "strictly" observant to 35% of the totally nonobservant. In the opposite direction, two-thirds of the strictly observant "definitely" object to negotiations over Jerusalem, compared to 20% of the nonobservant and 35% of the "somewhat" observant.

Among all the observance groups, however, only a minority support negotiations on Jerusalem: 5% among the "strictly" observant, 15% of the observant "to a great extent," 21% of the traditional, and 35% of the totally nonobservant. This distribution pattern remained unchanged when the question was repeated at the end of the interview.

The Meaning of Jerusalem

With the rise in religious observance, greater importance is attributed to Jerusalem, and respondents have a greater sense of belongingness to the city (μ = 0.49). A considerable difference was found between observant and nonobservant respondents in their assessment of the importance of Jerusalem from the following viewpoints: (1) the Jewish-religious point of view (μ = 0.71) and (2) as a center of the Jewish people and Judaism (μ = 0.51). On these two aspects, observant respondents attribute greater importance to Jerusalem than the nonobservant. However, with regard to the national aspects of the meaning of Jerusalem—"Jewish national-historical" and "a symbol of the State of Israel"—there is a small difference between observers and nonobservers, although here, too, the observant attribute somewhat more importance (monotonicity coefficients are 0.35 and 0.24 respectively). Only on one point of view is Jerusalem slightly more important to the nonobservant, namely, that Jerusalem "is a world center for all religions" (μ = –0.13).

Thus, among both religious and less religious respondents, Jerusalem is emblematic, above all, of the national-historic component of Jewish identity, and especially of the Jewish State. As for the other components of identity, the more religious emphasize the religious-ideological aspect, while the nonreligious, compared to the religious, emphasize the more universalistic component whereby Jerusalem is symbolic of a world center for all religions.

Similar tendencies appear in Jewish appraisal of the importance of Jerusalem as a national center for Palestinians. Nonobservant respondents believe somewhat more than the observant that Jerusalem is important to the Palestinians as a national center ($\mu = -0.32$). This belief diminishes from 74% of the totally non-observant who said "very important" and "important," to 44% of the "strictly" observant. Sixty-four percent of the "somewhat observant" and 57% of the "mostly observant" respondents chose these positive answers. However, only a minority of all the religiosity groups (16% to 25%) said that Jerusalem is "very important" as a national center for the Palestinians—in contrast to the majority in each of the observance groups who declare that Jerusalem is very important to them personally as a religious and national center of the Jewish people.

About half the sites within Jerusalem that were considered part of Jerusalem are more important to the observant (monotonicity coefficients range between 0.34 and 0.59). These are: the Temple Mount, the Wailing Wall, the Mount of Olives, the Jewish quarter in the Old City, and the Old City as a whole. It is noteworthy that each of these sites is "very important" to most of the respondents from all religiosity groups.

There are no meaningful differences between observers and nonobservers in their assessments of the importance of the following sites as part of Jerusalem: the non-Jewish quarters of the Old City, the Arab neighborhoods in downtown East Jerusalem, the Arab villages previously in the West Bank, the new Jewish neighborhoods (established after 1967), and the old Jewish neighborhoods (monotonicity coefficients range between 0.09 and 0.26).

It is worth reiterating that while the Jewish neighborhoods, both new and old, are "very important" to most respondents in all the religiosity groups, only a minority attribute such importance to the Arab neighborhoods as being part of Jerusalem, with the exception of the "non-Jewish quarters of the Old City" to which 45% of the "strictly" observant do attribute such importance, as compared to about one-third in each of the other observance groups.

Demography and Size of Jerusalem

There are hardly any differences between observers and nonobservers in their assessments relating to the demography and size of Jerusalem. However, the observant differ greatly from the others with respect to restricting construction of housing for the Arabs in order to prevent their becoming a majority in the future. On this point more of the observant support such restriction ("definitely support" and "support"), compared to the traditional and the totally nonobservant (75%, 66%, and 48% respectively—monotonicity coefficient = 0.40).

Prospects for Peace and the Role of Jerusalem in Achieving It

More observers than nonobservers hold the opinion that no concessions should be made in Jerusalem, even at the cost of giving up the possibility of peace with the Arabs: 75% of the "strictly" and "mostly" observant "definitely agree" and "agree" to no concessions, compared to 61% of the "somewhat" and 44% of the totally nonobservant ($\mu = 0.33$).

Nonobservant respondents believe more in the prospect for peace in the foreseeable future between Israel and the Arab world, and that a peace agreement with the Palestinians will indeed be a true and lasting peace. They also believe more that Jerusalem is the key to real peace, and that in order to achieve real peace with the Palestinians a compromise over Jerusalem should be made (monotonicity coefficients range between -0.38 and -0.46). The proportion of believers in the prospects for peace between Israel and the Arab world in the foreseeable future rises from 16% among the "strictly" observant to 46% among the totally nonobservant. However, only about one-third of the nonobservant believe that Jerusalem is the key to peace and that without a compromise over Jerusalem there will not be peace. In other words, a minority in all religiosity groups think that a compromise on Jerusalem is vital for achieving a true and lasting peace.

A similar but weaker trend was found in the correlations between religiosity and reasons for making concessions over Jerusalem (monotonicity coefficients ranging between -0.18 and -0.27). In other words, each of the reasons for a compromise is convincing somewhat more for the nonobservant than for the observant. As for the reasons against a compromise, stronger correlations were found. As expected, with increased religiosity there is also a rise in the convincing power of each of the reasons against making a compromise on Jerusalem (monotonicity coefficients ranging from 0.36 to 0.45).

The Status of Jerusalem

On the options proposed for the future status of Jerusalem, the nonobservant systematically reveal greater inclination than the observant to seriously consider each of them. All the correlations are moderate, and most of them range between -0.30 and -0.34.

Nonobservers, more than the observant, believe that the Palestinians have at least some legitimate rights with regard to Jerusalem, and that their claim over East Jerusalem as their capital is justified. These differences are moderate ($\mu = -0.37$ and $\mu = -0.35$ respectively). The nonobservant also give somewhat more support to each of the options for a Palestinian capital in the Jerusalem area, but the differences are very small ($\mu = -0.25$ for each of the options). In other words, none of the options gains massive support from the nonobservant. Establishing a new city for the Palestinian capital gains somewhat greater support among the nonobservant (33%) than does designating an Arab region in East Jerusalem for that purpose (28%). That is, only a minority of each of the religiosity groups support these two options. Contrariwise, about half the "somewhat" and the "mostly" observant express "definite" objection to these two options, and over 60% of the "strictly" observant express such objection.

The nonobservant give more support to the idea of establishing a Palestinian State ($\mu = -0.51$). The support for the establishment of a Palestinian state declines from 52% of the totally nonobservant to 5% of the "strictly" observant. Only one-third (33%) of the "somewhat" observers support the establishment of a Palestinian State.

Protest Acts Against Compromise on Jerusalem

In general, the observant respondents are more ready than the nonobservant to support protest actions against an unacceptable compromise over Jerusalem which might be made by a government supported by a non-Zionist majority in the Knesset. The "strictly" observant especially tend to support nonviolent actions that disrupt the functioning of society (69%) compared with 28% of the nonobservant ($\mu = 0.39$). A similar difference ($\mu = 0.37$) occurs with regard to use of force if necessary to prevent implementation of such a compromise; in this case, a minority in each of the religiosity groups would support such a protest action—from 30% among the "strictly" observant to 10% among the totally nonobservant.

Much smaller differences were found with regard to justification of violent actions against Palestinians or Jews (monotonicity coefficients ranging between 0.21 and 0.23 respectively), with only a negligible minority supporting such actions.

There are no notable differences by religiosity in personal readiness to participate in any actions against a compromise on Jerusalem that is unacceptable to the respondent. Of all the religioisty groups, only the "strictly" observant are an exception in that 26% of them stated that they would "definitely" participate in such protest actions, versus 8% to 13% among the other religiosity groups.

Country of Origin

Since country of birth cannot be ordered from high to low, the respondents were assigned to six groups according to their own countries of birth: (1) Israel, (2) former Soviet Union, (3) Eastern Europe (except former Soviet Union) (4) Western Europe [these are few in number ($N = 49$) and hence do not permit detailed discussion], (5) Middle East, and (6) North Africa.

It is of special interest to dwell on the attitudes of newcomers from the former Soviet Union ($N = 125$). The data indicate that these newcomers stand out on only a few items, but otherwise do not differ from the other origin groups. On the other hand, respondents born in North Africa do constitute a unique group in their attitudes on many of the topics, as do old-timers and European-born respondents (mainly Eastern Europe).

Involvement in the Peace Process and the Meaning of Jerusalem

Newcomers from the former Soviet Union are less involved in the peace process in general, as well as with respect to Jerusalem. Sixty-nine percent of them feel involved in the peace process, versus 80% to 89% of respondents from the other countries. Similarly, 80% and 90% respectively are involved with the topic of Jerusalem. Jerusalem is somewhat less important to newcomers from the Soviet Union, compared to the others: 66% of respondents from the former Soviet Union replied that Jerusalem is "very important" to them, versus 77% to 83% of the other groups who so replied. These newcomers also have a somewhat lesser sense of belongingness to the city compared to the others. However, no differences were found in the meaning of Jerusalem from the various viewpoints that were studied, the exception being the importance of Jerusalem as "a world center for all religions," an aspect to which respondents born in North Africa and in Western Europe attribute less importance compared to the others. Likewise, no striking differences were found by country of birth in attributing importance to the various sites as being part of Jerusalem. The ranking of sites by each ethnic group is the same as that for the sample as a whole.

Respondents of Eastern European origin (not the former Soviet Union) are the strongest supporters of conducting negotiations on Jerusalem within the peace process (35%), while the lowest support comes from North African Jews (11%). The rest of the groups fall between these two extreme groups, 20% to 26% of them supporting such negotiations. Moreover, the majority of North Africans (57%) "definitely" oppose any negotiations on Jerusalem, versus 28% to 36% of the other origin groups. A similar distribution recurred when this question was repeated at the end of the interview. Also, respondents from the various countries of birth differ in the extent of their agreement to the statement that "we should make no concessions over Jerusalem even if we have to give up peace." Respondents born in Europe, mainly in Eastern Europe (not former Soviet Union new immigrants), are divided on this topic, with only half of them agreeing, while in the other origin groups the majority (60% to 78%) agree to this statement. Especially striking on this point are respondents born in North Africa, more than two-thirds of whom are prepared to give up peace rather than make concessions over Jerusalem.

Prospects for Peace and the Role of Jerusalem in Addressing It

Respondents born in Eastern Europe are the most optimistic regarding the prospects for peace between Israel and the Arab world, and they also believe more than the others that a peace agreement with the Palestinians will be long-lasting (49% versus 30% to 33%). The most pessimistic on this topic are respondents born in North Africa, of whom only 23% believe that a peace agreement with the Palestinians will be long-lasting. On the other hand, only a minority (20% to 26%) of all the origin groups believe that a compromise over Jerusalem is the key to a true and lasting peace between Israel and the Arab countries, the most negative being those born in North Africa and the Middle East (16% and 17% respectively). In other words, there are hardly any differences on this point by country of origin— only a minority regard Jerusalem as the key to the peace process. Moreover, no differences by country of origin were found in assessments of the "convincing conditions" for real peace with the Arab countries ("that Saudi Arabia open an embassy in Jerusalem," and "establishing regular commercial relations with the Arab States").

No differences were found by country of origin with respect to the various "convincing reasons" for a compromise on Jerusalem, except one, namely, because extremists of the Moslem world will gain strength. This reason is somewhat more convincing to the newcomers from the Soviet Union, compared to the other origin groups (33% versus 14% to 25%). No differences were found, by country of birth, in the extent of the persuasive power of the reasons against a compromise over Jerusalem.

The Status of Jerusalem

It is interesting that respondents born in North Africa believe more than the others that there should be a full separation in daily life between Jews and Arabs in Jerusalem, while respondents born in Eastern Europe are least supportive of such a separation (63% and 40% respectively replied "very desirable" and "desirable"). Respondents from other origins are divided on this issue. On the other hand, respondents born in the Middle East and North Africa are least supportive of the establishment of a Palestinian State, compared to the other origin groups (22% versus 34% to 38%). The former also think less than the others that the Palestinians have any sort of legitimate rights with regard to Jerusalem (29% to 32% versus 40% to 43%). Especially striking in their extreme negation of Palestinian rights are those born in North Africa (38% versus 20% to 27% of the others). A similar pattern prevails with regard to justification of the Palestinians' claim for East Jerusalem as the capital of a Palestinian State: again, the North African Jews are the strongest opponents (half strongly oppose, versus one-third from the other origin groups). Nevertheless, there are no differences by country of birth with regard to the areas in Jerusalem and adjoining it which were suggested as options for a Palestinian capital; an absolute majority, whatever the country of birth, object to the two options that were proposed.

Respondents from the various countries of birth have similar attitudes regarding the various options for the future status of Jerusalem with but one exception, that "control of the Temple Mount will be under the Wakf as now." Fewer of the respondents from the Middle East and North Africa (17% to 22%) compared to the others (32% to 35%) would seriously consider this option. Similarly, for the Easterners it is more important that Jews be able to pray on the Temple Mount: 65% and 75% chose the answer "very important" compared with 54% to 59% from the other groups; an exception, again, are the Soviet newcomers, of whom only 46% considered it "very important" that Jews be able to pray on the Temple Mount.

Protest Acts Against a Compromise on Jerusalem

Respondents born in Eastern Europe (except the former Soviet Union) are the strongest opponents of any violent protest actions, no matter toward whom they are directed. The data show that the newcomers are least likely to justify lawful demonstrations in the event of a compromise over Jerusalem that is unacceptable to them, made by a government with a non-Jewish majority in the Knesset (62% of Soviets, compared with 71% to 78% of the other origin groups).

Respondents from all countries of birth divide similarly in their readiness to participate personally in a protest act against a compromise on Jerusalem.

Time in Country

All the correlations between time in the country and the attitudes toward Jerusalem are close to zero: Israeli-born, old-time immigrants and newcomers respond similarly on the variety of questions that were asked (Table 2.11).

4. Ideological Inclination and Attitudes on the Topic of Jerusalem

Of all the background variables presented in Table 2.11, voting intention is the one that correlates best with most of the topics that were investigated. In other words, this is first and foremost a political issue. Hence, this section is devoted to the inter-relations between political preference and attitudes toward the Jerusalem problem.

The coefficients given in Table 2.11 are based on the question: "If elections were held today, for which party would you vote?" Only respondents mentioning "Labor" or "Likud" were included in the analysis. Thus, this variable becomes a dichotomous one artificially ordered politically from left to right. Another question, relating to the ideological inclination of the respondents, reads: "To which of the following political/ideological movements do you feel closest?" The response categories were: (1) closer to the Labor movement; (2) closer to Meretz; (3) closer to Likud; (4) closer to parties right of Likud (Tsomet, Moledet); (5) closer to the religious parties.

The discussion here focuses on differences by voting intention, that is, between politically left (Labor) and politically right (Likud). We shall also dwell on differences defined by the question on ideological inclination when it proves helpful for obtaining a more refined distinction of the political orientation. Because of the importance of the topic, we present the distributions by ideological inclination in Appendix A-2.* The ideological question relates only to the ideological identification of respondents, and in any event does not necessarily correspond to voting intention and voting distribution, although, of course, these two questions are to some extent intercorrelated.

Involvement in the Peace Process and Attitudes Toward Negotiations on Jerusalem

The low coefficients in Table 2.11 show that voters of both Labor and Likud reveal a similar extent of involvement in the peace process in general and in the status of Jerusalem within this process. In addition, the cross-tabulations by ideological inclination show that respondents who feel right-of-Likud and to the religious parties are more involved on the topic of the future of Jerusalem than are respondents who identify with Likud, Labor, and Meretz (see Appendix A-2, p. 240). No differences were found by ideological inclination on involvement in the topic of peace in general.

Voters of Labor and Likud differ greatly in their attitudes toward holding negotiations on Jerusalem. Labor voters support these negotiations more than do Likud voters (μ = 0.64). While 37% of Labor supporters favor ("definitely for" and "for") negotiations on Jerusalem, only 10% of Likud, religious parties, and extreme right supporters favor such negotiations. Despite the striking difference between Labor and Likud on this topic, there is only a minority (albeit a discernible one) of those who feel close to Labor who support negotiations on Jerusalem— this, compared with a majority of those inclined toward Meretz (63%!) who support these negotiations. In other words, no political group in Israel, except Meretz (about 6% of party identifiers), has a majority that supports negotiations on Jerusalem within the framework of the peace process. This pattern recurred both at the beginning and at the end of the interview.

The Importance and Meaningfulness of Jerusalem

Four out of five aspects of the importance of Jerusalem were found to be somewhat more important for the right than for the left, especially those associated with religious and Jewish matters. There is hardly a difference between Labor voters and

---

*The number of respondents in the tables given in Appendix A-2 does not include those who did not respond to the question on ideological inclination; therefore, the total number of respondents is always less than 1,530, and varies from topic to topic in accordance with the number of respondents who did not answer each pair of questions, namely, the political-inclination cross-tabulated with each of the other questions. The same is true for all the tables in this part and in the appendixes.

Likud voters in their assessments of the importance of Jerusalem as a world center for all religions (μ = 0.19). The same trend is apparent with respect to the various sites in Jerusalem as being part of the city, although the differences vary in accordance with the particular site. All the differences are in the same direction: Likud voters attribute more importance than do Labor voters to each of the sites mentioned. Especially noteworthy are the differences regarding the Temple Mount, the Wailing Wall and the Old City (monotonicity coefficients with political affiliation are –0.53 and –0.51 respectively).

The data in Appendix A-2 show that despite the fact that supporters of Labor attribute less importance to Jerusalem compared to supporters of Likud, the extreme right, and the religious parties, the majority even of Labor supporters (56% to 77%) replied that Jerusalem is "very important" to them from each of the studied viewpoints. The only exception is the aspect of "a world center for all religions." In contrast, only a minority (31% to 44%) of Meretz supporters replied that Jerusalem is "very important" to them from the religious and Jewish aspects, and only for half of them is Jerusalem "very important" from a national-historical point of view. Fifty-eight percent of Meretz supporters replied that Jerusalem is "very important" to them as a symbol of the State of Israel, compared to between 77% and 90%, who said so from all the other political groups (Appendix A-2, p. 242). Similarly, only 42% of Meretz supporters expressed a strong sense of belonging to Jerusalem, compared to 60% to 92% in the other political groups.

In general, then, despite the differences between left and right, the majority in each of the political groups attributes very great importance to Jerusalem from the various viewpoints that were studied, even if the size of the majority differs between left and right. An exception is Meretz supporters, who break the national consensus for all aspects except that of Jerusalem being a symbol of the State of Israel.

With respect to the importance attributed to various sites as being "part of the city," it is worth noting that a number of sites evoke a consensus throughout the political spectrum including Meretz. These are: the Wailing Wall, the Jewish quarter of the Old City, the old Jewish neighborhoods, and the Old City. As for the Jewish neighborhoods established after 1967, there is a consensus throughout all the political parties (71% to 83% consider them "very important" as part of Jerusalem), except for Meretz supporters, whose opinions are divided: 48% replied "very important," but only a *small* minority answered "not so important" or "not at all important" (Appendix A-2, p. 243–245).

More Labor voters, compared to Likud, think that Jerusalem is important for the Palestinians as a national center (μ = 0.49). It should be noted, however, that only a minority of each of the political groups thinks that Jerusalem is "very important" for the Palestinians as a national center, but the size of this minority varies, from 12% among supporters of the right bloc to 37% among supporters of Meretz. It is interesting that on this point supporters of the religious parties are similar to those who support Labor, with about one-quarter (24%) of each of these groups holding the opinion that Jerusalem is "very important" for the Palestinians as a national center (Appendix A-2, p. 243, Q. 15).

Demography and Size of Jerusalem

No differences were found by ideological inclination in assessments relating to the size of Jerusalem and its demographic composition. Yet Likud voters are much more "disturbed" than Labor voters by the fact that 28% of residents of Jerusalem are Arabs. The Likud respondents give more support to restricting housing construction for Arabs for the purpose of preventing their becoming a majority in the city (monotonicity coefficients are –0.61 and –0.42 respectively; see also the tables on ideological inclination in Appendix A-2, p. 249–250).

Prospects for Peace and the Role of Jerusalem in Achieving Peace

Half of Labor supporters agree that "we should make no concessions over Jerusalem even if we have to give up on peace with the Arabs," but only 19% of these agree "definitely." By comparison, a majority of supporters of Likud, right-of-Likud, and the religious parties (69% to 75%) agreed, compared with over one-third (35%) of the Likud supporters and close to half of the extreme right who "definitely" agree (48% and 45% respectively). Only about one-fourth (24%) of Meretz supporters expressed agreement with this statement, with 8% holding the extreme affirmative view. Thus, at least half of the respondents throughout the political spectrum agree with the statement that "we should make no concessions over Jerusalem even if we have to give up on peace with the Arabs," with the exception of Meretz supporters, of whom one-fourth agree.

Ideological-political inclination in Israel is closely related with the assessment of the prospects for peace and with the perception of the role of Jerusalem in the achievement of peace. These correlations are among the strongest, ranging from 0.70 to 0.87. Labor voters, compared to Likud voters, believe much more in the prospects for peace with the Arab world in the foreseeable future, and that a peace agreement with the Palestinians will be true and long-lasting (monotonicity coefficients are 0.81 and 0.87 respectively). Somewhat weaker correlations, yet still notable, were found concerning the role of Jerusalem in the attainment of peace, where, again, Labor voters believe more than Likud voters that a compromise over Jerusalem is the key to true peace between Israel and the Arab countries; that in order to arrive at real peace with the Palestinians a compromise on Jerusalem must be made, and that for the sake of peaceful co-existence between Arabs and Jews in Jerusalem, a compromise on Jerusalem should be made (monotonicity coefficients are 0.68, 0.70 and 0.66 respectively). While a majority of Labor and Meretz supporters (63% and 77% respectively) believe in the prospects for true peace in the foreseeable future (replied "believe strongly" and "believe"), only a minority of supporters of the right and religious parties believe so (18% of Likud and religious parties, and 9% of the extreme right). This finding is worthy of attention, since, as we shall see later, support or objection to negotiations over Jerusalem is related, first and foremost, to attitudes regarding the prospects for true peace with the Arab world and with the Palestinians. Nevertheless, even among Labor supporters only 37% think that a compromise over Jerusalem is the key to real peace between Israel and the Arab countries; comparatively, an even smaller minority (about 10%) of the right and religious parties think so. However, more than half of Meretz supporters believe so (Appendix A-2, p. 252). The same is true with regard to the other questions relating to the role of Jerusalem in the peace process. In sum, while there is a clear contrast between left and right in the assessments of the prospects for true peace, only a minority throughout the political spectrum, except Meretz, believe that a compromise over Jerusalem is an undisputable condition for attaining peace. Among Meretz supporters, 52% to 56% believe so.

Reasons for and Against Compromise on Jerusalem

Four of the six reasons offered in favor of compromise over Jerusalem convinced only a minority of between 10% and 36% throughout the political spectrum, except for Meretz. Only a small minority among the right and religious parties are convinced versus a third among Labor and a majority among Meretz supporters. Indeed, Meretz supporters are convinced by all the reasons for a compromise but one, namely, that a compromise over Jerusalem will improve peace with Egypt.

A different pattern was obtained for the two last reasons for compromise, namely: "A compromise on Jerusalem will enhance personal safety of Israelis in Jerusalem" and "A compromise on Jerusalem will lead to international recognition of Jerusalem as the capital of Israel." With regard to these two reasons, Labor supporters are closer to Meretz supporters, with nearly half of them (46% and 43% respectively) saying that these reasons are convincing, whereas only 14% and 20% think so among the right and religious parties (Appendix A-2, pp. 255–256).

All the reasons presented for a compromise on Jerusalem are more convincing to Labor voters, compared to Likud voters (monotonicity coefficients ranging from 0.44 to 0.59). And conversely, all the reasons against a compromise are more convincing for Likud than for Labor voters (from –0.53 to –0.64).

The reasons *against* a compromise on Jerusalem generally gain strong support from a majority of respondents throughout the political spectrum ("very convincing" and "convincing") except Meretz supporters, but even among them about half support two of the "against" reasons, namely: (1) "Concessions in Jerusalem will only enhance the Palestinians' demands for more concessions" (47% of Meretz are convinced, versus 72% of Labor, and 90% to 92% of the right and religious parties); and (2) "If there is a compromise on Jerusalem, Jews will not have free access to the Old City" (50% of Meretz supporters are convinced, versus 59% of Labor, and 83% to 89% of the right and religious parties) (Appendix A-2, p. 257–258). In other words, despite the support of a great part of the left for these two "against" reasons, there still remains a wide gap between the judgments of left and right with respect to the reasons against a compromise on Jerusalem.

Options for the Status of Jerusalem

As expected, Labor voters are more prepared than Likud voters to consider each of the options presented to them for the future status of Jerusalem (monotonicity coefficients range between 0.43 and 0.63). As on other topics, here, too, Meretz supporters stand out in their readiness to consider the options, with most of them (52% to 61%) prepared to consider seriously ("very seriously" and "seriously") all the options, except two: "Turn the Old City into an international city under the United Nations" (35% of Meretz would consider), and "Give over East Jerusalem to Palestinian sovereignty while the Jewish neighborhoods in East Jerusalem will have special status under Israeli control" (37% of Meretz would consider seriously).

Only a minority of respondents from those who identified with the right and the religious parties would consider each of the options, the proportions of that minority differing for each option, ranging from 15% to 35% who would consider them; Likud supporters are more positive than are supporters of the extreme right and religious parties (Appendix A-2, p. 259–263).

As for supporters of Labor, the proportions willing to consider seriously the choice of options vary from a majority to a minority with regard to the several options. About two-thirds of Labor supporters are prepared to consider seriously the transfer of Arab settlements and villages previously in the West Bank to Palestinian sovereignty, with or without an exchange for the Jewish regions now in the West Bank. Half of them are even willing to consider seriously "to transfer the Arab neighborhoods of East Jerusalem except those that are inside the walls to Palestinian sovereignty." A considerable proportion (about 40%) of Labor supporters are ready to consider seriously the options that "control of the Temple Mount will be under the Wakf as is now," and "Retain Israeli sovereignty over East Jerusalem, while the Arab neighborhoods in East Jerusalem will have special status under Palestinian control." A much smaller minority would consider seriously the other options (Appendix A-2, p. 259–263).

The data on the "options" again point to the fact that the issue of Jerusalem is mainly a political one. Yet, although Labor supporters are more flexible than Likud and religious parties supporters on some of the options, they, too, are not very enthusiastic about most of the options presented for the future status of Jerusalem. Only Meretz respondents are prepared to make generous concessions.

Attitudes toward a Palestinian State and Its Capital

Labor voters, more than Likud voters, believe that the Palestinians have some legitimate rights with regard to Jerusalem, and that their claim for Jerusalem as their capital is justified; they also express greater support for the establishment of a Palestinian State (monotonicity coefficients are 0.64, 0.61 and 0.79 respectively). Labor voters also support more each of the two options presented to them for a Palestinian capital in the Jerusalem area, but the differences on these options between them and the Likud are more moderate than the differences in support of a Palestinian State (monotonicity coefficients are 0.42 and 0.43).

Inspection of the details in Appendix A-2 reveals that over half of Labor supporters (55%) and a majority of Meretz supporters (82%) think that the Palestinians have some legitimate rights with regard to Jerusalem, versus only a minority (22% to 27%) who think so among the right and religious parties. However, only a *minority* of the Labor supporters (29%) justify the Palestinians' claim of East Jerusalem as their capital, versus about two-thirds (62%) of Meretz supporters who justify it. Of course, only a negligible minority of the right and religious parties justify that claim (5% to 11%). Thus, the difference between Likud and Labor voters on this issue is in the size of the minority. Moreover, the Labor supporters of a Palestinian State are more reticent than among Meretz supporters: 57% and 79% respectively, with only 8% of Labor supporters who "definitely support" the establishment of a Palestinian State. Only a slight minority (3% to 16%) of supporters of the right bloc and of the religious parties approve the establishment of a Palestinian State (Appendix A-2, p. 264). In other words, the difference between left and right on this point is fundamental and is expressed by a majority versus a minority, although, as stated above, the Labor majority is relatively reticent in its support. Only a minority throughout the political spectrum, including Labor, support the two options for a Palestinian capital in the Jerusalem region. Yet, compared to about one-third of Labor who support these two options, only 7% to 16% do so among the right and religious parties. Again, the strongest support for a Palestinian capital in the Jerusalem region comes from supporters of Meretz, of whom about half (52% to 54%) expressed approval (Appendix A-2, p. 265).

To conclude, then, Labor supporters, compared to Likud, are much more liberal in their general attitudes toward Palestinians, admitting Palestinian rights and supporting the establishment of a Palestinian State. However, when the issue of Jerusalem is raised, only a minority of Labor are prepared to make concessions, although their objection is not as strong as among the supporters of the right and the religious parties.

Protest Acts Against a Compromise on Jerusalem

Except for lawful demonstrations, Likud voters are more likely than Labor to justify the various protest actions against an unacceptable compromise over Jerusalem made by a government that lacks a Zionist majority in the Knesset (monotonicity coefficients ranging between –0.47 and –0.60). The main difference is in justifying "nonviolent actions that disrupt the functioning of society," which is justified by only 25% and 18% of Labor and Meretz respectively, versus 49% who justify such actions among Likud supporters, 53% among adherents of the religious parties, and about two-thirds (66%) among the extreme right. Only a slight minority throughout the political spectrum justify any violent protest actions against Jews, but there is a considerable difference between right (24%) and left (6%) in the percentage who justify acting violently against palestinians should the Knesset propose an unacceptable compromise over Jerusalem (Appendix A-2, p. 266–267).

As for personal participation in protest actions, the main difference is between supporters of right-of-Likud and religious parties, on the one hand, and Likud, Labor, and Meretz on the other. Of the extreme right and of the religious parties, 53% and 37% respectively said they would personally participate in protest actions, compared to 30% of Likud, 19% of Labor, and 17% of Meretz who would personally take part in such actions. (Recent protest against the Wye Accord fitted this pattern.)

5. Attitudes Toward Negotiations on Jerusalem

The analysis, so far, has focused on group differences in the perceptions of the various aspects of the Jerusalem issue. But, for policy purposes, it is necessary to identify those aspects that are strongly correlated, and those that are only weakly correlated, with willingness to support conducting negotiations on Jerusalem.

The central criterion of this study is whether there is any support for negotiations on Jerusalem within the overall peace negotiations. The following question was asked: "Are you for or against negotiations on Jerusalem within the peace process?" The question was asked at the beginning of the interview, preceded by only two questions on personal involvement with the peace process and the future of Jerusalem, and was repeated verbatim at the end of the interview.

The percentage distributions of responses to this question, at the beginning and at the end of the interview, for the national and for the settler samples are as follows:

Shlomit Levy

Are you for or against negotiations on Jerusalem within the peace process?	National sample		Settlers sample	
	Beginning of interview	End of interview	Beginning of interview	End of interview
1. Definitely for	5	3	2	2
2. For	16	18	8	7
3. Against	42	36	32	31
4. Definitely against	36	43	59	60
Total (%)	100	100	100	100

Obviously, in light of the different backgrounds of the two samples (see the introductory section for a description of the samples), the settlers could be expected to be more definite in their negative attitudes toward conducting negotiations on Jerusalem, compared to the national sample.

It turns out, however, that a great majority in both samples object to negotiations on Jerusalem: 80% of the national sample and 90% of the settler sample. Moreover, in both samples there were hardly any changes in respondents' answers when the two interview-times are compared: A majority of 80% of the national sample object to the negotiations and so do 90% of the settler sample. Yet, while among the settler sample there is no change at all from the first to the second time in percent distributions, the national sample shows a small increase in those answering "definitely against," from 36% the first time to 43% the second time, the increase being on account of those responding the less extreme "against," which fell from 42% to 36%. In other words, the various options for a solution presented in the questionnaire, and the "for" and "against" reasons for compromise, not only failed to contribute toward a change in respondents' readiness for a compromise, but in fact sharpened the objection to a compromise.

Observing the joint (the two interview-times) distributions of anwers to the question in the national sample reveals that over two-thirds (68%) did not change their attitudes (either positively or negatively); of the remaining 32%, 20% changed during the interview in the negative direction and 12% changed in the positive direction. These findings strengthen the overall negative trend. In any event, the reliability of the question is very high, as expressed by the very strong correlation between the two interview-times ($\mu = 0.88$).

As for the settler sample, 70% of them did not change their opinion, and the remaining 30% divided almost equally between a more negative opinion (16%) and a more positive opinion (14%) (generally a more moderate objection).

The data show, moreover, that repetition of the question at the end of the interview has greater predictive power. In other words, the correlations of this question with the other assessments and attitudes on the topic are systematically higher than those obtained for the question when asked the first time. Hence, in our discussion of the correlations between the attitude toward negotiation on Jerusalem and other attitudes, we shall relate only to the data obtained at the end of the interview (Q. 78 in Appendix A-1, p. 235).

It is important to note furthermore that the extent of political involvement—in the sense of following the peace process and expressing interest on the future of Jerusalem—is hardly related to the attitude on negotiations over Jerusalem. This stems from the fact that respondents who are involved in politics may have quite different and even opposing attitudes on various political issues, and certainly on an issue as central as the future status of Jerusalem. This finding is in full accord with principal component theory (Guttman, 1954;* Levy, 1978**).

Let us now turn to the interrelationships between the attitude toward negotiations over Jerusalem and the various aspects of the Jerusalem issue that were studied. We shall again make use of monotonicity coefficients; when necessary for clarifying the discussion, we shall also present the relevant tables on which the coefficients are based.

Support for negotiations on Jerusalem within the peace process is related, first and foremost, to assessments of the prospects for peace and the role of Jerusalem in the attainment of a long-lasting peace. The more the respondents believe that Jerusalem is the key to true peace between Israel and the Arab states, and the more they believe that only a compromise on Jerusalem will lead to co-existence in Jerusalem and to real peace with the Palestinians, the more they support negotiations on Jerusalem within the peace process (monotonicity coefficients are 0.83, 0.86, and 0.87 respectively). Very strong correlations, although not as tight, were found between support for negotiations on Jerusalem and belief that there can be a true peace with the Palestinians and with the Arab world ($\mu = 0.71$ and $\mu = 0.62$ respectively). Recognition of the legitimacy of any sort of rights of Palestinians with regard to Jerusalem, justification of their claims over Jerusalem as their capital, and agreement that the capital of the Palestinian state (if established) will be in Jerusalem or within its region are also closely related to support for negotiations on Jerusalem (monotonicity coefficients are 0.75, 0.78, 0.71 and 0.68, respectively).

Hence, support for negotiations on Jerusalem is closely related to recognition of any rights of the Palestinians with regard to Jerusalem, to strong belief in prospects for true peace, and especially that such a peace can be achieved only if a compromise is made over Jerusalem. In light of these strong correlations, and the great importance of the topic, we shall present below additional clarifying data from the relevant tables (Table 2.12).

Striking throughout all the cross-tabulations presented in Table 2.12 is the polarization regarding negotiations on Jerusalem between extreme supporters and extreme opponents. This polarization is even stronger when the assessment is focused on the role of Jerusalem in the attainment of peace.

---

* L. Guttman, (1954). "The Principal Components of Scalable Attitudes," in P. F. Lazarsfeld (ed.), *Mathematical Thinking in the Social Sciences*, Glencoe, Ill.: The Free Press, pp. 216–257.
** S. Levy, (1978). "Involvement as a Component of Attitude: Theory and Political Examples," in S. Shye (ed.), *Theory Construction and Data Analysis in the Behavioral Sciences*. San Francisco: Jossey-Bass, pp. 300–324.

Table 2.12
Attitude toward negotiations on Jerusalem by assessments of prospects for peace, the role of Jerusalem in attaining peace, and recognition of Palestinian rights with regard to Jerusalem (in percentage)

	Are you for or against negotiations on Jerusalem within the peace process?			
	For*	Against	Definitely against	Total %
Percentage in sample	21	36	43	100
To what extent do you believe there can be true peace between Israel and the Arab world in the foreseeable future?				
Believe strongly	53	22	26	100
Believe	37	38	25	100
Don't believe so much	14	44	42	100
Don't believe at all	7	25	68	100
Do you believe that a peace agreement with the Palestinians will bring a true, long-term peace?				
Believe strongly	65	17	18	100
Believe	42	36	21	100
Don't believe so much	12	47	41	100
Don't believe at all	5	25	70	100
A compromise on Jerusalem is the key to true peace between Israel and the Arab States				
Definitely agree	79	15	6	100
Agree	62	25	12	100
Disagree	15	54	31	100
Definitely disagree	4	22	75	100
For true peace with the Palestinians we must compromise on Jerusalem				
Believe*	70	24	7	100
Don't believe so much	15	57	28	100
Don't believe at all	4	25	71	100
For co-existence between Arabs and Jews in Jerusalem we must compromise on Jerusalem				
Believe*	67	26	8	100
Don't believe so much	15	55	30	100
Don't believe at all	3	24	73	100
Do Palestinians have any sort of legitimate rights with regard to Jerusalem?				
Yes, definitely	69	18	13	100
Yes	38	39	23	100
No	11	51	38	100
Definitely no	5	15	81	100

*In view of the small number of respondents answering the extreme positive answer ("definitely for"/"believe strongly"), we have combined the two positive answers.

Attitudes toward negotiations on Jerusalem are closely related to many of the other topics under study. Thus, the greater the symbolic importance attributed to Jerusalem from each of the several viewpoints studied—except that of its being a center for all religions—the less the support for negotiations on Jerusalem within the peace process (monotonicity coefficients range from –0.58 to –0.63). A similar trend emerges regarding the importance attributed to various sites in Jerusalem, namely, the more a specific site is perceived as an important part of Jerusalem, the lower the support for negotiations on Jerusalem within the peace process. In this connection, the most outstanding sites are: the Wailing Wall (μ = –0.69), the Old City (–0.61), the Mount of Olives (–0.56), the Jewish quarter in the Old City (–0.51), and the Temple Mount (–0.50). It is important to note that these are "objective" findings, based not on subjective responses but on correlations between ostensibly different questions (importance attributed to sites as defining the city of Jerusalem and willingness to support the idea of negotiations over the city within the peace process). Substantively, these findings reveal the great importance that Israeli Jews attribute to the Old City and the holy places as identifying elements of Jerusalem. They imply that degrees of attachment to the symbolic 'center' of the city is more closely associated with the negotiating process than even degrees of attachment to residential areas, Jewish and non-Jewish.

Number of visits to Jerusalem, assessments of its demographic composition, and assessment of its size are hardly correlated to the attitude toward negotiations on Jerusalem. Table 2.13 presents the attitude toward negotiations on Jerusalem by assessments of its size.

In this connection it should be noted that the perception of the size of Jerusalem is not correlated with most of the issues studied; monotonicity coefficients range between 0.00 and 0.20, with the majority being close to zero.

As might be expected, the attitude toward negotiations on Jerusalem is closely related to the reasons for and against a compromise on Jerusalem, but the directions differ. The more positive the respondents' attitude toward conducting negotiations, the *higher* the convincing power of each of the reasons for a compromise (monotonicity coefficients ranging from 0.66 to 0.75); and, conversely, the more positive the attitude, the lower the convincing power of each of the reasons against a compromise (monotonicity coefficients range between –0.57 and –0.75). The most moderate correlation is with the "against"-claim that "Jerusalem is much more important for Judaism than for Islam," while the strongest correlation is with "concessions in Jerusalem will only enhance the Palestinians' demands for more concessions" (μ = –0.75).

Finally, again as expected, support for negotiations on Jerusalem is also positively correlated with each of the options proposed for the future status of Jerusalem (monotonicity coefficients ranging from 0.60 to 0.72, mostly between 0.68 and 0.72). The more respondents favor negotiations on Jerusalem within the peace process, the more they are prepared to consider seriously each of the options presented to them for its future status. The small difference in the size of the coefficients

Table 2.13
**Attitude toward negotiations on Jerusalem within the peace process
by assessment of its size (in percentages)**

| | Are you for or against negotiations on Jerusalem within the peace process? | | | |
	For*	Against	Definitely against	Total percentage
Percentage in sample	21	36	43	100
Of three descriptions of the borders of Jerusalem, which is the most appropriate?				
Two parts of the city that were united after the Six-Day War	21	28	51	100
The two parts + natural growth	21	37	42	100
The two parts + additional regions on the basis of various considerations	22	36	42	100
Compared to East Jerusalem under Jordanian rule up to the Six-Day War, what is the size of East Jerusalem today?				
About the same	24	43	33	100
Somewhat bigger	22	37	41	100
Much bigger	21	29	50	100

*In view of the small number of respondents answering "Definitely for," we have combined the two positive answers on support for negotiations.

points to the fact that respondents do not make much of a distinction among the various options, except perhaps for one, namely: "Establish a joint Palestinian-Jewish administration for the Old City without Israel having to yield its claim to sovereignty." While the correlation coefficient between that option and support for negotiations on Jerusalem is also not negligible ($\mu = 0.55$), it is more moderate compared to the others.

Moderate correlations were also found between readiness for a compromise on Jerusalem and justification of protest actions in case of an unacceptable compromise. In general, the greater the objection to negotiations, the greater the justification of protest actions, especially "nonviolent actions that disrupt the functioning of society," and "use of force if necessary to prevent implementation" (monotonicity coefficients are -0.38 and -0.37 respectively). Supporters and opponents of negotiations are similar in the extent of their justification of—or more precisely their opposition to—violent actions against Jews.

Those who oppose negotiations over Jerusalem are somewhat more prepared than supporters to participate personally in any protest action against a compromise on Jerusalem ($\mu = -0.43$).

6. The Status of Jerusalem in the Eyes of National, Settler, and SHAS Populations

In addition to the national sample, interviews were conducted with a special sample of 121 respondents from the settler population beyond the green line (see introductory section). Also, we have enlarged the number of the SHAS voters in order to study the attitudes of a faction which has a strong ethnic-religious background and which has been gaining strength in the past few years. Supporters of that party are mostly of North African origin and strictly adhere to the religious tradition. Because of the special social background of the settlers (see introductory section) and that of SHAS people, it is interesting to study their opinions in comparison with those of the national sample. It might be expected that the differences between the two samples would be in the same direction as those found by extent of religious observance, which, it will be recalled, is the social-demographic variable that is most strongly related to the studied topics (see third section). Also, the fact that the peace process raises immediate anxiety among the settlers regarding their future will certainly have bearing on their attitudes on the future of the status of Jerusalem. With regard to SHAS people, in view of their ethnic background, we may also expect differences similar to those obtained by country of birth (also described in the third section).

We shall conclude this study with a brief comparative analysis of the assessments of the various issues that were investigated regarding the future of Jerusalem, comparing the three specific populations—national, settlers, and SHAS.

The full distributions of responses from the national and the settler samples are presented in Appendix A. These data will be compared with the enlarged SHAS group. Since the latter does not constitute a scientifically extracted sample of that party, and in view of their small number ($N = 70$), the findings stemming from this comparison should be regarded with caution.

Involvement with the Peace Process and the Meaning of Jerusalem

The settlers are much more involved with the peace process in general and with the topic of the status of Jerusalem, as compared to the national population sample (Appendix A-1, p. 223). Compared to both, SHAS voters are much less involved in the peace process on both aspects. However, they, too, express more interest on the topic of Jerusalem than on the peace process as a whole. Almost all SHAS voters (96%) indicated that Jerusalem is "very important" for them personally and that they "definitely" feel a sense of belonging to the city, compared to 88% and 81% of the settlers, and 77% and 69% of the Jewish public within the green line. In other words, although Jerusalem is "very important" personally to a majority of respondents from the three groups, there are differences in the extent of importance that is attributed to Jerusalem, ordered in a descending direction as follows: SHAS, settlers, national. Differences were also found in the ranking of the importance of the meanings of Jerusalem from the five points of view given in Table 2.14.

The data in Table 2.14 indicate that there are almost no differences among the three samples in the extent of importance attributed to Jerusalem from a Jewish national point of view and as a symbol of the State of Israel. However, while the national sample and the settlers rank these two viewpoints at the top of the ranking, SHAS respondents give higher rank to the Jewish religion and Jerusalem as a center for the Jewish people and Judaism. Settlers attribute greater importance to the Jewish religious aspects than do respondents of the national sample, but not as much as SHAS affiliates; hence, the ranking in Table 2.14 is identical for the national sample and for the settlers, but differs for SHAS. These findings demonstrate that SHAS is a less "nation-oriented" faction, but serves a specific sector of the population, namely, the combination of Haredim (the ultra-orthodox) and easterners (especially from North Africa). In other words, SHAS represents Haredim of eastern ethnicity who are rejected by Ashkenazi Haredim, on the one hand, and who carry the torch for the deprived easterners, on the other. For this group Jerusalem is most important as a symbol of Judaism. In view of the increased power of this party in recent elections, it is worthwhile studying its attitudes on the political issue of the status of Jerusalem.

Least importance is attributed to Jerusalem as a world center for all religions by the three respondent groups. Half of the national sample regard Jerusalem as "very important" from this viewpoint as well, but it is "very important" for only about one-third of the settlers and of SHAS voters (35% and 36% respectively). In other words, the importance of the "universal" aspect of Jerusalem is lower among the groups characterized by high religious observance. It is noteworthy

Table 2.14
Ranking of importance of Jerusalem from five points of view
for the national sample, the settler sample, and SHAS voters
(percentage answering "very important")

	Importance of Jerusalem		
	National Sample	Settler sample	SHAS voters
As a symbol of the State of Israel	83	83	86
Jewish national-historical point of view	80	83	84
As a center for the Jewish people and Judaism	77	81	97
Jewish-religious point of view	68	73	99
As a world center for all religions	48	35	36

that there are hardly any differences between the settlers and the national sample in their assessments of the importance of Jerusalem as a national center for the Palestinians; about two-thirds of both groups think that Jerusalem is "very important" or "important" in that respect (66% and 63% respectively; Appendix A-1, p. 224), compared with only about one-third (36%) of SHAS voters.

With regard to the importance of sites in Jerusalem as part of the city, again we find great similarity between the national and settler samples, both in their ranking of their importance, as well as in the degree of importance. Only with respect to non-Jewish sites are there somewhat greater differences between these two groups: more of the settlers, compared to the national sample, think that these sites are important as part of the city. In any event, even among the settlers only a minority regard these sites as "very important" as part of Jerusalem (32% to 42% of the settlers, versus 23% to 26% of the national sample—Table 2.15). In spite of these differences, the ranking of the sites according to their importance as part of Jerusalem is similar for both the national sample and the settlers (Table 2.15). Discussion of this ranking is found in the first section, above.

In contrast to the national and settler samples, SHAS voters make fewer distinctions among the "Jewish" sites in the importance they attribute to them: almost all of them (90% to 100%) consider each of these sites as a "very important" part of

Table 2.15
Ranking of importance of sites in Jerusalem as part of the city
by the national sample, the settlers, and SHAS voters
(percentage answering "very important")

The site	Importance of sites as part of Jerusalem Percentage answering "very important"		
	National sample	Settler sample	SHAS voters
The Wailing Wall	91	92	100
The Old City	85	86	97
Old Jewish neighborhoods	80	84	93
The Jewish quarter in the Old City	79	79	90
Mount of Olives	77	80	91
The Temple Mount	75	81	99
New Jewish neighborhoods (established after 1967)	75	79	90
Non-Jewish quarters in the Old City	33	42	62
Arab neighborhoods in downtown East Jerusalem	23	32	43
Arab settlements and villages previously in the West Bank	20	32	44

Jerusalem. The main distinction, as in the other groups, is between the Jewish neighborhoods (new as well as old) and the non-Jewish neighborhoods. But, while non-Jewish neighborhoods within the Old City are considered "very important" for about two-thirds (62%) of SHAS voters, only 42% and one-third respectively among the settlers and national sample think so. As for the Arab neighborhoods outside the Old City, SHAS voters, too, attribute less importance; nevertheless, 44% of them think they are "very important" as part of Jerusalem. This minority is relatively larger in SHAS than among the settlers (32%) and the national sample (20% to 23%).

Thus, a majority of at least three-fourths in each of the three samples attributes great importance to all the "Jewish" sites, both old and new, as part of Jerusalem, with the Wailing Wall and the Old City topping the list; for SHAS the Temple Mount is also near the top. As for the Arab sites, fewer respondents attribute "great importance" to them as part of the city; an exception are the non-Jewish quarters in the Old City, to which more importance is attributed by the more observant respondents (settlers and particularly SHAS).

Prospects for Peace and the Role of a Compromise over Jerusalem in the Attainment of Peace

Only a minority of Israeli Jews believe that Israel and the Arab world can live peacefully in the foreseeable future. But, while 35% of the national sample and 29% of the settlers do believe so (replied "strongly believe" and "believe") only a meager proportion of SHAS voters (6%) are optimistic on this point. When respondents were asked if they believe that a peace agreement with the Palestinians will bring true and long-lasting peace, the proportion of believers in the settler sample dropped to 18%. In the national sample and SHAS voters no change was recorded in comparison to their assessments of the prospects for peace with the Arab world.

In light of these pessimistic views on the prospects for peace, two conditions were presented to the respondents. If fulfilled, would they be convinced that a real and long-lasting peace is possible with the Arab states? The conditions were: (1) that Saudi Arabia open an embassy in Jerusalem; and (2) that there will be regular commercial relations with Arab States. The data show that the second condition is convincing for just over half (53%) of the national sample and just under half (46%) for the settlers. The first condition, on the other hand, is convincing to a minority of about one-third of both samples (36% and 31% respectively). SHAS voters again stand out in their overall negative attitude and lack of distinction between Palestinians and Arab States; only 12% to 15% find each of the two conditions "convincing" or "very convicing" as evidence that real, long-term peace with the Arab world is possible.

Although 80% to 85% of Israeli Jews do not agree that a compromise on Jerusalem is the key to real peace between Israel and the Arab States, there are striking differences in the proportion of the extreme negative replies ("not at all") among the three samples: 38% of the national sample, 57% of the settler sample (Appendix A-1, p. 229), and 80% of SHAS voters. On the role of Jerusalem in the attainment of peace ("Do you believe that in order to arrive at a real peace with the *Palestinians* we must make a compromise on Jerusalem?"), the responses from the settlers and from SHAS voters get closer: 74% of the settlers and 83% of SHAS voters said "not at all," compared to 45% of the national sample who gave that extreme negative answer. The phenomenon of nondistinction by SHAS voters between Palestinians and other Arabs is again evident. Notably, almost all (90%) the settlers answered "definitely agree" and "agree" to give up on peace rather than make concessions on Jerusalem while a much smaller majority of the national sample and also of SHAS gave this answer (60% and 64% respectively, Appendix A-1, p. 227). This pattern should be regarded with caution both because it does not match the systematic trend found with respect to the other questions, and because the SHAS group is not a representative one and is small in number.

Despite the pessimism expressed regarding the prospects for peace, and the denial of the claim that Jerusalem has a central role in the achievement of peace, the majority of Israeli Jews object to separation between Arabs and Jews in Jerusalem by means of a wall, even for the sake of security. The settlers and SHAS voters are the most negative on this point, compared to the national sample (49%, 48%, and 19% respectively answered "definitely disagree," Q. 47 in Appendix A-1, p. 230). However, over half of the national sample (52%) and of the settlers (56%), and three-fourths of SHAS voters think it desirable that in daily life in Jerusalem there be a separation between Jews and Arabs in housing, places of entertainment, and so on.

Reasons for and Against a Compromise on Jerusalem

As noted in the first and fifth sections of this part, the majority of Israeli Jews (80%) object to negotiations on Jerusalem within the peace process. The objection is stronger among the settlers, with 90% of them objecting and 60% choosing the extreme negative answer "definitely object," versus 43% of the national sample who chose the extreme negative answer (Q. 78, Appendix A-1, p. 235). SHAS voters are the most extreme in their objection to negotiations over Jerusalem, with 86% who "definitely object" and only 1% who "support."

As will be recalled (section 1), respondents were presented with six possible reasons for, and four reasons against, a compromise on Jerusalem, and were asked to state to what extent they were convinced by each of them. Table 2.16 presents the reasons for and against with the percentages of the "convinced" in each of the three populations. A detailed discussion of the reasons for and against is given in section 1. As in Table 2.4, here, too, the reasons are ordered, separately for and against, by their "convincing" power for the national sample. The rankings in

Table 2.16

**Arguments for and against a compromise on Jerusalem
for the national sample, the settler sample, and SHAS voters
(percentage answering "very convincing" and "convincing")**

The argument	*Percentage answering "very convincing" and "convincing"*		
	National sample	*Settler sample*	*SHAS voters*
Arguments FOR compromise			
A compromise on Jerusalem will lead to international recognition of Jerusalem as the capital of Israel	29	17	10
A compromise on Jerusalem will enhance personal safety of Israelis in Jerusalem	21	13	13
A compromise on Jerusalem will honor the religious national rights of Palestinians in Jerusalem	23	10	7
Without a compromise on Jerusalem Moslem extremists will strengthen	23	11	10
Without a compromise on Jerusalem any Palestinian leadership that makes peace with Israel will be discredited among Palestinains	22	7	7
A compromise on Jerusalem will improve peace with Egypt	19	8	4
Arguments AGAINST compromise			
There should not be a compromise on Jerusalem because concessions on Jerusalem will enhance Palestinian demands	83	79	91
There should not be a compromise on Jerusalem because Jews will not have free access to the Old City	79	71	94
There should not be a compromise on Jerusalem because a city should not be divided because of a minority	70	60	65
There should not be a compromise on Jerusalem because Jerusalem is much more important for Judaism than for Islam	67	60	93

Table 2.16 are very similar to those of Table 2.4, where they are discussed in detail.

Only a few from each of the three groups are convinced by the for-compromise reasons, compared to a majority who are convinced by each of the against-compromise reasons. Systematically, more respondents of the national sample support each of the "for" reasons, compared to the settler sample and SHAS voters (19% to 29% in the national sample, versus 4% to 17% of the settlers and of the SHAS voters). The ranking of the for-compromise reasons is identical for the national and the settler samples, despite the small percentage of approvals in each. At the top of each ranking are the following two: "A compromise on Jerusalem will enhance the personal safety of Israelis in Jerusalem," and "A compromise on Jerusalem will lead to international recognition of Jerusalem as the capital of Israel." Surprisingly, perhaps, the data in Table 2.16 show that the settlers, compared to respondents from the national sample, are also somewhat less supportive of each of the four against reasons, but the ranking of the reasons for both groups is identical (the percentages of support are 67% to 83% for the national sample and 60% to 79% for the settlers). A higher proportion of SHAS voters support the reasons against a compromise on Jerusalem, compared to the national and settler samples. Almost all SHAS voters (91% to 94%) support the "against" reasons, the exception being "a city should not be divided or compromised on because of a minority that lives in it," for which support is expressed by only 65% of SHAS voters. This percentage is similar to that obtained for both the national and the settler samples, but in the SHAS ranking this reason is preceded by the reason "Jerusalem is much more important for Judaism than for Islam," for which support is expressed by 93% of SHAS versus 60% and 67% of the settlers and the national samples. Again we encounter the religious-Jewish emphasis given to Jerusalem by SHAS versus the extreme nationalistic emphasis expressed by the settlers.

The Status of Jerusalem

Table 2.17 presents in detail the ten options that were proposed for the future status of Jerusalem, with the percentages of those who would be willing to consider them seriously in the three population groups.

The discussion on the ranking of the options, and extent of support for them, is given in section 1. We shall focus here, rather, on the group differences. Table 2.17 indicates that the settlers are systematically less supportive of each of the options, as compared to the national sample, the proportion of supporters never exceeding 32%, which expresses the settlers' somewhat greater willingness to consider an exchange of Arab settlements in Jerusalem for Jewish areas in the West Bank. SHAS voters are generally even less supportive than the settlers, except in the case of four options, which neither settlers nor SHAS (6% to 9%) would consider seriously. These are: " Give the Palestinians sovereignty over the Arab neighborhoods of the Old City"; "Palestinians will get sovereignty of the Temple Mount in exchange for Palestinian recognition of Israel's sovereignty of the Wailing Wall"; "Give East Jerusalem to Palestinian sovereignty while Jewish neighborhoods in East Jerusalem have special status under Israeli control"; and "Turn the Old City into an international city under the United Nations."

Table 2.17
Options for the status of Jerusalem
(percentage answering "would consider very seriously" and "seriously"
for the national sample, settler sample, and SHAS voters)

To what extent would you consider each of the following proposals?	Consider "very seriously" and "seriously"		
	National sample	Settler sample	SHAS voters
Transfer to Palestinian sovereignty Arab settlements now within Jerusalem	44	27	19
Arab settlements now in Jerusalem go to Palestinian sovereignty in exchange for Jewish regions in the West Bank	44	32	15
Retain Israeli sovereignty over East Jerusalem, while Arab neighborhoods in East Jerusalem have special status under Palestinian control	35	22	17
Establish a joint Palestinian-Jewish administration of the Old City without Israel having to yield sovereignty	34	31	21
Transfer Arab neighborhoods of East Jerusalem, except those inside the walls of the Old City, to Palestinian sovereignty	34	21	17
Control of Temple Mount will be under the Wakf as now	31	15	14
Give the Palestinians sovereignty over the Arab neighborhoods of the Old City	23	9	9
Palestinians will get sovereignty of Temple Mount in exchange for Palestinian recognition of Israel's sovereignty of the Wailing Wall	20	9	9
Give East Jerusalem to Palestinian sovereignty while Jewish neighborhoods in East Jerusalem have special status under Israeli control	19	7	8
Turn the Old City into an international city under the United Nations	18	6	12

The ranking of the options is similar for the three populations, except for one difference which is worthy of attention, namely, "establish a joint Palestinian-Jewish administration for the Old City without Israel having to yield its claim to sovereignty." Although this option is also acceptable only to a minority of respondents, there is hardly any difference in the percentages of the settlers and of the national sample who would consider it seriously (31% and 34% respectively).

This option is ranked somewhat higher in the settler sample; moreover, it received the highest support among the SHAS voters (21%).

Attitudes Toward a Palestinian State and Its Capital

One-third of the national sample supports the establishment of a Palestinian State under the "present" circumstances, but only a slight proportion (3%) chose the extreme positive answer "definitely for." Eighteen percent of the settlers and 13% of SHAS voters support the establishment of a Palestinian State. In other words, here, too, recurs the above-described order: national → settlers → SHAS.

A similar pattern is revealed with respect to the assessment of the Palestinians' rights with regard to Jerusalem: 39% of Israeli Jews think that "the Palestinians have any sort of legitimate rights with regard to Jerusalem," versus 22% who think so among the settlers, and only 10% of SHAS voters. Only a tiny proportion (4% to 5%) chose the extreme positive answer "yes, definitely" in both the national and the settler samples, while not even one SHAS respondent chose that answer. Many fewer respondents think that the Palestinians' claim over East Jerusalem as their capital is justified—20%, 12%, and 1% respectively, from the national sample, the settlers, and SHAS. In other words, in each of the investigated groups, more respondents admit that the Palestinians have some legitimate rights with regard to Jerusalem, than those who justify their claim over East Jerusalem as their capital. In both cases, however, the percentages are low.

As will be recalled, two options were presented for the location of the Palestinian capital, if and when a Palestinian State is established. Table 2.18 presents respondents' answers to these two options.

Table 2.18
Proposals for the capital of a Palestinian state
(percentage answering "definitely support" and "support"
for the national sample, settler sample, and SHAS voters)

	Percentage answering "definitely support" and "support"		
	National sample	Settler Sample	SHAS voters
The capital of the Palestinian State will be an Arab region in East Jerusalem	20	10	4
The Palestinian capital will be a new city consisting of two parts: an area of East Jerusalem plus an area of the West Bank adjoining Jerusalem	23	18	5

Table 2.18 reveals that the two options are rejected by an absolute majority of each of the three groups, in the usual order: national sample → settlers → SHAS. It is interesting, however, to note that in the settler sample there is somewhat less objection with regard to the second option (a new city consisting of areas from East Jerusalem and the West Bank) as compared to the first option, which renders the difference between the settler and the national samples somewhat smaller on this option compared to the difference with regard to the first option.

Protest Actions Against a Compromise on Jerusalem

It will be recalled that respondents were presented with five alternative protest actions in case an Israeli government that lacks a Zionist majority in the Knesset makes a compromise on Jerusalem that is unacceptable to them. Respondents were requested to state to what extent each protest action was justified in their opinion. Table 2.19 presents these protest actions, with the proportion justifying them in each of the three population groups.

The only protest action that is acceptable to all three groups is "lawful demonstrations." Two-thirds of the settlers also justify "nonviolent actions that disrupt the functioning of society," versus 40% to 45% who justify such actions in the national sample and SHAS voters. The remaining protest actions are justified by a minority in each of the groups, and the least justified is "violent actions against other Jews." Nevertheless, it is worth noting that twice as many SHAS voters justify violent actions against Palestinians (33% of SHAS versus 13% and

Table 2.19
Justifying acts of protest
in the national sample, the settler sample, and SHAS voters
(percentage answering "very justified" and "justified")

	Percentage answering "very" justified" and "justified		
The act of protest	National sample	Settler Sample	SHAS voters
Lawful demonstrations	96	99	99
Nonviolent actions that disrupt the functioning of society	40	67	45
Use of force if necessary to prevent implementation	17	23	22
Violent actions directed toward Palestinians	16	13	33
Violent actions against other Jews, if necessary	6	3	7

16% in the settler and national samples). This finding is congruent with what is already known from previous Guttman Institute research, namely, that a higher proportion of easterners, compared to other ethnic groups, testify that they hate "most Arabs," and, SHAS voters, it will be recalled, are mostly of eastern origin.

In the case of a compromise over Jerusalem made by a Zionist majority in the Knesset, the settlers are again more supportive of unlawful but nonviolent demonstrations but to a much lower level than in the case of a decision based on a non-Zionist majority (38% of the settlers versus 20% of both the national sample and of SHAS voters; Question 88 in Appendix A-1, p. 237). The settlers are also the most prepared to personally participate in any action against a compromise on Jerusalem: 61% of them said "yes, definitely" and "yes," versus 27% who said so in the national sample and among SHAS voters. (Indeed, the settlers are in the vanguard of opposition to the Wye Accord, which, of course, affects them in particular.)

Highlights and Commentary

ELIHU KATZ

If public opinion had been consulted before the signing of the Oslo Accord, the overwhelming majority of Israeli Jews would have objected to the inclusion of Jerusalem within the peace negotiations. This was still the case in 1996 when about 60% supported the peace process in principle, but had a lot of trouble with the details. Even after the Rabin assassination, when a relatively optimistic mood about the prospects for peace again prevailed, this study finds that eight of ten Israeli Jews reject the idea of negotiating on Jerusalem within the peace process. Moreover, six of ten say they would opt to abandon the peace process altogether if concessions on Jerusalem were to be made.

At the same time, it should be noted that the mental map of the city in the minds of Israeli Jews does not completely coincide with the political map. Asked to identify areas of the city that "are important to you as part of Jerusalem," substantial numbers—ranging from 40% to 60%—designated the Arab and non-Jewish quarters as subjectively "not important parts of the city." Some 45% of Israeli Jews express de facto willingness to give serious consideration to proposals that would cede peripheral and unfamiliar Arab areas to the Palestinians.

This is the baseline that emerges from a national study of adult Israeli Jews conducted between September and January 1995–96. Initiated by the Center for International and Security Studies of the University of Maryland and conducted jointly with the Guttman Institute of Applied Social Research, the research is based on 1,530 face-to-face interviews with a representative sample of the Jewish population. Following the assassination on November 4, 1995, the size of the original sample was increased so that the influence on public opinion could be assessed by comparing the "before" and "after" subgroups.

The object of this study, therefore, was to make a more subtle assessment of the value system in which attitudes toward Jerusalem are anchored, but also of the lines along which negotiations might be undertaken. Our overall aim is to contribute a better understanding of Israeli opinion to the policymaker and, indeed, to the public itself.

Involvement in the Peace Process

This is not your run-of-the-mill survey in which citizens are asked opinions about matters on which they have little interest and little knowledge. Involvement in the peace process is very high among Israeli Jews and Arabs alike. Eighty percent of Israeli Jews consider themselves "involved" in the process, about one-third "highly involved." The proportion "involved" in the issue of negotiations over Jerusalem rises to 90%; 50% of the respondents rate themselves "highly involved."

By 1995, some 64% supported the peace process. But when it came to the details, Israeli Jews were not so sure. From other survey work before the last elections, we know that more than half supported Oslo 1 (Gaza and Jericho) and Oslo 2 (autonomy to certain cities in the West Bank). But fewer than 50% were prepared to go further. When queried, they also admitted to being unclear about what "further" actually means.

In fact, despite majority support for the process, the present survey finds that only 35% of Israeli Jews think peace will actually result (29% before Rabin's death, 42% afterward). Two-thirds are against a Palestinian State, but 78% think it will happen. This adds to a pessimistic note: A majority support the peace process but are doubtful about its outcome; a larger majority oppose the establishment of a Palestinian State, but believe they will be overruled. It appears that Israeli Jews want peace without Palestine, but fear they will get Palestine without peace.

What Is Jerusalem? The Mental Map

By every measure of centrality, Jerusalem is central to Israeli Jews, both symbolically and really. Virtually every Israeli Jew has visited Jerusalem; two-thirds do so frequently. Very high proportions (70% to 85%) consider Jerusalem symbolic of the Israeli State, of the Jewish people, and of Judaism. Interestingly, as we shall note again below, those residing outside Jerusalem emphasize its symbolic functions more than do Jerusalemites.

Israeli Jews are rather accurate in their perceptions of some aspects of the city's vital statistics, but they are ill-informed about others. More than half know the approximate size of the Arab population (28%); incorrect answers tended to underestimate the number of Arabs rather than to overestimate it. They guess wrong, however, in assuming that the proportion of Arabs has increased since 1967, when it has remained virtually unchanged. A majority answer accurately that the size of East Jerusalem has been enlarged since the Six-Day War, but they far underestimate the extent of the enlargement. (These estimates increased in accuracy among respondents who were interviewed following the Rabin assassination, as information on the peace process generally appeared to become more salient.)

That 28% of Jerusalemites are Arabs is considered "disturbing" to 60% of Israeli Jews. There is majority support for various proposals to restrict further Arab housing in Jerusalem, and to redistrict the city such that peripheral concentrations of Arabs are redefined as belonging outside. It is worth noting that this is a rare "hawkish" basis for acceptable negotiations over the future of the city.

For Israeli Jews, Jerusalem connotes the Wall (90%), the Old City (85%), the old Jewish neighborhoods (80%), the Jewish quarter in the Old City (79%), the Mount of Olives (77%), the Temple Mount (75%), and the new Jewish neighborhoods established after 1967 (76%). In other words, these Jewish sections of East Jerusalem are judged to be "very important" as part of the city by more than three-quarters of Israeli Jews. By contrast, one-third of Israeli Jews perceive the non-Jewish quarters of the Old City as "very important" to the city, and fewer still (21%) ascribe high importance to the Arab neighborhoods in downtown East Jerusalem (Wadi Jos, Sheikh Jarah, etc.) or "Arab settlements and villages previously part of the West Bank" (Um Tuba, Zur Baher, etc.) in their subjective map of Jerusalem. Most Israeli Jews have never visited these places during their frequent trips to the city.

This mental map is altogether consistent with the functions attributed to the city by Israeli Jews. For a large majority, as already noted, Jerusalem is very important as a center for the Jewish people and Judaism and as symbolic of the State itself. Some 70% of Israeli Jews say it is also important to them from a Jewish religious point of view. On the other hand, it is less important to them that the city is a center for others of the world's religions (even though it appears that the Rabin assassination—and the international attention it occasioned— increased this aspect of its importance dramatically).

Asked to assess the importance of Jerusalem as a national center for Palestinians, the modal response was "important" (19% "very important") and this proportion increased following the Rabin assassination. Thirty-nine percent acknowledged that the Palestinians have certain legitimate rights with respect to the city. There is thus some appreciation of Palestinian interest in Jerusalem.

Openness to Negotiations

Given these underpinnings, it is no surprise that only some 20% of Israeli Jews agree that the city named Jerusalem is a proper subject of negotiations. Moreover, this percentage remained unchanged when the question was asked a second time at the end of the thought-provoking interview. Those who favor negotiations also tend to believe that Jerusalem is a "key" to the successful resolution of the peace process. They come from the same minority who agree that "real peace can be obtained only if there is a compromise over Jerusalem," or that compromise is a prerequisite for the sake of Arab-Jewish co-existence within the city. Of course, they are among the 39% who affirm the rights of Palestinians in Jerusalem, and among the 33% who hold that long-term peace will ultimately result from negotiations with the Palestinians. Although these correlations are not perfect (monotonicity coefficients of 0.7 and 0.8), substantial proportions of those who hold each of these beliefs also affirm that Jerusalem belongs in the bargaining process. In short, this is the dovish view on the negotiability of Jerusalem, the view that tends to see the other side and to be available for compromise. Below, we shall say more about the identity of this minority.

The majority, however, is not at all convinced that compromise on Jerusalem is prerequisite to the peace process. They reject the idea that there is a necessary connection between negotiations over Jerusalem and peace or co-existence with the Arabs in general, with the Palestinians, or with the Arabs of Jerusalem. Indeed, a full two-thirds of Israeli Jews do not believe that a peace agreement with the Palestinians will result in true peace, and, in this light, negotiating over Jerusalem hardly makes sense.

This minority/majority division is also evident in response to a series of arguments for and against compromise over Jerusalem. With respect to six arguments favoring compromise and four arguments against, respondents were asked to indicate which of them they found "persuasive." Of the pro-compromise arguments, only two enlisted as much as 30% support: that "a compromise on Jerusalem will enhance the personal safety of Israelis in Jerusalem" and that "a compromise will lead to international recognition of Jerusalem as the capital of Israel." The remaining arguments for compromise were found to be convincing by even smaller numbers: that a compromise on Jerusalem would honor the religious and national rights of Palestinians, that it would temper Moslem extremism, that Palestinian leadership will be discredited otherwise, that it would improve the climate of peace with Egypt.

In contrast, the four arguments against compromise were found persuasive by two-thirds or more of respondents: that compromise will exacerbate Palestinian demands (83%), that compromise will inhibit Jewish access to the Old City (77%), that the presence of a minority in a city is no reason to compromise over the status of the city (70%), that Jerusalem is much more important for Judaism than for Islam. It is evident that the arguments emphasizing what will be "lost" by compromise are considered far more "persuasive" than the arguments emphasizing what might be gained, or more precisely, what will be lost if there is no compromise.

"Diplomacy"

Yet, in spite of these overwhelming expressions of opposition by Israeli Jews to the very idea that "Jerusalem" might be a candidate for compromise or negotiation, there is de facto willingness to consider pragmatic proposals that would relinquish certain non-Jewish quarters of the city—those the Jews exclude from their mental maps. Thus, a substantial 42% say they would "agree" (9% "definitely") "to cede the Arab neighborhoods of East Jerusalem to the Palestinians, if the Old City, the Mount of Olives, all of the Jewish neighborhoods of East Jerusalem, and Mount Scopus remain in Jerusalem as they are today." A much larger proportion (59%; 17% "definitely") support the following statement: "In order to ensure a Jewish majority, do you support or object to redefining the city limits so that Arab settlements and villages which are now within the borders of Jerusalem (such as Shuafat, Um Tuba, Zur Baher) will be outside the city?"

The specifics of these inclinations are evident in that part of the survey which asked respondents to play a game of "diplomacy," that is, to act as if they were members of a negotiating team considering the Jerusalem issue. If you were in such a position, they were asked, which of the following proposals would seem to you worthy of consideration? Ten options were presented, of which two were thought worthy of consideration by some 45% of the population—considerably more than the proportion who found any of the pro-compromise arguments persuasive. Both of these were proposals to cede Arab settlements now within Jerusalem city limits to Palestinian sovereignty.* Surprisingly, the second of these two—the proposal for a reciprocal exchange of Jewish regions in the West Bank for these Arab settlements in Jerusalem—did not make this option more worthy. This suggests that the relatively large support for these options is motivated by a desire to be rid of the Arab neighborhoods rather than to benefit from any exchange. In other words, it is likely that the "seriousness" accorded these proposals draws on hawkish as well as dovish elements.

Four additional options were deemed worthy of consideration by one-third of the respondents. Two of these are not easily distinguished from the previous two, except that they are more complex, and explicitly refer to "East Jerusalem" and the "Old City" whereas the previous two did not.** A third option proposes joint administration of the Old City under Israeli sovereignty, and the fourth would reaffirm control of the Temple Mount by the Wakf, as is now the case.

The remaining four options garnered serious attention from one-quarter of respondents or fewer: Palestinian sovereignty over the Arab neighborhoods in the Old City; Palestinian sovereignty over the Temple Mount and Israel sovereignty over the Western Wall; Palestinian sovereignty over East Jerusalem, excepting

---

* Q. 65: "to transfer to Palestinian sovereignty the Arab settlements and villages previously in the West Bank which are now within the border of Jerusalem (e.g., Shuafat, Um Tuba, Zur Baher, Bet Hanina, etc.).

** Q. 67: "to transfer the Arab neighborhoods of East Jerusalem except those that are inside the wall to Palestinian sovereignty." Q. 73: "retain Israeli sovereignty over East Jerusalem, while the Arab neighborhoods in East Jerusalem will have special status under Palestinian control."

Jewish neighborhoods; and internationalization of the Old City under the United Nations.

Finally, proposals to establish the capital of the Palestinian State in an Arab region of East Jerusalem, or in an area made up of some part of East Jerusalem and an adjoining territory in the West Bank, were supported by about 20%.

Hawks and Doves on Jerusalem: Who Are They?

Among the background variables, such as age, gender, education, ethnicity (country of origin), religiosity, and party affiliation, political inclination is by far the best predictor of these attitudes toward peace and negotiation. Thus, if "doves" and "hawks" may be defined as those who do and don't "believe that a peace agreement with the Palestinians will bring a long-term peace," the data reveal that two-thirds of those who feel close to Labor are "doves," compared with 14% of those who feel close to Likud. The small parties to the left of Labor are more dovish (77% of Meretz sympathizers) while those to the right of Likud and religious-party sympathizers harbor very few doves (7% to 10%). These proportions correspond more or less to the traditional distribution of hawks and doves on earlier issues, such as willingness to hold talks with the PLO (before Madrid) or willingness to cede territory for peace.

Dovish and hawkish attitudes toward Jerusalem reveal similar divergences by political inclinations. When the subject of negotiations over "Jerusalem" is raised frontally, 37% of Labor adherents (63% of Meretz) and 10% of Likud are in favor. When specific proposals are broached about relinquishing certain Arab quarters, support increases to 64% among Labor adherents and to 35% among those inclined to Likud. Left of Labor and right of Likud behave as expected on all questions, with the interesting exception of redefining city limits "to ensure a Jewish majority" which is supported by 77% of Labor adherents compared with about 55% of all the others from Meretz to the religious right.

Labor and Meretz supporters distribute similarly on matters such as the "persuasiveness" of the several reasons for including Jerusalem in the peace negotiations. Thus, about half of both labor (46%) and Meretz (52%) supporters agree that it can be argued that negotiating over Jerusalem will improve security in Jerusalem or improve chances for international recognition. On the whole, however, Meretz is far more "dovish" than Labor, and Labor more dovish than Likud. Thus, some 70% of Likud supporters would give up on the peace process rather than make concessions on Jerusalem, compared with 50% of Labor and 24% of Meretz. Eighty-two percent of Meretz supporters affirm that Palestinians have some sort of legitimate rights with regard to Jerusalem compared with 55% of Labor and 27% of Likud, 22% of the extreme right and 22% of the religious parties.

Labor supporters are more prepared than Likud supporters to consider each of the options for a redistricting of Jerusalem. Again, Meretz supporters stand out once more, in their readiness (ranging from 52% to 77%) to consider all the options except two: (1) internationalize the Old City or (2) give the Palestinians sovereignty over Jewish neighborhoods in East Jerusalem, restricting Israeli control to the Jewish neighborhoods.

What is striking about the dovish position of the Meretz supporters is that they feel less attached to Jerusalem, less involved. Whereas a majority of Labor supporters agree that Jerusalem is very important to them from a Jewish point of view, only 30% to 40% of Meretz supporters take this position. Most revealing is the distribution of answers to the question: "Do you feel a sense of belonging to Jerusalem?" Seventy-four percent of Likud supporters say "definitely yes," as do some 60% of Labor, but only 42% of Meretz.

Religiosity produces much the same results. The more religious the respondent, the more Jerusalem assumes personal importance, the greater the sense of belonging to the city, the more centrality is attributed to its symbolic role for the Jewish people and for Judaism, the less acceptable are the claims of the Palestinians—and, of course, the less negotiable is Jerusalem. Parenthetically, these data make it easy to understand how attitudes expressed by Meretz can be discredited as "non-Jewish."

Ethnicity enters the picture through religiosity and political party. Thus, the special analysis of a (nonrandom) sample of SHAS supporters shows the striking contrast between the staunch, hawkish support for the non-negotiability of Jerusalem among this enclave of North Africans (who splintered from the Likud in favor of their own ethnic-cum-religious party) and the old-time immigrants from East Europe. Thus, intending SHAS voters are vociferous in their objection to negotiating over Jerusalem; 86% "definitely object." This is a religious version of the attitude prevailing among respondents of North African origin, 57% of whom definitely object to negotiating on Jerusalem, the most extreme position taken by any of the origin groups. By contrast Eastern European old-timers are the most "dovish" of the origin groups; 35% of them support negotiating over Jerusalem within the peace talks, compared with 11% of the North Africans and 20% to 26% of the other origin groups. Similarly, while (only) half of the Europeans would abandon the peace effort rather than negotiate over Jerusalem, more than two-thirds of the North Africans would do so.

Newcomers from the Soviet Union have a lesser sense of the centrality of Jerusalem in their personal lives. They also feel somewhat less involved in the peace process than the other groups and less involved in the subject of Jerusalem.

Differences by Places of Residence

Comparing responses by place of respondent residence reveals some interesting differences, several of which have already been alluded to. It is not much of a surprise that Jerusalem residents feel more personally involved in the city and in

negotiations over it. It is more surprising perhaps, but understandable, that Jerusalemites experience their city less symbolically than residents of the other cities.
Thus, they attribute less importance to the function of the city as a world center
for all religions. The historic Old City and the Temple Mount are less important
in their subjective map of the city than they are for the Tel Avivans for example.

Jerusalemites are somewhat more likely to underestimate the size of the Arab
minority and to be less likely to think that the number of Arabs has increased since
1967. They are somewhat less likely than others to be disturbed by the number of
their Arab neighbors or to want to do anything about restricting expansion of their
housing.

There are small, but confusing, differences, between Jerusalem and Tel Aviv
residents on judgments of the "persuasiveness" of the arguments for and against
compromising on Jerusalem. The Tel Avivans tend to find the arguments for
compromise more convincing than the Jerusalemites, while the Jerusalemites find
the arguments against compromise somewhat less convincing. Taking account of
the series of questions on options for Jerusalem in the bargaining, the Tel Avivans,
on the whole, seem slightly more inclined to treat the various options seriously. It
is also the case that the Tel Avivans are slightly less pessimistic about the
outcome of the peace process than are Jerusalemites.

But these differences are negligible compared with the difference between
the settlers in Judea and Samaria and the population inside the green line. As
expected, the settlers are more hawkish on all of the issues, although they fall
short of the hawkishness of SHAS, for example. Indeed, the settlers show more
interest in the peace process and more regard for Palestinian rights than do SHAS
adherents.

Will Negotiations over Jerusalem Incite Protest?

Respondents were asked what forms of protest they would find justified if there
were a government decision to agree on some sort of compromise with respect to
Jerusalem. Five forms of protest were posed with the condition that the decision
was taken by a government with a non-Zionist majority in the Knesset. The data
show that almost all Israelis justify lawful demonstrations. The use of force to
prevent implementation was justified by 20% of Israeli Jews prior to the Rabin
assassination, but dropped to 8% afterward.

Political differences are evident here, too, but it should be borne in mind
that these data predate the 1996 elections. Thus, about one-fifth of Labor and
Meretz supporters justified the use of "nonviolent actions that disrupt the functioning of society" to express disapproval of a Knesset decision to compromise
compared with half of Likud supporters and even more of the extreme right.
Substantial proportions of the extreme right (53%) and of the religious parties

(37%) said they would participate personally in protest, compared to 30% of the Likud supporters and about one-fifth of Labor and Meretz.

Respondents from the settlements across the green line are distinguished by their support for "nonviolent actions that disrupt the functioning of society"; two-thirds of the settlers would justify such action compared with 40% of the national sample. Most of them would also participate personally in protesting a compromise on Jerusalem (61% "definitely" participate) compared with far smaller proportions of other groups.

In case of an unacceptable decision on Jerusalem, violent actions "directed against Palestinians" are justified by about 15% of the respondents, and half this number would justify "violent actions against other Jews, if necessary." The settlers fall below the national average in these respects.

Effect of the Rabin Assassination

The assassination of the prime minister augmented the dovish trend in Israel, at least during the weeks immediately following the event. The assassination introduced a period of greater openness to the other side, as well as a greater sense of involvement and knowledgeability with respect to issues that figure in the peace process. Thus, as has already been noted, facts and figures concerning Jerusalem were more accurately perceived by respondents who were interviewed following the assassination. There was a somewhat greater recognition of the importance of Jerusalem to the Palestinians, and a greater awareness of the universal interest in Jerusalem as a world religious center. In the wake of the assassination, the number of Israeli Jews who hold high promise for the peace process increased from 29% to 44%! There was also increased acceptance of the co-existence of Arabs and Jews in Jerusalem.

But as far as the place of Jerusalem in the negotiations is concerned, Rabin's murder had no influence. "Don't negotiate over Jerusalem" was reiterated by 80% of respondents both before and after Rabin's death. (The data analysis suggests that Rabin's assassination prevented a possible rise in the extreme negative response.) Sixty percent have also continued to agree with the position that no concessions should be made over Jerusalem, "even if we have to give up on peace with the Arabs." There was, however, a somewhat greater readiness to consider the various options for compromise presented in the hypothetical game of "diplomacy," but on the other hand, there was an even smaller minority prepared to hear talk of a Palestinian capital anywhere in the Jerusalem area.

Changes in opinion following the assassination express the aftermath of optimism and openness more than matters of substance over the negotiability of Jerusalem. It is a fair assumption that, as time elapsed, even the mood changes regressed to what they were earlier.

Implications of Results for Negotiating on Jerusalem

Jewish public opinion in Israel strongly objects in principle to the prospects of negotiations over Jerusalem. Sixty percent of Israeli Jews say they would ditch the peace process rather than make concessions on Jerusalem. Attachment to the city, symbolically and tangibly, is very high. It serves as a true "center" of identity in the sense of the late Edward Shils.

It may be argued that Israelis have retreated from hard-line attitudes on other issues in the peace process. Over the years, there has been a slow growth in the proportion willing to compromise over Gaza, parts of the West Bank, and even the Golan Heights. The Oslo Accord has achieved surprisingly high support, although going beyond Oslo 2 has yet to enlist a majority. It is also true that Israelis usually follow their elected leaders, even when their performance deviated from the consensus—the Begin–Sadat and Rabin–Arafat agreements are the two famous examples. But the fact is that attitudes toward relinquishing any part of Jerusalem for peace have not softened over the years,* and the present study suggests that this attitude is encased in a structure that includes strong personal attachment to the city and an acute awareness of its symbolic meaning for the Jewish people, for Judaism, and for the State of Israel. It seems a safe inference that frontal negotiation over the Jerusalem issue will arouse strong opposition. Indeed, the Peres camp was attacked in the recent election campaign for its alleged intention "to divide Jerusalem."

Thus, "negotiating over Jerusalem" *in principle* has the support of only one-fifth of the population. It should be reiterated that these come, primarily, from the ranks of the one-third who believe that true peace with the Palestinians is possible. The study also offers an operational definition of peace from the point of view of public opinion: more than half of Israeli Jews say that they would recognize peace in the establishment of commercial relations with the Arab States.

Nor do most Israeli Jews agree that compromise on Jerusalem is prerequisite to peace or co-existence. The most consistent position is that of Meretz supporters, who are more prepared than any other bloc to consider various options for accommodating Palestinian claims. They are also much more likely to recognize the legitimacy of such claims. From the point of view of public opinion, there simply is not a lot of principled potential on which to build; only 37% of Labor supporters agree that the subject of "Jerusalem" should be included in the peace negotiations, although it is important to note that three-quarters of Labor sympathizers would support territorial adjustments to make Jerusalem more Jewish!

Indirect appeals to public opinion would seem the more promising route. Thus, there is a substantial minority (some 40%) who are sensitive to the idea that Jerusalem has political and religious meaning to the Palestinians as well,

---

* From Guttman Institute surveys for the years 1993–96.

although this opinion is shared by only a quarter of Likud supporters and far fewer of the religious and the more radical right. But even here, no more than a third of the population would take "seriously" the demand for continued control of the Temple Mount by an Islamic religious authority, as is presently the case.

The potential for compromise, rather, lies in the substantial readiness—on the part of some 40%—to consider pragmatic proposals to yield certain "unimportant" parts of the city. These proposals attract support from almost two-thirds of Labor sympathizers and, surprisingly, from even one-third of Likud adherents! They are couched not in the language of principle, but in the pragmatic and instrumental language of municipal boundaries and demographics. They come wrapped in a desire to make the city more Jewish. Of the various options for compromise presented to respondents, the idea of transferring the peripheral Arab neighborhoods that are incorporated in present-day Jerusalem was taken "seriously" by 45%. This was the most popular of the options, and its meaning is underlined by the fact that interest in it was not enhanced by linking it to a trade for certain Jewish settlements in the territories. That a majority of Jews would feel more comfortable not having to share Jerusalem with Arabs is also evident in the fact that 60% of respondents say they are "disturbed" by the size of the Arab population in Jerusalem, even if Jerusalemites themselves are slightly less likely to be "very" disturbed than the rest of the country.

This readiness to consider relinquishing certain parts of the city does not extend, however, to the idea of inviting the Palestinian capital to establish itself next door. Eighty percent of the population objects (half "definitely objects") to the idea that some part of East Jerusalem might be allocated for a Palestinian capital; only the proverbial 20% approve.

PART III

The Status of Jerusalem in the Eyes of Palestinians

A *Survey Research Perspective*

NADER IZZAT SA'ID

An Analysis of Palestinian Opinion
on the Status of Jerusalem

NADER IZZAT SA'ID

This is the most extensive survey of Palestinian public opinion on the status of Jerusalem. A few years ago, the Jerusalem issue (like most political issues) was taboo to researchers. Among the various political issues, the Jerusalem issue has probably been the most sensitive one. There have been a few attempts at studying Palestinian public opinion on the question of Jerusalem.* However, these attempts, were either partial or superficial.

The present survey approaches the issue of Jerusalem using a comprehensive outlook. It deals with questions related to the city and its future from various angles of public opinion: perceptions, attitudes, involvement, belonging, behavior, expected behavior, support, and opposition. The survey deals with issues such as involvement in the peace process; the meaning of Jerusalem; knowledge of the geography and demography of the city; willingness (or unwillingness) to compromise; and the future status of Jerusalem.

This chapter will be devoted to an overview and analysis of the data from the national sample. The analysis will utilize variables such as region (i.e., Gaza—West Bank), religion, religiosity, political affiliation, and other demographic variables. The questionnaire instrument and the cross-tabulations are in Appendix B. The following is a discussion of the methodology utilized in the data collection and analysis stage.

---

* For serious polling attempts, see various polls conducted by the Jerusalem Media and Communication Center and the Center for Palestine Research and Studies. The latter Center repeatedly polled Palestinian attitudes on the "Abu Mazen–Beilin Plan" on Jerusalem.

Methodology

The data for this study came mainly from two sources: six focus groups and a survey of 870 respondents.

Focus Groups

The researchers organized six focus groups, the first of which was held April 27, 1996. Four groups were selected from the West Bank population and two from the Gaza population. The West Bank participants came from the up-north, the north, the middle, and the south. Gaza participants came from Gaza City and from the southern parts of the Strip. About thirty Palestinians, most of whom were well educated, participated in the discussions. One of the groups was comprised exclusively of women. The political and ideological affiliations of the participants were representative, as they came from such groups as liberals, conservatives, politically religious, independents, hard-core Fatah and supporters, pan-Arabists, and leftists.

   The results of the focus groups proved helpful for analytical purposes. They were also useful in the formulation of the questionnaire instrument and in the setting up of various research procedures.

The Sample

The total sample size for the survey is 870. It was selected from the population of Palestinians in the West Bank, Gaza, and Jerusalem. The sample design adopted has been stratified. A multistage procedure involving proportional as well as simple random sampling was used. To complete the sample design, the following steps were undertaken:

1. Dividing the area into three regions: the West Bank, Gaza, and Jerusalem.
2. Dividing each region into districts: nine (in the West Bank), five (in Gaza), one (in Jerusalem).
3. Listing of all localities in each district.
4. Classifying the localities according to population size and type (i.e. village, city, refugee camp). Each locality was given a number of chances for selection that is proportional to its population size (e.g., a city like Nablus was given one hundred chances for selection as its population size is approximately one hundred thousand, while a village like Anabta was given seven chances as its population size is approximately seven thousand). This ensured the representation of large cities as well as small localities.
5. Selecting the localities in a simple random manner.
6. Dividing each locality into a number of neighborhoods.

7. Selecting the neighborhoods in a simple random manner.
8. Drawing a map for the neighborhood and identifying all the houses located there.
9. Counting the number of houses in the neighborhood. Dividing the total number by the desired number of questionnaires for the neighborhood, resulting in a sampling interval used in selecting the specific houses where the researchers conducted the interviews.
10. Selecting the individuals in the sample according to "Kish" method. Kish (1965) offered a procedure for generating a probabilistic selection of respondents within the households. This procedure involves three steps:

    a. Ascertain how many people living in a household are eligible to be respondents (i.e., how many are 18 or older).
    b. Number these subjects in a consistent way in all households (i.e., order by increasing age).
    c. Match the number assigned to the youngest member with the number of the designated questionnaire through a table constructed beforehand. (This gives the researchers a number that indicates the family member that they were supposed to interview.)

Overall, the sample distribution fairly corresponded with the actual population distribution. Some weighting was done to produce a more representative sample. The variables weighted were education and region (see Table 3.1).

The Fieldwork

The fieldwork took place between August 27 and September 10, 1996. Experienced fieldworkers were recruited from a pool of researchers who work for some of the best survey research institutions. Overall, fifty fieldworkers were involved in the collection of data and participated in two training workshops. They were lectured on such issues as survey research, sample selection, and interviewing. The objectives of the study were also fully explained to them. The interviews were conducted by a team of fieldworkers (a male and a female) to ensure the representation of women in the sample and to minimize the dangers that might be encountered by the fieldworkers as a result of moving about the Palestinian territories. The fieldworkers encountered only five nonresponse cases, resulting in an insignificant nonresponse rate. Other respondents were hesitant to cooperate (as a result of fear or suspicion), but the fieldworkers were able to convince them of the academic nature and value of the research.

It should be noted that four questions used in this study were asked in a separate questionnaire in a different period of time (December 1996). Two of

Table 3.1
Sample distribution (all data after weighting/all percentages)

Region	%	Occupation	%	Place of Birth	%
Gaza	36.5	Student	8.2	In 1948 region	6.9
West Bank	63.5	Laborer	11.0	In West Bank or Gaza	90.2
District		Housewife	36.4	Outside the country	2.9
Jenin	5.4	Employee	10.1	Income	
Tulkarm	12.7	Merchant	6.5	Less than 200 JDs*	45.2
Nablus	7.2	Farmer	3.0	200–400 JDs	36.6
Ramallah	8.7	Craftsman	10.5	401–800 JDs	13.7
Jerusalem	11.4	Professional	3.7	+ 800 JDs	4.5
Bethlehem	8.0	Unemployed	8.0	Education	
Hebron	10.3	Retired	2.7	0–10 yrs.	37.4
Gaza North	7.2	Age		11–12 yrs.	34.4
Gaza City	12.4	18–22	11.8	Two-year college	13.8
Gaza Middle	9.6	23–30	28.4	University	14.5
Gaza South	7.0	31–39	19.3		
Gender		40–47	16.9		
Male	53.5	48–54	9.1		
Female	46.5	54+	14.5		

* A Jordanian dinar (JD) is worth about $1.4 U.S.

these questions were intended to be asked in the original questionnaire but were missed. The other two were not properly worded and had to be repeated.

The Results*

Involvement in the Peace Process

About 65% of the Palestinians follow the negotiations between Palestinians and Israelis. More than a third (36%) follow the negotiations "to a great extent" and 29% follow them "to some extent." About a third (35%) follow the negotiations "to a small extent" or don't follow them at all (Q. 1).

The data show that Palestinians are more interested in following the negotiations on the topic of the future of Jerusalem than on other issues. About 80% of

---

* For national and regional results, see Appendix B-1. For political affiliation cross-tabulations, see Appendix B-2. For religiosity cross-tabulations, see Appendix B-3. For religion cross-tabulations, see Appendix B-4.

the respondents said that they follow the topic of Jerusalem "to a great extent" or "to some extent" (Q. 2).

Interest in following the negotiations varies according to place of residence, as Gaza respondents show 6% more interest than West Bank respondents and 19% more interest than Jerusalem respondents. In contrast, interest in following the topic of Jerusalem within the peace process is equal in all three regions.

The Meaning of Jerusalem

The Importance of the City

The vast majority of Palestinians (99%) said that Jerusalem is "very important" (or "important") to them personally. Another 97% said that they feel a sense of belonging to the city (Q. 8, Q. 9). In Jerusalem this percentage was 100%. According to various variables no significant differences can be found in the degree of belonging. However, viewing Jerusalem as "important" varies, to some extent, according to religiosity. Ninety-six percent of those who described themselves as "very religious" said that Jerusalem is very important to them, compared with 78% of those who are "not at all religious." However, it must be mentioned that 20% of this last group said that Jerusalem was "important" to them, and only 2% said that it was "not important." And while 99% of the Muslim respondents and 97% of the Christian respondents feel that Jerusalem is "very important" or "important" to them, more Muslims are concentrated in the group of respondents who described Jerusalem as "very important."

Older Palestinians (over 54 years) were more inclined than all other age groups to say that Jerusalem is "very important" to them personally. Feeling a sense of belonging to Jerusalem is also directly correlated with age, as 91% of older Palestinians definitely feel a sense of belonging to the city compared with 71% of younger Palestinians (18 to 22 age group). This is probably due to the fact that a larger percentage of younger Palestinians never visited the city. Another reason for this reported importance is that older Palestinians tend to be more religious than their younger counterparts. Respondents with lower incomes tend to show more attachment to Jerusalem, as a larger percentage of them felt that the city is "very important" to them personally. Refugees show attachment to Jerusalem similar to that of the rest of the population. About 82% of the refugee population said that they definitely feel a sense of belonging to the city, compared to 79% of the nonrefugee population. No difference in the degree of attachment to Jerusalem could be found among the residents of refugee camps, cities, and villages. About 81% of the total sample in each area "definitely feel a sense of belonging" to the city (see Table 3.2).

Jerusalem (East Jerusalem) is not only important to Palestinians as a Palestinian sovereign area, but also as a capital of a Palestinian state. This reflects the

Table 3.2
Percentage of respondents who said that Jerusalem is very important to them and those who definitely feel a sense of belonging to the city according to a number of variables

	Very important	*Definitely feel a sense of belonging*
Gender		
Male	90%	81%
Female	94%	82%
Education		
0–10 yrs.	92%	84%
11–12 yrs.	94%	84%
Two-year college	91%	78%
University	89%	70%
Age		
18–22	91%	71%
23–30	92%	78%
31–38	89%	80%
39–46	92%	87%
47–54	92%	84%
Over 54	98%	91%
Income		
Less than 200 JDs	96%	85%
200–400 JDs	91%	82%
401–800 JDs	83%	73%
Over 800 JDs	83%	78%
Place of Birth		
In 1948 region	97%	86%
In West Bank or Gaza	91%	81%
Outside country	98%	89%
Refugee Status		
Refugee		82%
Nonrefugee		79%
Place of Residence		
Refugee camp		81%
Village		81%
City		80%

opinion of 97% of the respondents, who said that even if a satisfactory agreement "giving the Palestinians sovereign rights in East Jerusalem can be reached," in addition it is "very important" (90%) or "important" (7%) that "East Jerusalem be the capital of a Palestinian state" (Q. 59).

Jerusalem is so important to Palestinians that they are unwilling to "recognize Israeli's claim that it alone is sovereign over all of Jerusalem" even if doing so was "the only way a Palestinian state could come into existence." The majority of respondents (94%) said "no" (or "definitely no") to this proposal (Q. 7). In contrast, Palestinians view Jerusalem as a future Palestinian capital. About 46% of respondents view Jerusalem as a capital for a Palestinian national state. This percentage is as high as 60% among Jerusalem respondents. Another 42% of the respondents view Jerusalem as a capital for a Palestinian Islamic state. Only 12% of the respondents view Jerusalem as a capital for an "Islamic state" (Q. 16).

The Importance of the City from Various Points of View

As indicated in Table 3.3 the importance of Jerusalem to Palestinians varies according to various points of views. The data show that Jerusalem is mostly important from an Islamic religious point of view and from a Palestinian national-historical point of view. It is also important as a symbol of the future Palestinian state. Jerusalem is not as important, to Palestinians, as a center for all religions or as a center for the Arab people.

While the data show that, from various points of view, there is consensus among Palestinians on the importance of Jerusalem, differences can be found in Palestinians' evaluation of the degree of importance. As indicated in Table 3.3, Jerusalem is most important to Gaza respondents from an "Islamic religious" point of view. For West Bank respondents, Jerusalem is most important "as a symbol of the future Palestinian State" and from an "Islamic religious" point of view. The "very religious" feel the same way as West Bank respondents. In contrast, Jerusalem is least important to the "not at all religious" from a "religious" point of view and "as a center of the Arab people"; it is mostly important to them from a "Palestinian national-historical" point of view and "as a symbol of the future Palestinian state." No variance can be found between the views of Muslim and Christian respondents, except that Jerusalem is seen "as a center for all religions" by more Christians than Muslims.

The Importance of Jerusalem Sites "as Part of Jerusalem"

In Jerusalem, the most important sites are religious and historical in nature. About 94% of the respondents felt that the Haram al-Sharif is "very important" to them, as did 95% when asked separately about the al-Aqsa mosque and the Dome of the Rock. The next most important site to Palestinians is the Old City, especially the Islamic quarters. The least important sites are the old Jewish neighborhoods in the western part the of city, as well as the new Jewish neighborhoods and the Jewish quarter of the Old City. A third of Palestinians felt

Table 3.3
To what extent is Jerusalem important to you from the
following points of views? (percentage of those who said it is very important)

Point of view	National	West Bank	Gaza	Jerusalem	Very religious	Not religious	Islamists	Leftists	Fatah	Independents
As a symbol of the future Palestinian state	90%	88%	93%	77%	98%	85%	84%	89%	93%	88%
Islamic religious	90%	87%	97%	78%	98%	58%	97%	67%	95%	84%
Palestinian national-historical	89%	87%	93%	81%	93%	84%	89%	88%	90%	87%
As a center for all religions	77%	63%	85%	68%	81%	62%	73%	64%	84%	73%
As a center for the Arab people	74%	69%	83%	67%	89%	57%	72%	55%	79%	73%

that the Western Wall is very important to them, another 20% felt it is important (see Table 3.4).

For Gazans religious sites were the most important. For Jerusalemites the Old City as a whole was most important. West Bank respondents were more interested in the Christian and Jewish quarters of the Old City and in the Western Wall than Gaza respondents. As expected, Islamists were more interested in the religious sites than were the Leftists. Interest in the Jewish areas of the city was, basically, equal to the supporters of all political groups.

The "very religious" respondents show more interest than the less "religious" respondents in almost all Jerusalem sites. They tend to show the same interest in the Jewish areas of the city. There were also differences between Muslims and Christians in their evaluation of the various sites. Christian respondents show more interest in the Christian quarter of the city, the Mount of Olives, and the Jewish quarter of the city than Muslim respondents. They show equal interest in the Western Wall. However, it must be noted that the majority of Christians feel that the Islamic sites are "very important" to them, and many feel that they are "important." This confirms results showing that 97% of Christian respondents feel that Jerusalem is "very important" or "important" to them from an Islamic religious point of view.

Number of Visits to Jerusalem

From a Palestinian perspective attachment to Jerusalem cannot be expressed by the number of visits to the city. Since 1993, Palestinians (with the exception of Jerusalem residents) have been banned from entering Jerusalem, except after obtaining a permit from the Israeli military authorities. Permits to enter Jerusalem have been scarce and were only issued to Palestinians who met criteria that the Israelis changed sporadically. Some Palestinians visited Jerusalem without obtaining a permit. Those who were caught entering "illegally" were fined, beaten, imprisoned, or exposed to all these measures.

These restrictions had an impact on the frequency of Palestinian visits to Jerusalem. About 11% of the respondents (excluding residents of Jerusalem) never visited Jerusalem. In addition, about 40% of the respondents (excluding Jerusalem respondents) did not visit the city in more than four years (Q. 34, Q. 35). In Gaza, 22% of the respondents never visited Jerusalem, and 61% did not visit it in more than four years. Only 22% of the respondents visited the city during the year prior to this study. In Gaza this percentage was only 2%. Few Palestinians have visited the new Jewish settlements in East Jerusalem. More of them were able to visit the Jewish neighborhoods in West Jerusalem. As expected, younger Palestinians were less able to visit the city than older Palestinians. Far fewer females visited the city than did their male counterparts.

Table 3.4

How important as part of Jerusalem are the following? (percentage of those who said it is "very important")

The site	National	West Bank	Gaza	Jerusalem	Very religious	Not religious	Islamist	Leftist	Fatah	Independent
The Haram al-Sharif	94%	92%	98%	89%	99%	78%	98%	81%	97%	91%
al-Aqsa mosque and the Dome of the Rock	95%	93%	98%	91%	98%	79%	98%	81%	97%	92%
Mount of Olives	66%	62%	72%	65%	76%	60%	65%	58%	70%	61%
The Western Wall	34%	38%	26%	36%	41%	38%	38%	33%	34%	35%
The Islamic quarters of the Old City	85%	83%	89%	83%	94%	70%	91%	75%	86%	82%
The Christian quarters of the Old City	47%	55%	33%	62%	50%	69%				
The Jewish quarters of the Old City	24%	27%	17%	33%	21%	33%	23%	28%	24%	25%
Palestinian neighborhoods in downtown East Jerusalem (Wadi Jos, Sheikh, Jarah)	59%	54%	66%	70%	73%	57%	59%	51%	62%	56%

The new Jewish neighborhoods (e.g, Gilo, Ramot)	29%	26%	35%	30%	31%	31%	32%	26%	29%	28%
The older Jewish neighborhoods in the western part of the city (e.g., Rehavia, Talbieh, Beit Hakerem)	26%	22%	32%	26%	38%	23%	29%	23%	26%	25%
The Old City	86%	87%	85%	96%	92%	88%	87%	82%	86%	86%

The Importance of Jerusalem to Israelis

While Palestinians feel that Jerusalem is "important" to them, they don't feel that it is as "important" to Israelis. About 86% of the respondents said that "Jerusalem is not important to the Israelis as a national center" (Q.17). A greater percentage of Palestinians were willing to accept that Jerusalem "is important" to the Israelis as a religious center. About 36% of the respondents said that Jerusalem is important (or somewhat important) to the Israelis as a religious center. The rest (64%) didn't think that Jerusalem is important to the Israelis as a religious center (Q. 18). The gap between Palestinian attitudes (toward the religious importance and the national importance of Jerusalem to Israelis) might be explained by their belief that "because Judaism is a religion, Jews should not be thought of as constituting a people, and therefore are lacking national rights." About 70% of the respondents said "definitely yes" or "yes" to this statement. Surprisingly, as many as 30% of the respondents did not agree with this statement (Q. 46).

These attitudes are accompanied by Palestinians' belief that Jews have "no legitimate rights" with regard to Jerusalem. Only 20% of the respondents felt that Jews have "legitimate rights" in Jerusalem (Q. 58). About 80% said that Jews have "no legitimate rights" in Jerusalem. The majority of supporters of all political groups said that Jews have "no legitimate rights" with regard to Jerusalem. It was, however, noticeable that 29% of independents and 24% of leftists said that Jews have some "sort of legitimate rights with regards to Jerusalem." It is surprising to find that fewer Fatah supporters felt this way (about 17%). Similar results can be found among the Islamists. Thus, recognition of Jewish rights in Jerusalem was inversely correlated with degree of religiosity. The less religious are more willing to recognize the Jews as having some "sort of legitimate rights with regard to Jerusalem." About a third of the "not at all religious" said that Jews have some "sort of legitimate rights" compared with 16% of the "very religious.

Males were more willing to recognize that Jews "have some sort of legitimate rights" than females. The groups most willing to recognize such rights were: respondents with incomes ranging from 401 to 800 JDs (lower middle class) and respondents in the 31 to 38 age group. It was also noticeable that respondents born outside the country were the least willing to recognize that Jews "have some sort of legitimate rights with regard to Jerusalem" (see Table 3.5).

The Demography of Jerusalem

The majority of Palestinians said that they don't know what proportion of East Jerusalem is Jewish. Of those who gave an answer, only 11% knew that Jews comprise "about half" of the population. More Jerusalemites knew the answer to the question than all others. About 15% of the respondents said that Jews comprise "about two-thirds," and 21% said that they comprise less than half (Q. 40). Lack

Table 3.5
In your opinion, do Jews have any sort of legitimate rights
with regard to Jerusalem?

	Yes	No
Gender		
Male	23%	77%
Female	17%	83%
Education		
0–10 yrs.	23%	77%
11–12 yrs.	17%	83%
Two-year college	20%	80%
University	23%	77%
Age		
18–22	16%	84%
23–30	20%	80%
31–38	27%	73%
39–46	16%	84%
47–54	14%	86%
Over 54	24%	76%
Income		
Less than 200 JDs	16%	84%
200–400 JDs	21%	79%
401–800 JDs	31%	69%
Over 800 JDs	20%	80%
Place of Birth		
In 1948 region	22%	78%
In West Bank or Gaza	18%	82%
Outside country	15%	85%

of knowledge (and the underestimation) of the size of Jewish population might be due to the following factors:

1. The inability of most Palestinians to visit the city in the past few years;
2. Their lack of knowledge of what constitutes East Jerusalem;
3. The inability of Palestinians to fully grasp the extent of Jewish settlements, especially in and around Jerusalem.

The Geography of Jerusalem

The majority of Palestinians (70%) said that the Israeli government's definition of the geography of Jerusalem includes "the two parts of the city plus large additional

areas from the West Bank that were added to Jerusalem by the Israeli government" (Q.19). The majority of Palestinians (58%) considered the areas that had
been in the West Bank and later added to the city by the Israeli government as
part of Jerusalem. In comparison, 42% did not agree that these areas are part of
the city. A larger percentage of Palestinians (69%) considered the large areas of
Jewish settlements constructed by Israel since 1967 (e.g., Gilo, Ramot, Ramot
Eshkol, Pisgat Zeev) to be within East Jerusalem. In addition, 84% considered
that Palestinian village areas (e.g., Um Tuba and Zur Baher) to be part of Jerusalem (Q. 20, Q. 21, Q. 22).

The Role of Jerusalem in the Peace Process

Negotiations on Jerusalem

The majority of Palestinians support negotiations on Jerusalem within the peace
process. About 58% of them said that they are "definitely for" such negotiations;
another 22% said that they are "for" negotiations. Only 20% said that they were
"against" or "definitely against" negotiations on Jerusalem (Q. 3). The data show
that Gazans are more supportive of negotiations on Jerusalem within the peace
process. Degree of support for negotiations on Jerusalem is correlated with political
affiliation. Fatah supporters are more supportive of such negotiations, followed by
independents and Islamists. The least support for negotiations on Jerusalem came
from the leftists.

Support for negotiations on Jerusalem is directly correlated with degree of
religiosity. The "very religious" and those who are "somewhat religious" show more
support for negotiations than the "not at all religious."

A large percentage of Muslim respondents (47%) said that they were
"definitely for" negotiations on Jerusalem. Fewer Christians (35%) felt the same
way. All in all, 89% of Moslem respondents said that they were "definitely for" or
"for" negotiations, compared with 81% of Christian respondents.

Females are more supportive of negotiations on Jerusalem than males, as indicated in Table 3.6. The least educated and older respondents are most supportive
of such negotiations. Support for negotiations on Jerusalem reaches 90% among
older respondents and 91% among wealthier respondents.

The Importance of the Topic of
Jerusalem in the Negotiations

Palestinians feel that the topic of Jerusalem is very important in the negotiations. About 58% said that the topic of Jerusalem is "much more important"
or "more important" than other topics being negotiated (water, refugees, settlements). Another 41% felt that it is "equally important" to these other topics
(Q. 74).

Table 3.6
Are you "for" or "against" negotiations on Jerusalem within the peace process?

	For or definitely for	Against or definitely against
Gender		
Male	79%	21%
Female	86%	14%
Education		
0–10 yrs.	89%	11%
11–12 yrs.	75%	25%
Two-year college	80%	20%
University	76%	24%
Age		
18–22	78%	22%
23–30	78%	22%
31–38	79%	21%
39–46	84%	16%
47–54	84%	16%
Over 54 yrs.	90%	10%
Income		
Less than 200 JDs	84%	16%
200-400 JDs	80%	20%
401-800 JDs	74%	26%
Over 800 JDs	91%	9%
Place of Birth		
In 1948 region	85%	15%
In West Bank or Gaza	81%	19%
Outside country	86%	14%

Gaza respondents were more inclined to say that the Jerusalem topic is "more important" than all other topics. West Bank respondents (including Jerusalemites) were more inclined to say that the Jerusalem topic is "equally important" to other topics.

The Islamists, more than all others, stress the importance of the topic of Jerusalem in the negotiations. About 74% of them feel that this topic is "much more important" or "more important" than other topics. The leftists disagree: 50% of them said that the Jerusalem topic is "as important" as all other topics.

A majority (59%) of the very religious (many of whom are older and less educated respondents; divided among Fatah, Islamists, and independents) feel that the topic of Jerusalem is "more important" than other topics. A majority of the "not at all religious" (many of whom are leftists and independents) feel that the topic of Jerusalem is "as important" as all other issues.

Binding Agreement/Satisfaction with the Palestinian Authority

In general, an agreement over Jerusalem will be "more binding" or "much more binding" if reached under a Palestinian state, in the opinion of 45% of the respondents.* Only 25% said that such an agreement will be "more" or "much more binding" if achieved by the present negotiators. Less than one-third (30%) felt that such a variable will not make a difference (Q. 4). Gaza respondents, more than West Bank respondents, feel that an agreement is more binding under a Palestinian state.

About 60% of West Bank respondents and 68% of Jerusalem respondents were dissatisfied with the Palestinian Authority's concern with Jerusalem. In contrast, only 22% of Gazans felt the same way and 78% were very satisfied or satisfied (Q. 6). This positive evaluation might be an indication of Gazans' optimism that a Palestinian state with Jerusalem as its capital will soon emerge. (The same line is constantly repeated by the Palestinian official television airing from Gaza and is seen more in Gaza than in the West Bank.) West Bank respondents are not as optimistic, and therefore more anxious to see a quick resolution to the Jerusalem topic.

Fatah supporters are the most satisfied with the Palestinian Authority's concern with Jerusalem, followed by the independents, and the Islamists. The least satisfied are the leftists, as 74% of them said that they were "dissatisfied" or "very dissatisfied." This is compared with 62% among the Islamists. It was also noticeable that 28% of Fatah supporters and 50% of the independents felt the same way about the Authority's concern with Jerusalem.

Satisfaction with the Authority's attention to Jerusalem is directly correlated with the subject's degree of religiosity. About 38% of the "very religious" were "very satisfied" with the Authority's attention, compared with 10% of the "not at all religious."

True and Lasting Peace

The majority of Palestinians (65%) don't believe that there can be true peace between Israel and the Arab world in the foreseeable future (Q. 43). Jerusalem respondents were the least convinced that true peace can be achieved, followed immediately by West Bank respondents, and then Gaza respondents. The percentage of those who don't believe that lasting peace is possible declines from 65% to 56% if Israel shows willingness to compromise on Jerusalem. Furthermore, the majority of Palestinians (70%) support genuine and lasting peace with Israel

---

* The question did not specify if the agreement will be more binding to the respondent, or to Palestinians in general, or to the Israelis. Therefore, the answers to the question must viewed in broad terms.

in exchange for recognition of a Palestinian state with its capital in East Jerusalem and resolution of the refugee issue, "even though this will inevitably fall short of full justice for the Palestinians" (Q. 44).

The Islamists are the least likely to believe that there can be true peace between Israel and the Arab world in the foreseeable future. They are followed by the leftists and the independents. And while a majority of Fatah supporters feel the same way, a large group of them (45%) believe that there can be true peace in the foreseeable future.

Support for genuine and lasting peace is also correlated with political affiliation. Fifty-two percent of the supporters of Islamist groups are not willing to "support genuine and lasting peace with Israel in exchange for recognition of a Palestinian state with its capital in East Jerusalem, and a resolution of the refugee issue even though this will inevitably fall short of achieving full justice for the Palestinians." It is interesting to notice that a majority of leftists (67%) are willing to support such a solution. The majority of Fatah supporters (82%) and independents (72%) are willing to do the same.

Support for genuine and lasting peace is more widespread among males than females. (See Table 3.7 for the full version of the question and the results.) Such support is inversely correlated with education, as 72% of the least educated and 66% of the most educated support this proposal. In contrast, the relationship between age and support for the proposal is a direct one. A difference of 20% in support can be noticed between the youngest (61%) and the oldest (81%). More than other respondents, Palestinians with higher incomes (over 800 JDs) and those with incomes ranging from 200 to 400 Jds tend to support genuine and lasting peace based on the mentioned proposal. Support for the proposal is weakest among Palestinians born outside the country, as 40% of them disagree with it, compared with 25% among those born in the 1948 region.

Willingness (or Unwillingness) to Compromise on Jerusalem

Palestinians from all regions and political affiliations are calling on the Palestinian negotiators to be less compromising on the issue of Jerusalem. This is especially true in the West Bank (including Jerusalem). A quarter of Gaza respondents advise the negotiators to be somewhat more compromising. Calls for less compromise come from the Islamists and the leftists more than independents and Fatah supporters (Q. 5).

Males tend to call for less compromise than females. Close to a quarter (23%) of the least educated advise the Palestinian negotiators to be somewhat compromising. It was interesting to notice that the most educated are calling for less compromise, but at the same time a relatively large percentage of them (17%) advise the negotiators to be somewhat compromising. As noted in Table 3.8, older Palestinians tend to be more compromising than younger Palestinians. Willingness

Table 3.7
Do you support genuine and lasting peace with Israel in exchange for
recognition of a Palestinian state with its capital in East Jerusalem and
resolution of the refugee issue, even though this will inevitably
will fall short of full justice for the Palestinians?

	Agree or definitely agree	*Disagree or definitely disagree*
Gender		
Male	72%	28%
Female	68%	32%
Education		
0–10 yrs.	72%	28%
11–12 yrs.	69%	31%
Two-year college	69%	31%
University	66%	34%
Age		
18–22	61%	39%
23–30	65%	35%
31–38	67%	33%
39–46	77%	23%
47–54	76%	24%
Over 54	81%	19%
Income		
Less than 200 JDs	66%	34%
200–400 JDs	75%	25%
401–800 JDs	67%	33%
Over 800 JDs	78%	22%
Place of Birth		
In 1948 region	75%	25%
In West Bank or Gaza	70%	30%
Outside country	60%	40%

to compromise declines with income; respondents with the lower incomes are more willing to compromise (21%) than those with higher incomes (9%).

Reasons for Compromise

The most important reason for compromise on Jerusalem, in the opinion of Palestinians, is that compromise will bring peace. Around 65% of the respondents "agreed" or "strongly agreed" with this point of view (Q. 48). This is followed by the assertion that a compromise on Jerusalem will gain Palestinians more favorable outcomes on other issues in the negotiations, such as statehood, borders, and refugees. Around 64% of the respondents agreed with this assertion (Q. 49).

Table 3.8
If you were able to advise Palestinian negotiators with respect to Jerusalem, with respect to their willingness or unwillingness to reach a compromise with the Israelis, how would you advise them?

	Be much less compromising	Be less compromising	Be somewhat compromising
Gender			
Male	65%	25%	10%
Female	57%	25%	18%
Education			
0–10 yrs.	52%	25%	23%
11–12 yrs.	68%	23%	9%
Two-year college	66%	23%	11%
University	67%	17%	17%
Age			
18–22	60%	27%	13%
23–30	62%	25%	13%
31–38	61%	26%	13%
39–46	63%	26%	11%
47–54	60%	20%	20%
Over 54	62%	21%	17%
Income			
Less than 200 JDs	57%	22%	21%
200–400 JDs	66%	24%	10%
401–800 JDs	61%	31%	8%
Over 800 JDs	67%	24%	9%
Place of Birth			
In 1948 region	56%	28%	16%
In West Bank or Gaza	62%	25%	13%
Outside country	61%	18%	21%

Another reason for compromise on Jerusalem is that it will bring something tangible today. When strong, Palestinians hope to gain still more. This point of view is shared by 57% of the respondents (Q. 52). As many as 50% of the respondents feel that a compromise is needed because Palestinians are in the "weaker position" and have to compromise or they will get nothing (Q. 51).

From the Palestinian perspective, the least important reason for compromise relates to the assertion that "a compromise on Jerusalem is the right thing to do because Israelis also have a deep historical and religious attachment to Jerusalem." About 40% of the respondents "agreed" or "strongly agreed" with this assertion, while 60% disagreed or "strongly disagreed" (Q. 50).

Table 3.9
A compromise on Jerusalem is the right thing to do because Israelis also have deep historical and religious attachment to Jerusalem."

	Convincing	*Not convincing*
Gender		
Male	39%	61%
Female	41%	59%
Education		
0–10 yrs.	46%	54%
11–12 yrs.	39%	61%
Two-year college	36%	64%
University	29%	71%
Age		
18–22	41%	59%
23–30	36%	64%
31–38	39%	61%
39–46	35%	65%
47–54	45%	55%
Over 54	51%	49%
Income		
Less than 200 JDs		
200–400 JDs	41%	59%
401–800 JDs	40%	60%
Over 800 JDs	37%	63%
Place of Birth		
In 1948 region	43%	57%
In West Bank or Gaza	40%	60%
Outside country	32%	68%

It is interesting to note that degree of religiosity was not a significant factor in shaping this view. In fact, as much as 44% of the "very religious" "agreed" or "strongly agreed" with a compromise made on the basis that "Jews also have historical and religious attachment to Jerusalem." This view was shared by only 35% of the least religious respondents. And, while there was no difference between Muslims and Christians in the "strongly agree" category, a larger percentage of Christians were in the "agree" category.

Of all groups, the more educated were the least convinced in a compromise based on the assertion that "Jews also have historical and religious attachment to Jerusalem." As many as 71% of them were "not convinced" with this argument, compared with 54% of the less educated. It is interesting to find that as many as 51% of older Palestinians (over 54) were convinced by this argument. Furthermore, agreement with this argument came from those respondents who were born in the 1948 region more than respondents who were born outside the country (see Table 3.9).

Reasons Against Compromise

Palestinians were more in agreement with reasons against compromise than with reasons for compromise. The most important reason against compromise stemmed from the assertion that "Jerusalem in its entirety is the heart of Palestine" (Q. 57). About 87% of the respondents shared this point of view. About 74% of the respondents felt that Jerusalem is much more important for Islam than Judaism (Q. 53). A similar percentage of respondents felt that Israel has no right to Jerusalem at all, and that the actual historical connection of Jews to the city is minor (Q. 55, Q. 56). Fewer Palestinians (66%) felt that Jerusalem is an Islamic Wakf and therefore no compromise should be made in the negotiations over the city (Q. 54).

As noted from the data, Gaza respondents, more than West Bank respondents, tend to "strongly agree" with both reasons for and reasons against compromise. This is possibly because respondents in Gaza tend to be less sophisticated than those in the West Bank, as indicated by the data on education. The least educated tend to "agree" with all types of statements offered to them without questioning while the educated were more discerning. Those with less education also tend to be more optimistic.

It was also noticeable that the "very religious" find reasons against compromise more convincing than the "least religious." Around 63% of the "very religious" found the statement "there should not be any compromise on Jerusalem because Israel has no right to Jerusalem at all" a very convincing statement. Only 31% of the "least religious" found such a statement "very convincing."

Views against compromise are also related to political affiliation, as seen in the Islamists who found the reasons against compromise to be highly convincing. The most convincing reason against compromise for the Islamists was that "Israel has no right to Jerusalem at all," as 69% of them said that they found this a "very convincing" reason and an additional 19% found it "convincing." For the leftists and the independents, the most "convincing" reason against compromise is that "Jerusalem is much more important to Islam than to Judaism." For Fatah supporters, there were two important reasons against compromise: "Jerusalem is more important to Islam than Judaism," and "Israel has no right to Jerusalem at all."

No significant differences can be found with respect to the various variables, except that more than a third (36%) of the most educated were not convinced with this argument against compromise (see Table 3.10).

In general, Palestinian willingness to compromise over Jerusalem is not very high. Around 82% of them said that "we should make no concessions at all over Jerusalem even if we have to give up achieving a Palestinian state" (Q. 38). The percentage of those who "agree" (or "definitely agree") with this statement is

Table 3.10
"There shouldn't be any compromise on Jerusalem because
Israel has no right to Jerusalem at all."

	Convincing	Not convincing
Gender		
Male	72%	28%
Female	74%	26%
Education		
0–10 yrs.	75%	25%
11–12 yrs.	74%	26%
Two-year college	72%	28%
University	64%	36%
Age		
18–22	72%	28%
23–30	70%	30%
31–38	74%	26%
39–46	74%	26%
47–54	80%	20%
Over 54	72%	28%
Income		
Less than 200 JDs	77%	23%
200–400 JDs	71%	29%
401–800 JDs	67%	33%
Over 800 JDs	75%	25%
Place of Birth		
In 1948 region	75%	25%
In West Bank or Gaza	73%	27%
Outside country	72%	28%

higher (89%) among the "very religious" than among the "least religious." It should be noted, however, that 53% say they would accept a solution in which Israel has sovereignty over West Jerusalem and the State of Palestine has sovereignty over East Jerusalem. This may be because most Palestinians view this as "less of a concession," since the PLO and the Palestinian Authority have been referring to East (or Arab) Jerusalem as the capital for a Palestinian state for so long.

The Status of Jerusalem

In general, Palestinians were willing to seriously consider a number of proposals mentioned in the survey, including dividing the city and joint sovereignty if they were part of a Palestinian negotiating team.

Divided City

The majority of Palestinians (52%) will "seriously" (or "very seriously") consider a proposal that states that "West Jerusalem would be under Israeli sovereignty, and East Jerusalem would be under Palestinian sovereignty with a special arrangement for Israeli control of the Jewish neighborhoods in East Jerusalem. The Old City would be dealt with separately" (Q. 61). Around 16% of the respondents are willing to give this proposal some consideration. In contrast, one-third of the respondents will not take the proposal seriously or will "totally reject" it.

Respondents from all regions are equally willing to consider this proposal. A majority of Fatah supporters (59%) and independents (53%) are willing to "seriously" (or "very seriously") consider this proposal. Around 48% of the leftists are willing to "seriously" consider it. The Islamists are divided on this proposal: 41% of them are willing to "seriously" consider the proposal; 41% will "not seriously" consider it or will "totally reject" it; 18% will give the proposal some consideration. Degree of religiosity doesn't appear to be a significant factor in determining point of view on this proposal, as 52% of the "not at all religious" and 47% of the "very religious" are willing to "seriously" (or "very seriously") consider such a proposal.

Willingness to accept a divided city is confirmed by the fact that 53% of the respondents accept as a permanent solution of the Jerusalem question that "Israel has sovereignty over West Jerusalem and the State of Palestine has sovereignty over East Jerusalem" (Q. 39). This acceptance is higher in the West Bank than Gaza. A majority of independents, Fatah supporters, and leftists accept this proposal. In addition, one-third of the Islamists accept it.

With regard to dividing the city into two sovereign areas, males accepted this proposal more than females (a difference of 15%). The educated were more accepting of this proposal than the less educated. The difference between older and younger respondents with regard to this proposal is striking. As many as 64% of older respondents accept dividing the city, while only 27% of the younger respondents accept it (a 37% difference). Similar patterns are noted if we look at income, as 45% of the respondents with the lowest incomes accept dividing the city as a permanent solution, compared with 74% of the respondents with the highest incomes. Palestinians born in the 1948 region were more accepting of the proposal than other Palestinians (see Table 3.11).

Joint Sovereignty over an Undivided City

A proposal stating that "Israel and Palestine together would exercise joint sovereignty over an undivided city" would be seriously considered by 40% of the Palestinians if they were part of the negotiating team over Jerusalem. Around 16% will give the proposal "some consideration," while 45% will "not seriously consider" it or will "totally reject" it (Q. 60). The proposal was "seriously considered" by 43%

Table 3.11
Would you accept as a permanent solution of the Jerusalem question that Israel has sovereignty over West Jerusalem and the State of Palestine has sovereignty over East Jerusalem?

	Yes or definitely yes	*No or definitely no*
Gender		
Male	59%	41%
Female	44%	54%
Education		
0–10 yrs.	51%	49%
11–12 yrs.	48%	52%
Two-year college	60%	40%
University	59%	41%
Age		
18–22	27%	73%
23–30	45%	55%
31–38	56%	44%
39–46	66%	34%
47–54	56%	44%
Over 54	64%	36%
Income		
Less than 200 JDs	45%	55%
200–400 JDs	56%	46%
401–800 JDs	55%	45%
Over 800 JDs	74%	26%
Place of Birth		
In 1948 region	57%	43%
In West Bank or Gaza	52%	48%
Outside country	47%	53%

of West Bank respondents, 37% of Jerusalem respondents, and 34% of Gaza respondents. The difference between Gaza and West Bank respondents is partly due to their attitudes on the issue of separation between Jews and Arabs in the daily life of Jerusalem. A larger percentage (82%) of Gaza respondents felt that separation is "desirable" (or "very desirable"), compared with 67% of West Bank respondents.

The relationship between attitudes toward separation and the proposal on joint sovereignty is clear from the data. About 32% of those who strongly prefer separation will consider joint sovereignty "seriously" (or "very seriously"). In comparison, among those strongly opposed to separation in daily life, 47% would "seriously consider" joint sovereignty.

This argument doesn't hold true if we examine education. Support for separation is lower among the more educated (about 62% of the most educated support such separation compared with 75% of the least educated). Willingness to consider joint sovereignty is also lower among the more educated. This is possibly due to the inclination of the educated to distinguish between the social and the political. They are more willing to consider proposals that are social in nature, but less willing to consider political proposals. Support for separation also decreases with income, as 64% of those within the highest income category support separation compared with 80% of those within the lowest income category.

A larger percentage of Fatah supporters (45%) and independents (42%) are more willing to "seriously consider" joint sovereignty than the Islamists (30%) and the leftists (30%). The "very religious" and the "least religious" respondents share the same view on the proposal, as one-third of each group is willing to "seriously consider" joint sovereignty. Around 65% of the "very religious" and 48% of the "least religious" do not take this proposal "seriously" or "reject" it. Those who are "religious" or "somewhat religious" are more willing to consider the mentioned proposal.

Willingness to consider joint sovereignty is inversely correlated with education. A third of the university degree-holders are willing to consider joint sovereignty. This is compared with 43% of those who have zero to 10 years of education. It is interesting to find that willingness to consider this proposal declines with age. Older respondents (an otherwise more compromising group) are less willing to consider joint sovereignty than younger respondents (see Table 3.12).

Israeli Sovereignty over Jewish Neighborhoods in East Jerusalem

The majority of Palestinians (57%) refuse to "seriously consider" (or "reject totally") a proposal stating that "West Jerusalem and Jewish neighborhoods in East Jerusalem would be under Israeli sovereignty and the rest of East Jerusalem would be under Palestinian sovereignty, with the Old City dealt with separately" (Q. 61). Only 28% said that they are willing to "seriously consider" this proposal, and 15% are willing to "give it some consideration."

Lack of willingness to consider this proposal is widespread in both the West Bank and Gaza. A third of Fatah supporters are willing to consider it compared with 28% of independents, 23% of the leftists, and 20% of the Islamists.

Self-Rule Status in Palestinian Neighborhoods in East Jerusalem

An overwhelming majority of Palestinians (71%) refuse to "seriously" consider (or "reject totally") a proposal stating that "Israel would exercise sovereignty over East

Table 3.12
"Israel and Palestine together would exercise joint sovereignty over undivided city." Please state the extent to which you would seriously consider this proposal.

	Seriously or very seriously	Give it some consideration	No seriously or reject
Gender			
Male	39%	16%	45%
Female	41%	14%	45%
Education			
0–10 yrs.	43%	12%	45%
11–12 yrs.	37%	17%	46%
Two-year college	43%	14%	43%
University	33%	19%	52%
Age			
18–22	47%	17%	36%
23–30	38%	16%	54%
31–38	35%	16%	49%
39–46	39%	15%	46%
47–54	35%	13%	52%
Over 54			
Income			
Less than 200 JDs	40%	12%	48%
200–400 JDs	39%	21%	40%
401–800 JDs	35%	12%	53%
Over 800 JDs	40%	18%	42%
Place of Birth			
In 1948 region	32%	11%	57%
In West Bank or Gaza	40%	16%	44%
Outside country	38%	9%	53%

Jerusalem, but Palestinian neighborhoods would be given a special self-rule status." Around 44% "totally reject" this proposal (Q. 65). And while refusal to consider this proposal is widespread in all regions, it is considerably higher among Jerusalem respondents.

The Status of Abu Dis

A small majority of Palestinians (53%) are willing to "seriously" (or "very seriously") consider that Abu Dis (a Palestinian suburb) be added to Jerusalem and the Palestinian Parliament be housed in that region of the expanded city. Another 11%

are willing to give the proposal "some consideration." Around 36% will "not seriously" consider this proposal or "totally reject" it (Q. 67).

Consideration of this proposal does not mean that Palestinians are willing to accept Abu Dis as a substitute capital for Palestine. Around 76% of the Palestinian respondents rejected a proposal stating that "as an interim step the Palestinian capital be located in the Jerusalem suburb of Abu Dis, without relinquishing the Palestinian claim to sovereignty over East Jerusalem" (Q. 73). Such rejection is higher in the West Bank than in the Gaza Strip, as 80% of West Bank respondents rejected this proposal, compared with 67% of Gaza respondents. And while supporters of all political groups reject this proposal, 22% of Fatah supporters and 19% of independents accept it. Rejection for this proposal is widespread among the "very religious" as well as the "least religious."

Support for a Palestinian capital to be located in Abu Dis (as an interim step) declines with education. Only 13% of the most educated support this arrangement, compared with 27% of the least educated. In general, support for this arrangement increases with age. Support is highest among the 47–54 age group at 28%. A quarter of the respondents in the income category less than 200 JDs support such an arrangement. This is compared with 13% among respondents with incomes higher than 400 JDs. The least support for this proposal comes from respondents born outside the country (see Table 3.13).

Religious Sites

The majority of Palestinians (60%) would seriously consider keeping the control of the Haram al-Sharif under the Wakf as it is now (Q. 69). The largest group of respondents (50%) are willing to consider a proposal stating that "the Palestinians would get sovereignty over the Haram al-Sharif in exchange for Palestinian recognition of Israeli sovereignty over the Western Wall" (Q. 64). Willingness to consider this proposal is higher in Gaza than in the West Bank. It was also noticeable that 41% of the Islamists and the leftists are willing to consider this proposal, compared with 57% of Fatah supporters. It was also surprising to find that there was no significant difference between the "very religious" and the "least religious" in regard to this proposal.

Older respondents are most willing to consider this proposal. Support is higher among respondents with the lower income than those with higher income (see Table 3.14).

Palestinians were divided in their views on a related proposal. About 47% of the respondents are "not willing to consider" (or "reject totally") a proposal stating that " Palestinians would have sovereignty over al-Aqsa mosque and the Dome of the Rock, but with respect to the plateau itself sovereignty would be shared with the Israelis, although day-to-day administration of the plateau would be in Palestinians' hands alone" (Q. 68). Around 41% of the respondents are

Table 3.13
Assume that no definitive solution for the Jerusalem question can be found.
Would you support as an interim step that the Palestinian capital
be located in the Jerusalem suburb of Abu Dis, without
relinquishing the Palestinian claim to sovereignty over East Jerusalem?

	Yes	No	Others
Gender			
Male	19%	73%	8%
Female	19%	78%	3%
Education			
0–10 yrs.	27%	68%	5%
11–12 yrs.	14%	80%	6%
Two-year college	12%	80%	8%
University	13%	78%	9%
Age			
18–22	13%	81%	6%
23–30	14%	77%	9%
31–38	19%	77%	4%
39–46	24%	72%	4%
47–54	28%	71%	1%
Over 54	20%	71%	9%
Income			
Less than 200 JDs	25%	69%	6%
200–400 JDs	15%	78%	7%
401–800 JDs	13%	81%	6%
Over 800 JDs	13%	85%	2%
Place of Birth			
In 1948 region	14%	74%	12%
In West Bank or Gaza	19%	75%	6%
Outside country	10%	85%	5%

willing to consider this proposal in the negotiations. Another 12% will give the proposal some consideration. Residents of villages, refugee camps, and cities show similar attitudes toward this proposal. About 42% of refugee camp residents would consider (or seriously consider) the above-mentioned proposal. This is compared with 41% among city residents and village residents. About 43% of the refugee respondents would consider (or seriously consider) the proposal, compared with 40% of nonrefugees.

The most intense rejection was directed at a proposal stating that "Jews would be allowed to pray on the Haram al-Sharif which would be under the operational authority of the Wakf." A majority of 57% "rejected" this proposal

Table 3.14
"The Palestinians would get sovereignty over the Haram al-Sharif in exchange for Palestinian recognition of Israeli sovereignty over the Western Wall."
Please state the extent to which you would seriously consider this proposal.

	Seriously or very seriously	Give it some consideration	Not seriously or reject
Gender			
Male	48%	15%	37%
Female	53%	15%	32%
Education			
0–10 yrs.	55%	13%	32%
11–12 yrs.	44%	18%	27%
Two-year college	56%	13%	31%
University	48%	14%	38%
Age			
18–22	55%	13%	32%
23–30	44%	16%	40%
31–38	46%	15%	39%
39–46	53%	16%	31%
47–54	53%	12%	35%
Over 54	60%	12%	28%
Income			
Less than 200 JDs	58%	11%	31%
200–400 JDs	43%	17%	40%
401–800 JDs	44%	18%	38%
Over 800 JDs	43%	17%	40%
Place of Birth			
In 1948 region	54%	11%	35%
In West Bank or Gaza	50%	15%	35%
Outside country	44%	14%	42%

totally. Another 19% are "not willing to consider" this proposal seriously. Only 17% will consider such a proposal "seriously" (Q. 63).

The Old City

Palestinians were divided on the topic of the Old City of Jerusalem. As many as 47% of the respondents "reject totally" or would "not seriously consider" a proposal stating that "in the Old City, Israel would get sovereignty over Jewish neighborhoods and Palestine would get sovereignty over Palestinian neighborhoods" (Q. 62). Around 13% are willing to "give the proposal some consideration." About 40% are willing to "seriously" consider this proposal. Rejection of this proposal is

Table 3.15
"In the Old City, Israel would get sovereignty over the Jewish neighborhoods, and Palestine would get sovereignty over Palestinian neighborhoods." Please state the extent to which you would seriously consider this proposal?

	Seriously or very seriously	Give it some consideration	Not seriously or reject
Gender			
Male	39%	9%	52%
Female	41%	17%	42%
Education			
0–10 yrs.	41%	12%	47%
11–12 yrs.	40%	13%	47%
Two-year college	42%	12%	46%
University	31%	17%	52%
Age			
18–22	34%	12%	54%
23–30	39%	18%	43%
31–38	33%	14%	53%
39–46	45%	7%	48%
47–54	42%	11%	47%
Over 54	40%	11%	49%
Income			
Less than 200 JDs	43%	13%	44%
200–400 JDs	37%	15%	48%
401–800 JDs	33%	12%	55%
Over 800 JDs	33%	1%	56%
Place of Birth			
In 1948 region	45%	8%	47%
In West Bank or Gaza	39%	13%	48%
Outside country	30%	11%	59%

highest in Jerusalem (at 58%) followed by the rest of the West Bank (52%) and Gaza (40%).

Willingness to consider this proposal is higher among Fatah supporters and independents than among leftists and Islamists. The "least religious" respondents are the least "willing to consider" this proposal (23%) compared with 39% among the "most religious" and 41% among the "religious." No significant differences can be found between Muslims and Christians in regard to this proposal. Around 39% of the Muslim respondents and 38% of the Christian respondents are "willing to consider" this proposal.

Less than a third (31%) of the most educated are "willing to consider" this proposal. This is compared with 41% of the least educated. Older respondents are more "willing to consider" it than younger respondents. Palestinian willingness to consider this proposal declines with income, as 43% of the respondents with the least income and 33% of the respondents with the most income are willing to consider the proposal dealing with the Old City (see Table 3.15).

Sovereignty Belongs to God

Palestinians are willing to accept a proposal stating that "each side should stop arguing about sovereignty over holy sites in Jerusalem and agree that ultimate sovereignty belongs to God." About 64% of the respondents said "definitely yes" or "yes" to this proposal, and 36% said "no" or "definitely no" (Q. 70). This proposal is possibly the most abstract of all proposals, leaving room for varying interpretations. Concrete, related proposals will be needed to understand what Palestinians are agreeing (or disagreeing) with.

This willingness to accept that sovereignty belongs to God is not accompanied by similar support for a greater role for Jordan in the administration of the Islamic sites. Only 16% of the respondents agreed with the idea that Jordan should play a substantial role in the administration of the Islamic sites in Jerusalem (Q. 71). Surprisingly, this percentage was higher in Gaza than in the West Bank. Support for a more substantial role for Jordan increases with religiosity, as 24% of the "very religious" and only 8% of the "least religious" agree.

Close to a third (32%) of older respondents supported the idea that Jordan should play a more substantial role in the administration of the Islamic holy sites in the city. Only 10% of the respondents in the 31–38 age group shared this view. Support for a substantial role for Jordan declines with education, as 26% of the "least educated" and 8% of the "most educated" support the idea. Female respondents are more supportive of the idea than are males (see Table 3.16).

Protest Activities Against an "Unacceptable" Compromise on Jerusalem

The majority of Palestinians will "oppose" a compromise on Jerusalem that they do not approve of. As many as 66% said that if a Palestinian government accepts a compromise that they "do not approve of," they would "oppose" it. In contrast, 28% said that they will "accept" it with reservations. Only 6% said that they will "accept" it (Q. 75).

About 72% "agree" with the point of view that says "in the case of an unsatisfactory agreement on Jerusalem, Palestinians have the right to use all means necessary to block its implementation." Only 28% "disagree" with this point of view (Q. 77).

More female respondents than males "agree" that in the case of an unsatisfactory agreement on Jerusalem, Palestinians have the right to use all means necessary to block its implementation. And while agreement with this statement

Table 3.16
Do you support the idea that Jordan should play a substantial role in the administration of the Islamic holy sites in Jerusalem?

	Yes or definitely yes	*No or definitely no*
Gender		
Male	15%	85%
Female	20%	80%
Education		
0–10 yrs.	26%	74%
11–12 yrs.	13%	87%
Two-year college	12%	88%
University	8%	92%
Age		
18–22	16%	84%
23–30	12%	88%
31–38	10%	90%
39–46	18%	82%
47–54	24%	76%
Over 54	32%	68%
Income		
Less than 200 JDs	23%	77%
200–400 JDs	13%	87%
401–800 JDs	16%	84%
Over 800 JDs	2%	98%
Place of Birth		
In 1948 region	24%	76%
In West Bank or Gaza	17%	83%
Outside country	25%	75%

is high (74%) among the less educated, it declines to 66% among the most educated. Older respondents and those who were born in the 1948 region are more in agreement with the mentioned statement than all others (see Table 3.17).

On a personal level, as many as 62% said that "they will participate in any action against an agreement on Jerusalem that they do not approve of" (Q. 76). Readiness to participate in any action against an unsatisfactory agreement is higher in Jerusalem (74%) than in the rest of the West Bank (64%) and Gaza (60%). The leftists are the most willing to participate in protest action (86%), followed by the Islamists (77%) and Fatah supporters (66%). Independents are the least willing to participate in protest action (56%). Refugees show an almost similar degree of readiness to participate in protest action (61%) as nonrefugees (64%). Surprisingly, refugee camp residents were the least willing to express

Table 3.17

Do you agree with the point of view that says "in the case of an unsatisfactory agreement on Jerusalem, Palestinians have the right to use all means necessary to block its implementation"?

	Agree or definitely agree	*Disagree or definitely disagree*
Gender		
Male	68%	32%
Female	77%	23%
Education		
0–10 yrs.	74%	26%
11–12 yrs.	72%	28%
Two-year college	74%	26%
University	66%	34%
Age		
18–22	73%	27%
23–30	72%	28%
31–38	63%	37%
39–46	73%	27%
47–54	74%	26%
Over 54	81%	19%
Income		
Less than 200 JDs	76%	24%
200–400 JDs	67%	33%
401–800 JDs	71%	29%
Over 800 JDs	67%	33%
Place of Birth		
In 1948 region	81%	19%
In West Bank or Gaza	71%	29%
Outside country	73%	27%

readiness to protest, as 55% of them said that they will participate. This is compared with 66% in cities and 63% in villages.

Palestinian Attitudes on Jerusalem:
A Multilevel Analysis

The survey data show that a comprehensive understanding of Palestinian attitudes on Jerusalem requires a multilevel analysis based on various "groupings" of questions. The relationship among political, social, and demographic variables and attitudes depends greatly on the types of questions raised. The survey itself raised questions that included the following:

- Questions that show ideological positions and emotional attachment to Jerusalem.
- Questions that show willingness to recognize rights for Jews in the city.
- Questions that show support for peace and willingness to compromise.
- Questions that show willingness to consider specific (concrete) proposals.
- Questions that show willingness to consider proposals that are permanent in nature.

As the following analysis will reveal, what seem to be hard-line positions on issues of ideological and emotional nature, or unwillingness to recognize rights for Jews in Jerusalem, are not necessarily accompanied by hard-line attitudes toward the peace process and specific (concrete) proposals. In fact, a Palestinian who is very attached (emotionally) to Jerusalem and who is not willing to recognize rights for Jews in Jerusalem may also be willing to support the current peace process and to consider concrete proposals. This Palestinian, however, is less inclined to support proposals that are of permanent nature (proposals that might directly conflict with his or her ideological beliefs). On the contrary, those groups of Palestinians who are not as emotionally attached to Jerusalem tend to be more critical of the specific proposals (that deal with only parts of the issue). Those Palestinians are, however, more supportive of long-term solutions such as dividing the city or joint sovereignty.

The following section will provide an analysis of the two patterns mentioned in the previous paragraphs. Table 3.18 reveals that:

Gaza respondents	*are more attached to*	West Bank respondents
Women	*Jerusalem than*	Men
The less educated		The more educated
Lower-income respondents		Higher-income respondents
Older respondents		Younger respondents
The very religious		The least religious

Respondents listed in the first column, more than those listed in the second column, feel that Jerusalem is "very important to them personally"; that the Jerusalem topic is more important than all other topics; that Jerusalem is "important" as a symbol for the future Palestinian state; and that the Islamic quarter of the Old City is "very important." More than their counterparts Gazans, women, the less educated, older respondents, and the "very religious" think that no concessions over Jerusalem should be made at all, even if Palestinians have to give up achieving a Palestinian state. They are also more accepting of "the right to use all necessary means to block" the implementation of an unacceptable agreement.

Table 3.18
Ideological positions (sentimental attachment)

	Jerusalem is very important to me personally	The Jerusalem issue is much more important than all other issues	Jerusalem is very important as a symbol for the future Palestinian State	The islamic quarter of the Old City is very important	Should make no concessions at all over Jerusalem even if we have to give up achieving a Palestinian State (definitely agree)	In case of an acceptable agreement on Jerusalem, Palestinians have the right to use all means necessary to block its implementation (definitely agree)
West Bank	90%	40%	88%	83%	58%	40%
Gaza Strip	95%	61%	93%	89%	74%	51%
Male	90%	44%	89%	83%	62%	41%
Female	94%	50%	89%	86%	67%	45%
Less Education	92%	56%	92%	89%	70%	50%
More Education	89%	30%	84%	67%	51%	33%
High Income	82%	43%	82%	77%	46%	44%
Low Income	95%	56%	91%	89%	71%	50%
Younger	91%	51%	88%	74%	66%	37%
Older	97%	52%	95%	95%	72%	55%
Very Religious	96%	59%	98%	94%	79%	64%
Not Religious	78%	29%	85%	70%	56%	45%

*Less educated (0–10 years); more educated (University degree-holders); higher-income respondents (monthly income over 800 JDs); lower-income respondents (less than 200 JDs a month); younger respondents (18–22); older respondents (over 54); Resp:: respondents.

Table 3.19
Willingness to recognize Jewish "rights" in Jerusalem

	Because Judaism is a religion, Jews shouldn't be thought of as constituting a people, and therefore are lacking national rights (definitely, yes)	There shouldn't be any compromise on Jerusalem because Israel has no right to Jerusalem at all (very convincing)	Do Jews have any sort of legitimate rights with regard to Jerusalem? (definitely yes, or yes)
West Bank	28%	43%	22%
Gaza Strip	39%	59%	18%
Male	35%	47%	23%
Female	28%	48%	17%
Less Educated	37%	53%	23%
More Educated	31%	33%	23%
Higher Income	30%	36%	20%
Lower Income	35%	56%	16%
Younger	23%	44%	16%
Older	41%	52%	24%
Very religious	41%	66%	16%
Not at All Religious	35%	34%	30%

Feelings of attachment to Jerusalem are accompanied with less willingness to recognize rights for Jews in the city. The data show that:

Gaza respondents	are less willing to	West Bank respondents
Women	recognize rights for	Men
The less educated	Jews in Jerusalem	The more educated
Lower-income respondents	than	Higher-income respondents
Older respondents		Younger respondents
The very religious		The least religious

Respondents listed in the first column, more than those listed in the second column, feel that since Judaism is a religion, "Jews shouldn't be thought of as constituting a people, and therefore are lacking national rights." More than their counterparts, Gazans, women, the less educated, lower-income respondents, older respondents, and the "very religious" think that there shouldn't be a compromise on Jerusalem "because Israel has no right to Jerusalem at all." When asked if Jews have any sort of legitimate rights with regard to Jerusalem, the same pattern existed (see Table 3.19).

Table 3.20
Support for peace (and willingness to compromise)

	Are you for or against negotiations on Jerusalem within the peace process? (definitely for)	A compromise on Jerusalem is the right thing to do because israelis also have deep historical and religious attachment to Jerusalem (strongly agree or agree)	Advixe Palestinian negotiators to be somewhat more compromising	Would you participate in any action against an agreement on Jerusalem that you don't approve of? (no)
West Bank	56%	34%	7%	15%
Gaza Strip	70%	49%	25%	29%
Male	57%	39%	10%	15%
Female	59%	41%	18%	26%
Less Educated	70%	46%	23%	23%
More Educated	50%	29%	17%	17%
Higher Income	61%	41%	9%	—
Lower Income	63%	41%	21%	—
Younger	51%	41%	13%	21%
Older	65%	51%	17%	25%
Very Religious	62%	44%	16%	—
Not at All Religious	47%	35%	8%	—

Paradoxically, those same subgroups, although they show more attachment to Jerusalem and are in some instances less willing to recognize rights for Jews in Jerusalem, are more willing to support the peace process and to give concessions with regard to the city (see Table 3.20). This, however, does not mean that willingness to recognize rights for Jews in Jerusalem disposes people against compromise; within each group (e.g., Gaza respondents) those who acknowledge rights are more open to specific proposals than those who do not.

Gaza respondents	*are more supportive of*	West Bank respondents
Women	*negotiations and more*	Men
The less educated	*willing to compromise*	The more educated
Lower-income respondents	*than*	Higher-income respondents
Older respondents		Younger respondents
The very religious		The least religious

Respondents in the first column were more supportive of negotiations on Jerusalem within the peace process. The same applies to their willingness to compromise. A larger percentage of them advise Palestinian negotiators to be "somewhat more compromising." And while they are more supportive of the right of Palestinians to use all means necessary to block an unacceptable agreement, they are also less willing to participate in any action against an agreement on Jerusalem that they don't approve of.

Table 3.21
Willingness to consider specific proposals

	In the Old City, Israel would get sovereignty over Jewish neighborhood, and Palestine would get sovereignty over Palestinian neighborhoods (will consider very seriously	As an interim step, the Palestinian capital be located in Abu Dis, without relinquishing Palestinian claim to sovereignty over East Jerusalem (yes)	Palestine would get sovereignty over the Haram al-Sharif in exchange for Palestinian recognition of Israeli sovereignty over the Western Wall (will consider very seriously)	Joint administration of Old City (definitely yes, or yes)
West Bank	15%	13%	21%	25%
Gaza Strip	26%	27%	46%	33%
Male	20%	19%	29%	27%
Female	16%	19%	30%	29%
Less Educated	21%	27%	27%	27%
More Educated	13%	13%	33%	27%
Higher Income	18%	13%	18%	23%
Lower Income	24%	24%	41%	28%
Younger	23%	16%	29%	34%
Older	20%	20%	36%	24%
Very Religious	22%	15%	29%	19%
Not at All Religious	12%	11%	20%	27%

Both support for negotiations and willingness to compromise are accompanied by a similar willingness to consider specific and detailed proposals (that don't mention words such as "permanent" and "lasting"). As noted in Table 3.21:

Gaza respondents	*are more supportive of*	West Bank respondents
The less educated	*specific (concrete)*	The more educated
Lower-income respondents	*proposals than*	Higher-income respondents
Older respondents		Younger respondents
The very religious		The least religious

Respondents in the first column are willing to consider Israeli sovereignty over the Jewish neighborhoods in the Old City and Palestinian sovereignty over Palestinian neighborhoods more than respondents in the second column. The same applies to a proposal stating that Abu Dis become a Palestinian capital (as an interim step) and a proposal that Palestine would get sovereignty over the Haram al-Sharif in exchange for Israeli sovereignty over the Western Wall.

When these proposals involve permanent features, willingness to consider specific proposals is less clear among Gazans, women, the less educated, lower-income respondents, older respondents, and the "very religious." It seems that the notion of "permanency" challenges their strong ideological beliefs and their emotional attachment to the city.

For example, the data in Table 3.21 show that Gazans, women, and lower-income respondents show support for a proposal suggesting indefinite joint sovereignty over the Old City. At the same time, younger respondents and the less religious respondents support this proposal more than older respondents and the "very religious." Women and men feel the same way about the proposal.

The pattern witnessed with regards to specific proposals (listed in Table 3.21) is reversed when we examine proposals that emphasize permanence. Table 3.22 shows the following:

Gaza respondents	*are less willing to*	West Bank respondents
Women	*consider proposals that*	Men
Lower-income respondent	*are permanent in nature*	Higher-income respondents
The very religious	*than*	The least religious

This new pattern doesn't apply to the "age variable," as older respondents still show support for proposals (even if they involve permanent features). This is also true, to an extent, when looking at education, as the less educated "support genuine and lasting peace" more than the more educated.

Attitudes and Socioeconomic Variables

In summary, the following statements can be made about the various aspects of Palestinian public opinion toward Jerusalem.

Region (West Bank and Gaza)

Compared with West Bank respondents, Gazans are more emotionally attached to Jerusalem and less willing to recognize rights of Jews in the city. But they are

Table 3.22
Willingness to consider proposals that are permanent in nature

	Would you accept as a permanent solution of the Jerusalem question that Israel has sovereignty over West Jerusalem and the State of Palestine has sovereignty over East Jerusalem? (definitely yes, yes)	*Do you support genuine and lasing peace with Israel in exchange for recognition of a Palestinian State with its capital East Jerusalem, and resolution of the refugee issue, even though this will inevitably fall short of full justice for the Palestinians?* (definitely yes or yes)
West Bank	58%	71%
Gaza Strip	42%	68%
Male	59%	72%
Female	49%	68%
Less Educated	51%	72%
More Educated	59%	66%
Higher Income	64%	78%
Lower Income	45%	66%
Younger	27%	61%
Older	64%	81%
Very Religious	41%	60%
Not at All Religious	65%	73%

more willing to support negotiations and give concessions on specific proposals. They are, however, less supportive of "permanent" proposals.

Gender

Compared with their male counterparts, women are more emotionally attached to Jerusalem and less willing to recognize rights of Jews in the city. No significant differences can be detected between men and women in regard to their attitudes toward specific proposals. Women are, however, less supportive of "permanent" proposals than men.

Education

Compared with the more educated respondents, the less educated are more emotionally attached to Jerusalem and less willing to recognize rights for Jews in the city. The less educated are generally more willing to consider specific proposals than the more educated (with the exception of a proposal that gives sovereignty over the Western Wall to the Israelis and gives sovereignty over the Haram al-Sharif to Palestinians). A mixed pattern is detected when it comes to permanent proposals. The more educated accept dividing Jerusalem into two sovereign areas as a permanent solution. In contrast, the less educated are more willing to support "genuine and lasting peace" than the educated.

Income

Compared with higher-income respondents, lower-income respondents are more emotionally attached to Jerusalem and less willing to recognize rights for Jews in the city. But they are more willing to support negotiations and give concessions on specific proposals. They are, however, less supportive of "permanent" proposals.

Age

Compared with younger respondents, older respondents are more emotionally attached to Jerusalem. They are more willing to support negotiations and give concessions on specific proposals. Older Palestinians go against the dominant pattern in their views of "permanent" proposals, as they are more willing to support them than younger Palestinians.

Religiosity

Compared with the least religious respondents, the "very religious" are more emotionally attached to Jerusalem and less willing to recognize rights of Jews in the city. But they are more willing to support negotiations and give concessions on specific proposals. They are less supportive of indefinite joint sovereignty over the Old City. (This is consistent with their unsupportive attitudes toward joint sovereignty over the city, their views favoring separation between Jews and Palestinians in the daily life of the city, and their lack of support for "permanent" proposals.)

Myths About Palestinian Public Opinion on Jerusalem

The current study has challenged a number of "myths" about Palestinian public opinion on the Jerusalem issue.

The first myth: Since Palestinians are "in the weaker position," they are willing to give up on their demands with regard to Jerusalem.

The data show that while Palestinians show commitment to peace and realize that they are in "the weaker position," they are unwilling to compromise over basic demands (such as a Palestinian state with East Jerusalem as its capital).

The second myth: Palestinians residing in Jerusalem are not interested in resolving the Jerusalem issue and they don't wish to see the expansion of a Palestinian state into Jerusalem.

This myth is based on the assumption that since Jerusalemites are enjoying the benefits of Israeli social security, they don't want to give that up. In fact, the data reveal that Jerusalem residents show the same commitment (and sometimes more commitment) to the establishment of a Palestinian state with its capital in Jerusalem as their brethren Palestinians in the rest of the West Bank and Gaza.

The third myth: Christians and Muslims see Jerusalem from very different points of view.

This is not true, as 97% of Christians see Jerusalem as "very important" or "important" from an Islamic religious point of view (compared with 98% of Muslims). Ninety-eight percent of Christians see Jerusalem as "very important" or "important" from a Palestinian national-historical point of view (compared with 99% of Muslims). Again, 91% of Christians see Jerusalem as "very important" or "important" as a center of the Arab people (compared with 95% of Muslims). In addition, 99% of Christians see Jerusalem as "very important" as a symbol for the future Palestinian state (compared to 97% of Muslims). As expected, religion is a variable that explains some differences in points of view, as Christians, for example, attach more importance to Christian sites, and Muslims more importance to Islamic religious sites. And while there are other differences between Christians and Muslims, they both show a very strong commitment to a Palestinian state with Jerusalem as its capital.

The fourth myth: Religious Palestinians adopt more hard-line positions than the less religious.

This is one of the more prevalent myths (especially in the West). The data show that while the most religious Palestinians are most committed and attached to Jerusalem, they show more willingness to compromise over Jerusalem than the less religious. This is especially true with concrete proposals that don't challenge their ideological and emotional views of Jerusalem. Proposals that are "permanent" in nature are less supported by the religious respondents. The religious are willing to give concessions as long as that doesn't imply that they have to admit to "legitimate rights" for Jews in the city.

Of course, both religiosity and views on Jerusalem are related to other variables, such as political affiliation, age, and education. The very religious are divided among Fatah, independents, and Islamists. Many of them are older and less educated. Religiosity is constantly confused with "political religion." In fact, the majority of the "very religious" (54%) support Fatah or are independents. About 46% of them are supporters of Islamist political groups (such as Hamas and

Islamic Jihad "Islamists"). It must be noted that while the "Islamists" are less compromising than Fatah and the independents, they are no more "hard-line" in their positions than the leftists. It is interesting to find that in many cases the Islamists are more compromising than the leftists. For example, the majority of the Islamists (55%) said that they were definitely supportive of negotiations on Jerusalem, compared with 38% of the leftists and 51% of the independents. About 54% of them would consider ("very seriously," "seriously," or "give some consideration") to Palestinian sovereignty over the Haram al-Sharif in exchange for Israeli sovereignty over the Western Wall. About 48% of them would support "genuine and lasting peace with Israel in exchange for a Palestinian state with its capital in East Jerusalem, and resolution of the refugee issue, even though this will inevitably fall short of full justice for the Palestinians."

Conclusion

A thorough investigation of Palestinian attitudes toward Jerusalem revealed a strong and deep commitment to the city from all social and political groups in Palestinian society. It is not only that Palestinians feel that Jerusalem is very important to them personally, but they feel a sense of belonging to the city, and also believe that Jerusalem (or East Jerusalem) must be a capital for a Palestinian state.

Palestinian attitudes toward Jerusalem correspond very closely with the dominant political culture, and with the agendas offered by the PLO, the Palestinian National Authority, and the majority of political groups. They are also consistent with United Nations resolutions and international conventions.

And while Palestinians (including Jerusalem residents) have shown that Jerusalem is the key to real peace, a majority of them have shown willingness to give concessions on a number of issues so as to bring peace to the area. A large majority of Palestinians support negotiations on Jerusalem. They also support genuine and lasting peace as long as it is accompanied by the establishment of a Palestinian state with East Jerusalem as its capital and a solution to the refugee issue. A majority of Palestinians accept dividing the city into two sovereign areas: East Jerusalem (a capital for a Palestinian state) and West Jerusalem (a capital of Israel).

Finally, the data show that while Palestinians are supportive of negotiations and willing to consider a compromise over Jerusalem (i.e., accept a Palestinian state with Jerusalem as its capital), it is not clear if they are ready for the normalization of the current situation. It is true that they are willing to accept political solutions, but they are not ready to accept the social, cultural, and psychological implications of these solutions. Resolving the political aspects of the Arab-Israeli conflict (as difficult as it is) will prove to be more attainable than resolving the ideological, cultural, and psychological aspects of this conflict.

Central Findings and Conclusions*

1. Jerusalem is of enormous importance to Palestinians. Ninety-two percent say that it is "very important" to them personally, and 94% would not support "recognizing Israel's claim that it alone is sovereign over Jerusalem, even if that was the only way a Palestinian State could come into being."

2. Seventy-two percent agree that "in the case of an unacceptable agreement on Jerusalem, Palestinians have the right to use all means necessary to block its implementation."

3. Thus, it is extremely unlikely that real peace can be achieved if there is not a compromise on Jerusalem acceptable to both sides.

4. Most Palestinians support real peace, under certain conditions. Seventy percent of Palestinians "support genuine and lasting peace with Israel in exchange for recognition of a Palestinian state with its capital in East Jerusalem, and resolution of the refugee issue, even though this will inevitably fall short of full justice for the Palestinians." Within Gaza this is supported by 68% of the population.

5. Forty-eight percent of those who identify politically with the Islamic bloc also support genuine peace under the stated conditions.

6. Sixty percent of those Palestinians who identify themselves as "very religious" are also willing to support "genuine and lasting peace" with Israel on the above conditions.

7. Palestinians, like Israeli Jews, make major distinctions between the areas of the city that are very important to them "as part of Jerusalem" and those that are not.

---

* Drawn from both Segal's and Saʿid's chapters.

8. While 94% of Palestinians consider the Haram al-Sharif as "very important" to them "as part of Jerusalem," only 34% so consider the Western Wall.

9. A majority of Palestinians consider areas of Jewish residence as "not so important" or "not important at all" as "part of Jerusalem."

10. Few Palestinians (20%) believe that Jews have "any sort of legitimate rights with regard to Jerusalem." Those that acknowledge some Jewish rights in regard to Jerusalem are in some respects significantly more willing to accept compromise proposals that those that do not.

11. Even among those Palestinians that both support genuine peace and acknowledge some Jewish rights in regard to Jerusalem, only 24% would "seriously consider" a proposal in which Israel would have sovereignty over East Jerusalem, but Palestinian neighborhoods would be given a special self-rule status.

12. Palestinians who live in Jerusalem are also overwhelmingly opposed to Israeli sovereignty over East Jerusalem.

13. Palestinians are open to a variety of proposals with respect to the future status of the city. These include the following:

   • West Jerusalem would be under Israeli sovereignty and East Jerusalem under Palestinian sovereignty, with special arrangement for Israeli control of the Jewish neighborhoods in East Jerusalem (Old City dealt with separately).

   • The Palestinians would get sovereignty over the Haram al-Sharif in exchange for Palestinian recognition of Israeli sovereignty over the Western Wall.

   • Palestinians would have sovereignty over the al-Aqsa mosque and the Dome of the Rock, but with respect to the plateau itself, sovereignty would be shared with the Israelis, although day-to-day administration of the plateau would be in Palestinian hands alone.

   • Israel and Palestine would exercise joint sovereignty over an undivided city.

   • In the Old City, there would be Israeli sovereignty over the Jewish neighborhoods, and Palestinian sovereignty over the Palestinian neighborhoods.

14. Palestinians show strong opposition to Israeli sovereignty over the Jewish neighborhoods of East Jerusalem.

15. Overwhelmingly, Palestinians reject the idea that Jordan would play a substantial role in the administration of Islamic holy sites in Jerusalem.

PART IV

Is Jerusalem Negotiable?

JEROME M. SEGAL

Introduction

Successful negotiation of the Jerusalem question can be thought of as requiring the satisfaction of three necessary conditions, none of which is sufficient in itself:

- That both the Israeli and Palestinian governing leaderships seek to achieve a compromise settlement.
- That within each national community, there is general public support for those compromises that are acceptable to the leadership.
- That there be at least one set of compromises that is acceptable to both sides and that will not thoroughly violate the most deeply held values of a substantial minority within either community.*

Although the two research studies focus on the attitudes of the Palestinian and Israeli Jewish publics, it is important to briefly address the issue of political leadership. It seems clear from both studies that any Israeli or Palestinian leadership that does not seek a compromise solution on the Jerusalem issue will not be pushed into such compromises by their respective public. Israelis in general are skeptical about the wisdom of compromising on Jerusalem, and Palestinians are broadly reluctant to make substantial concessions. Issues such as Jerusalem as the Palestinian capital or the status of the Temple Mount engage such strong commitments on both sides that it would not be hard for a political leadership on either side to approach these issues in ways that would deadlock and doom any negotiation process. It is, however, important to see why both Israeli and Palestinian

---

* How large a minority has to be in order to possess an effective veto depends on many factors, including the determination of political leaders and the costs they are willing to bear.

leaders *should* want a full resolution of the Jerusalem question, even if this might involve painful compromises.

The Palestinian Interests in Full Resolution

For Palestinians there are two obvious reasons. First, they have much to gain. At present, Israel controls all of Jerusalem. As a result of a settlement, Palestinians would likely gain some sovereign rights in Jerusalem as well as administrative control within at least some of the areas where an agreement on sovereignty is not reached.

Second, unless the Jerusalem question is in some form resolved or put to rest it is hard to see how peace between Israel and the Palestinians can be attained, or if attained, remain stable. Thus the Palestinian interests in ending the conflict and in an environment that allows them to get on with the social and economic development project of a new state, also motivate resolution of the Jerusalem question.

Third, and perhaps less obviously, Palestinians will gain on other issues if the Jerusalem question is resolved. On first glance, the relationship may seem the opposite—were Palestinians to not press the Jerusalem issue, Israel would be more willing to accommodate Palestinians on other matters. But there is another dynamic at work as well. It is highly likely that, as the quid pro quo for various compromises on other issues, Israel will seek Palestinian agreement that the final accord is indeed final, that Palestinians agree, for now and forever, that no further claims for territory or compensation will be placed on Israel. If Israel insists on Palestinian agreement that the conflict has been "resolved in full," then, absent an accord on Jerusalem, Israel would be requiring of the Palestinians something that no Palestinian leadership would or could agree to. Thus, unless there is full resolution of the Jerusalem issue it is quite possible that other issues will not be subject to successful negotiation.

Israeli Options and the Desirability of Full Resolution

It is likely that Israel will seek Palestinian agreement on putting off (either indefinitely or for a specified period) the question of sovereignty over Jerusalem and instead seek agreement on an administrative framework that would delegate powers and identify limitations on unilateral actions. This approach would seek to neutralize Jerusalem by reconfiguring it as an unresolved international dispute between the two states, but one with respect to which they have reached some sort of modus vivendi.

As part of this approach Israel might agree to steps that would satisfy some Palestinian needs and increase stability. Thus, Israel could formally announce that the "mosque compound" on the Temple Mount is outside Israeli sovereignty.

(This was the position taken in the Yossi Beilin–Abu Mazen formulations of 1996.) It might agree to a "free passage" corridor between the Temple Mount and the West Bank. And Israel could announce a policy of restraint with respect to land confiscations and construction in and around Jerusalem. Such an approach gives the Palestinians something on issues that are particularly explosive. In exchange for such concrete steps, the Palestinian leadership might agree to put off the issue of sovereignty and deal with Jerusalem through an administrative agreement for the time being.

As tempting as this approach may be, it involves serious problems, and is not Israel's best option. One problem with an interim partial or administrative approach is that it involves negotiations that, in some respects, may be as much or even more arduous than negotiating full resolution. Indeed, it may simply not be possible to conclude an administrative agreement on Jerusalem that would be satisfactory to both Israelis and Palestinians. Such an agreement in Israeli eyes would have to avoid compromising their sovereignty, and in Palestinian eyes avoid compromising their claim to sovereignty. Issues such as construction, applicability of law, rights of entrance and exit, and so forth would have to be resolved administratively.

Assuming that such an agreement could be concluded, it would allow for a Palestinian state to come into existence without Jerusalem being resolved, and without any disclaimer on further claims. This would buy some time and allow events to move forward. However, the breathing space it will allow is likely to be short-lived.

It is inevitable that such an agreement would lend itself to multiple interpretations and possess areas of indeterminacy. While Israel and Palestine may agree on specific actions they will refrain from, they are likely to be constantly drawn into at least symbolic struggle over who has sovereignty, and there will remain a high likelihood of destabilizing incidents.

Internationally, with an existing Palestinian state, other countries will have to decide whether they recognize Jerusalem as Israel's capital, as Palestine's, or as the capital of both. And the Palestinian leadership will be under strong internal pressure to demonstrate that they have not in fact forsaken Jerusalem, that they have not acquiesced to an Israeli status quo. On the Israeli side, there will be constant charges that the government is "de facto" acquiescing in the redivision of the city.

For Palestinians there will be a question of where their capital is, even for an interim period. The current study showed very strong Palestinian opposition to accepting, even on an interim basis, an area outside Jerusalem, such as Abu Dis, as the capital. Also, there is the issue of the status of the 190,000 Palestinians who live in Jerusalem. It is doubtful that any Palestinian state would agree that it could not extend citizenship to these Palestinian residents of Jerusalem. Both of these issues will not sit still for long. Over time, it is likely that any interim agreement will break down, or that any isolated and subsequent negotiations on Jerusalem between the two states will deadlock.

The danger for both Israelis and Palestinians is that there will be a subsequent revitalization of the conflict, with Jerusalem rather than the West Bank/ Gaza as the essence of the struggle. In crystallizing the Jerusalem issue in this way, the situation can get even worse. Thus, when Jerusalem and only Jerusalem is the issue, it is quite possible that this will move Islamic states into a more confrontational mode, and serve to encourage the challenge of fundamentalists.

Within Israel, the isolation of the Jerusalem issue will offer new likelihood that Israel may move toward the right. Since any Israeli government will be in danger of being discredited if it seems willing to divide Jerusalem, the government will be under pressure to take positions, as well as unilateral steps, which make successful resolution of the issue impossible. Thus, an indefinite string of Har Homas might result.

Third, seeking an administrative solution not only runs the risks of both deadlock and worsened conflict down the line, it does so *without providing Israel with the benefits of a full solution*. The advantages to Israel of full resolution of the Jerusalem issue are very substantial. Full resolution will allow international recognition of Israeli sovereignty in Jerusalem and of Jerusalem as Israel's capital. It will open the door to a full resolution of the conflict, to a peace agreement in which "for now and forever" all further claims are relinquished. It will maximize the extent to which normalization with the Arab and Islamic world is possible, and may make possible at least a partial Islamic acceptance of "some legitimate Jewish rights in regard to Jerusalem." Finally, by making it possible for Palestinians to genuinely think of the conflict as having been fully resolved, it will allow them to move on, thus stabilizing and deepening the peace.

Such outcomes are of vast historic import and the opportunity to achieve them may not always be present. The key question, then, is not the desirability of a comprehensive and permanent Jerusalem accord, but rather the possibility of attaining it. Ultimately, Israel and the Palestinians may have to settle for a second best approach. However, this should not be lightly conceded. Second best, in this case, is significantly worse than a full settlement. Thus, the overriding importance of the issue under consideration in this section, "To what extent, if any, do the values, beliefs, and attitudes of Israelis and Palestinians make it impossible to fully negotiate resolution of the Jerusalem issue?"

Three Contexts for Negotiability

To gauge the extent to which, from the point of view of the two publics, the Jerusalem question is potentially negotiable, it is necessary to bring together an understanding of Palestinian perspectives with a similar understanding of Israeli perspectives. In our study of Israeli-Jews, it was found that:

- Israeli Jews generally are opposed to negotiations over Jerusalem (79%).
- Israeli Jews make major distinctions between those parts of the city that are "important to them as Jerusalem" and those parts of the city that are not.
- With respect to the parts of the city that are of lesser "importance as Jerusalem," there is a significant willingness to seriously consider transferring those areas to Palestinian sovereignty.
- Most Israeli Jews (66%) do not believe that a peace treaty with the Palestinians will lead to true and lasting peace.
- For those Israeli Jews who do believe that a peace treaty will lead to lasting peace, there is a substantially greater willingness to compromise over Jerusalem.
- Among those that do not believe that there can be true peace between Israel and the Arab world in the foreseeable future, a significant percentage are open to being convinced by events that true peace is possible.

Thus, the study of the Israeli Jewish public revealed an internal logic that is operative in determining the degree to which Israeli Jews are prepared to negotiate different aspects of the Jerusalem question. Most Israeli Jews do not believe that Palestinians have legitimate rights to Jerusalem. Thus, if they are to be motivated to compromise on Jerusalem, they will need to anticipate some substantial benefit from doing so. Achieving lasting peace with the Arab world would certainly qualify, but most Israelis don't believe that this is likely. Moreover, they fear that making any concessions on Jerusalem will only result in demands for further concessions. Thus, there is substantial resistance to compromise, except for those that do believe that peace with the Arab world is possible. And even for this group, there are some aspects of Jerusalem that are simply not up for negotiation.

The potential negotiability of the Jerusalem issue can be considered within several contexts that are successively more supportive of a negotiated outcome. The first we might label "the standard context," by which is meant that the underlying factors which determine Israeli and Palestinian willingness to compromise are roughly as they were at the time of the two studies. On the Israeli side, this means a situation in which only a minority (39%) believe that Palestinians have "any sort of legitimate rights in regard to Jerusalem," and in which a clear majority of Israeli Jews doubt that a peace treaty with the Palestinians will mean genuine and lasting peace. For Palestinians, this means only a small segment (20%) of the Palestinian public believes Jews have "any sort of legitimate rights in regard to Jerusalem," and a distinct majority (70%) support genuine and lasting peace with Israel in exchange for a Palestinian state with East Jerusalem as its capital and resolution of the refugee issue.

A second, more promising context is one of "enhanced Israeli confidence." This might be defined roughly as a situation in which the one-third of Israeli Jews who believe in the efficacy of a peace treaty to yield true peace has grown to two-thirds.

A third context, one in which both sides are most open to compromise, is one in which enhanced Israeli confidence is combined with enhanced Palestinian acceptance of some Jewish rights in regard to Jerusalem, say doubling from 20% of the population to 40% of the population, and Israeli Jewish acceptance of some Palestinian rights in regard to Jerusalem has expanded 50%, from 39% to 60%.

In a later section, consideration will be given to whether these second and third contexts are realistic and how they might be attained. For now, let us consider how the degree of negotiability of the Jerusalem question changes as the context shifts. Throughout it should be remembered that there is no magic in the numbers. The issue is not whether a numerical majority in this or that study supports a given proposal. This is so for several reasons. First, public support for specific proposals within a research inquiry is likely to be less than it would be if the proposal receives the support of the governing leadership. Second, proposals are likely to receive more support if they are part of a package that represents the outcome of a negotiations process.

More fundamentally, even majority public support in both communities may not be sufficient to ensure the negotiability of the proposal in question. If the opposition of a significant minority promises to be intense and enduring, this may deter policymakers from giving it serious consideration. Indeed, in a situation in which a shift of a small percentage of the electorate may change the outcome of an election, or the shift of a few members in Parliament may force new elections, intensely held minority positions get taken very seriously.

Resolving the Jerusalem question will, in the end, require strong, effective, and motivated leadership on both sides. Perhaps it is best to view public opinion as a constraint that limits even what such leaders can bring about. This inquiry into negotiability is then an inquiry into the extent, nature, and dynamics of that constraint.

The Standard Context:
Most Israeli Jews Doubt That a Peace Treaty Will Yield Genuine Peace

The two studies found that for both peoples certain parts of the city are of enormous importance "as part of Jerusalem" and other parts less so. The difficulty of negotiating the final status of any particular area bears a strong relationship to the extent to which that area is of great importance "as Jerusalem" for both sides. A good deal of the underlying potential for resolving the Jerusalem issue emerges from the fact that not all areas are of equal importance to both sides. These differences are captured in Diagram 4.1:

Diagram 4.1
**Relative importance to both Israeli-Jews and Palestinians of different parts of
Jerusalem (percentage answering "very important" as Jerusalem)**

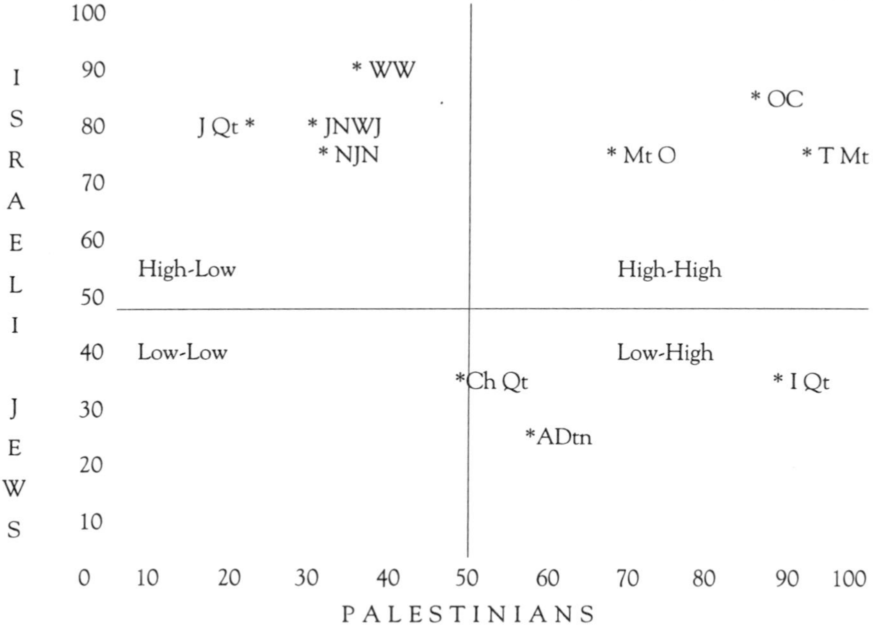

```
        100

    I    90              * WW
    S                                                      * OC
    R    80       J Qt *   * JNWJ
    A    70                * NJN              * Mt O        * T Mt

    E    60
    L            High-Low                    High-High
         50
    I ────────────────────────────────┼─────────────────────────
         40    Low-Low                      Low-High
                                    *Ch Qt                  * I Qt
    J    30
    E                                     *ADtn
         20
    W
    S    10

          0   10   20   30   40   50   60   70   80   90   100
                            PALESTINIANS
```

Key: Western Wall (WW); Old City (OC); Mount of Olives (Mt O); Jewish neighborhoods in West Jerusalem (JNWJ); new Jewish neighborhoods in East Jerusalem (NJN);
Jewish quarter in the Old City (J Qt); Islamic quarter in the Old City (I Qt); Christian
quarter of the Old City (C Qt); Arab downtown neighborhoods in East Jerusalem (ADtn).

The diagram allows us to see the relative importance of the different areas "as
Jerusalem" to the two peoples. It shows that what is important to the Palestinians
"as Jerusalem" is not always the same as what is important to Israeli Jews "as Jerusalem." The struggle over Jerusalem is most essentially a struggle over the areas in
the quadrant labeled "High-High," namely, the Old City as a whole, the Temple
Mount, and the Mount of Olives. Jewish neighborhoods in West Jerusalem, in East
Jerusalem, or the Old City are far less hotly contested. Nor is this most centrally a
struggle over Palestinian areas, whether it be Arab downtown neighborhoods or the
Christian or Islamic quarters of the Old City. Nor is it most essentially about the
outlying Arab village areas within the boundaries. (These are not shown in Diagram
4.1, but were of the least importance "as Jerusalem" to Israeli Jews.)

It should not be thought that this implies that achieving successful negotiations over these areas of lesser contention will be easy, or even possible. Rather,

Table 4.1
Ranking of the extent to which specific parts of the city are contested

	Percentage saying "very important as part of Jerusalem"	
	Israelis	Palestinians
Outlying areas of Palestinian residence (e.g. Um Tuba)	22	*
Arab downtown areas (e.g., Wadi Jos, Sheikh Jarah)	24	59
Jewish quarter of Old City	79	24
Jewish neighborhoods of West Jerusalem	81	26
New Jewish neighborhoods of East Jerusalem	76	29
Christian quarter of Old City	33	47
Islamic quarter of Old City	33	85
al-Aqsa mosque and Dome of the Rock	**	95
Western Wall	91	34
Mount of Olives	77	66
Temple Mount (Haram al-Sharif)	76	94
Old City (taken as a whole)	85	86

* Inadvertently, the study did not directly ask Palestinians how important to them "as Jerusalem" these areas were.
** The study of Israeli Jewish attitudes did not ask about the importance of the mosques (as opposed to the Temple Mount/Haram al-Sharif). The mosques themselves hold no religious significance for Jews and are widely referred to in the uncontested idiom of "Islamic holy places." The mosques are ranked here because of how Israeli Jews ranked the Islamic quarter as a whole. It is also worth noting in this context that the Yossi Beilin–Abu Mazen framework stated that the "mosque compound" would not be under Israeli sovereignty. That Beilin would agree to this supports the appropriateness of this ranking, but this should be confirmed in further research.

what is suggested is only that the relative degree of conflict in these areas is considerably less than over the central areas of contention.

Table 4.1 ranks the parts of the city with respect to the extent to which they are contested, using as a measure of "the degree of contestation" the lower of either the percentage of Israelis or the percentage of Palestinians identifying that area as "very important as part of Jerusalem."

Scanning Table 4.1, it can be seen that for the first nine areas considered (the outlying Palestinian village areas through the Western Wall) there is continuity. For each of these areas, *for at least one of the peoples*, a majority does not see the area in question as "very important as part of Jerusalem." However, with the Mount of Olives and the Temple Mount there is a quantum leap upward.

Here, for both peoples, the area is perceived as the essence of Jerusalem. And, of course, with respect to the Old City as a whole, this is also true. For each side, the Old City contains much of what is essential, although, to a very important degree, they differ on what this essence is.

As was stated above, it would be a mistake to assume that just because an area is not among the most intensely disputed parts of Jerusalem that a compromise solution acceptable to both sides can be found. In some instances this may be so; in other instances not. In this section I will offer an assessment, within the standard context, of what kinds of solutions appear to be consistent with what we have learned about how the two peoples view Jerusalem.

1. East Jerusalem, with the Exception of the Old City, the Mount of Olives, Mount Scopus, and the Jewish Neighborhoods

The study of Israeli Jews revealed that:

- No more than a fourth of Israeli Jews view the Arab neighborhoods as "very important as Jerusalem," although 40% to 45% view them as "important" or "very important as part of Jerusalem."
- Forty-five percent of Israeli Jews would seriously consider transferring the outlying village areas (e.g., Um Tuba, Zur Baher) to Palestinian sovereignty.
- Thirty-four percent would seriously consider transferring to Palestinian sovereignty the Arab neighborhoods of East Jerusalem outside the Old City.
- Forty-two percent said that they "would cede the Arab neighborhoods of East Jerusalem to the Palestinians" if the Old City, the Mount of Olives, all of the Jewish neighborhoods of East Jerusalem, and Mount Scopus "remain in Jerusalem."

The general picture that emerges on the Israeli side is that, within the standard context, Israel could agree to transfer the outlying village areas to Palestinian sovereignty. Arab downtown and peripheral areas are more problematic. Only one-third of Israeli Jews would take seriously a proposal for Palestinian sovereignty over these areas, and the 42% that said they would cede these areas did so within the context of a proposal in which virtually all of what was most important to Israel, including the Old City, would remain in Israeli hands. It is unrealistic to think that Palestinians would agree to this.

Viewed from the Palestinian side these more central areas of the city are quite important "as Jerusalem." Fifty-nine percent viewed Arab downtown and peripheral areas as "very important as part of Jerusalem" and another 33% viewed them as "important as part of Jerusalem." Further, when asked about a general proposal that would deny Palestinians any sovereignty in East Jerusalem, but would accord them "a special self-rule status," only 20% were prepared to take the proposal seriously.

Thus, it appears clear that, from a Palestinian point of view, there can be no resolution of the Jerusalem question without Palestinian sovereignty over these areas of Palestinian residence and commerce outside the Old City. Within the standard context this appears to be most possible for the outlying areas. It should be noted though that, even with respect to these parts of the city, over 20% of Israeli Jews would be yielding areas they view as "very important as part of Jerusalem." As for the more central areas (outside the Old City) it is unlikely that Israel would agree to Palestinian sovereignty within the standard context.

2. Jewish Neighborhoods in East Jerusalem, Outside the Old City

Israeli Jews view these areas as essential parts of Jerusalem:

- Seventy-six percent of Israeli Jews view them as "very important as Jerusalem" and another 19% view them as "important."
- When asked, "In your opinion are the new Jewish neighborhoods that were established since 1967 as much a part of Jerusalem as the older neighborhoods?", 94% of Israeli Jews said "yes" (35%) or "definitely yes" (59%).
- Only 19% of Israeli Jews would take seriously a proposal to "Give East Jerusalem to Palestinian sovereignty with the Jewish neighborhoods in East Jerusalem having a 'special status' under Israeli control."

Thus, what emerges is a clear picture that for Israeli Jews anything other than Israeli sovereignty over this part of East Jerusalem is a nonstarter.

On the Palestinian side the matter is less clear-cut. On the one hand, only 29% of Palestinians view these areas as "very important" as Jerusalem. This would suggest that Palestinians would at least take seriously a proposal that (leaving the Old City aside) would give them sovereignty over all of East Jerusalem except these Jewish neighborhoods in exchange for the Jewish neighborhoods falling under Israeli sovereignty. Yet this was not what we found.

Two questions were posed:

	Seriously consider	Reject/not seriously consider
61. West Jerusalem would be under Israeli sovereignty and East Jerusalem would be under Palestinian sovereignty, with a special arrangement for Israeli control of the Jewish neighborhoods in East Jerusalem. The Old City would be dealt with separately.	52	32

66. West Jerusalem and the Jewish neighborhoods in Eastern Jerusalem would be under Israeli sovereignty and the rest of East Jerusalem under Palestinian sovereignty, with the Old City dealt with separately.	28	57

The two proposals are identical except for the treatment of the Jewish neighborhoods. In the first they fall under Palestinian sovereignty but Israeli control. In the second they fall under Israeli sovereignty. The difference appears significant. Those willing to seriously consider the proposal fell from a majority of Palestinians to a clear minority, with those dismissing the proposal twice as numerous as those willing to take it seriously.

While Israeli sovereignty over these neighborhoods in East Jerusalem does not appear to cross a Palestinian red line, within the standard context, an agreement that provided for Israeli sovereignty over these neighborhoods would (all other things being equal) be opposed by most Palestinians. Nonetheless, in a real-world context, as part of an overall agreement that is supported by the Palestinian leadership and which counterbalances Palestinian concessions here with Israeli concessions elsewhere, it might be that general Palestinian acceptance could be attained.

3. The Old City: Jewish and Palestinian Neighborhoods

Taken as a whole, the Old City is at the core of what both Israeli Jews and Palestinians experience "as Jerusalem." Eighty-five percent of Israeli Jews find the Old City "very important as part of Jerusalem" and another 12% find it "important as part of Jerusalem"—leaving only 3% who do not. For Palestinians the numbers are virtually identical. Eighty-six percent find the Old City "very important as part of Jerusalem" and an additional 12% find it "important as part of Jerusalem."

Given that the Old City encompasses the four residential quarters as well as the Western Wall, the Temple Mount, the Dome of the Rock, and the al-Aqsa mosque, it is not surprising that it should be central to both Jewish and Palestinian experiences of Jerusalem.

What is striking, however, is the extent to which the degree of centrality "as Jerusalem" differs when the Old City is disaggregated into its component parts.

For Israeli Jews, the Jewish quarter is viewed as "very important as part of Jerusalem" by 79% of the population, with an additional 15% viewing it as "important as part of Jerusalem." On the other hand, the non-Jewish quarters were viewed as "very important as part of Jerusalem" by only 33% of Israeli Jews, with another 26% saying they were "important as part of Jerusalem."

For Palestinians, there is an analogous pattern. The Islamic quarter is viewed as "very important as part of Jerusalem" by 85% of the population, with an additional 13% viewing it as "important as part of Jerusalem." The Christian quarter is seen as "very important as part of Jerusalem" by 47% and "important as part of

Jerusalem" by an additional 33%. But the Jewish quarter is seen as very important as Jerusalem by only 24% of the Palestinian population, with an additional 17% seeing it as important.

Among Israeli Jews, some 40% view the non-Jewish quarters as "not so important" or "not at all important" "as Jerusalem." Fifty-nine percent of Palestinians responded similarly to the Jewish quarter.

When Israeli Jews were asked about giving the Palestinians sovereignty over the Palestinian neighborhoods in the Old City, only 23% were prepared to seriously consider the idea, and 55% rejected it outright. On the Palestinian side, a proposal for the Old City in which Israel would have sovereignty over the Jewish neighborhoods and Palestine would have sovereignty over Palestinian neighborhoods would be seriously considered by 40% of the population, and dismissed by 47% (20% saying they would not take the proposal seriously, and 27% saying they would reject it totally).

Thus we find some, but limited, support for dividing the sovereignty over the residential areas with the Old City. The opposition among Israelis and Palestinians is strong, but it is much stronger among Israelis. Within the standard context, the opposition to dividing sovereignty or to joint sovereignty appears sufficient to make these proposals unrealistic.

4. The Old City: The Western Wall, the Temple Mount, the Dome of the Rock/al-Aqsa Mosque

The relative centrality of these sites for Palestinians and Israeli Jews can be seen in Table 4.2.

Table 4.2 makes clear that for both Palestinians and Israeli Jews the religious sites within the Old City are absolutely central to their understanding of Jerusalem. For 91% of Israeli Jews, the Western Wall is "very important as part of Jerusalem" (and it is "important as part of Jerusalem" for an additional 8%.) For Palestinians, the Haram al-Sharif (the Temple Mount) and the two mosques are respectively viewed as "very important as part of Jerusalem" by 94% and 95% of the population.

For Israelis it is the Western Wall that is of premier importance. Here, only 2% of the population says it is either "not so important as part of Jerusalem" or "not important at all as part of Jerusalem." Yet when it comes to the Palestinians, the Western Wall is of distinctly lesser importance. Thirty-four percent of Palestinians say it is "very important as part of Jerusalem," and another 20% say it is "important as part of Jerusalem"; 40% say it is either "not so important as part of Jerusalem" or "not important at all as part of Jerusalem."

The study of Israeli Jews did not ask about the importance to them of the Islamic mosques on the Temple Mount. However, there are several reasons for assuming that the mosques themselves are not of importance (although the place where they stand is of great importance). The mosques are viewed as both historical

Table 4.2

**Importance "as part of Jerusalem" to Palestinians and Israeli Jews
of religious sites in the Old City**

	Importance "as part of Jerusalem"			
	Very important	Important	Not so important	Not at all important
The Temple Mount (Haram al-Sharif)				
Israeli Jews	75	18	5	2
Palestinians	94	5	1	0
The Western Wall				
Israeli Jews	91	8	1	1
Palestinians	34	20	18	28
al-Aqsa mosque and the Dome of the Rock				
Israeli Jews	—	—	—	—
Palestinians	95	5	0	0

and religious Islamic holy sites. Unlike certain other sites, such as the Tomb of the Patriarchs outside Hebron, these structures are viewed as exclusively Islamic in character and significance.

It is the Temple Mount/Haram al-Sharif which is the most contested area. Here only 1% of Palestinians say it is "not so important as part of Jerusalem" and only 7% of Israeli Jews view it as either "not so important as part of Jerusalem" or "not important at all as part of Jerusalem."

This fact, that the Temple Mount/Haram al-Sharif, but not the Western Wall, is of vital importance to both peoples is reflected in the different responses that Palestinians and Israeli Jews gave to the following proposal:

Palestinian sovereignty over the Temple Mount/Haram al-Sharif in exchange for Palestinian recognition of Israeli sovereignty over the Western Wall

Palestinian response		Israeli response	
Seriously* Consider	Dismiss**	Seriously Consider	Reject Outright
50%	35%	20%	58%

* "Seriously consider" includes "very seriously consider" as well.
** The category "dismiss" for Palestinians is the sum of those saying they would not seriously consider the proposal plus those saying they reject the proposal totally. The category "reject outright" for the Israelis was the sum of those saying they would not consider the proposal at all plus those who, given their objection to any compromise, refused to consider any of the options.

For the Palestinians, the claim to sovereignty over the Western Wall is something that is subject to negotiation and can be relinquished in exchange for sovereignty over the Temple Mount. For Israelis, this exchange is largely out of the question.*

These considerations serve to underline the difficulties that lie ahead in efforts to reach a final status accord with respect to the Old City and the Temple Mount in particular.

The Mount of Olives must also be added to the list of areas of extreme difficulty. Among Israeli Jews, only 5% said it was either "not so important to them as part of Jerusalem" or "not important at all as part of Jerusalem." Among Palestinians, the identical percentage (5%) also said it was "not so important to them as part of Jerusalem" or "not at all important as part of Jerusalem." In both cases the percentage saying it was "very important as part of Jerusalem" was high (66% of Palestinians, and 77% of Israeli Jews), but this is less than was found in respect to the Temple Mount/Haram al-Sharif.

Taking this standard context as the background, the studies of Israeli and Palestinian attitudes suggest that there are limited but still important areas in which agreement may be possible. Perhaps the outlying areas of the city might be transferred to Palestinian sovereignty, and possibly it could be agreed that Israel would have sovereignty over the Western Wall in exchange for Palestinian sovereignty over the mosque compound on the Temple Mount. But there is inadequate willingness among Israelis to support most of what Palestinians seek:

- Sovereignty over Arab downtown and peripheral areas
- Sovereignty over the Arab quarters of the Old City
- Sovereignty over the Temple Mount/Haram al-Sharif and the Mount of Olives
- Joint sovereignty over the city as a whole, or perhaps the Old City

At the same time, viewing the Palestinian responses to the current study it is clear that a majority (typically an overwhelming majority) of the Palestinian public would oppose compromises that accept the Israeli demands for:

- Sovereignty over Jewish neighborhoods in East Jerusalem
- Sovereignty over Arab downtown
- Sovereignty over the Old City
- Sovereignty over the Temple Mount and the Mount of Olives

Thus, the standard context is one in which *most of the Jerusalem question lies outside the range of what can be mutually agreed upon.* Moreover, even the proposal

---

* In no way should this be seen as giving credence to the view that Israelis seek to rebuild the Jewish Temple. Only a minute fringe element of Israeli society maintains this objective.

that each side maintain its claim to sovereignty while agreeing on joint administration of the Old City draws only limited support from either Israeli Jews or Palestinians.

Context Two: Enhanced Israeli Confidence in the Efficacy of a Peace Treaty

The shift to a hypothetical context of enhanced confidence (in which two-thirds, rather than one-third, of Israeli Jews believe in the efficacy of a peace treaty to yield long-term peace) would produce changes in Israeli support for compromise proposals. How great might this increased willingness to compromise be? No doubt it overstates the magnitude of this change to assume that the willingness to compromise of the newly added third would be the same as that of the third that already believes in the efficacy of a peace treaty. Nonetheless it is instructive to note how radically the willingness to compromise differs between those that believe in the efficacy of a peace treaty and those that do not. This can be seen in Table 4.3.

Table 4.3 indicates that among those that believe in the efficacy of a peace treaty, a majority would seriously consider Palestinian sovereignty over Arab areas outside the Old City, as well as joint administration of the Old City (without Israel giving up its claim to sovereignty). In addition, there is a plurality that would seriously consider Palestinian sovereignty over the Arab areas of the Old City. However, even for this most dovish third of Israeli Jews, only a minority would seriously consider Palestinian sovereignty over the Temple Mount or Palestinian sovereignty (with Israeli control) over the Jewish neighborhoods of East Jerusalem outside the Old City.

What this suggests is that if it were possible to move from the standard context to one of enhanced Israeli confidence in genuine peace, then, potentially, compromises could be found that would include Palestinian sovereignty over Arab downtown areas. With respect to the Old City (excluding the Temple Mount question), some formula for either joint administration or divided or joint sovereignty might also be found, with the Israelis more likely to support joint administration and the Palestinians more likely to support shared sovereignty or each side having sovereignty over the neighborhoods it populates.

As for the Jewish neighborhoods of East Jerusalem, it seems clear that even in a context most supportive of compromise, Israelis will not agree to anything less than sovereign control. And similarly, even with enhanced Israeli trust, there is no serious disposition to yield the Temple Mount to Palestinian sovereignty.

Third Context: Enhanced Israeli Confidence and Enhanced Palestinian and Israeli Recognition of Each Other's Rights in Regard to Jerusalem

Consider, then, a third context in which there is not only enhanced Israeli trust of the second context but enhanced mutual recognition of the rights of the other. Consider first the Palestinians.

Table 4.3
Israeli Jews: in relation to beliefs about whether a peace agreement with the Palestinians will lead to true long-term peace, the percentage who seriously consider (line one) and who flatly reject (line two) each proposal

		Will a peace agreement lead to peace?		
		Believe it will	Don't believe it will	National average
Group I				
Palestinian sovereignty over Arab villages in East Jerusalem (e.g., Shuafat, Um Tuba, Zur Baher)	Seriously Consider	67	35	45
	Flatly Reject	16	46	36
Group II				
Autonomy for Arab areas in East Jerusalem	Seriously Consider	50	28	35
	Flatly Reject	28	51	44
Arab areas in East Jerusalem outside Old City to Palestinian sovereignty.	Seriously Consider	53	24	34
	Flatly Reject	24	54	44
Joint administration of Old City without yielding on sovereignty.	Seriously Consider	50	26	34
	Flatly Reject	26	49	41
Temple Mount under Wakf as now	Seriously Consider	48	23	31
	Flatly Reject	30	56	48
Group III				
Palestinian sovereignty over Arab neighborhoods in Old City	Seriously Consider	41	13	23
	Flatly Reject	35	65	55
Palestinian sovereignty over Temple Mount, Israeli over Western Wall	Seriously Consider	37	13	20
	Flatly Reject	42	67	58
East Jerusalem under Palestinian sovereignty with Jewish neighborhoods of East Jerusalem given a special status under Israeli control	Seriously Consider	33	12	19
	Flatly Reject	43	71	62
Old City internationalized under United Nations	Seriously Consider	30	12	18
	Flatly Reject	47	72	64

Table 4.4
Alternative Palestinian positions on peace and Jewish rights—percentage willing to consider specific proposals "seriously" or "very seriously" ("SC") and (second line) percentage that would "not seriously consider" or "reject totally" (R)

		Three types of response*			
Support genuine peace with Israel		*Yes*	*Yes*	*No*	
Do Jews have some legitimate rights in regard to Jerusalem?		*Yes*	*No*	*No*	*Total population*
Compromise Proposal					
61. West Jerusalem under Israeli sovereigntyand East Jerusalem under Palestinian sovereignty, with special arrangement for Israeli control of the Jewish neighborhoods in East Jerusalem.	SC	78	56	32	52
Old City dealt with separately.	R	14	27	50	32
64. The Palestinians would get sovereignty over Haram al-Sharif in exchange for Palestinian recognition of Israeli	SC	65	50	39	50
sovereignty over the Western Wall.	R	17	34	49	35
60. Israel and Palestine together exercise	SC	60	39	27	40
joint sovereignty over an undivided city.	R	25	44	63	45
62. In the Old City, Israel sovereignty over the Jewish neighborhoods, and Palestine sovereignty over the Palestinian	SC	50	42	29	40
neighborhoods.	R	31	47	59	47
66. West Jerusalem and the Jewish neighborhoods in East Jerusalem under Israeli sovereignty, and the rest of East Jerusalemunder Palestinian sovereignty;	SC	35	31	19	28
Old City dealt with separately.	R	47	54	71	57
65. Israel would exercise sovereignty over East Jerusalem, but Palestinian neighborhoods would be given a special	SC	24	21	15	20
self-rule status.	R	65	70	78	71
63. Jews would be allowed to pray on Haram al-Sharif, which would be under	SC	23	16	17	17
operational authority of the Wakf.	R	68	77	79	76
Percentage of the total population		16	54	25	

*Those saying no to peace but yes to rights were too small a group to be included in this breakdown

It was seen earlier that there are major differences between Palestinians who are prepared to live in genuine peace with Israel and those that are not, and similarly major differences between those Palestinians who believe that Jews have "some sort of legitimate rights in regard to Jerusalem" and those that do not.

Table 4.4 focuses on the three groups of Palestinians that make up 95% of the population:

- The 16% that both support genuine peace and acknowledge some Jewish rights in regard to Jerusalem.
- The 54% that support genuine peace but do not acknowledge any Jewish rights in regard to Jerusalem.
- The 25% that neither supports genuine peace nor acknowledges Jewish rights in regard to Jerusalem.

From Table 4.4 we can develop a measure of the relative willingness to compromise that we find among Palestinians in the general public and among the three subgroups. This is presented in Table 4.5.

Table 4.5
Relative willingness of Palestinians to accept compromise proposals

Compromise proposal	Ratio (expressed as a decimal) of those that would seriously consider each proposal to those that dismiss the proposal, according to support for genuine peace and acknowledgment of some Jewish rights in regard to Jerusalem:			
	Peace and Jewish rights	Peace and no rights	No peace No rights	General public
61. West Jerusalem under Israeli sovereignty and East Jerusalem under Palestinian sovereignty, with special arrangement for Israeli control of the Jewish neighborhoods in East Jerusalem. Old City dealt with separately.	5.571	2.074	.640	1.625
64. The Palestinians would get sovereignty over the Haram al-Sharif in exchange for Palestinian recognition of Israeli sovereignty over the Western Wall.	3.823	1.470	.795	1.428
60. Israel and Palestine together exercise joint sovereignty over an undivided city.	2.400	.886	.425	.888
62. In the Old City, Israel sovereignty over the Jewish neighborhoods, and Palestine sovereignty over Palestinian neighborhoods.	1.612	.893	.491	.851
66. West Jerusalem and the Jewish neighborhoods in East Jerusalem under Israeli sovereignty, and the rest of East Jerusalem under Palestinian sovereignty; Old City dealt with separately.	.744	.574	.267	.491
65. Israel would exercise sovereignty over East Jerusalem, but Palestinian neighborhoods would be given a special self-rule status.	.369	.300	.192	.281
63. Jews would be allowed to pray on the Haram al-Sharif which would be under operational authority of the Wakf.	.338	.207	.215	.223

Diagram 4.2

Willingness of Palestinian Subgroups to accept compromise proposals

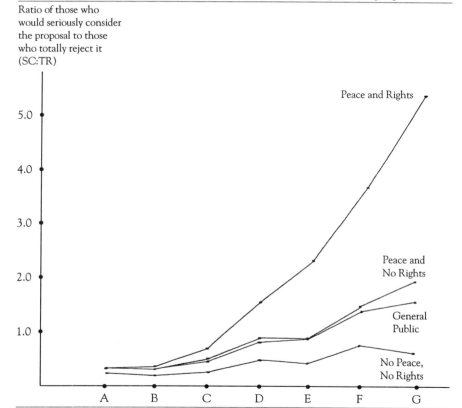

Ratio of those who
would seriously consider
the proposal to those
who totally reject it
(SC:TR)

Proposals:
A. Jews would be allowed to pray on the Haram al-Sharif, which would be under operational authority of the Wakf.
B. Israel would exercise sovereignty over East Jerusalem, but Palestinian neighborhoods
would be given a special self-rule status.
C. West Jerusalem and the Jewish neighborhoods in East Jerusalem under Israeli sover-
eignty, and the rest of East Jerusalem under Palestinian sovereignty; Old City dealt with
separately.
D. In the Old City, Israeli sovereignty over the Jewish neighborhoods, and Palestine
sovereignty over Palestinian neighborhoods.
E. Israel and Palestine together exercise joint sovereignty over an undivided city.
F. The Palestinians would get sovereignty over the Haram al-Sharif in exchange for Pale-
stinian recognition of Israeli sovereignty over the Western Wall.
G. West Jerusalem under Israeli sovereignty and East Jerusalem under Palestinian sover-
eignty, with special arrangement for Israeli control of the Jewish neighborhoods in East
Jerusalem. Old City dealt with separately.

Diagram 4.2 shows how the acceptability of these compromise proposals to these sub-groups varies with the acceptability of the proposal to the general public:

In Diagram 4.2 we immediately see the greater willingness to compromise of those who both support genuine peace with Israel and recognize some Jewish rights in relation to Jerusalem. The diagram also illustrates how great the difference remains between those who support genuine peace and those who do not among those that do not acknowledge Jewish rights.

Among those who support genuine peace but do not acknowledge any Jewish rights in regard to Jerusalem, the difference with the general public is very small. One reason for this is simply that since 70% of the general population supports genuine peace with Israel, the effect of this factor is already largely reflected in the attitudes of the general public. The implication of this is that *there is not much upward potential for increased general willingness to compromise to be obtained by seeking increases in the percentage of Palestinians willing to live in genuine peace with Israel.* On the other hand, one could hypothetically entertain the idea of a doubling of the percentage of Palestinians who believe Jews have some rights in regard to Jerusalem, (from the present 20% to 40%), and this is how the third context has been defined with respect to change on the Palestinian side.

How much of a difference would this make? The diagram illustrates the high degree of acceptability of certain proposals among those that both support peace and acknowledge that Jews have "some sort of rights with regard to Jerusalem." Doubling the percentage of Palestinians in this group would enhance the likelihood of Palestinian agreement to Israeli sovereignty over the Western Wall, Israeli sovereignty over Jewish neighborhoods inside the Old City, and joint sovereignty over the entire city, including the Old City. On the other hand, as Diagram 4.2 shows, those Palestinians who recognize Jewish rights do not have a generally enhanced willingness to compromise which uniformly affects every proposal. With respect to proposals that are generally unacceptable to the Palestinian public, the degree of acceptability to this 16% that recognizes Jewish rights comes closer to that of the public as a whole. Moreover, in absolute terms, the widely unacceptable proposals are also unacceptable to this group. For instance, while there is some greater willingness (of those who support genuine peace and acknowledge Jewish rights) to accept Israeli sovereignty over Jewish neighborhoods of East Jerusalem outside the Old City (Q. 66), even within this group this is a minority position. And given the centrality of the Temple Mount/Haram al-Sharif, there is no reason to believe that there would be any appreciable reduction in opposition to Israeli sovereignty over the Temple Mount. Further, those who recognize Jewish rights and support genuine peace are not appreciably different from the general population when it comes to the high importance given to East Jerusalem as the capital of the Palestinian state.

Let us now consider the implication of a shift in the percentage of Israelis that recognize some legitimate Palestinian rights in regard to Jerusalem. This can be gathered from Table 4.6.

Table 4.6

Israeli Jews: in relation to beliefs about whether a peace agreement with the Palestinians will lead to true long-term peace, and whether the Palestinians have any legitimate rights in regard to Jerusalem, the percentage who seriously consider (line one) and who flatly reject (line two) each proposal

		Four types of response				
Will a peace agreement lead to peace?		Yes	Yes	No	No	
Do Palestinians have any sort of legitimate rights in regard to Jerusalem?		Yes	No	Yes	No	*National average*
Group I						
Palestinian sovereignty over Arab village in East Jerusalem (e.g., Shuafat, Um Tuba, Zur Baher)	Seriously Consider	79	47	52	27	45
	Flatly Reject	10	27	30	52	36
Group II						
Autonomy for Arab areas in East Jerusalem	Seriously Consider	55	41	41	23	35
	Flatly Reject	22	38	36	56	44
Arab areas in East Jerusalem outside Old City to Palestinian sovereignty.	Seriously Consider	53	37	39	19	34
	Flatly Reject	16	38	38	59	44
Joint administration of Old City without yielding claim to sovereignty.	Seriously Consider	54	41	40	20	34
	Flatly Reject	22	33	36	55	41
Temple Mount under Wakf as now	Seriously Consider	56	34	34	18	31
	Flatly Reject	23	44	40	62	48
Group III						
Palestinian sovereignty over Arab neighborhoods in Old City	Seriously Consider	51	24	22	10	23
	Flatly Reject	24	52	45	70	55
Palestinian sovereignty over Temple Mount, Israeli over Western Wall	Seriously Consider	46	21	25	7	20
	Flatly Reject	33	56	55	71	58
East Jerusalem under Palestinian sovereignty with Jewish neighborhoods of East Jerusalem given a special status under Israeli control	Seriously Consider	38	23	20	9	19
	Flatly Reject	35	59	65	73	62
Old City internationalized under United Nations	Seriously Consider	34	26	18	10	18
	Flatly Reject	41	58	68	74	64
Percentage of the Total Population		21	12	18	49	

Table 4.6 divides the Israeli Jewish public into four groups based on their responses to two key questions having to do with the efficacy of a peace treaty and with Palestinian rights.

Roughly half of Israeli Jews neither believe that a peace treaty will lead to real peace, nor that Palestinians have some legitimate rights in relation to Jerusalem.

Thus, for this group, there is little reason to compromise on Jerusalem. And thus Table 4.6 shows, as might be predicted, that this half of the Jewish population thoroughly rejects every approach to compromise on Jerusalem that was considered.

The three remaining groups, making up 51% of the Israeli Jewish population, either believe in the efficacy of a peace treaty, believe that Palestinians have some rights in regard to Jerusalem, or believe both. Among the 21% that believe both, there is dominant openness to every proposal under consideration, with the exception of internationalizing the Old City under the United Nations.

Interestingly, for the two remaining groups (together constituting 30%) of the population, their responses are strikingly similar. For Israeli Jews who believe either that Palestinians have some legitimate rights in regard to Jerusalem or that a peace treaty will bring real peace (but not both) there is considerable openness to proposals that would move the two sides closer to negotiated resolution of the Jerusalem question.

In reading Table 4.6, the first two columns may be viewed as the optimists with respect to the implications of a peace treaty. The difference between the first and the second columns shows the difference between optimists who believe that Palestinians have some legitimate rights in regard to Jerusalem, and optimists that do not. The difference is very powerful, representing in some instances a doubling of the percentage willing to consider seriously the proposal in question.

Similarly, one can view the last two columns as the pessimists with respect to the efficacy of a peace treaty, and here, too, the difference among the pessimists, depending on whether they recognize some Palestinian rights in regard to Jerusalem, is also dramatic. Indeed, it is even more powerful among the pessimists than among the optimists.

The conclusion is inescapable. Regardless of one's views on the efficacy of a peace treaty, believing that Palestinians have some legitimate rights to Jerusalem is a very powerful factor in affecting willingness to compromise. In this regard, it should be pointed out that of those "broad-minded pessimists" who don't believe in the likelihood of peace yet recognize some Palestinian rights, fully half identify with the Likud Party.

Looking at specific proposals, and considering a situation (the third context) in which the size of the no-no group declines in favor of the other three, it becomes reasonable to believe that proposals such as joint administration of the Old City and Palestinian sovereignty over Arab areas outside the Old City become viable.

But when we look at proposals such as Palestinian sovereignty over Arab neighborhoods in the Old City, Palestinian sovereignty over the Temple Mount/ Haram al-Sharif, or Palestinian sovereignty over Jewish neighborhoods of East Jerusalem (with Israel control), these continue to look unrealistic. Even among the two middle groups, no more than 25% of the population is willing to seriously consider such proposals.

Table 4.6 thus suggests that new possibilities for the negotiability of Jerusalem can be opened up either by a substantial increase in the percentage of Israeli Jews believing in the efficacy of a peace treaty or by a substantial increase in the percentage of Israeli Jews believing that Palestinians have some legitimate rights to Jerusalem. Both factors appear powerful and seem to be of similar magnitude in affecting willingness to compromise.

Table 4.7 shows for various elements in a potential Jerusalem negotiation, how the viability (in relation to public opinion) shifts among the three contexts considered.

Approaches That Might Be Promising in Negotiations

Other than shifts toward more supportive contexts for negotiations, there are specific approaches to some of the more difficult issues that may prove fruitful in the negotiations.

The Boundaries of Jerusalem

Among the possible approaches to finding a compromise on Jerusalem that is acceptable to both sides is the idea of redefining the borders of Jerusalem—either making the city larger, or smaller, or changing its definition in some way.

The Palestinian study posed several questions that bear on city boundaries and proposals for changing those boundaries. Three questions had to do with those areas of the West Bank that were for the first time included within Jerusalem when Israel redefined the municipal boundaries of the city a few days after the end of the 1967 War. These areas comprise 90% of what is generally referred to as East Jerusalem. The remaining 10% includes the Old City and Arab downtown areas. Within the 90% are the Jewish housing projects constructed since 1967 as well as Arab village areas that were included within the city.

> Q. 20: After the Six-Day War in 1967, Israel expanded the city limits of Jerusalem to include large areas that had been under Jordanian control, but had never been within the city limits. Do you consider such areas to be part of Jerusalem?

> 1. Definitely yes   39%
> 2. Yes   19%
> 3. No   27%
> 4. Definitely no   15%

> Q. 21: Do you consider the Jewish areas settled after 1967 (Gilo, Ramot, Ramot Eshkol, Pisgat Zeev) as part of Jerusalem?

Table 4.7
Viability of elements of Jerusalem proposal within three alternative contexts

Proposal elements		Alternative contexts		
		Standard	Second	Third
1. Palestinian sovereignty over the outlying Arab neighborhoods of East Jerusalem (e.g., Um Tuma, Zur Baher).	IS	Highly possible	Yes	Yes
	PAL	Yes	Yes	Yes
2. Palestinian sovereignty over the downtown Arab neighborhoods of East Jerusalem outside the Old City.	IS	Some possibility	Highly possible	Highly possible
	PAL	Yes	Yes	Yes
3. Israeli sovereignty over Jewish neighborhoods of East Jerusalem (outside Old City).	IS	Yes	Yes	Yes
	PAL	No	No	Some Possibility
4. Palestinian sovereignty over the mosque compound on the Temple Mount/Haram al-Sharif and Israeli sovereignty over the Western Wall.*	IS	Yes	Yes	Yes
	PAL	Yes	Yes	Yes
5. With respect to the Temple Mount/Haram al-Sharif (plateau) and the Mount of Olives it is agreed that the ultimate sovereignty belongs to God.	IS	Some possibility	Some possibility	Some possibility
	PAL	Yes	Yes	Yes
6. Both States retain their claim to sovereignty over the Old City and agree on an administrative framework.	IS	Some possibility	Yes	Yes
	PAL	No	No	Some possibility
7. Palestinian sovereignty over Arab neighborhoods in the Old City and Israeli sovereignty over Jewish neighborhoods in the Old City.	IS	No	No	Some possibility
	PAL	Some possibility	Some possibility	Highly possible

* Requires further research.

1. Definitely yes   47%
2. Yes   22%
3. No   19%
4. Definitely no   13%

Q. 22: Do you consider Palestinian village areas such as Um Tuba and Zur Baher to be part of Jerusalem?

1. Definitely yes   53%
2. Yes   31%
3. No   12%
4. Definitely no   4%

It is interesting to note that when the question is phrased in general terms (as in Q. 20) with respect to areas unilaterally placed within the city boundaries by the Israelis, 42% of Palestinians say that they don't consider these areas part of Jerusalem ("Al-Quds"). However, when the question is put in terms of specific areas of Jewish residence, the number viewing these areas as outside Jerusalem falls to 32%, and when asked about Palestinian areas it falls to 16%. This suggests two thing. First, when emphasis is placed on "who gets to define Jerusalem," Palestinians would be most open to a redefinition different from how Israelis defined Jerusalem. Second, were there a proposal to exclude certain areas, Palestinians would be considerably more likely to support excluding areas of Jewish residence.

Question 41 specifically addressed the issue of redefinition of boundaries.

Q. 41: In order to attain a Palestinian majority in Jerusalem, do you support or oppose considering the Jewish settlements built after 1967 as areas outside of the city boundaries?

1. Definitely support   14%
2. Support   24%
3. Object   41%
4. Definitely object   21%

Here redefinition was linked to the objective of attaining a Palestinian majority within the city. With that as the identified purpose, 38% of Palestinians favor excluding the post-1967 Jewish neighborhoods of East Jerusalem from the city. One idea which has surfaced is that there might be a second city called "Al-Quds" which was not congruent with "Yerushalayim."*

The response to the question suggests that it might be possible for Al-Quds to be defined in such a way as to exclude these Jewish neighborhoods. In this

---

* In this regard, see: Ian S. Lustick, "Reinventing Jerusalem," *Foreign Policy* 93 (winter 1993–94): 41–59; and Adnan Abu Odeh, "Two Capitals in an Undivided Jerusalem," *Foreign Affairs* 70 (1992).

respect it is to be noted that only 21% of the population strongly objected to the redefinition idea.

This response is also noteworthy when it is remembered that only 28% of Palestinians were prepared to seriously consider the proposal in Question 66 in which Israelis would have had sovereignty over not just West Jerusalem but the Jewish neighborhoods of East Jerusalem (outside the Old City) as well. Further, 57% of Palestinians dismissed that proposal. Thus, the responses suggest that to some extent a redefinition of what is Jerusalem may play a useful purpose in moving toward compromises acceptable to both sides.

Question 42 posed the issue of a redefinition of the city boundaries, again in order to attain a Palestinian majority.

> Q. 42: In order to attain a Palestinian majority within the city, would you support redefining the city limits so that Palestinian areas adjacent to the city such as Abu Dis and el Eizariya are included within the city?

1. Definitely support	42%
2. Support	43%
3. Object	9%
4. Definitely object	6%

Here the response was overwhelmingly positive, with 85% of Palestinians in favor of redefinition and only 6% definitely opposed to it. What this makes clear is that for certain purposes, Palestinians will overwhelmingly view changing the boundaries of the city, in certain ways, as a desirable policy option. In principle, then, the boundaries themselves are not sacred lines.

Among Israeli Jews it was found that there is a similar attitude toward the municipal boundaries. These were expanded in 1967 and again in 1993, and there are proposals in the Knesset to expand them farther. In the parallel study Israeli Jews were asked to consider changes that would result in a smaller Jerusalem:

> In order to ensure a Jewish majority, do you support or object to redefining the city limits so that Arab settlements and villages which are now within the borders of Jerusalem (such as Shuafat, Um Tuba, Zur Baher) will be outside the city?

Israeli Jews responded:

1. Definitely support	17%
2. Support	42%
3. Object	34%
4. Definitely object	7%

Thus 59% supported the idea. Of the 41% that opposed it, only 7% of Israeli Jews were strongly opposed, and of these a significant number were on the left. Virtually no one views the municipal boundaries as sacred lines.

Sidestepping the Sovereignty Issue

If a peace agreement has to identify who is sovereign over each part of Jerusalem, it will be more difficult to come to an agreement than if there are ways of sidestepping the sovereignty issue.

One approach to avoiding a specification of one party or the other as sovereign is to say that both are sovereign, that is, that sovereignty is held jointly. This concept, known as condominium in international law, is rare, but has existed.

In the study there were two points at which Palestinians were asked about joint sovereignty.

Q. 60: How seriously would you take the following proposal as permanent arrangements: Israel and Palestine together would exercise joint sovereignty over an undivided city?

1. Very seriously	22%
2. Seriously	18%
3. Give some consideration	16%
4. Not seriously	22%
5. Reject totally	23%

Q. 68: Palestinians would have sovereignty over the al-Aqsa mosque and the Dome of the Rock but, with respect to the plateau itself, sovereignty would be shared with the Israelis, although day-to-day administration of the plateau would be in Palestinian hands.

1. Very seriously	23%
2. Seriously	18%
3. Give some consideration	12%
4. Not seriously	15%
5. Reject totally	32%

Both questions demonstrate that among Palestinians there is an appreciable openness to the idea of joint sovereignty. The latter question is important in an additional way. It shows that, although it is rarely articulated, Palestinians do make a distinction between the mosques on the Temple Mount and the plateau itself. This distinction opens a significant space within which compromise might be found, even for this most difficult issue.

A second approach to sidestepping the sovereignty issue is to allow each side to maintain its claim to sovereignty, leave the issue unresolved, and instead arrive at an administrative agreement. Question 72 posed just this idea with respect to the Old City.

Q. 72: Suppose that negotiations fail to resolve the question of sovereignty over the Old City. Would you support an agreement whereby the two States would jointly administer the Old City indefinitely?

1. Definitely yes   6%
2. Yes   21%
3. No   39%
4. Definitely no   34%

While this proposal, in practical terms, may seem quite similar to that for joint sovereignty, it meets with a far more negative reaction among Palestinians. It is not clear why this is so. Perhaps there is skepticism about what joint administration would actually mean, absent an agreement on joint sovereignty.

As we saw earlier, among Israeli Jews a proposal for joint administration of the Old City, without Israel having to give up its claim to sovereignty, would be taken seriously by a third of the population. However, among those that believe in the efficacy of a peace treaty (context 2) it is taken seriously by 50% and rejected only by 26%.

A third approach which allows sidestepping the sovereignty issue is to simply say that "sovereignty belongs to God." This of course does not address how the area in question is to be handled, but presumably with the sovereignty issue put to one side, an agreement on administration is required.

Table 4.8
Palestinian responses to Q. 70: There is a proposal that each side should stop arguing about sovereignty over holy sites in Jerusalem and agree that ultimate sovereignty belongs to God. Is this proposal acceptable to you?

	Definitely yes	*Yes*	*No*	*Definitely no*
National	44	20	21	15
Gaza	65	14	16	5
Islamist	60	17	15	8
Leftist	25	10	31	31
Fatah	49	21	20	10
Independent	36	23	24	17
Very Religious	70	18	10	2
Religious	49	22	19	10
Not Religious	35	19	27	19
Not at All religious	21	17	26	36
Support genuine peace	43	22	22	12
Do not support genuine peace	56	14	16	14

A proposal of this sort was part of both studies. Palestinian responses are examined in Table 4.8.

Palestinian support for this approach is strikingly widespread. Not only is it supported by 64% of the population, but each of the varied groupings considered above, with the exception of those who are not at all religious, give this approach majority support. Further, it is supported by 77% of the Islamists, and by 70% of those who do not support genuine peace with Israel (on condition of a Palestinian state with its capital in East Jerusalem, etc.).

From the above, it is clear that for Palestinians, there are acceptable approaches that allow the sovereignty issue to be sidestepped by either joint sovereignty or putting the sovereignty issue aside by saying that God is the ultimate sovereign.

It is not clear that there is equal potential for sidestepping the sovereignty issue on the Israeli side. When we similarly explored this "sovereignty belongs to God" approach among Israeli Jews, we found:

> There is a proposal that each side should stop arguing about sovereignty over the Temple Mount and agree that sovereignty belongs to God. Is this approach acceptable to you?

Israeli Jews responded:

1. Definitely yes	9%
2. Yes	26%
3. No	32%
4. Definitely no	33%

Even with this 65% to 35% opposition there may be some potential here. First, the 35% open to this approach should be compared to the mere 20% willing to seriously consider Palestinian sovereignty over the Temple Mount in exchange for recognition of Israeli sovereignty over the Western Wall. Second, it is striking that rejection of this approach was highest among the totally nonobservant, and acceptance was highest among the strictly observant.

	Israeli Jews: Religiosity			
	Strictly observant	To a great extent	Observe somewhat	Totally nonobservant
There is a proposal that each side should stop arguing about sovereignty over the Temple Mount and agree that sovereignty belongs to God. Is this approach acceptable to you?				
1. Definitely yes	20	8	8	8
2. Yes	22	28	27	23
3. No	30	37	33	28
4. Definitely no	28	28	32	41

In this regard it is also worth noting that as religious observance decreased so did the personal importance attributed to the Temple Mount. Thus, the more important the Temple Mount was to a respondent, the more likely she or he was to find some merit in the "sovereignty belongs to God" approach. The approach does not meet with majority support from any group yet, given the strong responsiveness among Palestinians, it is worthy of further exploration.

Before leaving this discussion of the "sovereignty belongs to God" approach, a word should be said about objections raised by some analysts (e.g., Meron Benvenisti). It is argued that this approach is not viable because the phrase "sovereignty belongs to God" has neither clear meaning nor precedent in international law. Indeed, some would view it as mere empty words. Be this as it may, this does not show that a "sovereignty belongs to God" approach is of limited value. Indeed, one might argue just the contrary, that such a phrase is exactly what one needs if one is seeking to sidestep the sovereignty issue. And the history of the conflict demonstrates the powerful role that ill-defined and perhaps undefinable language can play. The best example of this is the phrase "right to exist" when applied to a nation-state. For almost twenty years it was part of U.S. law that no government official might negotiate with the PLO until that organization recognized "Israel's right to exist." Not only was this locution unprecedented in international law, but throughout that period, and indeed continuing to this day, it has never been clarified whether this means "a right to have come into existence" or "a right to remain in existence." To ask the Palestinians to accept the latter could on some interpretations be merely a request that they agree that Israel is covered by more familiar rights such as the rights of existing states to live in peace and security. But if the phrase "right to exist" also covers the right to come into existence, then Palestinians were being asked to affirm the moral legitimacy of the Zionist project. It is noteworthy that when the PLO met the U.S. conditions in 1988 they avoided a simple affirmation of Israeli's right to exist, no doubt in part because it continued to be unclear what they would be affirming. Because the United States at that point was seeking to open dialogue, PLO affirmations were deemed sufficient. The point here is that just as such linguistic formulas have been capable of playing a major role in keeping parties from dialogue and negotiations, so too can other linguistic formulas play a valuable role in navigating around the troublesome sovereignty issue, provided that that is the will of the parties.

A Model of a Compromise on Jerusalem

The above considerations can be brought together in a model of a comprehensive compromise on Jerusalem. What is set out below is intended to be consistent with the data from the two studies. It should not be taken as the only compromise that is compatible, but it is instructive to see that there is at least one such potential compromise, and what it looks like.

In setting this out, the following assumptions are made:

- The background situation is the third context (two-thirds of Israeli Jews believe in the efficacy of a peace treaty, and 40% of Palestinians and 60% of Israel's Jews recognize that the other has some sort of legitimate rights in regard to Jerusalem).
- This proposal is reached through negotiations between Israel and the Palestinian authorities, and thus it has the support of both.

Features of the compromise:

1. From an Israeli point of view, the boundaries of "Yerushalayim" are redefined so as to exclude from the city the Arab-populated areas of East Jerusalem outside the Old City. Thus, the new boundaries of Yerushalayim include the Old City, Mount Scopus, the Mount of Olives, West Jerusalem, and the Jewish neighborhoods of East Jerusalem.

2. From a Palestinian point of view, the boundaries of Al-Quds are redefined. Al-Quds will include the Old City, the Mount of Olives, the Arab-populated areas of East Jerusalem, and Abu Dis.

3. Sovereignty will also extend to corridors and roads necessary to avoid enclaves.

4. Thus, rather than Yerushalayim and Al-Quds being two names for a single area, they will refer to two areas that overlap. What they will have in common is the Mount of Olives and the Old City.

5. With some exceptions (detailed below), both states would retain their claim to sovereignty over the Old City. Until such indefinite time as the two states might resolve this disagreement, the areas would be governed by an administrative agreement giving Israel political authority over the Jewish quarter and Palestine political authority over the Arab quarters.

6. Palestine would have sovereignty over the mosque compound on the Temple Mount and Israel would have sovereignty over the Western Wall.

7. With respect to the Temple Mount and the Mount of Olives, it would be agreed that ultimate sovereignty belongs to God, and that Palestine would exercise primary administrative authority over the Temple Mount and Israel would exercise primary administrative authority over the Mount of Olives.

Variants on this framework are of course possible. For instance, the "sovereignty belongs to God" approach might be applied to the entire Old City, or perhaps there might be an agreement that the Old City is under the joint sovereignty of the two states. Both of these may prove acceptable to Palestinians, but are less likely than the above proposal to win Israeli support. In any of these cases there would still be the need for an administrative agreement allocating spheres of authority.

It should be noted that the above proposal does not address the issue of Jerusalem as the capital of Palestine. This is deliberate, for several reasons. First, it will be extremely difficult to gain Israeli agreement to making Jerusalem the capital of Palestine. Tying this to the other aspects of the Jerusalem question might result in a package that was beyond what can be sustained. Second, once Israeli and Palestinian sovereignty over the nonoverlapping parts of Yerushalayim and Al-Quds are agreed on, the designation by either country of its capital and the location of its Parliament outside the overlapping area should be treated by Israel, Palestine, and the international community as a unilateral decision within the prerogative of either state.

Finally, there is another reason for not pushing to the fore the issue of Jerusalem as the Palestinian capital. Israeli agreement to redefinition of Yerushalayim so as to exclude Arab-populated areas is likely to be more forthcoming as it becomes more clear that the 160,000 Palestinians living in these areas of East Jerusalem outside the Old City will be citizens of the state of Palestine. In the study of Israeli Jewish attitudes the question was posed:

> Let's assume that a Palestinian state is established and Jerusalem remains united under Israeli sovereignty. In such circumstances there is a reasonable chance that the Arab residents of East Jerusalem will become citizens of a Palestinian state. To what extent do you consider this a problem?

The response was:

1. A very big problem	41%
2. Some problem	34%
3. A small problem	10%
4. No problem at all	13%
5. On the contrary, it is very desirable	3%

Most Israelis believe that there will be a Palestinian state, and it is clear to most observers that unless this does occur there can be no resolution of the conflict. In the elections to the Palestinian Authority the Palestinian residents of Jerusalem (who are not Israeli citizens) were permitted to vote. This recognition of their political rights foreshadowed their ultimately becoming citizens of Palestine. The strong Israeli discomfort with having this large population of "foreign nationals" within Israel's capital should serve to reinforce the desire to "make Jerusalem more Jewish," which is also the motivation that lies behind the strong support noted earlier for the proposal to exclude outlying Arab areas from Jerusalem.

Even avoiding the issue of Jerusalem as the Palestinian capital, it must be borne in mind that this model proposal is in no way attainable in the standard context. On almost every point it would be forcefully opposed by substantial numbers of Israelis or Palestinians or both. Moreover, in the standard context, this is true of any likely variant proposal that seeks to be comprehensive. The central issue with respect to negotiability is not then a matter of this detail or that, but *whether it is possible to move from the standard context to one in which proposals of this sort might be acceptable to both sides.*

The Potential for Moving from the Standard Context to One More Favorable to Negotiations

As has been pointed out, the two studies suggest four factors that are central to the willingness of Israelis and Palestinians to support various compromise proposals:

- For the Israelis: whether they believe that a peace treaty with the Palestinians will lead to true peace.
- For the Israelis: whether they believe that Palestinians have some legitimate rights in regard to Jerusalem.
- For the Palestinians: whether they support genuine and lasting peace with Israel (on the proviso that there is a Palestinian state with Jerusalem as its capital and some resolution of the refugee question).
- For the Palestinians: whether they believe that Jews have any sort of legitimate rights in regard to Jerusalem.

Of these four factors, the greatest potential for movement toward negotiability appears to lie with the first, whether Israelis believe that a peace treaty with the Palestinians will lead to genuine peace. This is so for a variety of reasons:

- When Israeli Jews believe that genuine peace will result from a peace treaty, they are significantly more willing to compromise.
- Only one-third of Israeli Jews believe in the efficacy of a peace treaty; thus there is substantial potential for change. With respect to Palestinian support for genuine peace, this is already the position of 70% of the population, so there is little upward potential.
- Israeli Jews seem to be open to being convinced by events that real peace is indeed possible. It is probably more difficult to shift either Israeli or Palestinian views about the rights of the other people than it is to affect their views on the possibility of lasting peace.

On this last point, it is worth considering Table 4.9.

The columns of numbers in the table should be read as answering the question: Of those who "believe strongly" (or other column heading) that true peace will result from a peace agreement, how convincing of "long-term peace" would they find "opening of a Saudi embassy in Jerusalem" or "regular commercial relations with Arab states"?

The table shows that those who already hold strong beliefs ("believe strongly" or "don't believe at all") with respect to the possibility of peace are either strongly supported in their beliefs or relatively unaffected in their beliefs by the hypothetical

Table 4.9
Israeli Jews: Would it convince you that real, long-term peace is possible?

	To what extent do you believe there can be true peace between Israel and the Arab world in the foreseeable future?				
	Believe strongly	Believe	Don't believe so much	Don't believe at all	Total
To what extent would it convince you that long-term peace with the Arab world is possible if Saudi Arabia opens an embassy in Jerusalem?					
Very convincing	30%	16%	7%	4%	10%
Convincing	34%	38%	22%	16%	26%
Not so convincing	25%	21%	42%	31%	32%
Not at all convincing	11%	25%	29%	49%	32%
Total	100%	100%	100%	100%	100%
To what extent would it convince you that long-term peace with the Arab world is possible if there were regular commercial relations with Arab States?					
Very convincing	45%	26%	10%	8%	16%
Convincing	39%	50%	38%	23%	38%
Not so convincing	11%	17%	34%	30%	26%
Not at all convincing	5%	7%	18%	38%	20%
Total	100%	100%	100%	100%	100%
Percentage of Total	6%	29%	36%	28%	100%

developments. Thus, of those that "believe strongly" that peace is possible, 64% would find the opening of a Saudi embassy in Jerusalem "convincing" or "very convincing," and 84% would find regular commercial relations "convincing" or "very convincing." Similarly, of those that "don't believe at all" in the possibility of peace, 80% would find the opening of a Saudi embassy "not so convincing" or "not at all convincing, and 68% would find regular commercial relations "not so convincing" or "not at all convincing."

Perhaps of more interest than those with very strong beliefs with respect to the possibility of true peace are those two groups in the middle—those that "believe" and those that "don't believe so much" that peace is possible. These groups make up roughly two-thirds of the population. Of those who presently "don't believe so much" that there can be true peace in the foreseeable future, 29% would find it "convincing" or "very convincing" if Saudi Arabia opened an embassy in Jerusalem, and 48% would find it "convincing" or "very convincing" if there were regular commercial relations with Arab States. And of those that say they "believe" (as opposed to "believe strongly") in the possibility of peace, 54% would be strengthened in that belief by the opening of a Saudi embassy in Jerusalem, and 76% strengthened in that belief by regular commercial relations.

It would be a mistake, however, to read this in a mechanical fashion, as if all that has to happen is that trade be opened between Israel and the Arab world and suddenly the Jerusalem question will be subject to resolution. Rather, the data might better be understood as indicating that even a matter as sensitive as Jerusalem is governed to a large extent by pragmatic considerations. Israelis need to be convinced that it is really in their long-term interests to compromise on Jerusalem. They need to be convinced that Palestinian demands are not open-ended, that compromising on Jerusalem won't simply whet the Palestinian appetite for further compromises, as 88% of Israeli Jews expressed the fear that it would.

Looked at from another angle, were the Israeli government to decide to genuinely negotiate the toughest aspects of the Jerusalem question (e.g., sovereignty over the Old City), it would be in a unique position to seek in those negotiations what it most wants: a definitive end to the conflict.

A "definitive-ending" focus would, of course, involve an explicit statement that what was negotiated was a definitive end to the conflict. While important, this is not sufficient. From an Israeli point of view several other elements need to be brought into play. These include:

- resolution of the claimed "right of return" of Palestinian refugees
- relations with the Arab states and the status of Israel within the Islamic world
- the next generation in both Palestine and the Arab countries.

Right of Return

The right of return issue is particularly problematic. Successive United Nations Resolutions have affirmed the right of refugees to return to their homes within Israel. Yet the numbers are such that Israelis equate any wholesale return with the elimination of Israel as a Jewish state. While it is widely understood that the refugees will not in significant numbers return to Israel, receiving financial compensation instead, Palestinian leaders, even in exchange for compensation, are not prepared to actually renounce a right of return. But is there some step that Palestinians could take on the refugee issue that would signify for Israelis a closing of the conflict?

One possibility is that the Palestinians would go beyond their present recognition of "Israel's right to exist in peace and security" and recognize that Israel has a right to exist *as a Jewish state*. Were Palestinians to take this step, they would be undertaking a re-conceptualization of the right of return issue. At present,

Palestinians claim a right of return, knowing, as a pragmatic matter, that they lack the power to bring about its implementation. But if there is recognition of Israel's right to exist as a Jewish state, then the situation is redefined as a conflict of rights. Under these circumstances the right of return is a qualified right, a right appropriately constrained by the fact that its wholesale satisfaction would lead to the violation of another right. This allows for a different kind of acceptance of the otherwise brute reality of non-implementation.

But would Palestinians affirm Israel's Jewishness? Sceptics may doubt it. Yet a foundation already exists for Palestinian recognition of Israel's right to remain a Jewish state. In November 1988, the Palestine National Council, (the PLO's highest decision making authority) issued the Palestinian Declaration of Independence which acknowledged the United Nations 1947 Partition Resolution as part of international law. This same resolution, which called for two states, is also referenced in Israel's Declaration of Independence. Strikingly, in the text of the Palestinian Declaration, the PLO explicitly noted that the partition resolution provided "for two states, one Arab and one Jewish." It is this recognition that not just Israel, but Israel's Jewishness, is grounded in international law that Palestinian leaders can draw upon were they to decide to move in this direction.

The issue is one of motivation and political feasibility. Except in exchange for an equally powerful Israeli concession, the Palestinian leadership would not and could not take such a step. Politically they can't simply announce that the right of return is suddenly a qualified right. They can't simply tell the Palestinian refugees that as an alternative to returning to homes within Israel they can "return" to the State of Palestine. There has to be some major counter-balancing concession on the Israeli side. Linking the refugee issue to the Jerusalem question offers an answer. If a "return" to the State of Palestine includes a return to the heart of the homeland, Al Quds, it can signify a new beginning rather than a stage in the old struggle. Here each party would have a powerful rationale for equally powerful concessions. For Palestinians, accepting Israel's right to remain a Jewish state is validated as the price required to ensure that the State of Palestine includes Jerusalem. For Israelis sharing Jerusalem is validated as the price required to end the conflict.

The Wider Arab and Islamic World

As part of a "definitive-ending" focus, Israel might seek not just an agreement with the Palestinians, but changes in its relations with the Arab and Islamic world. Jerusalem negotiations are a particularly appropriate venue for achieving such changes, for several reasons. First because the issue of Jerusalem transcends the Israeli-Palestinian conflict. Second, because from both a wider Arab and Islamic perspective, the Palestinians carry something of "a proxy," representing those wider concerns and interests. (This was reenforced recently when Jordan relented in its traditional claim to represent Islamic interests in the Jerusalem negotiations.)

In negotiations with the Palestinians on Jerusalem, Israel could choose to underscore this "proxy" role, and as a pre-condition for an agreement's going into effect require specific commitments and endorsements. These might include widespread Arab recognition that West Jerusalem is the sovereign capital of Israel, and widespread Islamic acceptance that Israel has a right to exist as a Jewish state with sovereignty in Jerusalem.

This later objective, Islamic acceptance of Israel as a Jewish state with sovereignty in Jerusalem, if attained would be of major historic import. To seek such an outcome from the Jerusalem negotiations would be a scaling-up of ambitions; it would be seeking a turning point in Jewish-Islamic mutual understanding. There is, of course, no guarantee that efforts in this direction would be successful. The fact that among Palestinians, especially among those most religious, there was very strong support for a "sovereignty belongs to God" approach suggests that this might similarly resonate within the wider Islamic world as a way of dealing with sovereignty over the Old City.

The Next Generation

Definitively ending the conflict, above all else, involves addressing how the moral dimensions of the conflict are perceived and transmitted, generation to generation. Israelis know that overwhelmingly Palestinians continue to see the conflict in stark terms: the land was theirs, the Jews stole it. There is, of course, no way to guarantee that an entire people will ever come to a more nuanced understanding of the conflict. But the two sides can undertake a process that will deeply affect many.

As discussed above, only 20% of Palestinians acknowledge any sort of legitimate Jewish rights in regard to Jerusalem. The study also found that only to a very limited extent do Palestinians recognize either the importance of Jerusalem to Israelis or the degree of Jewish historical and religious connectedness to Jerusalem:

17. The Israelis say that Jerusalem is important to them as a national center, to what extent it this true?

1. Definitely not true	63%
2. Not true	23%
3. To some extent true	12%
4. Definitely true	2%

18. The Israelis say that Jerusalem is important to them from a religious point of view, to what extent is this true?

1. Definitely not true	44%
2. Not true	20%
3. To some extent true	33%
4. Definitely true	3%

56. There should not be any compromise on Jerusalem because the actual historical connection of the Jewish people to the city is minor.

1. Very convincing   44%
2. Convincing   30%
3. Not convincing   24%
4. Not at all convincing   2%

For whatever reason, it was found in the Israeli study that there was greater appreciation of the importance of Jerusalem to Palestinians among Israeli Jews:

In your opinion to what extent is Jerusalem important to the Palestinians as a national center?

1. Very important   19%
2. Important   44%
3. Not so important   20%
4. Not at all important   17%

Possibly this greater, although still limited, awareness among Israeli Jews of the significance of Jerusalem to Palestinians helps explain why 39% of Israeli Jews say "yes" when asked if "Palestinians have any sort of legitimate rights with regard to Jerusalem," compared to the 20% of Palestinians responding analogously.

In any event both studies show strikingly limited appreciation of the importance of the city to the other people. This is, of course, indicative of the much broader problem of how the two peoples understand each others history, religion and narrative of the conflict. As a third element that would signal a definitive ending of the conflict, the Jerusalem negotiations should seek agreement on a transformed schooling process (kindergarten through college). This should also involve Jordan and Egypt. The focus should be on bringing the entire next generation of Israelis and Palestinians into sustained contact with each other, to hear from each other the human stories that can make foreign narratives comprehensible.

Each of these areas, refugees, the larger regional context, and school curricula, are already part of the complex of negotiations. What is being suggested is that they need to be tightly linked to the Jerusalem issue and cast in a far more ambitious perspective. They need to be seen as elements in a grand compromise that ends the conflict. Only within an historic accord of this magnitude will Israelis be prepared to share the Old City of Jerusalem, and only within the context of a true ending that includes Jerusalem will the Palestinians and the wider Arab/Islamic world be genuinely forthcoming on the elements that give reality to the words in a peace agreement.

Central Findings and Conclusions

1. Because of the emotional intensity of the Jerusalem issue, Israeli or Palestinian leaders who seek to avoid compromises on Jerusalem will find strong support among their people. Successful negotiation will require that both leaderships seek a compromise solution.

2. The underlying negotiability of the Jerusalem issue emerges from two facts: (1) both Israelis and Palestinians make major distinctions between those parts of the city that are of great importance to them "as part of Jerusalem" and the parts that are of lesser importance, and (2) they value the areas differently. Thus, for Israeli Jews the areas where Palestinians live, including such areas inside the Old City, are of distinctly lesser importance while for Palestinians the areas where Israelis live, including those within the Old City, are of distinctly lesser importance.

3. With respect to religious sites, Israeli Jews give premier importance to the Western Wall; this is of lesser importance to Palestinians. The two areas that are of great importance to both peoples are the Temple Mount and the Mount of Olives (and, unless it is disaggregated, the Old City as a whole).

4. Nonetheless, under current conditions, compromise proposals acceptable to both peoples are likely to be found with respect to only a very limited part of the Jerusalem question. This includes the outlying Palestinian residential regions within the municipal boundaries (e.g., Um Tuba, Zur Baher), of which 45% of Israeli Jews say they would seriously consider Palestinian sovereignty. It may also be possible to conclude an agreement whereby Palestinians would get sovereignty over the mosque compound on the Temple Mount in exchange for Palestinian recognition of Israeli sovereignty over the Western Wall, although this was not fully explored in the two studies.

5. The greatest potential for expanding the negotiability of Jerusalem lies in the possibility of a significant expansion of the percentage of Israeli Jews who believe that a peace treaty with the Palestinians will lead to real peace (presently one-third). Among those that doubt that lasting peace with the Arab world is possible, a significant number indicate that they would be convinced by real changes, such as the development of commercial relations and the opening of Arab embassies in Israel.

6. An important increase in negotiability would also result from increases in the 39% of Israeli Jews who presently believe that Palestinians have some "sort of legitimate rights in regard to Jerusalem" and in the 20% of Palestinians who believe that Jews have some "sort of legitimate rights in regard to Jerusalem."

7. With significant, but not utopian, changes in these areas, especially with increases in Israeli confidence in the efficacy of a peace agreement, the Jerusalem issue becomes much more negotiable. Proposals such as Israeli sovereignty over

areas of Jewish residence and Palestinian sovereignty over areas of Palestinian residence become possible options, even within the Old City.

8. For both peoples there are also approaches that would assist in making Jerusalem negotiable. Thus, in order to make Jerusalem more Jewish, 59% of Israeli Jews would support redefining the municipal boundaries in ways that exclude outlying Palestinian residential areas of East Jerusalem. Similarly, in order to make the city more Palestinian, 38% of Palestinians would support redefining the boundaries to exclude areas of Jewish settlement constructed since 1967. This opens the door for two overlapping cities, "Yerushalayim" and "Al-Quds," which have only limited areas in common.

9. There is also a potential for sidestepping the question of sovereignty over the Temple Mount and the Mount of Olives by taking the approach that "ultimate sovereignty belongs to God." This resonated extremely strongly among almost all groups of Palestinians, including 77% of Islamists. It received less than majority support only among leftists and those who are "not at all religious." Among Israeli Jews, this approach was supported by 35% of the population, and among those who are strictly observant, 42%.

10. Independent of the issue of Palestinian sovereignty, the issue of Jerusalem as the capital of Palestine is a major issue in its own right. For 90% of Palestinians, this is "very important." Among Israeli Jews, 80% are opposed to a Palestinian capital that encompasses any part of East Jerusalem. This is probably best dealt with by viewing the designation of a national capital as the prerogative of any state with respect to its sovereign territory.

11. Roughly half of Israeli Jews neither believe that a peace treaty with the Palestinians will bring genuine peace nor that Palestinians have any sort of legitimate rights in regard to Jerusalem. Correspondingly, half of the Israeli Jewish population believes one or both of these.

12. Among Israeli Jews, the willingness to compromise on Jerusalem is almost identical when those who do not believe Palestinians have rights in regard to Jerusalem but believe in the efficacy of a peace treaty (exclusivist optimists) are compared with those that do believe Palestinians have rights in regard to Jerusalem, but do not believe in the efficacy of a peace treaty (inclusivist pessimists). This suggests that "fairness" and "pursuit of peace" may have similar degrees of power in motivating compromise.

13. Thus, for both Palestinians and Israelis, acknowledgment of the rights of the other emerges as a significant factor in motivating compromise, and because those who do acknowledge the rights of the other constitute minorities in both communities, this is an area with rich potential for expanding the degree of negotiability of the Jerusalem issue.

Appendix A
Data from Study of Israeli-Jews

**Questionnaire and distribution of responses in percentages
for the national sample and the settler sample**

5. To what extent do you follow the negotiations between the Israeli government and Palestinians?

Settler sample	National sample	
49	35	1. To a great extent
36	46	2. To some extent
13	13	3. To a small extent
2	6	4. Not at all
100%	100%	

6. To what extent do you follow the topic of the future of Jerusalem within the peace process?

75	52	1. To a great extent
18	36	2. To some extent
7	9	3. Somewhat
—	3	4. Not at all
100%	100%	

7. Are you for or against negotiations on Jerusalem within the peace process?

2	5	1. Definitely for
8	16	2. For
32	42	3. Against
59	36	4. Definitely against
100%	100%	

8. How important is Jerusalem to you personally?

Settler sample	National sample	
88	77	1. Very important
12	21	2. Important
-	2	3. Not so important
1	—	4. Not at all important
100%	100%	

9. Do you feel a sense of belonging to Jerusalem?

81	69	1. Definitely yes
17	29	2. Yes
2	2	3. No
1	1	4. Not at all
100%	100%	

10–14. To what extent is Jerusalem important to you from each of the following points of view?

		Very important	Important	Not so important	Not at all important	Total
10. From the Jewish-religious point of view						
	National	68	21	7	4	100%
	Settlers	73	20	6	2	100%
11. From the Jewish national-historical point of view						
	National	80	17	3	1	100%
	Settlers	83	17	1	—	100%
12. As a center of the Jewish people and of Judaism						
	National	77	19	4	1	100%
	Settlers	81	14	3	1	100%
13. As a world center for all religions						
	National	48	27	17	8	100%
	Settlers	35	33	21	11	100%
14. As a symbol of the State of Israel						
	National	83	14	2	1	100%
	Settlers	83	15	1	1	100%

15. In your opinion, to what extent is Jerusalem important to the Palestinians as a national center?

Settler sample	National sample	
26	19	1. Very important
40	44	2. Important
20	20	3. Not so important
14	17	4. Not at all important
100%	100%	

16–25. I will read a list of places in Jerusalem. Please tell me, for each of them, to what extent is or isn't it important to you as part of Jerusalem?

	Very important	Important	Not so important	Not at all important	Did not hear of this place	Total
			Important to you as part of Jerusalem			
16. The Temple Mount						
National	75	18	5	2	1	100%
Settlers	81	16	2	1	—	100%
17. The Western Wall						
National	91	8	1	1	—	100%
Settlers	92	7	—	1	—	100%
18. Mount of Olives						
National	77	17	4	1	—	100%
Settlers	80	18	2	—	—	100%
19. The Jewish quarter in the Old City						
National	79	15	4	2	—	100%
Settlers	79	20	—	1	—	100%
20. Non-Jewish quarters in the Old City						
National	33	26	25	15	1	100%
Settlers	42	31	22	6	—	100%
21. Arab neighborhoods in downtown East Jerusalem (Wadi Jos, Sheikh Jarah, etc.)						
National	23	21	28	24	4	100%
Settlers	32	26	28	11	3	100%
22. Arab settlements and villages, previously in the West Bank, which are now included within Jerusalem (e.g., Um Tuba, Zur Baher, etc.)						
National	20	21	28	25	5	100%
Settlers	32	28	22	18	1	100%
23. The new Jewish neighborhoods established after 1967 (Gilo, Ramot, Ramot Eshkol, French Hill, Pisgat Zeev, East Talpiot, etc.)						
National	75	19	3	1	1	100%
Settlers	79	18	2	1	—	100%
24. The old Jewish neighborhoods (e.g., Rehavia, Talbieh, Beit Hakerem, Bayit Vagan, Yemin Moshe, Nahlaot, Musrarah, Bucharim, Me'ah Shearim, etc.)						
National	80	17	2	1	1	100%
Settlers	84	15	1	—	—	100%
25. The Old City						
National	85	12	2	1	⸱	100%
Settlers	86	13	1	—	—	100%

26. In your opinion, are the new Jewish neighborhoods that were established since 1967 as much a part of Jerusalem as the older neighborhoods?

Settler sample	National sample	
72	59	1. Definitely yes
26	35	2. Yes
2	5	3. No
1	1	4. Definitely not
100%	100%	

27. Have you ever visited Jerusalem?

—	1	1. Never
—	11	2. Once
6	20	3. A few times
24	27	4. Quite a lot of times
68	33	5. Very many times
2	9	6. I live in Jerusalem
100%	100%	

28. When was the last time you visited the Old City of Jerusalem?

—	2	1. I have never visited the Old City of Jerusalem
8	16	2. Before the intifada (before 1987)
3	6	3. 6 to 7 years ago
3	8	4. 4 to 5 years ago
9	14	5. 2 to 3 years ago
18	14	6. A year ago
37	23	7. A few months ago
23	17	8. In the past month
—	—	9. I live in the Old City
100%	100%	

29. Have you ever visited any of the Arab villages that are now included within the boarders of Jerusalem, such as Zur Baher, Beit Hanina, Um Tuba, etc.?

44	70	1. Never
19	9	2. Once
21	14	3. A few times
4	3	4. Quite a lot of times
—	1	5. Very many times
2	2	6. Never heard of these places, could be that I have visited them
10	1	7. Never heard of it and I definitely didn't visit them
100%	100%	

30. Have you ever visited any of the neighborhoods of East Jerusalem, such as Wadi Jos or Sheikh Jarah?

Settler sample	National sample	
38	65	1. Never
13	11	2. Once
24	16	3. A few times
7	3	4. Quite a lot of times
3	2	5. Very many times
4	3	6. Never heard of these places, could be that I have visited them
11	1	7. Never heard of it and I definitely didn't visit them
100%	100%	

31. There are people who say that we should make no concessions on Jerusalem even if we have to give up on peace with the Arabs. To what extent do you agree or disagree with this statement?

57	29	1. Definitely agree
33	31	2. Agree
6	27	3. Disagree
3	12	4. Definitely disagree
100%	100%	

32. As far as you know, nowadays, what proportion of Jerusalemites are Arabs?

4	5	1. A very small minority (not more than 5% to 10%)
26	27	2. Only 15% to 20% are Arabs
44	49	3. Around 30% are Arabs
5	6	4. About half of Jerusalemites are Arabs (Jews and Arabs about the same)
	2	5. Most Jerusalemites are Arabs
21	12	6. Don't know
100%	100%	

33. As far as you know, has the proportion of Arabs in Jerusalem increased or decreased since 1967?

26	23	1. Increased greatly
34	53	2. Increased somewhat
8	6	3. Neither increased nor decreased (principally the same)
10	3	4. Decreased somewhat
2	1	5. Decreased greatly
20	13	6. Don't know
100%	100%	

34. More than a quarter (28%) of the inhabitants of Jerusalem are Arabs. Does this disturb you or not?

Settler sample	National sample	
35	28	1. Disturbs very much
35	33	2. Disturbs
26	34	3. Does not disturb
4	5	4. Does not disturb at all
100%	100%	

35. If Jerusalem remains united, there is a possibility, perhaps, that in the future the Arabs will become a majority. In this regard please indicate to what extent do you support or object to restricting construction of housing for the Arabs (not give building permits) so that they are forced to leave the city.

34	23	1. Definitely support
35	42	2. Support
23	29	3. Object
8	6	4. Definitely object
100%	100%	

36. In order to ensure a Jewish majority, do you support or object to redefining the city limits so that Arab settlements and villages which are now within the borders of Jerusalem (such as Shuafat, Um Tuba, Zur Baher) will be outside the city?

16	17	1. Definitely support
42	42	2. Support
26	34	3. Object
16	7	4. Definitely object
100%	100%	

37. I will read to you three descriptions of the borders of Jerusalem. Of these three, as far as you know, which description is the most appropriate?

13	19	1. Jerusalem consists of the two parts of the city that were united after the Six-Day War.
18	20	2. Jerusalem consists of the two parts of the city that were united, plus the natural urban growth.
51	49	3. Jerusalem consists of the two parts of the city that were united, plus additional regions that were added on the basis of security, political, and other considerations.
12	13	4. I don't know.
100%	100%	

38. Compared to what was called East Jerusalem when it was under Jordanian rule up to the Six-Day War (1967), what is the size of East Jerusalem nowadays?

12	13	1. About the same as it was at the time Jerusalem was united
42	47	2. Somewhat bigger
30	21	3. Much bigger
16	19	4. I don't know
100%	100%	

39. Let's assume that a Palestinian state is established and Jerusalem remains united under Israeli sovereignty. In such circumstances there is a reasonable chance that the Arab residents of East Jerusalem will become citizens of a Palestinian state. To what extent do you consider this a problem?

Settler sample	*National sample*	
49	41	1. A very big problem
27	34	2. Some problem
7	10	3. A small problem
12	13	4. No problem at all
5	3	5. On the contrary, it is very desirable
100%	100%	

40. To what extent do you believe there can be true peace between Israel and the Arab world in the foreseeable future?

1	6	1. Believe strongly
28	29	2. Believe
36	36	3. Don't believe so much
36	28	4. Don't believe at all
100%	100%	

41. Do you believe that a peace agreement with the Palestinians will bring a true, long-term peace?

2	5	1. Believe strongly
16	28	2. Believe
39	36	3. Don't believe so much
44	31	4. Don't believe at all
100%	100%	

42. Do you agree or disagree that a compromise on Jerusalem is the key to true peace between Israel and the Arab states?

2	3	1. Definitely agree
13	17	2. Agree
27	42	3. Disagree
57	38	4. Definitely disagree
100%	100%	

43. To what extent do you believe that in order to make possible true peace with the Palestinians we must make a compromise over Jerusalem?

2	3	1. Strongly believe
7	17	2. Believe
17	35	3. Don't believe so much
74	45	4. Don't believe at all
100%	100%	

44. To what extent do you believe that for the sake of co-existence between Arabs and Jews in Jerusalem we must make a compromise over Jerusalem?

Settler sample	National sample	
—	3	1. Strongly believe
9	18	2. Believe
24	37	3. Don't believe so much
67	42	4. Don't believe at all
100%	100%	

45. Do you agree or disagree that there is a better chance of arriving at peaceful co-existence with the Palestinian residents of Jerusalem than with the Palestinians of the West Bank (Judea and Samaria)?

1	5	1. Definitely agree
34	39	2. Agree
42	42	3. Don't agree
23	14	4. Definitely don't agree
100%	100%	

46. Do you agree or disagree that the only way to achieve security is by putting up a wall to separate Israel from the territories?

9	16	1. Definitely agree
15	32	2. Agree
29	41	3. Don't agree
47	12	4. Definitely don't agree
100%	100%	

47. Do you agree or disagree to such a separation between Jews and Arabs in Jerusalem?

3	7	1. Definitely agree
10	23	2. Agree
38	51	3. Disagree
49	19	4. Definitely disagree
100%	100%	

48. To what extent do you agree or disagree with the claim that in daily life in Jerusalem there is in fact a separation between Jews and Arabs—in housing, entertainment, shopping, etc.?

16	14	1. Definitely agree
48	42	2. Agree
31	38	3. Disagree
5	6	4. Definitely disagree
100%	100%	

49. In your opinion, is it desirable that in the daily life of Jerusalem there be a separation between Jews and Arabs in residence, entertainment, etc.?

Settler sample	National sample	
24	18	1. Very desirable
32	34	2. Desirable
37	42	3. Not desirable
7	7	4. Very undesirable
100%	100%	

50. To what extent would you agree to cede the Arab neighborhoods of East Jerusalem to the Palestinians if the Old City, the Mount of Olives, all of the Jewish neighborhoods of East Jerusalem, and Mount Scopus remain in Jerusalem, as they are today?

2	9	1. Definitely agree
24	33	2. Agree
34	31	3. Disagree
37	26	4. Definitely disagree
100%	100%	

51–56 People state various reasons why it is worthwhile to compromise on Jerusalem. With regard to each of the following reasons, please state to what extent it convinces you that a compromise with the Palestinians over Jerusalem is worthwhile.

	Very convincing	Convincing	Not so convincing	Not at all convincing	Total

51. Without a compromise on Jerusalem the Muslim extremists will strengthen. Do you find this convincing as a reason for compromise?

	Very convincing	Convincing	Not so convincing	Not at all convincing	Total
National	5	18	29	48	100%
Settlers	3	8	23	67	100%

52. Without a compromise on Jerusalem any Palestinian leadership that makes peace with Israel will be discredited among Palestinians. Do you find this reason convincing?

	Very convincing	Convincing	Not so convincing	Not at all convincing	Total
National	5	17	30	47	100%
Settlers	1	6	28	66	100%

53. A compromise on Jerusalem will improve peace with Egypt. Do you find this reason convincing?

	Very convincing	Convincing	Not so convincing	Not at all convincing	Total
National	5	14	29	53	100%
Settlers	—	8	15	78	100%

54. A compromise will honor the religious and national rights of the Palestinians in Jerusalem. Do you find this reason convincing?

	Very convincing	Convincing	Not so convincing	Not at all convincing	Total
National	5	18	30	47	100%
Settlers	—	10	16	74	100%

	Very convincing	Convincing	Not so convincing	Not at all convincing	Total

55. A compromise on Jerusalem will enhance the personal safety of Israelis in Jerusalem. Do you find this reason convincing?

	Very convincing	Convincing	Not so convincing	Not at all convincing	Total
National	10	21	28	42	100%
Settlers	5	8	23	64	100%

56. A compromise on Jerusalem will lead to international recognition of Jerusalem as the capital of Israel. Do you find this reason convincing?

	Very convincing	Convincing	Not so convincing	Not at all convincing	Total
National	11	18	25	47	100%
Settlers	4	13	18	65	100%

57–60 I will now read to you various arguments *against* a compromise on Jerusalem. With regard to each of the following reasons, please state to what extent it convinces you that *no* compromise should be made on Jerusalem.

	Convinces me that no compromise should be made				
	Very convincing	Convincing	Not so convincing	Not at all convincing	Total

57. There should not be a compromise on Jerusalem because Jerusalem is much more important for Judaism than for Islam. Do you or don't you find this a convincing reason?

	Very convincing	Convincing	Not so convincing	Not at all convincing	Total
National	41	26	18	15	100%
Settlers	42	18	22	19	100%

58. There should not be a compromise on Jerusalem because a city should not be divided or compromised on because of a minority that lives in it. Do you or don't you find this a convincing reason?

	Very convincing	Convincing	Not so convincing	Not at all convincing	Total
National	39	31	20	11	100%
Settlers	45	15	23	18	100%

59. There should not be a compromise on Jerusalem because concessions on Jerusalem will only enhance the Palestinians' demands for more concessions. Do you or don't you find this a convincing reason?

	Very convincing	Convincing	Not so convincing	Not at all convincing	Total
National	58	25	10	7	100%
Settlers	61	18	9	12	100%

60. There should not be a compromise on Jerusalem because if there is a compromise on Jerusalem, Jews will not have a free access to the Old City. Do you or don't you find this a convincing reason?

	Very convincing	Convincing	Not so convincing	Not at all convincing	Total
National	52	25	13	10	100%
Settlers	48	23	13	16	100%

61. In your opinion, do the Palestinians have any sort of legitimate rights with regard to Jerusalem?

Settler sample	National sample	
4	5	1. Yes, definitely
18	34	2. Yes
32	35	3. No
46	26	4. Definitely no
100%	100%	

62. To what extent, in your opinion, is the Palestinians' claim for East Jerusalem as a capital justified?

1	2	1. Definitely justified
11	18	2. Justified
31	43	3. Not justified
58	37	4. Definitely not justified
100%	100%	

63–64. To what extent would each of the following convince you that real, long-term peace with the Arab world is possible?

	Very convincing	Convincing	Not so convincing	Not at all convincing	Total
63. That Saudi Arabia open an embassy in Jerusalem					
National	10	26	32	32	100%
Settlers	7	24	28	42	100%
64. Regular commercial relations with Arab states					
National	16	37	26	20	100%
Settlers	8	38	21	34	100%

65–74. Let's assume that you were part of the negotiating team on Jerusalem. Please state to what extent you would seriously consider each of the following proposals.

	I would consider the proposal				Don't read	
	Very seriously	Seriously	Not so seriously	Not at all	Object to compromise, won't consider	Total
65. To transfer to Palestinian sovereignty the Arab settlements and villages previously in the West Bank which are now within the borders of Jerusalem (e.g., Shuafat, Um Tuba, Zur Baher, Beit Hanina, etc.)						
National	14	31	19	20	16	100%
Settlers	6	21	21	18	33	100%

| | I would consider the proposal | | | | Don't read | |
	Very seriously	Seriously	Not so seriously	Not at all	Object to compromise, won't consider	Total
66. The Arab settlements and villages previously in the West Bank which now are within the borders of Jerusalem will come under Palestinian sovereignty in exchange for the Jewish regions in the West Bank (e.g., Ma'aleh Edumim and Givat Zeev will become part of Jerusalem)						
National	14	30	17	24	16	100%
Settlers	11	21	17	21	30	100%
67. To transfer the Arab neighborhoods of East Jerusalem except those that are inside the walls to Palestinian sovereignty						
National	10	24	23	27	17	100%
Settlers	5	16	18	28	33	100%
68. Give the Palestinians sovereignty over the Arab neighborhoods of the Old City						
National	7	16	22	36	19	100%
Settlers	2	7	14	36	42	100%
69. The control of the Temple Mount will be under the Wakf as is now						
National	9	22	22	29	19	100%
Settlers	2	13	14	28	43	100%
70. The Palestinians will get sovereignty of the Temple Mount in exchange for Palestinian recognition of Israel's sovereignty of the Wailing Wall						
National	5	15	21	36	22	100%
Settlers	2	7	12	37	42	100%
71. Turn the Old City into an international city under the United Nations						
National	5	13	18	40	24	100%
Settlers	1	5	8	35	51	100%
72. Give East Jerusalem to Palestinian sovereignty while the Jewish neighborhoods in East Jerusalem will have "special status" under Israeli control						
National	5	14	19	40	22	100%
Settlers	2	5	8	40	45	100%
73. Retain Israeli sovereignty over East Jerusalem, while the Arab neighborhoods in East Jerusalem will have "special status" under Palestinian control						
National	8	27	22	26	18	100%
Settlers	2	20	17	27	33	100%
74. Establish a joint Palestinian-Jewish administration for the Old City without Israel having to yield its claim to sovereignty						
National	9	25	25	41	*	100%
Settlers	5	26	13	55	*	100%

* The response category was mistakenly omitted.

75. To what extent is it important to you that Jews can pray on the Temple Mount?

Settler sample	National sample	
68	59	1. Very important
21	27	2. Important
7	10	3. Not so important
5	4	4. Not at all important
100%	100%	

76. There is a proposal that each side should stop arguing about sovereignty over the Temple Mount and agree that sovereignty belongs to God. Is this approach acceptable to you?

8	9	1. Definitely yes
13	26	2. Yes
36	32	3. No
43	33	4. Definitely no
100%	100%	

77. Under present circumstances, do you support or object to the establishment of a Palestinian state?

—	5	1. Definitely support
18	28	2. Support
35	35	3. Object
47	32	4. Definitely object
100%	100%	

78. Are you for or against negotiations on Jerusalem within the peace process?

2	3	1. Definitely for
7	18	2. For
31	36	3. Against
60	43	4. Definitely against
100%	100%	

79. In the light of recent developments, will a Palestinian state eventually be established?

17	18	1. Will surely be established
60	60	1. I think so
20	16	3. I don't think so
3	6	4. Will surely not be established
100%	100%	

80–81 Let's assume that with time a Palestinian state will be established. If that is the case, to what extent do you support or object to each of the following?

	Definitely support	Support	Object	Definitely object	Total
80. That an Arab region in East Jerusalem will be designated as the capital of the Palestinian state					
National	4	16	30	50	100%
Settlers	—	10	17	73	100%

81. That the Palestinian capital will be a new city consisting of two parts: an area of East Jerusalem plus an area of the West Bank adjoining Jerusalem (such as Abu Dis) and will be named "Al-Quds"

	Definitely support	Support	Object	Definitely object	Total
National	4	19	29	48	100%
Settlers	2	16	17	65	100%

82. In comparison with other topics that are being negotiated with the Palestinians, such as water rights, returning of Palestinian refugees, and the status of the settlements, is the topic of Jerusalem more or less important than these topics?

Settler sample	National sample	
27	42	1. The topic of Jerusalem is much more important compared to other topics
37	24	2. More important
35	31	3. The topic of Jerusalem is as important as the other topics
2	2	4. Less important than other topics
—	1	5. Much less important than other topics
100%	100%	

83–87. If an Israeli government which hasn't got a Zionist majority in the Knesset arrives at a compromise on Jerusalem which you think is wrong, please state to what extent each of the following forms of protest is justified in your eyes.

	Very justified	Justified	Not so justified	Not al all justified	Total
83. Lawful demonstration					
National	71	25	2	2	100%
Settlers	83	17	1	—	100%
84. Nonviolent actions that disrupt the functioning of society					
National	19	21	18	42	100%
Settlers	38	29	28	5	100%
85. Use of force if necessary to prevent implementation					
National	7	10	16	67	100%
Settlers	12	11	28	50	100%

		Very justified	Justified	Not so justified	Not al all justified	Total
86. Violent actions directed against Palestinians						
	National	10	6	14	69	100%
	Settlers	7	6	21	66	100%
87. Violent actions against other Jews, if necessary						
	National	3	3	7	87	100%
	Settlers	2	1	10	88	100%

88. If a Zionist majority in the Knesset approves a decision on Jerusalem to which you object, what kind of protest would you justify in that case?

Settler sample	National sample	
2	6	1. I would not justify any kind of protest
57	71	2. Only lawful demonstrations
38	20	3. Lawful demonstration and also unlawful but nonviolent demonstration
4	3	4. Lawful demonstration and also unlawful, even violent, protest
100%	100%	

89. Would you, personally, participate in any action against a compromise on Jerusalem that you don't approve of?

33	12	1. Yes, definitely
28	15	2. Yes
22	27	3. Perhaps yes
2	4	4. Perhaps no
10	31	5. No
5	11	6. Definitely no
100%	100%	

Background questions

94. Is there a telephone in your home and do you have a car?

Settler sample	National sample	
75	63	1. There is a telephone at home and a car
25	33	2. There is a telephone at home but no car
—	1	3. No telephone at home and I have a car
—	2	4. No telephone and no car
100%	100%	

95. Gender (for coding only)

45	49	1. Male
55	51	2. Female
100%	100%	

96. How many years of schooling did you have?

Settler sample	National sample	
—	—	1. No schooling at all
—	1	2. Up to and including 4 years
1	7	3. 7 to 8 years
2	10	4. 9 to 10 years
3	7	5. 11 years
43	40	6. 12 years
26	17	7. 13+ years (no academic degree)
26	18	8. Full university education
100%	100%	

97. To which of the following political/ideological movements (streams) do you feel closest?

13	33	1. Closer to the Labor movement
2	6	2. Closer to Meretz
29	43	3. Closer to Likud
28	11	4. Closer to parties/movements that are right of Likud (Tzomet, Moledet)
27	7	5. Closer to the religious parties
100%	100%	

98. How old are you?

18	17	1. 20–24
11	13	2. 25–29
18	10	3. 30–34
18	12	4. 35–39
15	12	5. 40–44
12	9	6. 45–49
6	6	7. 50–54
2	9	8. 55–64
1	12	9. 65+
100%	100%	

99. Which of the following income levels is closest to the *gross monthly income* that you and your family members living with you have all together?

4	3	1. Up to 1,000 NIS per month
—	7	2. 1,001 to 2,000 NIS per month
9	17	3. 2,001 to 3,000 NIS per month
14	19	4. 3,001 to 4,000 NIS per month
14	21	5. 4,001 to 5,000 NIS per month
10	9	6. 5,001 to 6,000 NIS per month
6	6	7. 6,001 to 7,000 NIS per month
11	5	8. 7.001 to 8.000 NIS per month
31	14	9. Over 8,000 NIS per month
100%	100%	

100. Do you observe the religious tradition?

Settler sample	National sample	
27	10	1. I strictly observe the religious tradition
30	18	2. I observe to a great extent
29	48	3. I observe somewhat
14	24	4. I don't observe at all
100%	100%	

101. Where were you born and where was your father born? (*Interviewer:* Be sure to write down the name of the country and code accordingly here and in Question 102).

Respondent   Respondent's father

(Name of country)			(Name of country)
24	17	1. Israel	Israel
29	29	2. Israel	Asia-Africa
22	15	3. Israel	Europe-America
8	18	4. Asia-Africa	Asia-Africa
18	21	5. Europe-America	Europe-America
100%	100%		

102. The respondent's country of birth (code according to the respondent's answer regarding country of birth—name of the country in the left column of Question 101).

75	60	1. Israeli-born
4	8	2. Former Soviet Union
3	9	3. Eastern Europe (except former Soviet Union)
6	3	4. Western Europe
3	1	5. United States
2	6	6. Middle East
4	10	7. North Africa
—	—	8. Ethiopia
3	2	9. Other
100%	100%	

103. When did you immigrate to Israel?

75	62	1. Israeli-born
—	2	2. Before 1940
2	3	3. 1941–47
4	11	4. 1948–54
3	5	5. 1955–60
3	6	6. 1961–67
3	3	7. 1968–73
5	2	8. 1974–79
7	7	9. 1980 and later
100%	100%	

Appendix A-2
Cross-tabulation of all replies by ideological tendency

	Closer to Labor	Closer to Meretz	Closer to Likud	Closer to right of Likud	Closer to religious parties	Total
5. To what extent do you follow the negotiations between the Israeli government and the Palestinians?						
To a great extent	40	35	35	38	36	37
To some extent	47	52	45	45	43	46
To a small extent	10	11	13	11	18	12
Not at all	3	2	7	7	3	5
Total	100	100	100	100	100	100
N	437	84	577	146	95	1339
6. To what extent do you follow the topic of the future of Jerusalem within the peace process?						
To a great extent	52	47	51	64	71	54
To some extent	38	47	36	26	20	35
Somewhat	8	6	9	8	7	8
Not at all	2	0	4	3	1	3
Total	100	100	100	100	100	100
N	435	85	573	146	94	1333
7. Are you for or against negotiations on Jerusalem within the peace process?						
Definitely for	8	20	3	2	4	6
For	29	43	7	5	3	16
Against	42	29	46	36	28	41
Definitely against	21	8	44	58	64	37
Total	100	100	100	100	100	100
N	436	84	575	146	95	1336

8. How important is Jerusalem to you personally?

Very important	70	54	83	86	94	78
Important	29	39	16	13	5	20
Not so important	1	5	1	1	0	1
Not at all important	0	2	0	0	1	0
Total	100	100	100	100	100	100
N	437	85	576	146	96	1340

9. Do you feel a sense of belonging to Jerusalem?

Definitely yes	60	42	74	80	92	70
Yes	37	46	24	18	7	28
No	2	9	2	1	1	2
Not at all	1	2	0	1	0	1
Total	100	100	100	100	100	100
N	437	85	576	146	96	1340

10. To what extent is Jerusalem important to you from the Jewish-religious point of view?

Very important	56	31	74	75	95	67
Important	25	29	21	19	4	22
Not so important	13	19	4	3	1	7
Not at all important	6	21	1	3	0	4
Total	100	100	100	100	100	100
N	434	85	570	146	96	1331

11. To what extent is Jerusalem important to you from the Jewish national-historical point of view?

Very important	72	51	84	87	93	79
Important	25	36	14	10	6	18
Not so important	2	9	2	3	1	3
Not at all important	1	4	0	0	0	1
Total	100	100	100	100	100	100
N	435	85	570	143	96	1329

	Closer to Labor	Closer to Meretz	Closer to Likud	Closer to right of Likud	Closer to religious parties	Total
12. To what extent is Jerusalem important to you as a center of the Jewish people and of Judaism?						
Very important	69	44	82	85	92	76
Important	25	32	16	13	7	19
Not so important	6	15	1	1	1	4
Not at all important	0	9	0	1	0	1
Total	100	100	100	100	100	100
N	435	85	571	143	95	1329
13. To what extent is Jerusalem important to you as a world center for all religions?						
Very important	49	42	48	41	41	47
Important	31	31	26	26	24	28
Not so important	16	19	16	23	22	17
Not at all important	4	8	10	10	14	8
Total	100	100	100	100	100	100
N	435	85	568	143	96	1327
14. To what extent is Jerusalem important to you as a symbol of the State of Israel?						
Very important	77	58	88	90	85	82
Important	19	31	10	9	11	14
Not so important	4	7	1	1	2	3
Not at all important	0	5	0	0	1	1
Total	100	100	100	100	100	100
N	435	85	572	144	96	1332

15. In your opinion, to what extent is Jerusalem important to the Palestinians as a national center?

Very important	24	37	14	12	24	19
Important	49	51	40	40	37	44
Not so important	19	10	22	18	20	20
Not at all important	8	2	24	29	19	17
Total	100	100	100	100	100	100
N	421	82	540	139	89	1271

16. To what extent is the Temple Mount important to you as part of Jerusalem?

Very important	64	49	82	82	94	75
Important	26	28	14	16	4	18
Not so important	8	13	3	1	1	5
Not at all important	2	9	1	1	1	2
Total	100	100	100	100	100	100
N	434	85	571	145	96	1331

17. To what extent is the Western Wall important to you as part of Jerusalem?

Very important	85	72	95	95	100	91
Important	13	18	5	5	0	8
Not so important	2	5	1	0	0	1
Not at all important	0	6	0	0	0	1
Total	100	100	100	100	100	100
N	438	85	577	145	96	1341

	Closer to Labor	Closer to Meretz	Closer to Likud	Closer to right of Likud	Closer to religious parties	Total
18. To what extent is the Mount of Olives important to you as part of Jerusalem?						
Very important	67	49	83	85	94	77
Important	25	29	13	15	4	17
Not so important	6	19	4	0	1	5
Not at all important	2	4	1	0	1	1
Total	100	100	100	100	100	100
N	436	84	571	145	95	1331
19. To what extent is Jewish Quarter in the Old City important to you as part of Jerusalem?						
Very important	71	59	85	88	88	79
Important	21	24	13	8	10	15
Not so important	6	8	2	4	1	4
Not at all important	2	9	1	1	1	2
Total	100	100	100	100	100	100
N	437	85	567	146	94	1329
20. To what extent are the non-Jewish quarters in the Old City important to you as part of Jerusalem?						
Very important	23	17	38	54	39	34
Important	26	24	24	22	33	25
Not so important	34	33	22	16	21	26
Not at all important	17	26	15	8	8	15
Total	100	100	100	100	100	200
N	432	84	561	144	92	1313

21. *To what extent are Arab neighborhoods in downtown East Jerusalem important to you as part of Jerusalem?*

Very important	14	9	28	38	38	24
Important	18	16	22	26	25	21
Not so important	38	33	26	21	27	30
Not at all important	30	43	24	16	11	25
Total	100	100	100	100	100	100
N	421	82	548	141	93	1285

22. *To what extent are Arab settlements which are now included within Jerusalem important to you as part of Jerusalem?*

Very important	10	8	26	35	34	21
Important	17	8	24	25	26	21
Not so important	38	37	27	23	25	31
Not at all important	35	47	23	16	14	27
Total	100	100	100	100	100	100
N	413	78	544	142	91	1268

23. *To what extent are the new Jewish neighborhoods established after 1967 important to you as part of Jerusalem?*

Very important	71	48	79	83	83	75
Important	22	39	18	15	14	20
Not so important	6	10	2	2	1	4
Not at all important	1	4	1	0	2	1
Total	100	100	100	100	100	100
N	436	83	571	145	93	1328

	Closer to Labor	Closer to Meretz	Closer to Likud	Closer to right of Likud	Closer to religious parties	Total
24. To what extent are the old Jewish neighborhoods important to you as part of Jerusalem?						
Very important	78	63	83	90	84	81
Important	20	30	15	9	13	17
Not so important	1	6	2	1	3	2
Not at all important	1	1	1	0	0	1
Total	100	100	100	100	100	100
N	434	84	568	143	92	1321
25. To what extent is the Old city important to you as part of Jerusalem?						
Very important	79	62	90	92	91	85
Important	17	29	9	8	8	13
Not so important	4	5	1	0	1	2
Not at all important	1	4	1	0	0	1
Total	100	100	100	100	100	100
N	436	85	575	146	95	1337
26. Are new Jewish neighborhoods established since 1967 as much part of Jerusalem as the older neighborhoods?						
Definitely yes	52	34	63	80	69	60
Yes	41	43	33	18	28	34
No	6	17	3	2	3	5
Definitely not	1	6	3	0	0	1
Total	100	100	100	100	100	100
N	436	83	572	145	96	1332

27. *Have you ever visited Jerusalem?*

Never	1	0	1	0	1	1
Once	10	11	10	6	6	9
A few times	24	14	24	19	5	22
Quite a lot of times	31	42	30	23	28	30
Very many times	34	32	34	53	59	37
Total	100	100	100	100	100	100
N	395	71	538	127	79	1210

28. *When was the last time you visited the Old City of Jerusalem?*

Never visited Old City	1	1	2	0	1	1
Before intifada (1987)	20	13	17	10	15	17
6 to 7 years ago	8	6	6	3	3	6
4 to 5 years ago	8	9	8	9	3	8
2 to 3 years ago	15	15	14	12	8	14
A year ago	15	11	13	16	9	14
A few months ago	20	25	25	23	28	24
In the past month	13	20	13	26	32	16
Total	100	100	100	100	100	100
N	436	85	575	146	95	1337

29. *Have you ever visited any of the Arab villages now included within the borders of Jerusalem?*

Never	74	69	74	65	65	72
Once	9	15	8	10	12	9
A few times	14	15	13	20	18	15
Quite a lot of times	2	0	3	4	3	3
Very many times	1	1	1	1	2	1
Total	100	100	100	100	100	100
N	425	81	552	143	94	1295

	Closer to Labor	Closer to Meretz	Closer to Likud	Closer to right of Likud	Closer to religious parties	Total
30. Have you ever visited any of the neighborhoods of East Jerusalem?						
Never	68	61	69	62	53	67
Once	12	14	11	8	17	12
A few times	14	20	15	24	24	17
Quite a lot of times	3	3	3	5	4	3
Very many times	2	3	2	1	2	2
Total	100	100	100	100	100	100
N	422	80	554	143	96	1295
31. To what extent do you agree that we should make no concessions on Jerusalem even if we have to give up peace?						
Definitely agree	19	8	35	48	45	30
Agree	31	16	34	27	24	30
Disagree	39	51	19	11	17	26
Definitely disagree	11	25	12	14	14	13
Total	100	100	100	100	100	100
N	434	85	575	144	95	1333
32. As far as you know nowadays, what proportion of Jerusalemites are Arabs?						
A very small minority	3	5	5	9	12	5
Only 15% to 20% are Arabs	29	21	32	39	45	32
Around 30% are Arabs	61	66	53	43	39	55
About half are Arabs	6	8	7	8	2	6
Most of them are Arabs	1	0	3	0	1	2
Total	100	100	100	100	100	100
N	385	80	498	127	84	1174

33. *As far as you know has the proportion of Arabs in Jerusalem increased or decreased since 1967?*

Increased greatly	22	14	31	35	28	27
Increased somewhat	62	71	58	52	62	60
Principally the same	10	7	6	6	3	7
Decreased somewhat	4	8	3	5	6	4
Decreased greatly	2	0	2	2	1	2
Total	100	100	100	100	100	100
N	381	73	501	129	86	1170

34. *More than a quarter—28% of the inhabitants of Jerusalem are Arabs. Does this disturb you?*

Disturbs very much	13	4	38	45	42	29
Disturbs	35	21	35	34	29	34
Does not disturb	46	55	23	17	26	32
Does not disturb at all	6	20	3	3	3	5
Total	100	100	100	100	100	100
N	435	85	574	145	96	1335

35. *To avoid an Arab majority, to what extent do you support restricting construction of housing for Arabs?*

Definitely support	11	5	31	35	36	24
Support	44	26	43	39	40	41
Object	39	46	22	19	20	29
Definitely object	6	23	4	7	4	6
Total	100	100	100	100	100	100
N	423	84	569	146	95	1317

	Closer to Labor	Closer to Meretz	Closer to Likud	Closer to right of Likud	Closer to religious parties	Total
36. To ensure a Jewish majority, do you support redefining city limits so Arab settlements will be outside the city?						
Definitely support	16	18	20	19	16	18
Support	51	36	37	41	39	42
Object	29	40	35	28	41	33
Definitely object	5	6	8	12	4	7
Total	100	100	100	100	100	100
N	429	83	572	145	93	1322
37. Of three descriptions of the borders of Jerusalem which description is the most appropriate?						
2 united parts	16	20	26	21	22	21
2 parts + natural growth	23	18	21	22	23	22
2 parts + regions	60	62	53	58	54	57
Total	100	100	100	100	100	100
N	387	76	492	120	81	1156
38. Compared to East Jerusalem under Jordanian rule up to the Six-Day War, what is the size of East Jerusalem nowadays?						
About the same	19	13	14	17	20	16
Somewhat bigger	58	62	58	52	43	57
Much bigger	23	25	28	31	37	27
Total	100	100	100	100	100	100
N	360	71	463	112	76	1082

39. *Do you consider it a problem if Arabs of East Jerusalem become citizens of a Palestinian State if Jerusalem remains united under Israel?*

A very big problem	27	12	51	52	58	41
Some problem	39	41	30	34	20	33
A small problem	14	11	7	5	8	10
No problem at all	16	31	10	8	11	13
It is very desirable	3	6	2	1	2	2
Total	100	100	100	100	100	100
N	437	85	575	143	96	1336

40. *To what extent do you believe there can be true peace between Israel and the Arab world in the foreseeable future?*

Believe strongly	12	22	3	1	1	7
Believe	51	55	15	8	17	29
Don't believe so much	28	16	43	37	33	35
Don't believe at all	9	6	38	53	49	29
Total	100	100	100	100	100	100
N	437	85	578	146	96	1342

41. *Do you believe that a peace agreement with the Palestinians will bring a true long-term peace?*

Believe strongly	11	19	2	1	1	6
Believe	52	58	12	6	9	27
Don't believe so much	28	19	44	28	41	35
Don't believe at all	9	4	42	65	49	32
Total	100	100	100	100	100	100
N	437	84	577	145	96	1339

42. Do you agree or disagree that compromise on Jerusalem is the key to true peace between Israel and Arab States?

	Closer to Labor	Closer to Meretz	Closer to Likud	Closer to right of Likud	Closer to religious parties	Total
Definitely agree	6	11	1	1	1	3
Agree	31	41	9	5	8	18
Disagree	44	37	42	36	31	41
Definitely disagree	19	11	48	58	60	38
Total	100	100	100	100	100	100
N	436	83	576	146	95	1336

43. To what extent do you believe that for true peace with the Palestinians we must compromise on Jerusalem?

	Closer to Labor	Closer to Meretz	Closer to Likud	Closer to right of Likud	Closer to religious parties	Total
Believe strongly	6	11	1	2	1	3
Believe	31	45	9	5	8	18
Don't believe so much	37	33	35	23	24	34
Don't believe at all	26	11	56	70	67	46
Total	100	100	100	100	100	100
N	436	84	573	145	96	1334

44. To what extent do you believe that for co-existence between Arabs and Jews in Jerusalem we must compromise on Jerusalem?

	Closer to Labor	Closer to Meretz	Closer to Likud	Closer to right of Likud	Closer to religious parties	Total
Believe strongly	6	12	1	1	1	3
Believe	33	42	9	5	5	18
Don't believe so much	36	36	40	26	26	36
Don't believe at all	26	11	50	68	68	43
Total	100	100	100	100	100	100
N	437	84	571	146	96	1334

45. Do you agree there is better chance of peaceful co-existence with Palestinians of Jerusalem than with Palestinians of West Bank?

Definitely agree	7	6	5	6	3	5
Agree	48	52	35	20	29	38
Disagree	38	37	44	49	37	41
Definitely disagree	8	5	17	25	31	15
Total	100	100	100	100	100	100
N	429	81	567	144	94	1315

46. Do you agree that the only way to achieve security is by putting up a wall to separate Israel from territories?

Definitely agree	15	10	19	15	10	16
Agree	33	31	32	32	31	32
Disagree	44	45	38	32	34	40
Definitely disagree	8	14	11	21	26	12
Total	100	100	100	100	100	100
N	439	84	575	146	94	1338

47. Do you agree or disagree to such a separation between Jews and Arabs in Jerusalem?

Definitely agree	6	0	9	10	4	7
Agree	23	17	25	22	19	23
Disagree	55	61	48	46	46	51
Definitely disagree	16	23	18	23	30	19
Total	100	100	100	100	100	100
N	436	84	574	144	93	1331

	Closer to Labor	Closer to Meretz	Closer to Likud	Closer to right of Likud	Closer to religious parties	Total
48. Do you agree or disagree that in daily life in Jerusalem there is in fact separation between Jews and Arabs?						
Definitely agree	15	22	12	18	11	14
Agree	47	44	42	35	41	43
Disagree	35	31	38	40	40	37
Definitely disagree	4	4	7	7	8	6
Total	100	100	100	100	100	100
N	432	85	572	145	96	1330
49. Is it desirable that in the daily life of Jerusalem there be a separation between Jews and Arabs in residence, etc.?						
Very desirable	13	12	21	24	27	19
Desirable	33	20	35	38	34	33
Not desirable	48	57	36	33	30	41
Very undesirable	6	11	9	5	8	7
Total	100	100	100	100	100	100
N	438	83	573	144	96	1334
50. Do you agree to cede Arab neighborhoods of East Jerusalem to Palestinians if Old City, Mount of Olives, etc. remain in Jerusalem as today?						
Definitely agree	16	29	6	3	3	10
Agree	46	49	26	17	23	33
Disagree	27	18	34	35	30	30
Definitely disagree	11	4	35	45	44	27
Total	100	100	100	100	100	100
N	432	83	572	146	96	1329

51. *Is it convincing that without compromise on Jerusalem Muslim extremists will strengthen?*

Very convincing	8	7	4	3	4	5
Convincing	26	42	12	6	6	17
Not so convincing	31	21	30	22	32	29
Not at all convincing	35	29	54	69	58	48
Total	100	100	100	100	100	100
N	436	85	577	144	95	1337

52. *Is it convincing that without compromise on Jerusalem any Palestinian leader that makes peace will be discredited among Palestinians?*

Very convincing	8	18	2	2	3	5
Convincing	28	35	10	8	10	17
Not so convincing	35	32	30	20	25	30
Not at all convincing	29	15	57	69	61	47
Total	100	100	100	100	100	100
N	436	84	570	142	96	1328

53. *Is it convincing that a compromise on Jerusalem will improve peace with Egypt?*

Very convincing	7	13	2	3	3	5
Convincing	22	22	10	3	6	14
Not so convincing	34	33	30	22	19	30
Not at all convincing	37	32	58	73	72	52
Total	100	100	100	100	100	100
N	436	85	575	143	95	1334

	Closer to Labor	Closer to Meretz	Closer to Likud	Closer to right of Likud	Closer to religious parties	Total
54. Is it convincing that a compromise will honor the religious and national rights of Palestinians in Jerusalem?						
Very convincing	8	24	2	3	4	5
Convincing	28	34	12	8	9	18
Not so convincing	33	26	30	23	23	30
Not at all convincing	31	16	56	66	63	47
Total	100	100	100	100	100	100
N	435	85	574	143	95	1332
55. Is it convincing that a compromise on Jerusalem will enhance personal safety of Israelis in Jerusalem?						
Very convincing	15	27	6	3	7	10
Convincing	31	25	16	11	12	21
Not so convincing	28	28	31	24	21	28
Not at all convincing	26	20	48	62	60	41
Total	100	100	100	100	100	100
N	436	85	577	143	95	1336
56. Is it convincing that a compromise on Jerusalem will lead to international recognition of Jerusalem as capital of Israel?						
Very convincing	16	26	7	6	8	11
Convincing	27	26	13	8	14	18
Not so convincing	26	21	26	17	19	24
Not at all convincing	31	27	54	69	59	47
Total	100	100	100	100	100	100
N	437	85	577	143	95	1337

57. *Is it convincing there should not be compromise on Jerusalem because Jerusalem is much more important for Judaism than for Islam?*

Very convincing	29	19	48	43	51	40
Convincing	19	12	32	36	26	26
Not so convincing	26	27	13	11	15	18
Not at all convincing	25	42	7	10	8	16
Total	100	100	100	100	100	100
N	433	85	572	145	95	1330

58. *Is it convincing there should not be compromise on Jerusalem because a city should not be divided because of a minority?*

Very convincing	27	8	47	49	52	38
Convincing	30	28	34	29	21	31
Not so convincing	26	28	13	17	19	19
Not at all convincing	18	35	6	6	8	12
Total	100	100	100	100	100	100
N-	433	85	572	145	96	1331

59. *Is it convincing there should not be compromise on Jerusalem because concessions on Jerusalem will enhance Palestinian demands?*

Very convincing	42	22	68	79	67	58
Convincing	30	25	24	14	22	25
Not so convincing	15	26	5	3	6	10
Not at all convincing	13	27	2	3	4	8
Total	100	100	100	100	100	100
N	433	85	571	145	95	1329

	Closer to Labor	Closer to Meretz	Closer to Likud	Closer to right of Likud	Closer to religious parties	Total
60. Is it convincing there should not be compromise on Jerusalem because Jews won't have free access to the Old City?						
Very convincing	35	29	63	63	56	51
Convincing	24	21	26	26	27	25
Not so convincing	22	18	7	7	13	13
Not at all convincing	18	32	4	4	4	10
Total	100	100	100	100	100	100
N	432	84	570	144	95	1325
61. In your opinion do Palestinians have any sort of legitimate rights with regard to Jerusalem?						
Yes, definitely	8	18	2	1	1	5
Yes	47	64	25	21	21	34
No	33	16	37	38	35	35
Definitely no	11	2	36	40	43	27
Total	100	100	100	100	100	100
N	433	85	575	146	94	1333
62. To what extent in your opinion is the Palestinian claim for East Jerusalem as a capital justified?						
Definitely justified	3	8	1	1	0	2
Justified	26	54	10	8	5	18
Not justified	49	29	41	40	46	43
Definitely not justified	22	10	48	50	49	37
Total	100	100	100	100	100	100
N	430	84	575	146	96	1331

63. *Is it convincing that real, long-term peace with Arab world is possible if Saudi Arabia opens an embassy in Jerusalem?*

Very convincing	16	18	7	6	5	10
Convincing	37	39	22	13	20	27
Not so convincing	26	24	35	41	32	32
Not at all convincing	21	20	36	40	43	31
Total	100	100	100	100	100	100
N	432	85	574	144	95	1330

64. *Is it convincing that peace with Arab world is possible if there are commercial relations with Arab States?*

Very convincing	24	32	12	8	6	16
Convincing	50	55	31	26	26	38
Not so convincing	17	9	33	32	36	26
Not at all convincing	9	4	25	34	32	20
Total	100	100	100	100	100	100
N	434	85	572	144	95	1330

65. *In negotiations on Jerusalem would you consider transferring to Palestinian sovereignty Arab settlements now within Jerusalem?*

Consider very seriously	20	42	10	6	2	14
Consider seriously	44	33	25	20	17	30
Not so seriously	16	12	20	18	25	18
Not at all	13	12	26	27	25	21
Won't consider	7	1	19	29	31	16
Total	100	100	100	100	100	100
N	429	85	567	143	96	1320

66. Would you consider that Arab settlements now in Jerusalem go to Palestinian sovereignty in exchange for Jewish regions in the West Bank?

	Closer to Labor	Closer to Meretz	Closer to Likud	Closer to right of Likud	Closer to religious parties	Total
Consider very seriously	19	46	10	6	4	15
Consider seriously	42	25	25	17	20	29
Not so seriously	16	13	17	18	15	16
Not at all	14	13	30	28	31	24
Won't consider	8	4	18	30	31	16
Total	100	100	100	100	100	100
N	428	85	567	143	95	1318

67. Would you consider transferring Arab neighborhoods of East Jerusalem except those inside the walls to Palestinian sovereignty?

	Closer to Labor	Closer to Meretz	Closer to Likud	Closer to right of Likud	Closer to religious parties	Total
Consider very seriously	15	33	6	5	3	10
Consider seriously	35	40	18	12	12	24
Not so seriously	24	13	23	17	18	22
Not at all	18	13	33	33	35	27
Won't consider	8	1	20	33	31	17
Total	100	100	100	100	100	100
N	429	85	564	143	93	1314

68. *In negotiations on Jerusalem would you consider giving the Palestinian sovereignty over the Arab neighborhoods of the Old City?*

Consider very seriously	9	22	4	3	3	7
Consider seriously	25	32	11	5	5	16
Not so seriously	27	21	21	12	18	22
Not at all	29	21	43	42	40	37
Won't consider	11	4	22	38	34	20
Total	100	100	100	100	100	100
N	428	85	565	142	95	1315

69. *In negotiations on Jerusalem would you consider that control of the Temple Mount will be under the Wakf as is now?*

Consider very seriously	12	33	6	4	3	9
Consider seriously	34	28	17	10	11	22
Not so seriously	23	19	21	17	14	21
Not at all	22	15	33	34	39	29
Won't consider	10	5	22	34	34	19
Total	100	100	100	100	100	100
N	425	85	563	143	95	1311

70. *Would you consider that Palestinians will get sovereignty of the Temple Mount in exchange for Palestinians recognition of Israel's sovereignty of Wailing Wall?*

Consider very seriously	8	26	2	1	2	5
Consider seriously	23	33	10	6	3	15
Not so seriously	25	9	21	13	18	21
Not at all	33	25	42	40	40	37
Won't consider	11	7	25	40	37	22
Total	100	100	100	100	100	100
N	429	85	564	141	95	1314

	Closer to Labor	Closer to Meretz	Closer to Likud	Closer to right of Likud	Closer to religious parties	Total
71. In negotiations on Jerusalem would you consider turning the Old City into an international city under the United Nations?						
Consider very seriously	8	15	3	1	1	5
Consider seriously	17	20	10	9	7	13
Not so seriously	20	29	17	7	12	17
Not at all	39	25	42	44	42	40
Won't consider	16	11	28	39	38	25
Total	100	100	100	100	100	100
N	431	85	566	140	95	1317
72. Would you consider giving East Jerusalem to Palestinian sovereignty while Jewish neighborhoods in East Jerusalem have special status under Israeli control?						
Consider very seriously	8	13	2	3	4	5
Consider seriously	19	24	10	8	6	14
Not so seriously	23	28	17	9	11	19
Not at all	35	31	44	42	45	40
Won't consider	14	5	26	38	34	23
Total	100	100	100	100	100	100
N	431	85	567	142	95	1320

73. *Would you consider retaining Israeli sovereignty over East Jerusalem while Arab neighborhoods in East Jerusalem have special status under Palestinian control?*

Consider very seriously	11	20	5	7	1	8
Consider seriously	34	41	25	15	16	27
Not so seriously	25	18	19	21	20	21
Not at all	20	20	29	27	34	26
Won't consider	9	1	22	30	29	18
Total	100	100	100	100	100	106
N	428	85	565	143	95	1316

74. *Would you consider establishing joint Palestinian-Jewish administration for Old City without Israeli having to yield sovereignty?*

Consider very seriously	13	20	7	5	3	10
Consider seriously	34	32	19	15	20	24
Not so seriously	24	25	25	23	24	25
Not at all	28	24	49	57	53	41
Total	100	100	100	100	100	100
N	426	85	548	137	91	1287

75. *To what extent is it important to you that Jews can pray on the Temple Mount?*

Very important	46	29	68	71	69	59
Important	33	32	25	23	14	27
Not so important	16	22	5	5	7	10
Not at all important	6	16	2	1	10	5
Total	100	100	100	100	100	100
N	435	85	564	146	94	1324

	Closer to Labor	Closer to Meretz	Closer to Likud	Closer to right of Likud	Closer to religious parties	Total
76. Is it acceptable to you that each side stop arguing about sovereignty over the Temple Mount and agree it belongs to God?						
Definitely yes	7	11	8	7	12	8
Yes	25	19	26	20	24	24
No	34	31	32	39	30	34
Definitely no	33	39	34	34	34	34
Total	100	100	100	100	100	100
N	430	84	564	145	92	1315
77. Under present circumstances, do you support or object to the establishment of a Palestinian state?						
Definitely support	8	27	1	2	0	5
Support	49	52	15	11	3	27
Object	31	15	37	31	45	34
Definitely object	12	5	45	56	52	33
Total	100	100	100	100	100	100
N	437	84	571	146	96	1334
78. Are you for or against negotiations on Jerusalem within the peace process?						
Definitely for	5	19	1	1	0	3
For	35	42	7	3	3	18
Against	38	31	34	34	29	35
Definitely against	23	7	57	62	68	44
Total	100	100	100	100	100	100
N	432	83	574	146	96	1331

79. *In the light of recent developments, will a Palestinian state eventually be established?*

Surely be established	24	36	15	18	6	19
I think so	62	58	61	44	62	59
I don't think so	11	6	16	31	23	16
Surely not established	4	0	8	7	9	6
Total	100	100	100	100	100	100
N	434	84	568	146	94	1326

80. *If a Palestinian state is established, do you support the idea that an Arab region in East Jerusalem be designated as the Palestinian capital?*

Definitely support	5	13	2	1	1	3
Support	25	39	11	6	6	17
Object	31	20	32	35	36	31
Definitely object	39	28	55	59	56	49
Total	100	100	100	100	100	100
N	432	85	569	143	96	1325

81. *If a Palestinian state is established, do you support the idea that the Palestinian capital be an area of East Jerusalem plus an area of West Bank adjoining Jerusalem?*

Definitely support	5	14	2	2	1	4
Support	29	44	14	5	11	20
Object	29	17	30	34	40	30
Definitely object	37	25	54	59	48	47
Total	100	100	100	100	100	100
N	433	84	571	143	95	1326

	Closer to Labor	Closer to Meretz	Closer to Likud	Closer to right of Likud	Closer to religious parties	Total
82. In comparison with other topics being negotiated—water rights, refugees etc.—is the topic of Jerusalem more or less important?						
Much more important	35	15	51	43	58	43
More important	28	29	22	23	21	25
As other topics	33	46	24	33	20	29
Less important	3	8	1	1	1	2
Much less important	1	1	1	1	0	1
Total	100	100	100	100	100	100
N	436	85	567	145	95	1328
83. To what extent is a lawful demonstration justified if a non-Zionist Knesset majority arrives at a compromise on Jerusalem?						
Very justified	65	64	74	80	76	71
Justified	29	29	24	18	23	25
Not so justified	3	5	1	0	1	2
Not at all justified	3	2	1	1	0	2
Total	100	100	100	100	100	100
N	434	84	573	146	95	1332
84. To what extent are nonviolent actions justified if a non-Zionist Knesset majority arrives at a compromise on Jerusalem?						
Very justified	11	6	24	35	26	20
Justified	14	12	25	31	27	21
Not so justified	22	30	15	16	19	19
Not at all justified	53	52	36	18	27	40
Total	100	100	100	100	100	100
N	435	84	567	145	95	1326

85. *Is use of force for preventing implementation justified if a non-Zionist Knesset majority arrives at a compromise on Jerusalem?*

Very justified	2	1	9	15	11	7
Justified	6	4	12	16	15	10
Not so justified	13	7	18	16	22	16
Not at all justified	79	88	60	52	53	67
Total	100	100	100	100	100	100
N	434	84	568	142	95	1323

86. *Are violent actions against Palestinians justified if a non-Zionist Knesset majority arrives at a compromise on Jerusalem?*

Very justified	4	2	16	11	8	10
Justified	3	4	8	13	7	7
Not so justified	11	6	17	15	21	14
Not at all justified	81	88	59	61	63	69
Total	100	100	100	100	100	100
N	434	84	567	144	95	1324

87. *Are violent actions against other Jews justified if a non-Zionist Knesset majority arrives at a compromise on Jerusalem?*

Very justified	0	0	4	5	1	3
Justified	2	2	4	1	3	3
Not so justified	6	5	7	10	13	7
Not at all justified	92	93	85	84	83	87
Total	100	100	100	100	100	100
N	433	84	565	142	94	1318

	Closer to Labor	Closer to Meretz	Closer to Likud	Closer to right of Likud	Closer to religious parties	Total
88. If the Knesset with a Zionist majority approves decision on Jerusalem to which you object, what protest would you justify?						
Not justify any protest	8	7	5	5	2	6
Lawful demonstrations	79	85	68	49	61	70
Lawful + nonviolent	12	8	22	38	32	20
Lawful + unlawful violent	1	0	5	8	4	4
Total	100	100	100	100	100	100
N	433	84	570	146	93	1326
89. Would you participate in any action against a compromise on Jerusalem that you don't approve of?						
Yes, definitely	6	6	14	28	17	12
Yes	11	13	16	25	20	15
Perhaps yes	27	18	31	26	28	28
Perhaps no	4	6	5	1	4	4
No	37	43	27	15	20	29
Definitely not	16	14	8	4	10	11
Total	100	100	100	100	100	100
N	435	84	573	144	93	1329

Appendix A-3
Cross-tabulation of all replies by religious observance

	Strictly observant	To a great extent	Observe somewhat	Totally nonobservant	Total
5. To what extent do you follow the negotiations between the Israeli government and the Palestinians?					
To a great extent	36	40	33	35	35
To some extent	37	44	48	48	46
To a small extent	19	10	12	13	13
Not at all	8	6	7	4	6
Total	100	100	100	100	100
N	146	276	724	360	1506
6. To what extent do you follow the topic of the future of Jerusalem within the peace process?					
To a great extent	68	59	48	46	52
To some extent	19	30	39	43	36
Somewhat	7	8	10	9	9
Not at all	6	4	3	2	3
Total	100	100	100	100	100
N	145	274	721	361	1501
7. Are you for or against negotiations on Jerusalem within the peace process?					
Definitely for	2	5	4	10	5
For	3	10	17	25	16
Against	29	38	45	45	42
Definitely against	66	47	35	20	36
Total	100	100	100	100	100
N	145	274	721	359	1499

	Strictly observant	To a great extent	Observe somewhat	Totally nonobservant	Total
8. How important is Jerusalem to you personally?					
Very important	93	91	76	66	78
Important	5	8	23	31	20
Not so important	1	1	1	3	1
Not at all important	1	0	0	1	0
Total	100	100	100	100	100
N	147	277	723	361	1508
9. Do you feel a sense of belonging to Jerusalem?					
Definitely yes	92	80	67	54	69
Yes	7	18	31	39	28
No	1	0	2	5	2
Not at all	0	1	0	2	1
Total	100	100	100	100	100
N	147	277	723	360	1507
10. To what extent is Jerusalem important to you from the Jewish-religious point of view?					
Very important	95	83	67	46	68
Important	5	16	24	27	21
Not so important	0	2	7	15	7
Not at all important	0	0	2	13	4
Total	100	100	100	100	100
N	145	276	718	359	1498

11. *To what extent is Jerusalem important to you from the Jewish national-historical point of view?*

Very important	92	84	80	71	80
Important	6	13	18	24	17
Not so important	2	3	2	4	3
Not at all important	0	0	1	1	1
Total	100	100	100	100	100
N	145	276	717	358	1496

12. *To what extent is Jerusalem important to you as a center of the Jewish people and of Judaism?*

Very important	92	84	78	64	77
Important	7	16	19	24	18
Not so important	1	1	2	9	4
Not at all important	0	0	1	3	1
Total	100	100	100	100	100
N	145	276	717	357	1495

13. *To what extent is Jerusalem important to you as a world center for all religions?*

Very important	48	46	47	52	48
Important	19	27	29	26	27
Not so important	17	20	17	15	17
Not at all important	17	7	7	6	8
Total	100	100	100	100	100
N	145	275	715	358	1493

	Strictly observant	To a great extent	Observe somewhat	Totally nonobservant	Total
14. To what extent is Jerusalem important to you as a symbol of the State of Israel?					
Very important	87	87	85	75	83
Important	10	11	13	19	14
Not so important	2	2	2	4	2
Not at all important	1	0	0	2	1
Total	100	100	100	100	100
N	145	278	719	357	1499
15. In your opinion, to what extent is Jerusalem important to the Palestinians as a national center?					
Very important	16	17	17	25	19
Important	28	40	47	49	44
Not so important	20	19	21	17	20
Not at all important	36	24	15	9	17
Total	100	100	100	100	100
N	138	257	686	346	1427
16. To what extent is the Temple Mount important to you as part of Jerusalem?					
Very important	89	79	76	65	75
Important	8	16	19	24	18
Not so important	3	4	3	8	5
Not at all important	1	1	1	3	2
Total	100	100	100	100	100
N	146	275	716	357	1494

17. *To what extent is the Western Wall important to you as part of Jerusalem?*

Very important	99	94	92	82	91
Important	1	5	7	14	8
Not so important	0	0	1	2	1
Not at all important	0	0	0	2	1
Total	100	100	100	100	100
N	147	278	725	357	1507

18. *To what extent is the Mount of Olives important to you as part of Jerusalem?*

Very important	94	83	77	65	77
Important	4	14	18	25	17
Not so important	2	3	3	8	4
Not at all important	0	1	1	1	1
Total	100	100	100	100	100
N	145	276	723	353	1497

19. *To what extent is the Jewish Quarter in the Old City important to you as part of Jerusalem?*

Very important	92	83	79	70	79
Important	7	15	16	20	16
Not so important	1	2	4	6	4
Not at all important	0	0	1	4	2
Total	100	100	100	100	100
N	144	274	720	357	1495

	Strictly observant	To a great extent	Observe somewhat	Totally nonobservant	Total
20. To what extent are the non-Jewish quarters in the Old City important to you as part of Jerusalem?					
Very important	45	31	33	32	33
Important	25	27	26	26	26
Not so important	22	23	26	27	25
Not at all important	8	19	15	16	15
Total	100	100	100	100	100
N	139	274	709	352	1474
21. To what extent are Arab neighborhoods in downtown East Jerusalem important to you as part of Jerusalem?					
Very important	34	24	24	21	24
Important	25	20	23	21	22
Not so important	24	27	31	29	29
Not at all important	17	28	22	29	25
Total	100	100	100	100	100
N	138	267	690	347	1442
22. To what extent are Arab settlements which are now included within Jerusalem important to you as part of Jerusalem?					
Very important	31	23	21	18	21
Important	28	20	24	18	22
Not so important	22	27	32	31	30
Not at all important	19	30	24	33	27
Total	100	100	100	100	100
N	138	262	682	342	1424

23. *To what extent are the new Jewish neighborhoods established after 1967 important to you as part of Jerusalem?*

Very important	87	77	77	69	76
Important	13	19	19	24	19
Not so important	0	4	4	4	4
Not at all important	1	1	1	2	1
Total	100	100	100	100	100
N	144	274	718	357	1493

24. *To what extent are the old Jewish neighborhoods important to you as part of Jerusalem?*

Very important	89	81	81	76	81
Important	10	17	16	22	17
Not so important	1	1	2	1	2
Not at all important	0	1	1	1	1
Total	100	100	100	100	100
N	144	272	715	356	1487

25. *To what extent is the Old City important to you as part of Jerusalem?*

Very important	94	86	86	79	85
Important	6	13	12	16	12
Not so important	0	1	2	3	2
Not at all important	0	1	0	2	1
Total	100	100	100	100	100
N	146	278	720	358	1502

	Strictly observant	To a great extent	Observe somewhat	Totally nonobservant	Total
26. Are new Jewish neighborhoods established since 1967 as much part of Jerusalem as the older neighborhoods?					
Definitely yes	77	62	57	53	59
Yes	19	34	38	36	35
No	3	4	4	8	5
Definitely not	1	0	1	3	1
Total	100	100	100	100	100
N	146	273	721	359	1499
27. Have you ever visited Jerusalem?					
Never	1	1	1	1	1
Once	4	7	14	14	12
A few times	6	21	24	24	22
Quite a lot of times	26	29	29	32	29
Very many times	62	42	33	29	36
Total	100	100	100	100	100
N	114	253	676	323	1366
28. When was the last time you visited the Old City of Jerusalem?					
Never visited Old City	3	1	1	3	2
Before intifada (1987)	13	20	15	16	16
6 to 7 years ago	4	5	5	10	6
4 to 5 years ago	4	8	9	8	8
2 to 3 years ago	5	14	16	14	14
A year ago	5	12	17	15	14
A few months ago	33	23	24	18	23
In the past month	33	16	14	16	17
Total	100	100	100	100	100
N	144	276	724	359	1503

29. *Have you ever visited any of the Arab villages now included within the borders of Jerusalem?*

Never	66	72	76	68	73
Once	6	11	8	11	9
A few times	19	13	13	17	14
Quite a lot of times	5	3	2	3	3
Very many times	4	0	1	1	1
Total	100	100	100	100	100
N	142	264	701	352	1459

30. *Have you ever visited any of the neighborhoods of East Jerusalem?*

Never	58	69	73	59	67
Once	10	12	9	14	11
A few times	22	14	14	20	16
Quite a lot of times	6	3	2	5	3
Very many times	4	2	2	1	2
Total	100	100	100	100	100
N	144	263	699	353	1459

31. *To what extent do you agree that we should make no concessions over Jerusalem even if we have to give up peace?*

Definitely agree	50	40	26	18	29
Agree	25	32	35	26	31
Disagree	10	16	28	41	27
Definitely disagree	15	12	11	15	12
Total	100	100	100	100	100
N	144	274	717	356	1491

	Strictly observant	To a great extent	Observe somewhat	Totally nonobservant	Total
32. As far as you know nowadays, what proportion of Jerusalmites are Arabs?					
A very small minority	13	8	4	3	5
Only 15% to 20% are Arabs	37	36	30	27	31
Around 30% are Arabs	43	48	58	62	56
About half are Arabs	6	7	6	6	6
Most of them are Arabs	2	2	2	1	2
Total	100	100	100	100	100
N	123	234	635	321	1313
33. As far as you know has the proportion of Arabs in Jerusalem increased or decreased since 1967?					
Increased greatly	38	31	25	23	27
Increased somewhat	50	58	62	65	61
Principally the same	4	5	9	6	7
Decreased somewhat	8	3	3	5	4
Decreased greatly	1	2	1	2	1
Total	100	100	100	100	100
N	128	234	636	308	1306
34. More than a quarter—28%—of the inhabitants of Jerusalem are Arabs. Does this disturb you?					
Disturbs very much	41	36	27	19	28
Disturbs	28	36	33	32	33
Does not disturb	27	25	36	41	34
Does not disturb at all	5	3	5	8	5
Total	100	100	100	100	100
N	147	276	719	361	1503

35. To avoid an Arab majority, to what extent do you support restricting construction of housing for Arabs?

Definitely support	44	36	19	13	23
Support	31	40	47	35	42
Object	20	19	29	41	29
Definitely object	4	5	5	10	6
Total	100	100	100	100	100
N	143	271	708	355	1477

36. To ensure a Jewish majority, do you support redefining city limits so Arab settlements will be outside the city?

Definitely support	22	24	14	16	17
Support	45	41	44	38	42
Object	30	27	35	39	34
Definitely object	3	8	7	7	7
Total	100	100	100	100	100
N	143	274	717	349	1483

37. Of three descriptions of the borders of Jerusalem, which description is the most appropriate?

2 united parts	26	24	22	16	21
2 parts + natural growth	20	22	23	23	23
2 parts + regions	54	54	55	61	56
Total	100	100	100	100	100
N	124	231	624	323	1302

38. Compared to East Jerusalem under Jordanian rule up to the Six-Day War what is the size of East Jerusalem nowadays?

About the same	20	19	14	13	16
Somewhat bigger	42	54	60	62	58
Much bigger	38	27	25	24	27
Total	100	100	100	100	200
N	117	210	589	289	1205

	Strictly observant	To a great extent	Observe somewhat	Totally nonobservant	Total
39. Do you consider it a problem if Arabs of East Jerusalem become citizens of a Palestinian state if Jerusalem remains united under Israel?					
A very big problem	60	45	40	32	41
Some problem	25	38	34	34	34
A small problem	4	8	11	11	10
No problem at all	10	8	13	18	13
It is very desirable	1	2	2	4	3
Total	100	100	100	100	100
N	146	277	720	358	1501
40. To what extent do you believe there can be true peace between Israel and the Arab world in the foreseeable future?					
Believe strongly	2	3	6	12	6
Believe	14	29	30	34	29
Don't believe so much	31	36	37	36	36
Don't believe at all	53	32	28	17	28
Total	100	100	100	100	100
N	147	278	723	361	1509
41. Do you believe that a peace agreement with the Palestinians will bring a true, long-term peace?					
Believe strongly	1	3	4	12	5
Believe	7	24	29	36	28
Don't believe so much	33	36	37	34	36
Don't believe at all	59	37	30	18	31
Total	100	100	100	100	100
N	144	276	726	360	1506

42. *Do you agree or disagree that compromise on Jerusalem is the key to true peace between Israel and the Arab States?*

Definitely agreed	1	3	2	7	3
Agree	7	15	16	26	17
Disagree	26	40	45	43	42
Definitely disagree	66	41	38	24	38
Total	100	100	100	100	100
N	145	277	722	357	1501

43. *To what extent do you believe that for true peace with the Palestinians we must compromise on Jerusalem?*

Believe strongly	1	2	2	6	3
Believe	4	14	16	28	17
Don't believe so much	19	33	39	35	35
Don't believe at all	75	51	43	31	45
Total	100	100	100	100	100
N	146	275	720	359	1500

44. *To what extent do you believe that for co-existence between Arabs and Jews in Jerusalem we must compromise on Jerusalem?*

Believe strongly	1	3	2	7	3
Believe	5	14	16	29	18
Don't believe so much	21	38	40	35	37
Don't believe at all	74	45	41	29	42
Total	100	100	100	100	100
N	145	277	719	359	1500

45. Do you agree there is better chance of peaceful co-existence with Palestinians of Jerusalem than with Palestinians of the West Bank?

	Strictly observant	To a great extent	Observe somewhat	Totally nonobservant	Total
Definitely agree	5	5	5	6	5
Agree	25	37	39	44	39
Disagree	36	40	44	41	42
Definitely disagree	34	18	12	8	14
Total	100	100	100	100	100
N	141	273	712	350	1476

46. Do you agree that the only way to achieve security is by putting up a wall to separate Israel from territories?

	Strictly observant	To a great extent	Observe somewhat	Totally nonobservant	Total
Definitely agree	19	17	14	16	16
Agree	28	39	34	24	32
Disagree	30	30	42	50	40
Definitely disagree	24	14	10	10	12
Total	100	100	100	100	100
N	145	274	720	357	1496

47. Do you agree or disagree to such a separation between Jews and Arabs in Jerusalem?

	Strictly observant	To a great extent	Observe somewhat	Totally nonobservant	Total
Definitely agree	15	9	6	4	7
Agree	23	32	21	18	23
Disagree	34	40	56	59	52
Definitely disagree	28	19	17	18	19
Total	100	100	100	100	100
N	142	275	721	358	1496

48. *Do you agree or disagree that in daily life in Jerusalem there is in fact separation between Jews and Arabs?*

Definitely agree	19	13	12	17	14
Agree	36	46	44	37	42
Disagree	35	32	39	42	38
Definitely disagree	10	9	5	4	6
Total	100	100	100	100	100
N	145	277	717	351	1490

49. *Is it desirable that in the daily life of Jerusalem there be a separation between Jews and Arabs in residence, etc.?*

Very desirable	39	22	16	9	18
Desirable	28	41	35	28	34
Not desirable	27	27	43	56	42
Very undesirable	7	10	6	8	7
Total	100	100	100	100	100
N	145	275	723	359	1502

50. *Do you agree to cede Arab neighborhoods of East Jerusalem to Palestinians if the Old City, the Mount of Olives, etc., remain in Jerusalem as today?*

Definitely agree	8	8	7	15	9
Agree	19	31	35	37	33
Disagree	21	30	34	31	31
Definitely disagree	53	31	24	17	27
Total	100	100	100	100	100
N	145	273	718	357	1493

	Strictly observant	To a great extent	Observe somewhat	Totally nonobservant	Total
51. Is it convincing that without compromise on Jerusalem Muslim extremists will strengthen?					
Very convincing	5	5	4	9	5
Convincing	6	15	19	22	18
Not so convincing	26	29	30	28	29
Not at all convincing	63	51	48	42	48
Total	100	100	100	100	100
N	145	275	723	361	1504
52. Is it convincing that without compromise on Jerusalem any Palestinian leader that makes peace will be discredited among Palestinians?					
Very convincing	3	4	5	8	5
Convincing	12	17	15	23	17
Not so convincing	18	28	33	33	31
Not at all convincing	67	51	48	36	47
Total	100	100	100	100	100
N	146	272	719	359	1496
53. Is it convincing that a compromise on Jerusalem will improve peace with Egypt?					
Very convincing	3	4	4	7	5
Convincing	8	14	13	18	14
Not so convincing	14	30	31	31	29
Not at all convincing	75	51	52	44	52
Total	100	100	100	100	100
N	145	274	722	361	1502

54. *Is it convincing that a compromise will honor the religious-national rights of Palestinians in Jerusalem?*

Very convincing	3	3	4	11	5
Convincing	10	19	16	24	18
Not so convincing	18	32	31	30	30
Not at all convincing	69	47	49	35	47
Total	100	100	100	100	100
N	145	275	718	361	1499

55. *Is it convincing that a compromise on Jerusalem will enhance the personal safety of Israelis in Jerusalem?*

Very convincing	9	10	7	17	10
Convincing	8	21	21	23	20
Not so convincing	19	29	29	28	28
Not at all convincing	63	40	43	32	42
Total	100	100	100	100	100
N	145	275	722	362	1504

56. *Is it convincing that a compromise on Jerusalem will lead to international recognition of Jerusalem as the capital of Israel?*

Very convincing	8	11	9	15	11
Convincing	15	21	15	22	18
Not so convincing	14	22	27	25	25
Not at all convincing	63	47	49	38	47
Total	100	100	100	100	100
N	145	275	722	362	1504

	Strictly observant	To a great extent	Observe somewhat	Totally nonobservant	Total
57. Is it convincing there should not be compromise on Jerusalem because Jerusalem is much more important for Judaism than for Islam?					
Very convincing	65	43	41	29	41
Convincing	24	35	28	17	26
Not so convincing	6	14	18	25	18
Not at all convincing	6	8	13	30	15
Total	100	100	100	100	100
N	144	276	718	359	1497
58. Is it convincing there should not be compromise on Jerusalem because a city should not be divided because of a minority?					
Very convincing	63	40	38	29	38
Convincing	23	34	33	26	31
Not so convincing	9	20	19	25	19
Not at all convincing	5	6	10	20	11
Total	100	100	100	100	100
N	145	276	718	360	1499
59. Is it convincing there should not be compromise on Jerusalem because concessions on Jerusalem will enhance Palestinian demands?					
Very convincing	83	61	60	43	58
Convincing	14	29	25	26	25
Not so convincing	0	8	10	14	10
Not at all convincing	3	3	4	17	7
Total	100	100	100	100	100
N	144	276	717	360	1497

60. *Is it convincing there should not be compromise on Jerusalem because Jews won't have free access to the Old City?*

Very convincing	75	54	51	41	52
Convincing	17	28	28	21	25
Not so convincing	4	12	12	19	13
Not at all convincing	4	6	9	19	10
Total	100	100	100	100	100
N	144	274	715	359	1492

61. *In your opinion do Palestinians have any sort of legitimate rights with regard to Jerusalem?*

Yes, definitely	0	3	3	10	5
Yes	19	30	35	42	34
No	34	39	36	30	35
Definitely no	48	28	26	18	26
Total	100	100	100	100	100
N	145	275	719	361	1500

62. *To what extent in your opinion is the Palestinian claim for East Jerusalem as a capital justified?*

Definitely justified	1	1	2	4	2
Justified	7	15	16	29	18
Not justified	32	47	46	40	43
Definitely not justified	61	38	36	28	37
Total	100	100	100	100	100
N	146	277	716	357	1496

	Strictly observant	To a great extent	Observe somewhat	Totally nonobservant	Total
63. Is it convincing that real, long-term peace with Arab world is possible if Saudi Arabia opens an embassy in Jerusalem?					
Very convincing	3	12	9	13	10
Convincing	15	25	25	31	26
Not so convincing	31	35	32	29	32
Not at all convincing	51	28	33	27	32
Total	100	100	100	100	100
N	144	272	719	360	1495
64. Is it convincing that peace with the Arab world is possible if there are commercial relations with Arab States?					
Very convincing	8	16	15	21	16
Convincing	24	37	38	42	38
Not so convincing	26	30	27	23	26
Not at all convincing	42	18	19	14	20
Total	100	100	100	100	100
N	145	274	718	360	1497
65. In negotiations on Jerusalem would you consider transferring to Palestinian sovereignty Arab settlements now within Jerusalem?					
Consider very seriously	5	16	11	22	14
Consider seriously	21	24	35	35	31
Not so seriously	18	19	18	20	19
Not at all	23	21	23	14	20
Won't consider	34	20	14	10	16
Total	100	100	100	100	100
N	145	272	711	358	1486

66. *Would you consider the idea that Arab settlements now in Jerusalem go to Palestinian sovereignty in exchange for Jewish regions in the West Bank?*

Consider very seriously	6	11	12	21	14
Consider seriously	22	27	30	33	29
Not so seriously	14	17	18	19	17
Not at all	24	25	27	16	24
Won't consider	34	20	13	11	16
Total	100	100	100	100	100
N	144	271	709	360	1484

67. *Would you consider transferring Arab neighborhoods of East Jerusalem except those inside the walls to Palestinian sovereignty?*

Consider very seriously	4	10	8	15	10
Consider seriously	13	19	25	29	24
Not so seriously	18	23	21	25	22
Not at all	31	27	30	19	27
Won't consider	34	21	15	11	17
Total	100	100	100	100	100
N	143	270	708	357	1478

68. *In negotiations on Jerusalem would you consider giving the Palestinians sovereignty over the Arab neighborhoods of the Old City?*

Consider very seriously	3	6	6	11	7
Consider seriously	8	15	14	23	16
Not so seriously	16	20	22	25	22
Not at all	38	35	40	28	36
Won't consider	35	24	17	14	19
Total	100	100	100	100	100
N	144	271	708	357	1480

	Strictly observant	To a great extent	Observe somewhat	Totally nonobservant	Total
69. In negotiations on Jerusalem would you consider the idea that control of the Temple Mount will be under the Wakf as is now?					
Consider very seriously	3	7	7	17	9
Consider seriously	13	15	23	30	22
Not so seriously	15	23	23	21	22
Not at all	34	32	31	19	29
Won't consider	35	23	17	13	19
Total	100	100	100	100	100
N	144	270	704	356	1474
70. Would you consider the idea that Palestinians will get sovereignty of the Temple Mount in exchange for Palestinian recognition of Israel's sovereignty of Wailing Wall?					
Consider very seriously	1	3	4	11	5
Consider seriously	6	11	17	19	15
Not so seriously	19	20	21	23	21
Not at all	34	38	39	31	37
Won't consider	40	29	19	15	22
Total	100	100	100	100	100
N	144	268	707	357	1476

71. *In negotiations on Jerusalem would you consider turning the Old City into an international city under the United Nations?*

Consider very seriously	3	4	3	10	5
Consider seriously	6	11	13	19	13
Not so seriously	10	13	19	22	18
Not at all	38	43	43	31	40
Won't consider	44	29	22	18	24
Total	100	100	100	100	100
N	144	272	707	359	1482

72. *Would you consider giving East Jerusalem to Palestinian sovereignty while Jewish neighborhoods in East Jerusalem have special status under Israeli control?*

Consider very seriously	3	3	4	9	5
Consider seriously	6	15	13	17	14
Not so seriously	13	17	18	25	19
Not at all	37	39	45	30	40
Won't consider	41	26	19	18	22
Total	100	100	100	100	100
N	144	271	709	359	1483

73. *Would you consider retaining Israeli sovereignty over East Jerusalem while Arab neighborhoods in East Jerusalem have special status under Palestinian control?*

Consider very seriously	1	4	8	13	8
Consider seriously	18	26	27	31	27
Not so seriously	18	22	21	24	22
Not at all	28	26	29	19	26
Won't consider	35	21	15	12	18
Total	100	100	100	100	100
N	144	270	708	357	1479

	Strictly observant	To a great extent	Observe somewhat	Totally nonobservant	Total
74. Would you consider establishing joint Palestinian-Jewish administration for Old City without Israel having to yield sovereignty?					
Consider very seriously	7	6	8	15	9
Consider seriously	15	25	24	28	24
Not so seriously	24	28	25	22	25
Not at all	54	41	43	34	42
Total	100	100	100	100	100
N	136	257	698	357	1448
75. To what extent is it important to you that Jews can pray on the Temple Mount?					
Very important	74	67	59	45	59
Important	11	26	30	28	27
Not so important	7	5	8	19	10
Not at all important	7	2	3	8	4
Total	100	100	100	100	100
N	140	275	712	361	1488
76. Is it acceptable to you that each side stop arguing about sovereignty over the Temple Mount and agree it belongs to God?					
Definitely yes	20	8	8	8	9
Yes	22	28	27	23	26
No	30	37	33	28	32
Definitely no	28	28	32	41	33
Total	100	100	100	100	100
N	140	268	712	356	1476

77. *Under present circumstances, do you support or object to the establishment of a Palestinian state?*

Definitely support	1	4	3	11	5
Support	4	19	30	41	28
Object	36	36	38	28	35
Definitely object	60	42	29	20	32
Total	100	100	100	100	100
N	146	276	716	357	1495

78. *Are you for or against negotiations on Jerusalem within the peace process?*

Definitely for	1	4	2	8	3
For	3	9	18	30	18
Against	22	35	39	34	36
Definitely against	73	53	41	28	43
Total	100	100	100	100	100
N	147	277	718	355	1497

79. *In the light of recent developments, will a Palestinian state eventually be established?*

Surely be established	13	13	18	25	18
I think so	44	62	63	59	60
I don't think so	27	20	15	11	16
Surely not established	15	6	4	4	6
Total	100	100	100	100	100
N	143	271	716	357	1487

	Strictly observant	To a great extent	Observe somewhat	Totally nonobservant	Total
80. If a Palestinian state is established, do you support that an Arab region in East Jerusalem be designated as Palestinian capital?					
Definitely support	1	3	3	6	4
Support	8	14	15	22	16
Object	26	35	32	26	30
Definitely object	66	49	50	45	50
Total	100	100	100	100	100
N	145	274	714	356	1489
81. If a Palestinian state is established, do you support that Palestinian capital be an area of East Jerusalem plus an area of West Bank adjoining Jerusalem?					
Definitely support	1	4	3	6	4
Support	10	14	19	27	19
Object	28	33	30	26	29
Definitely object	61	48	48	41	48
Total	100	100	100	100	100
N	144	273	717	354	1488
82. In comparison with other topics being negotiated—water rights, refugees etc.—is the topic of Jerusalem more or less important?					
Much more important	61	53	39	32	42
More important	18	22	25	26	24
As other topics	19	22	33	38	31
Less important	1	1	2	4	2
Much less important	1		1	1	1
Total	100	100	100	100	100
N	144	273	718	358	1493

83. *To what extent is a lawful demonstration justified if a non-Zionist Knesset majority arrives at a compromise on Jerusalem?*

Very justified	83	69	72	67	71
Justified	14	27	24	29	25
Not so justified	2	3	2	2	2
Not at all justified	1	1	2	2	2
Total	100	100	100	100	100
N	144	277	719	359	1499

84. *To what extent are nonviolent actions justified if a non-Zionist Knesset majority arrives at a compromise on Jerusalem?*

Very justified	39	21	18	12	19
Justified	30	27	20	16	21
Not so justified	10	19	19	18	18
Not at all justified	22	33	43	55	42
Total	100	100	100	100	100
N	144	273	716	358	1491

85. *Is use of force for preventing implementation justified if a non-Zionist Knesset majority arrives at a compromise on Jerusalem?*

Very justified	15	7	7	4	7
Justified	13	16	8	6	9
Not so justified	26	21	15	12	16
Not at all justified	47	56	71	78	67
Total	100	100	100	100	100
N	144	275	714	356	1489

	Strictly observant	To a great extent	Observe somewhat	Totally nonobservant	Total
86. Are violent actions against Palestinians justified if a non-Zionist Knesset majority arrives at a compromise on Jerusalem?					
Very justified	11	11	11	8	10
Justified	9	10	5	6	7
Not so justified	20	20	13	9	14
Not at all justified	60	59	71	77	69
Total	100	100	100	100	100
N	143	274	715	358	1490
87. Are violent actions against other Jews justified if a non-Zionist Knesset majority arrives at a compromise on Jerusalem?					
Very justified	3	3	3	1	3
Justified	3	4	2	2	3
Not so justified	10	11	6	8	7
Not at all justified	84	82	89	89	87
Total	100	100	100	100	100
N	143	272	709	358	1482
88. If a Knesset with a Zionist majority approves decision on Jerusalem to which you object what protest would you justify?					
Not justify any protest	8	6	6	6	6
Lawful demonstrations	53	67	71	80	71
Lawful + non-violent	32	23	19	12	20
Lawful + unlawful violent	7	4	3	2	3
Total	100	100	100	100	100
N	143	275	715	359	1492

89. *Would you participate in any action against a compromise on*
Jerusalem that you don't approve of?

Yes, definitely	26	13	10	8	12
Yes	16	19	13	14	15
Perhaps yes	20	29	27	29	27
Perhaps no	2	5	4	3	4
No	21	24	34	35	31
Definitely not	15	10	11	11	11
Total	100	100	100	100	100
N	141	277	719	359	1496

Appendix B
Data from Study of Palestinians

Appendix B-1
National sample and region

(All questions/all percentages)		National	West Bank*	Gaza	Jerusalem
1) To what extent do you follow the negotiations between Palestinians and Israelis?	1. To a great extent	36	32	45	28
	2. To some extent	29	31	24	22
	3. To a small extent	22	23	20	26
	4. Not at all	13	14	11	24
2) To what extent do you follow mthe topic of the future of Jerusalem within the peace process?	1. To a great extent	59	54	63	57
	2. To some extent	21	23	17	18
	3. To a small extent	13	13	13	13
	4. Not at all	7	7	7	12
3) Are you for or against negotiations on Jerusalem within the peace process?	1. Definitely for	58	51	70	44
	2. For	22	25	18	30
	3. Against	12	15	6	15
	4. Definitely against	8	9	6	11
4) Will an agreement over Jerusalem be more binding if it is reached by the current negotiators, or if reached by a Palestinian state?	1. Much more binding under a Palestinian state	36	27	52	25
	2. More binding under a Palestinian state	9	9	9	6
	3. Will not make a difference	30	37	19	36
	4. More binding if reached by the current negotiators	12	12	12	20

---

* The Jerusalem sample is part of the West Bank sample. Therefore, the results of the national sample represent the weighted average for the West Bank sample and the Gaza sample only.

299

(All questions/all percentages)		National	West Bank*	Gaza	Jerusalem
	5. Much more binding if reached by the current negotiators	13	16	9	14
5) If you were able to advise Palestinian negotiators with respect to Jerusalem, with respect to their willingness to reach a with the Israelis, how would you advise them?	1. Be much less compromising	62	66	54	66
	2. Be less compromising	25	27	21	22
	3. Be somewhat more compromising	14	7	25	12
6) To what extent are you satisfied with the PNA concern with Jerusalem?	1. Very satisfied	24	10	47	7
	2. Satisfied	31	30	31	25
	3. Not satisfied	26	33	14	26
	4. Not satisfied at all	19	27	8	42
7) If the only way a Palestinian state could come into existence was by recognizing Israel's claim that it only is sovereign over all of Jerusalem, would you support that?	1. Definitely no	75	71	80	65
	2. No	19	22	14	23
	3. Yes	5	5	5	11
	4. Definitely yes	1	2	1	1
8) How important is Jerusalem to you personally?	1. Very important	92	90	95	89
	2. Important	7	9	4	10
	3. Not so important	1	1	1	1
	4. Not at all important	—	—	—	—
9) Do you feel a sense of personal belonging to Jerusalem?	1. Definitely yes	81	76	89	87
	2. Yes	16	20	8	13
	3. No	2	3	1	—
	4. Not at all	1	1	2	—
10) What is the most serious problem facing East Jerusalem?	1. The increase of Jewish population	8	6	11	5
	2. The expropriation of Palestinian land	6	4	10	4
	3. The acute social problems	—	—	—	1
	4. 1 + 2	34	33	36	23
	5. All are equally serious	52	57	43	67

To what extent is Jerusalem important to you from each of the following points of view?

		National	West Bank*	Gaza	Jerusalem
11) Islamic religious	1. Very important	90	87	97	78
	2. Important	9	11	3	19
	3. Not so important	1	2	—	3
	4. Not at all important	—	—	—	—

(All questions/all percentages)		National	West Bank*	Gaza	Jerusalem
12) Palestinian national-historical	1. Very important	89	87	93	81
	2. Important	10	11	7	18
	3. Not so important	1	1	—	1
	4. Not at all important	—	1	—	—
13) As a center for the Arab people	1. Very important	74	69	83	67
	2. Important	21	25	14	22
	3. Not so important	4	5	2	10
	4. Not at all important	1	1	1	1
14) As a center for all religions	1. Very important	77	73	85	68
	2. Important	18	22	12	23
	3. Not so important	3	3	2	6
	4. Not at all important	2	2	1	3
15) As a symbol of the future Palestinian state	1. Very important	90	88	93	77
	2. Important	8	9	5	17
	3. Not so important	1	1	1	4
	4. Not at all important	1	2	1	2
16) Do you view Jerusalem as acapital for:	1. A Palestinian state?	46	54	33	60
	2. A Palestinian-Islamic state?	42	34	54	22
	3. An Islamic state?	12	12	13	18
17) The Israelis say that Jeruslame is important to them as a national center. To what extent is this true?	1. Definitely not true	63	57	74	63
	2. Not true	23	27	16	19
	3. To some extent true	12	14	9	14
	4. Definitely true	2	2	1	4
18) The Israelis say that Jerusalem is important to them from a religious point of view. To what extent is this true?	1. Definitely not true	44	36	58	47
	2. Not true	20	21	18	14
	3. To some extent true	33	39	22	32
	4. Definitely true	3	4	2	7
19) Which one of these three descriptions of the area represents most accurately the Israeli government views as constituting Jerusalem?	1. The two parts of the city that had been divided until the Six-Day War, in 1967	17	16	18	20
	2. The two parts of the city that had been divided until the Six-Day War, in 1967, plus natural urban growth	13	13	15	13
	3. The two parts of the city plus large additional areas from the West Bank that were added to Jerusalem by the Israeli government.	70	71	67	67

(All questions/all percentages)		National	West Bank*	Gaza	Jerusalem
20) After the Six-Day War in 1967, Israel expanded the city limits of Jerusalem to include large areas that had been under Jordanian control, but had never been within the city limits. Do you consider such areas to be part of Jerusalem?	1. Definitely yes	39	29	56	43
	2. Yes	19	23	13	16
	3. No	27	30	21	24
	4. Definitely no	15	19	10	17
21) Do you consider the Jewish areas settled after 1967 (Gilo, Ramot, Ramot Eshkol, Pisgat Zeev) as part of Jerusalem?	1. Definitely yes	47	42	55	60
	2. Yes	22	23	20	14
	3. No	19	21	16	19
	4. Definitely no	13	15	9	7
22) Do you consider Palestinian village areas such as Um Tuba and Zur Baher to be part of Jerusalem?	1. Definitely yes	53	48	62	71
	2. Yes	31	34	26	20
	3. No	12	14	9	8
	4. Definitely no	4	5	2	1

I will read a list of places in Jerusalem. Please tell me, for each one of them, to what extent is or isn't it important to you as part of Jerusalem?

		National	West Bank*	Gaza	Jerusalem
23) Haram al-Sharif plateau	1. Very important	94	92	98	89
	2. Important	5	7	2	9
	3. Not so important	1	1	—	2
	4. Not at all important	—	—	—	—
24) al-Aqsa mosque and the Dome of the Rock	1. Very important	95	93	98	91
	2. Important	5	6	2	7
	3. Not so important	—	1	—	2
	4. Not at all important	—	—	—	—
25) Mount of Olives	1. Very important	66	62	72	65
	2. Important	29	33	23	33
	3. Not so important	4	4	4	2
	4. Not at all important	1	1	1	—
26) The Western Wall	1. Very important	34	38	26	36
	2. Important	20	23	15	23
	3. Not so important	18	18	19	16
	4. Not at all important	28	21	40	25
27) The Islamic quarters of the Old City	1. Very important	85	83	89	83
	2. Important	13	14	10	16
	3. Not so important	2	2	1	1
	4. Not at all important	—	1	—	—
28) The Christian quarters of the Old City	1. Very important	47	55	33	62
	2. Important	30	31	28	28
	3. Not so important	13	11	18	8
	4. Not at all important	10	3	21	2

(All questions/all percentages)		National	West Bank*	Gaza	Jerusalem

I will read a list of places in Jerusalem. Please tell me, for each one of them, to what extent is or isn't it important to you as part of Jerusalem?

		National	West Bank*	Gaza	Jerusalem
29) The Jewish quarters of the Old City	1. Very important	24	27	17	33
	2. Important	17	17	16	16
	3. Not so important	21	23	19	19
	4. Not at all important	38	33	48	32
30) Palestinian neighborhoods in downtown East Jerusalem (Wadi Jos, Sheikh Jarah, etc.)	1. Very important	59	54	66	70
	2. Important	33	37	28	28
	3. Not so important	6	7	4	1
	4. Not at all important	2	2	2	2
31) The new Jewish neighborhoods established after 1967 which are included by the Israelis in Jerusalem (e.g., Gilo, Ramot, etc.)	1. Very important	29	26	35	30
	2. Important	18	19	16	25
	3. Not so important	15	16	12	14
	4. Not at all important	38	39	37	31
32) The older Jewish neighborhoods in the western part of the city (e.g., Rehavia, Talbeih, Beit Hakerem, etc.)	1. Very important	26	22	32	26
	2. Important	18	20	15	29
	3. Not so important	19	21	14	21
	4. Not at all important	37	37	38	24
33) The Old City	1. Very important	86	87	85	96
	2. Important	12	11	13	4
	3. Not so important	1	1	1	—
	4. Not at all important	1	1	1	—
34) Have you ever visited Jerusalem?*	1. Never	11	3	22	NA
	2. Once	8	3	14	
	3. A few times	26	25	28	
	4. Quite a few times	43	50	33	
	5. Very many times	12	19	3	
35) When was the last time you visited the Old City of Jerusalem?	1. I have never visited it	11	3	22	NA
	2. Before the Intifada	22	10	39	
	3. 6 to 7 years ago	6	6	8	
	4. 4 to 5 years ago	11	8	14	
	5. 2 to 3 years ago	14	15	12	
	6. A year ago	16	25	3	
	7. Some months ago	12	20	2	
	8. In the past month	8	13	—	
36) Have you ever visited any of the Jewish areas that were built on land included in the city after 1967, such as Ramot, Pisgat Zeev, Gilo, etc.?	1. Never	79	72	90	39
	2. Once	7	10	3	8
	3. A few times	8	10	5	23
	4. Quite a few times	5	7	2	19
	5. Very many times	1	2	—	11

* The results for questions 34 and 35 exclude respondents resideing in Jerusalem.

(All questions/all percentages)		National	West Bank*	Gaza	Jerusalem
37) Have you ever visited any of the Jewish neighborhoods in the western part of the city?	1. Never	44	30	70	2
	2. Once	13	14	12	3
	3. A few times	23	30	10	28
	4. Quite a few times	14	17	8	32
	5. Very many times	6	9	—	35
38) There are people who say that we should make no concessions at all over Jerusalem even if we have to give up achieving a Palestinian state. To what extent do you agree or disagree with this statement?	1. Definitely agree	64	58	74	61
	2. Agree	18	22	13	16
	3. Disagree	12	14	9	17
	4. Definitely disagree	6	6	4	6
39) Would you accept as a permanent solution of the Jerusalem question that Israel has sovereignty over West Jerusalem and the State of Palestine has sovereignty over East Jerusalem?	1. Definitely yes	15	13	18	12
	2. Yes	38	45	24	45
	3. No	25	23	27	20
	4. Definitely no	23	19	31	23
40) As far as you know, nowadays, what proportion of East Jerusalem are Israelis?	1. About 10%	7	6	8	5
	2. About 25%	14	17	10	16
	3. About half	11	13	9	24
	4. About two-thirds	15	13	16	18
	5. Don't know	53	51	57	37
41) In order to attain a Palestinian majority in Jerusalem, do you support or oppose considering the Jewish settlements built after 1967 as areas outside the city boundaries?	1. Definitely support	14	14	12	19
	2. Support	24	31	13	27
	3. Object	41	37	50	29
	4. Definitely object	21	18	25	25
42) In order to attain a Palestinian majority within the city, would you support redefining the city limits so that Palestinian areas adjacent to the city, such as Abu Dis and el Eizariya, are included within the city?	1. Definitely support	42	38	51	28
	2. Support	43	45	38	51
	3. Object	9	10	7	15
	4. Definitely object	6	7	4	6
43) To what extent do you believe that there can be true peace between Israel and the Arab world in the foreseeable future?	1. Believe strongly	4	2	6	1
	2. Believe	31	28	36	19
	3. Don't believe so much	29	33	23	38
	4. Don't believe at all	36	37	36	42

(All questions/all percentages)		National	West Bank*	Gaza	Jerusalem
44) Do you support genuine and lasting peace with Israel in exchange for recognition of a Palestinian state with its capital in East Jerusalem, and resolution of the refugee issue, even though this will inevitably fall short of full justice for the Palestinians?	1. Definitely yes	26	21	35	25
	2. Yes	44	50	33	43
	3. No	17	16	19	15
	4. Definitely no	13	13	13	17
45) Do you believe that a genuine Israeli willingness to compromise on Jerusalem would lead to true and lasting peace between Israel and the Arab world?	1. Definitely agree	7	6	10	3
	2. Agree	37	39	33	35
	3. Disagree	39	37	41	30
	4. Definitely disagree	17	18	16	32
46) Do you agree with the claim that because Judaism is a religion, Jews should not be thought of as consti-tuting people, and therefore are lacking in national rights?	1. Definitely yes	32	28	39	36
	2. Yes	38	43	31	35
	3. No	23	21	25	18
	4. Definitely no	7	8	5	11
47) In your opinion, is it desirable that in the daily life of Jerusalem, there be a separation between Jews and Arabs in residence, entertainment, etc.?	1. Very desirable	37	26	57	30
	2. Desirable	35	41	25	32
	3. Not desirable	22	26	16	26
	4. Very undesirable	6	8	3	12

People state various reasons in favor of compromise on Jerusalem, with regard to each of the following. Please state to what extent do you agree with the point of view.

		National	West Bank*	Gaza	Jerusalem
48) Certain compromises could be made on Jerusalem in order to bring peace; with no compromise there will never be peace.	1. Strongly agree	19	12	33	13
	2. Agree	46	51	37	46
	3. Don't agree	22	23	21	18
	4. Strongly disagree	13	15	9	23
49) Palestinians should make some compromises on Jerusalem if doing so gains more favorable out-comes on other issues in the negotiations, such as statehood, refugees, and borders.	1. Strongly agree	20	12	35	11
	2. Agree	44	46	39	39
	3. Don't agree	24	28	17	24
	4. Strongly disagree	12	15	8	26

(All questions/all percentages)		National	West Bank*	Gaza	Jerusalem

People state various reasons in favor of compromise on Jerusalem, with regard to each of the following. Please state to what extent do you agree with the point of view.

		National	West Bank*	Gaza	Jerusalem
50) A compromise on Jerusakem is the right thing to do because Israelis also have deep historical and religious attachments to Jerusalem.	1. Strongly agree	6	2	13	3
	2. Agree	34	32	36	32
	3. Don't agree	38	41	33	28
	4. Strongly disagree	22	25	18	37
51) Since we are in the weaker position, we have to compromise on Jerusalem, otherwise we will get nothing.	1. Strongly agree	19	11	32	12
	2. Agree	37	41	31	40
	3. Don't agree	26	30	21	17
	4. Strongly disagree	18	18	16	31
52) Compromise will gain us something tangible today even though we are weak; when we are strong we can gain still more.	1. Strongly agree	22	13	38	13
	2. Agree	35	35	36	27
	3. Don't agree	26	33	14	25
	4. Strongly disagree	17	19	12	35

I will now read to you various arguments against any compromise on Jerusalem. With regard to each of them, please state the extent to which you find it a convincing reason against any compromise.

		National	West Bank*	Gaza	Jerusalem
53) There should not be any compromise on Jerusalem because it is much more important for Islam than Judaism.	1. Very convincing	51	42	66	54
	2. Convincing	24	27	21	14
	3. Not convincing	22	27	13	26
	4. Not at all convincing	3	4	—	6
54) There should not be any compromise on Jerusalem because it is an Islamic Wakf.	1. Very convincing	41	31	58	34
	2. Convincing	25	27	22	19
	3. Not convincing	30	36	19	32
	4. Not at all convincing	4	6	1	15
55) There should not be any compromise on Jerusalem because Israel has no right to Jerusalem at all.	1. Very convincing	49	43	59	52
	2. Convincing	24	27	17	21
	3. Not convincing	26	28	23	23
	4. Not at all convincing	1	2	1	4
56) There should not be any compromise on Jerusalem because the actual historical connection to the Jewish people to the city is minor.	1. Very convincing	44	37	57	49
	2. Convincing	30	34	23	27
	3. Not convincing	24	27	19	19
	4. Not at all convincing	2	2	1	5
57) There should not be any compromise on Jerusalem because Jerusalem in its entirely is the heart of Palestine.	1. Very convincing	62	52	78	61
	2. Convincing	25	32	13	24
	3. Not convincing	12	15	8	13
	4. Not at all convincing	1	1	1	2

(All questions/all percentages)		National	West Bank*	Gaza	Jerusalem
58) In your opinion, do Jews have any sort of legitimate rights with regard to Jerusalem?	1. Definitely yes	2	2	2	2
	2. Yes	18	20	16	18
	3. No	28	32	22	31
	4. Definitely no	52	46	61	49
59) Assume that a satisfactory agreement giving the Palestinians sovereign rights in East Jerusalem can be reached. important to you is it that, in addition, East Jerusalem be a Palestinian capital?	1. Very important	90	86	98	79
	2. Important	7	11	2	18
	3. Not too important	2	3	—	1
	4. Not important at all	1	1	—	2

Let's assume that you were part of the negotiating team over Jerusalem. Please state the extent to which you would seriously consider each of the following proposals as permanent arrangements.

		National	West Bank*	Gaza	Jerusalem
60) Israel and Palestine together would exercise joint sovereignty over undivided city.	1. Very seriously	22	22	21	16
	2. Seriously	18	21	13	21
	3. Give the proposal some consideration	16	16	15	13
	4. Not seriously	22	19	28	20
	5. Reject totally	23	22	23	30
61) West Jerusalem would be under Israeli sovereignty, and East Jerusalem would be under Palestinian sovereignty with a special arrangement for Israeli control of the Jewish neighborhoods in East Jerusalem. The Old City would be dealt with separately.	1. Very seriously	23	21	27	18
	2. Seriously	29	33	23	34
	3. Give the proposal some consideration	16	17	14	15
	4. Not seriously	16	13	19	10
	5. Reject totally	16	16	17	23
62) In the Old City, Israel would get sovereignty over the Jewish neighborhoods, and Palestine would get sovereignty over Palestinian neighborhoods.	1. Very seriously	19	15	26	12
	2. Seriously	21	21	20	21
	3. Give the proposal some consideration	13	12	14	10
	4. Not seriously	20	21	20	13
	5. Reject totally	27	31	20	45
63) Jews would be allowed to pray on Haram al-Sharif, which would be under operational authority of the Wakf.	1. Very seriously	12	15	7	12
	2. Seriously	5	6	4	6
	3. Give the proposal some consideration	7	7	6	2
	4. Not seriously	19	17	21	6
	5. Reject totally	57	55	62	74

(All questions/all percentages)		National	West Bank*	Gaza	Jerusalem

Let's assume that you were part of the negotiating team over Jerusalem. Please state the extent to which you would seriously consider each of the following proposals as permanent arrangements.

		National	West Bank*	Gaza	Jerusalem
64) The Palestinians would get sovereignty over the Haram al-Sharif in exchange for Palestinian recognition of Israeli sovereignty over the Western Wall.	1. Very seriously	30	21	46	19
	2. Seriously	20	22	17	21
	3. Give the proposal some consideration	15	17	11	15
	4. Not seriously	16	19	10	18
	5. Reject totally	19	21	16	27
65) Israel would exercise sovereignty over East Jerusalem, but Palestinian neighborhoods would be given a special self-rule status.	1. Very seriously	10	11	9	8
	2. Seriously	10	8	12	5
	3. Give the proposal some consideration	9	8	11	9
	4. Not seriously	27	22	36	14
	5. Reject totally	44	51	32	63
66) West Jerusalem and the Jewish neighborhoods in East Jerusalem would be under Israeli sovereignty and the rest of East Jerusalem under Palestinian sovereignty, with the Old City dealt with separately.	1. Very seriously	13	12	13	13
	2. Seriously	15	16	15	15
	3. Give the proposal some consideration	15	17	11	16
	4. Not seriously	28	26	33	16
	5. Reject totally	29	30	28	40
67) Abu Dis would be added to Jerusalem and the Palestinian Parliament would be located in that region of the expanded city.	1. Very seriously	34	22	55	25
	2. Seriously	19	20	18	16
	3. Give the proposal some consideration	11	13	8	14
	4. Not seriously	15	18	11	12
	5. Reject totally	21	27	8	33
68) Palestinians would have sovereignty over al-Aqsa mosque and the Dome of the Rock, but with respect to the plateau itself, sovereignty would be shared with the Israelis, although day-to-day administration of the plateau would be in Palestinian hands alone.	1. Very seriously	23	22	25	11
	2. Seriously	18	19	14	31
	3. Give the proposal some consideration	12	14	10	8
	4. Not seriously	15	14	17	23
	5. Reject totally	32	31	34	27
69) The control of the Haram al-Sharif would be under the Wakf as it is now.	1. Very seriously	32	28	39	11
	2. Seriously	28	31	24	49
	3. Give the proposal some consideration	12	12	11	16
	4. Not seriously	11	10	11	13
	5. Reject totally	17	19	15	11

(All questions/all percentages)		National	West Bank*	Gaza	Jerusalem
70) There is a proposal that each side should stop arguing about sovereignty over holy sites in Jerusalem and agree that ultimate sovereignty belongs to God. Is this proposal acceptable to you?	1. Definitely yes	44	33	65	31
	2. Yes	20	23	14	16
	3. No	21	24	16	23
	4. Definitely no	15	20	5	30
71) Do you support the idea that Jordan should play a substantial role in the administration of the Islamic holy sites in Jerusalem?	1. Definitely yes	6	5	9	6
	2. Yes	10	8	12	10
	3. No	31	33	27	28
	4. Definitely no	53	54	53	56
72) Suppose that negotiations fail to resolve the question of sovereignty over the Old City. Would you support an agreement whereby the two states would jointly administer the Old City indefinitely?	1. Definitely yes	6	4	11	2
	2. Yes	21	21	22	26
	3. No	39	42	33	31
	4. Definitely no	34	33	34	41
73) Assume that no definitive solution to the Jerusalem question can be found. Would you support as an interim step that the Palestinian capital be located in the Jerusalem suburb of Abu Dis, without relinquishing the Palestinian claim to sovereignty over East Jerusalem?	1. Yes	18	13	27	21
	2. No	76	80	67	72
	3. Others	6	7	6	7
74) In comparison with other topics that are being negotiated with the Israelis, such as water rights, return of Palestinian refugees, and the status of settlements, is the topic of Jerusalem more or less important than these other topics?	1. Much more important 2. More important	47	40	61	39
	3. As important	11	12	10	9
	4. Less important	41	47	28	47
	5. Much less important	1	1	1	5
		—	—	—	—
75) If a Palestinian government accepts a compromise on Jerusalem that you don't approve of, how will you react?	1. Will definitely oppose	31	32	31	40
	2. Will oppose	35	36	33	29
	3. Will accept with reservations	28	29	26	26
	4. Will accept	6	4	11	5

(All questions/all percentages)		National	West Bank*	Gaza	Jerusalem
76) Would you participate in any action against an agreement on Jerusalem that you don't approve of?	1. Definitely yes	41	38	45	51
	2. Yes	21	26	15	18
	3. Perhaps yes	18	21	11	18
	4. No	20	15	29	13
77) Do you agree with the point of view that says "in the case of an unacceptable agreement on Jerusalem, Palestinians have the right to use all means necessary to block its implementation"?	1. Definitely agree	44	40	51	38
	2. Agree	28	31	23	35
	3. Disagree	22	22	22	18
	4. Definitely disagree	6	7	4	9
78) Which one of the following political blocs best represents your point of view?	1. Islamic	21	21	21	15
	2. Leftist	10	14	4	16
	3. Fatah	37	31	45	21
	4. Independents	32	34	30	48

Appendix B-2
Cross-tabulation by political affiliation

(All percentages)		Islamist	Leftist	Fatah	Independent
3) Are you for or against negotiations on Jerusalem within the peace process?	1. Definitely for	55	38	73	51
	2. For	14	29	20	29
	3. Against	15	17	6	14
	4. Definitely against	16	16	1	6
5) If you were able to advise Palestinian negotiators with respect to Jerusalem, with respect to their willingness to reach a compromise with the Israelis, how would you advise them?	1. Be much less compromising	71	70	58	58
	2. Be less compromising	22	25	25	28
	3. Be somewhat compromising	7	5	17	14
6) To what extent are you satisfied with the PNA concern with Jerusalem?	1. Very satisfied	18	3	33	19
	2. Satisfied	20	23	39	31
	3. Not satisfied	28	45	20	30
	4. Not satisfied at all	34	29	8	20
7) If the only way a Palestinian state could come into existence was by recognizing Israel's claim that it only is sovereign over all of Jerusalem, would you support that?	1. Definitely no	82	73	74	67
	2. No	12	24	19	26
	3. Yes	3	2	6	6
	4. Definitely yes	3	1	1	1
8) How important is Jerusalem to you personally?	1. Very important	97	88	94	86
	2. Important	3	10	5	12
	3. Not so important	—	1	1	2
	4. Not at all important	—	1	—	—
10) What is the most serious problem facing East Jerusalem?	1. The increase of Jewish population	7	6	9	6
	2. The expropriation of Palestinian land	5	8	5	6
	3. The acute social problems	—	—	1	—
	4. 1 + 2	34	34	38	32
	5. All are equally serious	54	53	47	56

To what extent is Jerusalem important to you from each of the following points of view?

11) Islamic religious	1. Very important	97	67	95	84
	2. Important	2	26	4	14
	3. Not so important	1	5	1	2
	4. Not at all important	—	2	—	—

Political Affiliation		Islamist	Leftist	Fatah	Independent
12) Palestinian national-historical	1. Very important	89	88	90	87
	2. Important	8	10	9	12
	3. Not so important	—	1	1	1
	4. Not at all important	3	1	—	—
13) As a center for the Arab people	1. Very important	72	55	79	73
	2. Important	21	38	16	21
	3. Not so important	5	2	5	5
	4. Not at all important	2	5	—	1
14) As a center for all religions	1. Very important	73	64	84	73
	2. Important	21	29	12	23
	3. Not so important	2	3	3	3
	4. Not at all important	4	4	1	1
15) As a symbol of the future Palestinian state	1. Very important	84	89	93	88
	2. Important	9	9	7	9
	3. Not so important	2	1	—	1
	4. Not at all important	5	1	—	2
16) Do you view Jerusalem as a capital for:	1. A Palestinian state?	15	73	59	54
	2. A Palestinian-Islamic state?	58	25	40	36
	3. An Islamic state?	28	2	6	10
17) The Israelis say that Jerusalem is important to them as a religious center. To what extent is this true?	1. Not true at all	50	36	47	47
	2. Not true	21	21	22	24
	3. True to an extent	16	26	20	17
	4. Very true	13	17	11	13
18) The Israelis say that Jerusalem is important to them from a religious point of view. To what extent is this true?	1. Not true at all	54	35	46	35
	2. Not true	17	18	25	17
	3. True to an extent	26	42	28	42
	4. Very true	3	5	2	6

I will read a list of places in Jerusalem. Please tell me, for each one of them, to what extent is or isn't it important to you as part of Jerusalem?

		Islamist	Leftist	Fatah	Independent
23) Haram al-Sharif	1. Very important	98	81	97	91
	2. Important	2	14	2	8
	3. Not so important	—	3	—	1
	4. Not at all important	—	2	—	—
24) al-Aqsa mosque and the Dome of the Rock	1. Very important	98	81	97	92
	2. Important	2	14	3	7
	3. Not so important	—	3	—	1
	4. Not at all important	—	2	—	—
25) Mount of Olives	1. Very important	65	58	70	61
	2. Important	30	37	27	32
	3. Not so important	5	2	2	5
	4. Not at all important	—	3	1	2

Political Affiliation		Islamist	Leftist	Fatah	Independent
26) The Western Wall	1. Very important	38	33	34	35
	2. Important	22	21	18	20
	3. Not so important	13	18	21	20
	4. Not at all important	26	28	27	24
27) The Islamic quarters of the Old City	1. Very important	91	75	86	82
	2. Important	9	17	12	16
	3. Not so important	—	5	1	2
	4. Not at all important	—	3	1	—
29) The Jewish quarters of the Old City	1. Very important	23	28	24	25
	2. Important	15	20	17	20
	3. Not so important	23	24	21	22
	4. Not at all important	39	29	38	34
30) Palestinian neighborhoods in downtown East Jerusalem (Wadi Jos, Sheikh Jarah, etc.)	1. Very important	59	51	62	56
	2. Important	33	38	32	34
	3. Not so important	7	5	5	8
	4. Not at all important	1	7	2	3
31) The new Jewish neighborhoods established after 1967 which are included by the Israelis in Jerusalem (e.g., Gilo, Ramot, etc.)	1. Very important	32	26	29	28
	2. Important	16	13	17	24
	3. Not so important	15	22	15	15
	4. Not at all important	37	40	39	33
32) The older Jewish neighborhoods in the western part of the city (e.g., Rehavia, Talbieh, Beit Hakerem, etc.)	1. Very important	29	23	26	25
	2. Important	18	22	17	20
	3. Not so important	15	25	20	23
	4. Not at all important	38	31	38	32
33) The Old City	1. Very important	87	82	86	86
	2. Important	11	15	13	11
	3. Not so important	1		1	2
	4. Not at all important	1	3		2
38) There are people who say that we should make no concessions at all over Jerusalem even if we have to give up achieving a Palestinian state. To what extent do you agree or disagree with this statement?	1. Definitely agree	80	60	60	53
	2. Agree	12	23	19	25
	3. Disagree	4	12	16	16
	4. Definitely disagree	5	6	5	6
39) Would you accept as a permanent solution of the Jerusalem question that Israel has sovereignty over West Jerusalem and the State of Palestine has sovereignty over East Jerusalem?	1. Definitely yes	9	13	20	14
	2. Yes	24	40	39	46
	3. No	25	28	24	22
	4. Definitely no	42	19	18	17

Political Affiliation		Islamist	Leftist	Fatah	Independent
42) In order to attain a Palestinian majority within the city, would you support rede fining the city limits so that Palestinian areas adjacent to the city, such as Abu Dis and el Eizariya are included within the city?	1. Definitely support	41	38	49	36
	2. Support	32	40	40	48
	3. Object	15	3	8	10
	4. Definitely object	12	19	3	6
43) To what extent do you believe that there can be true peace between Israel and the Arab world in theforeseeable future?	1. Believe strongly	5	2	4	2
	2. Believe	19	19	41	30
	3. Don't believe so much	18	46	28	39
	4. Don't believe at all	58	33	28	29
44) Do you support genuine and lasting peace with Israel in exchange for recognition of a Palestinian State with its capital in East Jerusalem, andresolution of the refugee issue, even though this will inevitably fall short of full justice for the Palestinians?	1. Definitely yes	17	20	33	23
	2. Yes	31	47	49	49
	3. No	26	24	12	16
	4. Definitely no	26	9	6	12
45) Do you believe that a genuine Israeli willingness to compromise on Jerusalem would lead to true and lasting between Israel and the Arab world?	1. Definitely agree	4	11	10	5
	2. Agree	26	23	40	43
	3. Disagree	35	50	39	39
	4. Definitely disagree	35	16	10	12
46) Do you agree with the claim that because Judaism is a religion, Jews should not be thought of as constituting a people, and therefore are lacking in national rights?	1. Definitely yes	38	36	32	27
	2. Yes	33	35	40	42
	3. No	17	20	24	27
	4. Definitely no	12	10	5	4
47) In your opinion, is it desirable that in the daily life of Jerusalem there be a separation between Jews and Arabs in residence, entertainment, etc.?	1. Very desirable	44	30	38	29
	2. Desirable	33	41	36	35
	3. Not desirable	18	25	21	29
	4. Very undesirable	5	5	5	8

Political Affiliation		Islamist	Leftist	Fatah	Independent

People state various reasons in favor of compromise on Jerusalem. With regard to each of the following, please state to what extent do you agree with the point of view.

		Islamist	Leftist	Fatah	Independent
48) Certain compromises	1. Strongly agree	14	9	27	17
could be made on Jerusalem	2. Agree	28	41	53	52
in order to bring peace; with	3. Don't agree	31	35	16	20
no com promise there will	4. Strongly disagree	27	15	4	11
never be peace.					
49) Palestinians should make	1. Strongly agree	13	8	28	17
some compromises on Jeru-	2. Agree	30	37	50	52
salem if doing so gains more	3. Don't agree	32	44	16	23
favorable outcomes on other	4. Strongly disagree	24	12	6	10
issues in the negotiations, such					
as statehood, refugees, and					
borders.					
50) A compromise on Jeru-	1. Strongly agree	5	3	9	5
salem is the right thing to do	2. Agree	22	32	35	39
because Israelis also have deep	3. Don't agree	35	43	42	39
historical and religious attach-	4. Strongly disagree	38	22	15	17
ments to Jerusalem.					
51) Since we are in the weaker	1. Strongly agree	13	16	23	18
position, we have to compro-	2. Agree	24	30	42	43
mise on Jerusalem, otherwise	3. Don't agree	33	37	23	23
we will get nothing.	4. Strongly disagree	31	17	12	16
52) Compromise will gain us	1. Strongly agree	17	13	28	19
something tangible today even	2. Agree	25	31	40	39
though we are weak; when we	3. Don't agree	29	39	24	26
sare trong we can gain still	4. Strongly disagree	30	17	9	16
more.					

I will now read to you various arguments against any compromise on Jerusalem. With regard to each of them, please state the extent to which you find it a convincing reason against any compromise.

		Islamist	Leftist	Fatah	Independent
53) There should not be any	1. Very convincing	62	42	46	46
compromise on Jerusalem	2. Convincing	25	22	28	22
because it is much more	3. Not convincing	7	31	26	29
important for Islam than	4. Not at all	6	6	1	4
Judaism.	convincing				

I will now read to you various arguments against any compromise on Jerusalem. With regard to each of them, please state the extent to which you find it a convincing reason against any compromise.

		Islamist	Leftist	Fatah	Independent
54) There should not be any	1. Very convincing	61	24	37	32
compromise on Jerusalem	2. Convincing	23	22	27	25
because it is an Islamic Wakf.	3. Not convincing	14	42	35	36
	4. Not at all	2	13	1	7
	convincing				

Political Affiliation		Islamist	Leftist	Fatah	Independent
55) There should not be any compromise on Jerusalem because Israel has no right to Jerusalem at all.	1. Very convincing	69	38	46	38
	2. Convincing	19	26	25	27
	3. Not convincing	9	33	29	34
	4. Not at all convincing	3	3	1	2
56) There should not be any compromise on Jerusalem because the actual historical connection of the Jewish people to the city is minor.	1. Very convincing	63	33	42	34
	2. Convincing	24	31	33	31
	3. Not convincing	12	33	25	33
	4. Not at all convincing	2	3	1	3
58) In your opinion, do Jews have any sort of legitimate rights with regard to Jerusalem?	1. Definitely yes	3	3	2	1
	2. Yes	12	21	15	28
	3. No	16	31	32	30
	4. Definitely no	69	46	51	41
59) Assume that a satisfactory agreement giving the Palestinians sovereign rights in East Jerusalem can be reached. How important to you is it, that in addition, East Jerusalem be a Palestinian capital?	1. Very important	88	89	94	86
	2. Important	8	8	6	11
	3. Not too important	3	1	—	2
	4. Not important at all	1	2	—	1

Let's assume that you were part of the negotiating team over Jerusalem. Please state the extent to which you would seriously consider each of the following proposals as permanent arrangements.

		Islamist	Leftist	Fatah	Independent
60) Israel and Palestine together would exercise joint sovereignty over an undivided city.	1. Very seriously	17	8	28	21
	2. Seriously	13	22	17	21
	3. Give the proposal some consideration	10	19	19	15
	4. Not seriously	26	22	18	25
	5. Reject totally	34	29	18	18
61) West Jerusalem would be under Israeli sovereignty, and East Jerusalem would be under Palestinian sovereignty with a special arrangement for Israeli control of the Jewish neighborhoods in East Jerusalem. The Old City would be dealt with separately.	1. Very seriously	18	14	29	23
	2. Seriously	23	34	30	30
	3. Give the proposal some consideration	18	19	14	18
	4. Not seriously	15	15	15	15
	5. Reject totally	26	18	12	14
62) In the Old City, Israel would get sovereignty over the Jewish neighborhoods, and Palestine would get sovereignty over Palestinian neighborhoods.	1. Very seriously	15	11	24	17
	2. Seriously	16	26	20	24
	3. Give the proposal some consideration	12	14	15	12
	4. Not seriously	21	19	21	19
	5. Reject totally	36	30	20	28

Political Affiliation		Islamist	Leftist	Fatah	Independent
63) Jews would be allowed to pray on Haram al-Sharif, which would be under the operational authority of the Wakf.	1. Very seriously	12	12	15	9
	2. Seriously	5	7	6	6
	3. Give the proposal some consideration	6	11	7	8
	4. Not seriously	16	26	14	21
	5. Reject totally	61	44	58	56
64) The Palestinians would get sovereignty over Haram al-Sharif in exchange for Palestinian recognition of Israeli sovereignty over the Western Wall.	1. Very seriously	23	26	36	27
	2. Seriously	18	15	21	24
	3. Give the proposal some consideration	13	19	16	13
	4. Not seriously	17	18	13	19
	5. Reject totally	29	22	14	17
65) Israel would exercise sovereignty over East Jerusalem, but Palestinian neighborhoods would be given a special self-rule status.	1. Very seriously	7	8	11	10
	2. Seriously	7	14	10	10
	3. Give the proposal some consideration	9	10	10	8
	4. Not seriously	21	18	28	29
	5. Reject totally	56	50	41	43

Lets assume that you were part on the negotiating team over Jerusalem. Please state the extent to which you would serious consider each of the following proposals as permanent arrangements.

		Islamist	Leftist	Fatah	Independent
66) West Jerusalem and the Jewish neighborhoods in East Jerusalem would be under Israeli sovereignty and the rest of East Jerusalem under Palestinian sovereignty, with the Old City dealt with separately.	1. Very seriously	13	5	14	13
	2. Seriously	7	18	19	15
	3. Give the proposal some consideration	14	16	12	18
	4. Not seriously	28	24	31	27
	5. Reject totally	38	37	24	27
67) Abu Dis would be added to Jerusalem and the Palestinian Parliament would be located in that region of the expanded city.	1. Very seriously	35	25	42	28
	2. Seriously	14	19	19	22
	3. Give the proposal some consideration	7	11	14	11
	4. Not seriously	16	14	12	20
	5. Reject totally	28	31	13	19
68) Palestinians would have sovereignty over the al-Aqsa mosque and the Dome of the Rock, but with respect to the plateau itself sovereignty would be shared with the Israelis, although day-to-day administration of the plateau would be in Palestinian hands alone.	1. Very seriously	25	13	26	19
	2. Seriously	14	10	19	20
	3. Give the proposal some consideration	10	7	12	14
	4. Not seriously	6	13	16	15
	5. Reject totally	45	57	27	32

Political Affiliation		Islamist	Leftist	Fatah	Independent
69) The control of Haram al-Sharif would be under the Wakf as it is now.	1. Very seriously	33	20	33	33
	2. Seriously	26	17	30	27
	3. Give the proposal some consideration	12	7	14	11
	4. Not seriously	5	13	8	12
	5. Reject totally	23	43	15	17
70) There is a proposal that each side should stop arguing about sovereignty over holy sites in Jerusalem and agree that ultimage sovereignty belongs to God. Is this proposal acceptable to you?	1. Definitely yes	60	25	49	36
	2. Yes	17	10	21	23
	3. No	15	31	20	24
	4. Definitely no	8	34	10	17
71) Do you support the idea that Jordan should play a substantial role in the administration of the Islamic holy sites in Jerusalem?	1. Definitely yes	8	8	5	7
	2. Yes	15	2	10	11
	3. No	28	34	29	33
	4. Definitely no	49	56	56	49
73) Assume that no definitive solution to the Jerusalem question can be found. Would you support an interim step that the Palestinian capital be located in the Jerusalem suburb of Abu Dis, without relinquishing the Palestinian claim to sovereignty over East Jerusalem?	1. Yes	12	9	22	19
	2. No	83	79	71	75
	3. Others	5	12	7	6
74) In comparison with other topics that are being negotiated with the Israelis, such as water rights, return of Palestinian refugees, and the status of settlements, is the topic of Jerusalem more or less important than these other topics?	1. Much more important	64	34	49	38
	2. More important	10	13	9	14
	3. As important	26	50	41	46
	4. Less important	—	1	1	2
	5. Much less important	—	2	—	—
75) If a Palestinian government accepts a compromise on Jerusalem that you don't approve of, how will you react?	1. Will definitely oppose	47	36	26	26
	2. Will oppose	34	30	33	40
	3. Will accept with reservations	17	32	34	26
	4. Will accept	3	2	8	8
76) Would you participate in any action against an agreement on Jerusalem that you don't approve of?	1. Definitely yes	49	57	44	36
	2. Yes	28	29	22	20
	3. Perhaps yes	8	9	17	20
	4. No	15	15	17	24

Political Affiliation		Islamist	Leftist	Fatah	Independent
77) Do you agree with the point of view that says "in the case of an unacceptable agreement on Jerusalem, Palestinians have the right to use all means necessary to block its implementation"?	1. Definitely agree	66	43	37	33
	2. Agree	19	29	29	36
	3. Agree with reservations	11	21	28	24
	4. Agree	4	7	6	7

Appendix B-3
Cross-tabulation by religiosity

(All percentages)		Very religious	Religious	Not religious	Not at all religious
3) Are you for or against	1. Definitely for	62	60	57	47
negotiations on Jerusalem	2. For	18	22	23	28
within the peace process?	3. Against	11	11	13	11
	4. Definitely against	9	7	7	14
5) If you were able to advise	1. Be much less compromising	65	64	57	69
Palestinian negotiators with respect to Jerusalem, with	2. Be less compromising	19	22	33	23
respect to their willingness or unwillingness to reach a compromise with the Israelis, how would you advise them?	3. Be somewhat compromising	16	14	10	8
6) To what extent are you	1. Very satisfied	38	24	15	10
satisfied with the PNA	2. Satisfied	23	31	35	19
concern with Jerusalem?	3. Unsatisfied	19	26	32	36
	4. Unsatisfied at all	20	19	18	35
7) If the only way a Palestinian	1. Definitely no	78	78	70	64
state could come in to existence	2. No	15	16	23	27
was by recognizing Israel's	3. Yes	5	4	7	6
claim that it only is sovereign over all of Jerusalem, would you support that?	4. Definitely yes	2	2	—	3
8) How important is Jerusalem	1. Very important	96	95	89	78
to you personally?	2. Important	3	5	10	20
	3. Not so important	1	—	1	1
	4. Not at all important	—	—	—	1
10) What is the most serious	1. The increase of Jewish population	13	9	4	3
problem facing East Jerusalem?	2. The expropriation of Palestinian land	5	6	4	8
	3. The acute social problems	—	—	—	—
	4.1 + 2	31	35	36	33
	5. All are equally serious	52	50	56	56
To what extent is Jerusalem important to you from each of the following points of view?					
11) Islamic religious	1. Very important	98	94	88	58
	2. Important	2	6	11	31
	3. Not so important	—	—	1	9
	4. Not at all important	—	—	—	2

(All percentages)		Very religious	Religious	Not religious	Not at all religious
12) Palestinian national-historical	1. Very important	93	90	87	84
	2. Important	6	9	12	13
	3. Not so important	—	1	—	1
	4. Not at all important	1	—	1	2
13) As a center for the Arab people	1. Very important	89	77	65	57
	2. Important	10	18	28	29
	3. Not so important	1	4	6	9
	4. Not at all important	—	1	1	5
14) As a center for all religions	1. Very important	81	79	76	62
	2. Important	17	17	18	30
	3. Not so important	2	3	3	5
	4. Not at all important	—	1	3	3
15) As a symbol of the future Palestinian state	1. Very important	98	89	88	85
	2. Important	1	8	9	13
	3. Not so important	1	1	2	—
	4. Not at all important	—	2	1	2
16) Do you view Jerusalem as a capital for:	1. A Palestinian state	32	35	59	86
	2. A Palestinian-Islamic state?	50	52	30	11
	3. An Islamic state	18	13	11	3
17) The Israelis say that Jerusalem is important to them as a national center. To what extent is this true?	1. Not true at all	82	64	53	53
	2. Not true	14	23	27	26
	3. True to an extent	3	12	16	18
	4. Very true	1	1	4	3
18) The Israelis say that Jerusalem is important to them from a religious point of view. To what extent is this true?	1. Not true at all	65	46	34	30
	2. Not true	11	22	21	15
	3. True to an extent	22	30	38	47
	4. Very true	2	2	7	8

I will read a list of places in Jerusalem. Please tell me, for each one of them, to what extent is or isn't it important to you as part of Jerusalem?

23) The Haram al-Sharif	1. Very important	99	96	93	78
	2. Important	—	3	7	18
	3. Not so important	1	—	—	3
	4. Not at all important	—	1	—	1

(All percentages)		Very religious	Religious	Not religious	Not at all religious
24) al-Aqsa mosque and the Dome of the Rock	1. Very important	98	97	93	79
	2. Important	1	3	7	17
	3. Not so important	1	—	—	3
	4. Not at all important	—	—	—	1
25) Mount of Olives	1. Very important	76	67	58	60
	2. Important	20	29	37	32
	3. Not so important	2	3	5	3
	4. Not at all important	2	1	—	5
26) The Western Wall	1. Very important	41	33	34	38
	2. Important	18	19	21	21
	3. Not so important	14	19	21	18
	4. Not at all important	27	29	24	23
27) The Islamic quarters of the Old City	1. Very important	94	88	81	70
	2. Important	6	11	16	24
	3. Not so important	—	—	3	5
	4. Not at all important	—	1	—	1
28) The Christian quarters of the Old City	1. Very important	50	41	50	69
	2. Important	24	31	34	26
	3. Not so important	13	17	10	4
	4. Not at all important	13	11	6	1
29) The Jewish quarters of the Old City	1. Very important	21	22	26	33
	2. Important	15	15	20	19
	3. Not so important	17	20	27	22
	4. Not at all important	47	43	27	26
30) Palestinian neighborhoods in downtown East Jerusalem (Wadi Jos, Sheikh Jarah, etc.)	1. Very important	73	59	51	57
	2. Important	25	33	39	34
	3. Not so important	2	6	8	5
	4. Not at all important	—	2	2	4
31) The new Jewish neighborhoods established after 1967 which are included by the Israelis in Jerusalem (e.g., Gilo, Ramot, etc.)	1. Very important	31	30	26	31
	2. Important	15	19	19	16
	3. Not so important	18	13	19	16
	4. Not at all important	36	38	36	37

(All percentages)		Very religious	Religious	Not religious	Not at all religious
32) The older Jewish neighbor-hoods in the western part of the city (Rehavia, Talbieh, Beit Hakerem, etc.)	1. Very important	38	26	21	23
	2. Important	12	17	22	21
	3. Not so important	18	18	23	19
	4. Not at all important	32	31	34	37
33) The Old City	1. Very important	92	86	84	88
	2. Important	6	12	14	11
	3. Not so important	1	1	1	—
	4. Not at all important	1	1	1	1
38) There are people who say that we should make no con-cessions at all over Jerusalem even if we have give up achieving a Palestinian state. To what extent do you agree or disagree with this statement?	1. Definitely agree	79	67	51	56
	2. Agree	10	17	27	22
	3. Disagree	6	11	16	19
	4. Definitely disagree	5	5	6	3
39) Would you accept as a permanent solution of the Jerusalem question that Israel has sovereignty over West Jerusalem and the State of Palestine has sovereignty over East Jerusalem?	1. Definitely yes	12	14	17	12
	2. Yes	29	36	41	53
	3. No	24	25	27	12
	4. Definitely no	35	25	15	23
43) To what extent do you believe that there can be true peace between Isreal and the Arab world in the foreseeable future?	1. Believe strongly	4	3	3	4
	2. Believe	21	27	30	18
	3. Don't believe so much	22	36	37	45
	4. Don't believe at all	53	34	30	33
44) Do you support genuine and lasting peace with Israel in exchange for recognition of a Palestinian state with its capi-tal in East Jerusalem, and reso-lution of the refugee issue, even though this will inevitably fall short of full justice for the Palestinians?	1. Definitely yes	25	25	25	24
	2. Yes	35	42	49	49
	3. No	18	17	19	19
	4. Definitely no	22	16	7	8
45) Do you believe that a genuine Israeli willingness to compromise on Jerusalem would lead to true and lasting peace between Israel and the Arab world?	1. Definitely agree	6	7	6	13
	2. Agree	28	37	41	29
	3. Disagree	38	40	40	37
	4. Definitely disagree	28	16	13	21

(All percentages)		Very religious	Religious	Not religious	Not at all religious
46) Do you agree with the claim that because Judaism is a religion, Jews should not be thought of as constituting a people, and therefore are lacking in national rights?	1. Definitely yes	41	31	29	35
	2. Yes	31	39	41	33
	3. No	17	23	26	25
	4. Definitely no	12	7	4	7

People state various reasons in favor of compromise on Jerusalem. With regard to each of the following please state to what extent you agree with the point of view.

		Very religious	Religious	Not religious	Not at all religious
47) In your opinion, is it desirable that in the daily life of Jerusalem, there be a separation between Jews and Arabs in residence, entertainment, etc.?	1. Very desirable	45	40	29	22
	2. Desirable	33	37	36	36
	3. Not desirable	18	19	29	31
	4. Very undesirable	4	4	6	11
48) Certain compromises could be made on Jerusalem in order to bring peace; with no compromise there will never be peace.	1. Strongly agree	20	19	18	17
	2. Agree	37	46	51	41
	3. Don't agree	21	24	22	20
	4. Strongly disagree	22	11	9	22
49) Palestinians should make some compromises on Jerusalem if doing so gains more favorable outcomes on other issues in the negotiations, such as statehood, refugees, and borders.	1. Strongly agree	21	22	15	12
	2. Agree	40	43	52	35
	3. Don't agree	19	24	25	33
	4. Strongly disagree	20	11	8	20
50) A compromise on Jerusalem is the right thing to do because Israelis also have deep historical and religious attachments to Jerusalem.	1. Strongly agree	6	6	6	5
	2. Agree	38	33	30	30
	3. Don't agree	23	40	48	37
	4. Strongly disagree	33	21	16	28
51) Since we are in the weaker position, we have to compromise on Jerusalem, otherwise we will get nothing.	1. Strongly agree	19	19	16	18
	2. Agree	30	39	40	28
	3. Don't agree	26	24	28	33
	4. Strongly disagree	25	17	16	21
52) Compromise will gain us something tangible today even though we are weak; when we are strong we can gain still more.	1. Strongly agree	22	24	17	16
	2. Agree	35	39	33	23
	3. Don't agree	18	23	33	40
	4. Strongly disagree	25	14	17	21

(All percentages)		Very religious	Religious	Not religious	Not at all religious

I will now read to you various arguments against any compromise on Jerusalem. With regard to each of them, please state the extent to which you find it a convincing reason against any compromise.

		Very religious	Religious	Not religious	Not at all religious
53) There should not be any compromise on Jerusalem because it is much more important for Islam than Judaism.	1. Very convincing	67	54	42	27
	2. Convincing	17	26	27	18
	3. Not convincing	11	18	27	52
	4. Not at all convincing	5	2	4	3
54) There should not be any compromise on Jerusalem Because it is an Islamic Wakf.	1. Very convincing	65	45	30	14
	2. Convincing	17	26	29	20
	3. Not convincing	16	28	34	57
	4. Not at all convincing	2	2	7	9
55) There should not be any compromise on Jerusalem because Israel has no right to Jerusalem at all.	1. Very convincing	66	53	37	34
	2. Convincing	18	22	29	27
	3. Not convincing	16	24	33	35
	4. Not at all convincing	—	1	2	4
56) There should not be any compromise on Jerusalem because the actual historical connection of the Jewish people to the city is minor.	1. Very convincing	63	46	34	31
	2. Convincing	22	30	34	27
	3. Not convincing	14	22	30	38
	4. Not at all convincing	1	2	2	4
57) There should not be any compromise on Jerusalem because Jerusalem in its entirety is the heart of Palestine.	1. Very convincing	77	63	53	43
	2. Convincing	14	24	31	31
	3. Not convincing	8	12	15	24
	4. Not at all convincing	1	1	1	2
58) In your opinion, do Jews have any sort of legitimate rights with regard to Jerusalem?	1. Definitely yes	2	2	1	2
	2. Yes	14	16	22	28
	3. No	18	27	34	30
	4. Definitely no	67	55	43	40
59) Assume that a satisfactory agreement giving the Palestinians sovereign rights in East Jerusalem can be reached. How imortant to you is it, that in addition, East Jerusalem be a Palestinian capital?	1. Very important	91	91	90	80
	2. Important	6	8	8	15
	3. Not too important	2	1	2	3
	4. Not important at all	1	—	—	2

(All percentages)		Very religious	Religious	Not religious	Not at all religious

Let's assume that you were part of the negotiating team over Jerusalem. Please state the extent to which you would seriously consider each of the following proposals as permanent arrangements.

		Very religious	Religious	Not religious	Not at all religious
60) Israel and Palestine together would exercise joint sovereignty over undivided city.	1. Very seriously	22	20	22	20
	2. Seriously	11	18	21	14
	3. Give the proposal some consideration	12	14	19	18
	4. Not seriously	24	23	20	23
	5. Reject totally	32	24	18	25
61) West Jerusalem would be under Israeli sovereignty, and East Jerusalem would be under Palestinian sovereignty with a special arrangement for Israeli control of the Jewish neighborhoods in East Jerusalem. The Old City would be dealt with separately.	1. Very seriously	26	21	24	24
	2. Seriously	21	31	31	28
	3. Give the proposal some consideration	15	15	19	17
	4. Not seriously	16	17	14	12
	5. Reject totally	22	16	12	20
62) In the Old City, Israel would get sovereignty over the Jewish neighborhoods, and Palestine would get sovereignty over Palestinian neighborhoods.	1. Very seriously	22	18	19	12
	2. Seriously	17	23	22	11
	3. Give the proposal some consideration	14	11	16	14
	4. Not seriously	18	22	19	24
	5. Reject totally	30	27	24	39
63) Jews would be allowed to pray on Haram al-Sharif, which would be under operational authority of the Wakf.	1. Very seriously	13	11	16	10
	2. Seriously	2	5	8	6
	3. Give the proposal some consideration	8	5	9	10
	4. Not seriously	16	19	16	20
	5. Reject totally	61	60	52	54
64) The Palestinians would get sovereignty over the Haram al-Sharif in exchange for Palestinian recognition of Israeli sovereignty over the Western Wall.	1. Very seriously	29	32	29	20
	2. Seriously	14	22	20	25
	3. Give the proposal some consideration	12	12	18	16
	4. Not seriously	15	15	17	20
	5. Reject totally	30	19	16	19
65) Israel would exercise sovereignty over East Jerusalem, but Palestinian neighborhoods would be given a special self-rule status.	1. Very seriously	12	8	11	13
	2. Seriously	4	11	11	6
	3. Give the proposal some consideration	13	9	9	6
	4. Not seriously	28	27	24	28
	5. Reject totally	44	46	45	47

(All percentages)		Very religious	Religious	Not religious	Not at all religious

Let's assume that you were part of the negotiating team over Jerusalem. Please state the extent to which you would seriously consider each of the following proposals as permanent arrangements.

		Very religious	Religious	Not religious	Not at all religious
66) West Jerusalem and the Jewish neighborhoods in East Jerusalem would be under Israeli sovereignty and the rest of East Jerusalem under Palestinian sovereignty, with the Old City dealt with separately.	1. Very seriously	15	9	17	18
	2. Seriously	8	16	18	12
	3. Give the proposal some consideration	12	17	14	12
	4. Not seriously	31	29	26	26
	5. Reject totally	34	30	25	32
67) Abu Dis would be added to Jerusalem and the Palestinian parliament would be located in that region of the expanded city.	1. Very seriously	40	35	31	30
	2. Seriously	20	20	21	8
	3. Give the proposal some consideration	9	10	14	9
	4. Not seriously	11	17	14	18
	5. Reject totally	20	18	20	35
70) There is a proposal that each side should stop arguing about sovereignty over holy sites in Jerusalem and agree ultimate sovereignty belongs to God. Is this proposal acceptable to you?	1. Definitely yes	70	49	35	21
	2. Yes	18	22	19	17
	3. No	10	19	27	26
	4. Definitely no	2	10	19	36
71) Do you support the idea that Jordan should play a substantial role in the administration of the Islamic holy sites in Jerusalem?	1. Definitely yes	6	8	4	5
	2. Yes	18	11	8	3
	3. No	26	31	35	25
	4. Definitely no	51	50	54	67
73) Assume that no definitive solution to the Jerusalem question can be found. Would you support as an interim step that the Palestinian capital be located in the Jerusalem suburb of Abu Dis without relinquishing the Palestinian claim to sovereignty over East Jerusalem?	1. Yes	15	19	20	11
	2. No	79	76	73	79
	3. Others	6	5	7	10
74) In comparison with other topics that are being negotiated with the Israelis, such as water rights, return of Palestinian refugees, and the status of settlements, is the topic of Jerusalem more or less important than these other topics?	1. Much more important	59	53	38	29
	2. More important	8	9	15	14
	3. As important	33	37	45	54
	4. Less important	—	1	2	2
	5. Much less important	—	—	—	1

(All percentages)		Very religious	Religious	Not religious	Not at all religious
77) Do you agree with the point of view that says "in the case of an acceptable agreement on Jerusalem, Palestinians have the right to use all means necessary to block its implementation"?	1. Definitely agree	64	44	31	45
	2. Agree				
	3. Agree with reservations	17	31	33	22
		13	20	31	23
	4. Agree	6	5	5	10
78) Which one of the following political blocs best represent your point of view?	1. Islamic	46	25	11	5
	2. Leftist	—	6	13	37
	3. Fatah	25	41	36	25
	4. Independents	29	28	40	33

Appendix B-4
Cross-tabulation by religion

(All percentages)		Muslim	Christian
3) Are you for or against negotiations on Jerusalem within the peace process?	1. Definitely for	47	35
	2. For	32	46
	3. Against	10	13
	4. Definitely against	11	6
5) If you were able to advise Palestinian negotiators with respect to Jerusalem, with respect to their willingness to reach a compromise with the Israelis, how would you advise them?	1. Be much less compromising	63	51
	2. Be less compromising	25	36
	3. Be somewhat compromising	12	13
6) To what extent are you satisfied with the PNA concern with Jerusalem?	1. Very satisfied	22	9
	2. Satisfied	29	46
	3. Not satisfied	28	31
	4. Not satisfied at all	21	14
7) If the only way a Palestinian state could come into existence was by recognizing Israel's claim that it only is sovereign over all of Jerusalem, would you support that?	1. Definitely no	76	47
	2. No	18	44
	3. Yes	5	9
	4. Definitely yes	1	—
8) How important is Jerusalem to you personally?	1. Very important	92	84
	2. Important	7	13
	3. Not so important	1	13
	4. Not at all important	—	—
10) What is the most serious problem facing East Jerusalem?	1. The increase of Jewish population	7	3
	2. The expropriation of Palestinian land	5	10
	3. The acute social problems	—	—
	4. 1 + 2	36	24
	5. All are equally serious	52	62

To what extent is Jerusalem important to you from each of the following points of view?

		Muslim	Christian
11) Islamic religious	1. Very important	89	86
	2. Important	9	11
	3. Not so important	2	3
	4. Not at all important	—	—
12) Palestinian national-historical	1. Very important	89	87
	2. Important	10	11
	3. Not so important	1	2
	4. Not at all important	—	—

(All percentages)		Muslim	Christian
13) As a center for the Arab people	1. Very important	73	71
	2. Important	22	20
	3. Not so important	5	6
	4. Not at all important	—	3
14) As a center for all religions	1. Very important	76	86
	2. Important	19	13
	3. Not so important	3	1
	4. Not at all important	2	—
15) As a symbol of the future Palestinian state	1. Very important	89	84
	2. Important	8	15
	3. Not so important	1	1
	4. Not at all important	2	—
16) Do you view Jerusalem as a capital for:	1. A Palestinian state?	44	98
	2. A Palestinian-Islamic state?	43	2
	3. An Islamic state?	13	—
17) The Israelis say that Jerusalem is important to them as a national cente. To what extent is this true?	1. Not true at all	63	47
	2. Not true	23	35
	3. True to an extent	12	16
	4. Very true	2	2
18) The Israelis say that Jerusalem is important to them from a religious point of view. To what extent is this true?	1. Not true at all	45	22
	2. Not true	20	13
	3. True to an extent	31	59
	4. Very true	4	6
22) Do you consider Palestinian village areas such as Um Tuo and Zur Baher to be part of Jerusalem?	1. Definitely yes	55	29
	2. Yes	30	40
	3. No	12	25
	4. Definitely no	3	6

I will read a list of places in Jerusalem. Please tell me, for each one of them, to what extent is or isn't it important to you as part of Jerusalem?

23) The Haram al-Sharif	1. Very important	96	65
	2. Important	4	26
	3. Not so important	—	5
	4. Not at all important	—	4
24) al-Aqsa mosque and the Dome of the Rock	1. Very important	96	67
	2. Important	4	26
	3. Not so important	—	4
	4. Not at all important	—	3
25) Mount of Olives	1. Very important	64	75
	2. Important	31	18
	3. Not so important	4	4
	4. Not at all important	1	3

(All percentages)		Muslim	Christian
26) The Western Wall	1. Very important	35	36
	2. Important	20	9
	3. Not so important	19	20
	4. Not at all important	26	35
27) The Islamic quarters of the Old City	1. Very important	87	64
	2. Important	12	27
	3. Not so important	1	4
	4. Not at all important	—	5
28) The Christian quarters of the Old City	1. Very important	46	80
	2. Important	32	16
	3. Not so important	14	2
	4. Not at all important	9	2
29) The Jewish quarters of the Old City	1. Very important	24	29
	2. Important	18	15
	3. Not so important	22	24
	4. Not at all important	36	32
30) Palestinian neighborhoods in downtown East Jerusalem (Wadi Jos, Sheikh Jarah, etc.)	1. Very important	59	43
	2. Important	33	44
	3. Not so important	6	6
	4. Not at all important	2	7
31) The new Jewish neighborhoods established after 1967 which are included by the Israelis in Jerusalem(e.g., Gilo, Ramot etc.)	1. Very important	31	7
	2. Important	18	16
	3. Not so important	15	20
	4. Not at all important	36	57
32) The older Jewish neighborhoods in the Western part of the city (e.g., Rehavia, Talbieh, Beit Hakerem, etc.)	1. Very important	26	15
	2. Important	19	9
	3. Not so important	20	22
	4. Not at all important	35	55
33) The Old City	1. Very important	87	80
	2. Important	12	17
	3. Not so important	1	—
	4. Not at all important	—	3
37) Have you ever visited any of the Jewish neighborhoods in the Western part of the City?	1. Never	45	13
	2. Once	14	9
	3. A few times	22	46
	4. Quite a few times	13	26
	5. Very many times	6	6
38) There are people who say that we should make no concessions at all over Jerusalem even if we have to give up achieving a Palestinina state. To what extent do you agree or disagree with this statement?	1. Definitely agree	64	40
	2. Agree	19	27
	3. Disagree	12	26
	4. Definitely disagree	5	7

(All percentages)		Muslim	Christian
39) Would you accept as a permanent solution of the Jerusalem question that Israel has sovereignty over West Jerusalem and the State of Palestine has sovereignty over East Jerusalem?	1. Definitely yes 2. Yes 3. No 4. Definitely no	15 37 24 24	20 56 20 4
43) To what extent do you believe that there can be true peace between Israel and the Arab world in the foreseeable future?	1. Believe strongly 2. Believe 3. Don't believe so much 4. Don't believe at all	3 29 31 37	2 47 31 20
44) Do you support genuine and lasting peace with Israel in exchange for recognition of a Palestinian state with its capital in East Jerusalem, and resolution of the refugee issue, even though this will inevitably fall short of full justice for the Palestinians?	1. Definitely yes 2. Yes 3. No 4. Definitely no	26 43 18 14	18 67 13 2
46) Do you agree with the claim that because Judaism is a religion Jews should not be thought of as constituting a people, and therefore are lacking in national rights?	1. Definitely yes 2. Yes 3. No 4. Definitely no	33 38 22 7	18 35 46 1
47) In your opinion, is it desirable that in the daily life of Jerusalem there be a separation between Jews and Arabs in residence, entertainment, etc.	1. Very desirable 2. Desirable 3. Not desirable 4. Very undesirable	37 35 22 6	13 36 49 2

People state various reasons in favor of compromise on Jerusalem. With regard to each of the following, please state to what extent do you agree with the point of view.

		Muslim	Christian
48) Certain compromises could be made on Jerusalem in order to bring peace; with no compromise there will never be peace.	1. Strongly agree 2. Agree 3. Don't agree 4. Strongly disagree	19 45 23 13	16 64 15 5
49) Palestinians should make some compromises on Jerusalem if doing so gains more favorable outcomes on other issues in the negotiations, such as statehood, refugees, and borders.	1. Strongly agree 2. Agree 3. Don't agree 4. Strongly disagree	19 43 25 13	16 58 20 6

(All percentages)		Muslim	Christian
50) A compromise on Jerusalem ris the ight thing to do because Israelis also have deep historical and religious attachments to Jerusalem.	1. Strongly agree	6	6
	2. Agree	31	58
	3. Don't agree	40	27
	4. Strongly disagree	23	9
51) Since we are in the weaker position, we have to compromise on Jerusalem, otherwise we will get nothing.	1. Strongly agree	18	13
	2. Agree	36	58
	3. Don't agree	27	22
	4. Strongly disagree	19	7

Please state the extent to which you find it a convincing reason against any compromise.

		Muslim	Christian
53) There should not be any compromise on Jerusalem because it is much more important for Islam than Judaism.	1. Very convincing	52	13
	2. Convincing	25	9
	3. Not convincing	20	69
	4. Not at all convincing	3	9
54) There should not be any compromise on Jerusalem because it is an Islamic Wakf.	1. Very convincing	42	4
	2. Convincing	26	9
	3. Not convincing	29	66
	4. Not at all convincing	3	21
55) There should not be any compromise on Jerusalem because Israel has no right to Jerusalem at all.	1. Very convincing	50	15
	2. Convincing	24	22
	3. Not convincing	24	62
	4. Not at all convincing	2	1
56) There should not be any compromise on Jerusalem because the actual historical connection of the Jewish people to the city is minor.	1. Very convincing	45	9
	2. Convincing	30	22
	3. Not convincing	23	64
	4. Not at all convincing	2	5
57) There should not be any compromise on Jerusalem because Jerusalem in its entirety is the heart of Palestine.	1. Very convincing	62	26
	2. Convincing	25	40
	3. Not convincing	12	29
	4. Not at all convincing	1	5
58) In your opinion, do Jews have any sort of legitimate rights with regard to Jerusalem?	1. Definitely yes	2	2
	2. Yes	17	36
	3. No	28	44
	4. Definitely no	53	18

Let's assume that you were part of the negotiating team over Jerusalem. Please state the extent to which you would seriously consider each of the following proposals as permanent arrangements.

		Muslim	Christian
60) Israel and Palestine together would exercise joint sovereignty over undivided city.	1. Very seriously	21	26
	2. Seriously	16	44
	3. Give/some consideration	16	13
	4. Not seriously	23	10
	5. Reject totally	24	7

(All percentages)		Muslim	Christian
61) West Jerusalem would be under Israeli sovereignty, and East Jerusalem would be under Palestinian sovereignty with a special arrangement for Israeli control of the Jewiwh neighborhoods in EastJerusalem. The Old City would be dealt with separately.	1. Very seriously	23	31
	2. Seriously	28	44
	3. Give/some consideration	17	9
	4. Not seriously	15	13
	5. Reject totally	17	3
62) In the Old City, Israel would get sovereignty over the Jewish neighborhoods, and Palestine would get sovereignty over Palestinian neighborhoods.	1. Very seriously	19	16
	2. Seriously	20	22
	3. Give/some consideration	13	18
	4. Not seriously	20	24
	5. Reject totally	28	20
63) Jews would be allowed to pray on Haram al-Sharif, which would be under operational authority of the Wakf.	1. Very seriously	13	11
	2. Seriously	5	9
	3. Give/some consideration	6	20
	4. Not seriously	16	36
	5. Reject totally	60	24
64) The Palestinians would get sovereignty over the Haram al-Sharif in exchange for Palestinian recognition of Israeli sovereignty over the Western Wall.	1. Very seriously	30	24
	2. Seriously	20	38
	3. Give/some consideration	14	13
	4. Not seriously	16	16
	5. Reject totally	20	9
65) Israel would exercise sovereignty over East Jerusalem, but Palestinian neighborhoods would be given special self-rule status.	1. Very seriously	10	13
	2. Seriously	10	7
	3. Give/some consideration	9	13
	4. Not seriously	25	36
	5. Reject totally	46	31

Let's assume that you were part of the negotiating team over Jerusalem. Please state the extent to which you would seriously consider each of the following proposals as permanent arrangements.

66) West Jerusalem and the Jewish neighborhoods in East Jerusalem would be under Israeli sovereignty and the rest of East Jerusalem under Palestinian sovereignty, with the Old City dealt with separately.	1. Very seriously	12	22
	2. Seriously	15	22
	3. Give/some consideration	15	14
	4. Not seriously	28	22
	5. Reject totally	30	20
67) Abu Dis would be added to Jerusalem and the Palestinian Parliament would be located in that region of the expanded city.	1. Very seriously	34	26
	2. Seriously	19	22
	3. Give/some consideration	11	11
	4. Not seriously	15	20
	5. Reject totally	21	21

(All percentages)		Muslim	Christian
68) Palestinians would have sovereignty over the al-Aqsa mosque and the Dome of the Rock, but with respect to the plateau itself sovereignty would be shared with the Israelis, although day-to-day administration of the plateau would be in Palestinian hands alone.	1. Very seriously	23	11
	2. Seriously	18	14
	3. Give the proposal some consideration	12	17
	4. Not seriously	15	19
	5. Reject totally	32	39
69) The control of the Haram al-Sharif would be under the Wakf as it is now.	1. Very seriously	33	12
	2. Seriously	29	12
	3. Give the proposal some consideration	12	15
	4. Not seriously	10	15
	5. Reject totally	16	46
70) There is a proposal that each side should stop arguing about sovereignty over holy sites in Jerusalem and agree that ultimate sovereignty belongs to God. Is this proposal acceptable to you?	1. Definitely yes	46	25
	2. Yes	19	28
	3. No	20	32
	4. Definitely no	15	15
71) Do you support the idea that Jordan should play a substantial role in the administration of the Islamic hold sites in Jerusalem?	1. Definitely yes	6	9
	2. Yes	10	11
	3. No	30	44
	4. Definitely no	54	36
73) Assume that no definitive solution to the Jerusalem question can be found. Would you support as an interim step that the Palestinian capital be located in the Jerusalem suburb of Abu Dis, without relinquishing the Palestinian claim to sovereignty over East Jerusalem?	1. Yes	18	11
	2. No	75	84
	3. Others	7	5
74) In comparison with other topics that are being negotiated with the Israelis, such as water rights, return of Palestinian refugees, and the status of settlements, is the topic of Jerusalem more or less important than these other topics?	1. Much more important	48	27
	2. More important	12	4
	3. As important	38	67
	4. Less important	2	—
	5. Much less important	—	2

(All percentages)		Muslim	Christian
75) If a Palestinian government accepts a compromise on Jerusalem that you don't approve of, how will you react?	1. Will definitely oppose	32	22
	2. Will oppose	35	32
	3. Will accept with reservations	26	41
	4. Will accept	7	5
78) Which one of the following political blocs best represents your point of view?	1 Islamic	22	—
	2. Leftist	10	23
	3. Fatah	36	33
	4. Independents	32	44

About the Authors

Jerome M. Segal is the director of the Jerusalem Project at the University of Maryland's Center for International and Security Studies. He is also a Research Scholar at the Institute for Philosophy and Public Policy, School of Public Affairs, University of Maryland. He is the author of *Graceful Simplicity: Towards a Philosophy and Politics of Simple Living* (New York: Henry Holt, 1999), *Agency and Alienation* (Lanham, Md.: Rowman and Littlefield, 1996), and *Creating the Palestinian State: A Strategy for Peace* (Chicago: Lawrence Hill, 1989). During the 1970s and early 1980s he was a policy analyst working for the House of Representatives and subsequently for the Agency for International Development. He is the founder and director of The Jewish Peace Lobby.

Shlomit Levy is senior research associate of the Guttman Center for Applied Social Research, now an affiliate of the Israel Democracy Institute. She also lectures at the Baerwald School of Social Work at the Hebrew University. She is editor of *Louis Guttman on Theory and Methodology: Selected Writings* (Aldershot: Dartmouth, 1994), and co-author of "Beliefs, Observances and Social Interaction among Israeli Jews: The Guttman Report," in Liebman and Katz, eds., *The Jewishness of Israelis* (Albany: SUNY Press, 1997), and *The Structure of Social Values* (Jerusalem: Israel Institute of Applied Social Research, 1987).

Nader Izzat Saʿid is the director of the Development Studies Program at Bir Zeit University. He was the team leader for the Palestinian Human Development Report, funded by the United Nations Development Program. He initiated and established the largest survey research unit in the Arab world and supervised the first election exit poll in an Arabic speaking country. He has written extensively on public opinion, development and gender, and has trained researches in public opinion studies in a number of countries including Venezuela, Egypt, Jordan and the United States. He holds a doctorate in sociology from Western Michigan University.

337

Elihu Katz is Trustee Professor of Communication at the University of Pennsylvania, emeritus professor of sociology and communication at the Hebrew University, and former scientific director of the Guttman Institute of Applied Social Research. He is co-editor (with Charles Liebman) of *The Jewishness of Israelis: Responses to the Guttman Report* (Albany: SUNY Press, 1997), and co-editor (with Yael Warshel) of *Election Studies: What's Their Use?* (Boulder: Westview, 2000).

Index